Psychological Disorders of Children

of Children

A Behavioral Approach
to Theory, Research,
and Therapy

McGraw-Hill Series in Psychology

CONSULTING EDITOR

Norman Garmezy

By the same author:

Psychological Aspects of Learning Disabilities and Reading Disorders

Learning Disability: The Unrealized Potential

Psychological Disorders of Children

A Behavioral Approach to Theory, Research, and Therapy

Second Edition

Alan O. Ross

Professor of Psychology
State University of New York
Stony Brook

McGraw-Hill Book Company

New York   St. Louis   San Francisco   Auckland   Bogotá   Hamburg
Johannesburg   London   Madrid   Mexico   Montreal   New Delhi
Panama   Paris   São Paulo   Singapore   Sydney   Tokyo   Toronto

PSYCHOLOGICAL DISORDERS OF CHILDREN
A Behavioral Approach to Theory, Research, and Therapy

1 2 3 4 5 6 7 8 9 0   FGFG   7 8 3 2 1 0 9

This book was set in Times Roman by Automated Composition Service, Inc.
The editors were Richard R. Wright and Barry Benjamin;
the production supervisor was Richard A. Ausburn.
Fairfield Graphics was printer and binder.

Library of Congress Cataloging in Publication Data

Ross, Alan O
    Psychological disorders of children.

    (McGraw-Hill series in psychology)
    Bibliography: p.
    Includes indexes.
    1. Child psychiatry.   I. Title.
RJ499.R66   1980   618.9′28′9   79-14791
ISBN 0-07-053883-2

TO ISLE
—for sharing

Contents

Preface

The opportunity to prepare a revision of the 1974 edition of this book gratifies me on two counts. There is, first, the private pleasure which comes from knowing that one's book has earned the right to a revision. The other source of gratification is the awareness that the behavioral approach to clinical child psychology with which I identify so strongly has advanced with such celerity that my book had become obsolescent in the brief span of four years. It is exciting to be a part of such a vital field. Working on this revision has highlighted for me the fact that advances in theory, research, and practice have kept pace with each other. This is a very healthy sign.

The book continues to be addressed to advanced undergraduates and to beginning graduate students in psychology and such related fields as social work, special education, and child psychiatry. The reader should have some background in the behavioral sciences and familiarity with the principles of behavior, particularly those which find expression in current theories of learning. For the benefit of those who do not share this background, I have reviewed the most essential of these principles in Chapter 4 in order to facilitate the assimilation of the material which follows.

The behavioral point of view, from which this book is written, is not the radical behaviorism that categorically excludes from consideration any event that is not subject to direct observation. The orientation that guided my writing places a great deal of emphasis on the all-important role of the social environment in shaping and maintaining human behavior, but it also makes room for such concepts as self-control, self-observation, observational learning, and cognitive mediation as well as for a limited number of operationally defined constructs, such as anxiety and anger. Some readers may recognize this as the approach of social learning theorists, and I gladly acknowledge the influence, not only of my own teachers, John Dollard and Neal Miller, but also of Albert Bandura and his students. Whatever my approach might be labeled, I hope that it reflects a firm commitment to hew as closely as possible to the data from available research.

In the field of psychological disorders of children, research-based knowledge is, unfortunately, more readily available in some topic areas than in others. As a result, the chapters of this book are not of equal length. Where there is a dearth of data, there are few pages; where there is a profusion of data, there are many pages. I chose not to compensate for a paucity of knowledge by the presentation of armchair speculations or colorful case histories. In most instances, the investigators whose work I discuss operate in a frame of reference that is cognate to my own. At times, however, as in the chapters on early infantile autism and juvenile delinquency, I have presented the theoretical formulations of authors who take a different approach. The justification for this is that these writers stay sufficiently close to research-based data that their ideas deserve a hearing, particularly since they may well have a seminal influence on further research.

Aside from the obvious revising and updating in the content of almost every page, this second edition differs from the first in several important ways. Partly in response to comments by perceptive readers and partly as a result of having used this book in my own classes, I was moved to write three entirely new chapters. One deals with the important issue of ethics, values, and the rights of children. While I wrote an article dealing with the rights of children as long ago as 1958, and thus did not need to have my own consciousness raised, I felt that a separate chapter on this topic was both timely and essential, considering some of the highly publicized abuses perpetrated by people who claim to be using the methods of behavior therapy.

The second new chapter is the one on behavioral assessment. This addition reflects the fact that very little had been done in this area when I wrote the earlier edition. The development of methods for behavioral assessment was an important agenda item to which several of us were then trying to call attention. Since that time, much good material has become available, so the chapter on assessment turned out to be one of the longest in this volume.

The third entirely new chapter in this revision is the one on hyperactivity. I wrote this chapter in part because a great deal of research on this topic has been published during the past three or four years. A more important reason for a separate chapter, however, was that I did not wish to discuss hyperactivity in the chapter on learning disabilities because I am convinced that the two problems are not the same and that linking them under the same heading retards progress in both areas.

As for the chapter on learning disabilities, it too has undergone substantial rewriting, reflecting not only the increased interest of research investigators in this important area but also my desire to adopt the terminology on which most writers in the field now seem to have agreed. I have therefore abandoned the expression "learning dysfunction" with which I had earlier labeled the problem now covered by "learning disability."

Two further differences between the first and the second editions of this text bear pointing out. One is that instead of dealing with the treatment of psychological disorders in separate chapters, I have integrated this discussion into the chapters where the various disorders are presented. This integration has eliminated some redundancy and made it possible to follow the presentation of a problem immediately with a discussion of what can be done about it.

The other change, which those who are familiar with the first edition will notice, is that I no longer resort to the dichotomy of deficient and excess behavior in organizing the book. While this dichotomy continues to be useful in conceptualizing specific problem behaviors, its use creates difficulties when one wishes to discuss the psychological disorders of children under chapter headings that adhere to traditional categorical labels, such as early infantile autism. Children assigned to these categories exhibit both deficient and excess behavior. It therefore makes little sense to relegate early infantile autism to a segment labeled deficient behavior as I had done in the first edition at the price of some conceptual acrobatics and at the cost of no little consternation on the part of earlier readers, to whom I here apologize.

As was the earlier version of this book, this one is dedicated with love, admiration, and gratitude to Ilse Wallis Ross, my wife, whose steadfast support is so very important to me. Her abiding interest in people and remarkable clinical acumen as a social worker continue to provide a needed and constructive foil to my enthusiasm for scientific objectivity.

ACKNOWLEDGMENTS

For granting me permission to quote from their writings, I am indebted to Drs. Wesley C. Becker, Lovick C. Miller, and Donald R. Peterson. Corporate holders of copyrights who permitted me to quote from their material and whose courtesy is hereby acknowledged are: Academic Press, American Association for the Advancement of Science, American Psychological Association, American Psychosomatic Association, Association for Advancement of Behavior Therapy, Dorsey Press, Hoeber Medical Division of Harper and Row, McGraw-Hill Book Company, and The Society for Research in Child Development. Where requested, statements regarding copyright credits appear in the appropriate places in the text.

Alan O. Ross

Psychological Disorders of Children

A Behavioral Approach to Theory, Research, and Therapy

Introduction

THE BEHAVIORAL APPROACH

When scientists desire to study a phenomenon of nature, this phenomenon must be observable. Speculation about the phenomenon may serve the scientists for a while, but ultimately these speculations must be checked against observations. Similarly, indirect observation of a phenomenon may, for a time, be all the scientists have available, but ultimately direct observation will be necessary if their inferences are to be confirmed. In the case of the natural phenomenon that is the human being, the only thing we can observe is behavior. History is the record of our behavior. When we construct tools, build houses, create works of art, speak to one another, or teach our children, we are emitting behavior. Behavior can be observed and recorded, hence, scientifically studied, and this scientific study of behavior is psychology, the science of behavior.

All behavior, whether sublime or profane, unique or commonplace, normal or deviant, follows the same principles. Many of these principles are now known, while others remain to be discovered; yet, enough of them are known to venture a presentation of the psychological disorders of children based on the psychological principles of behavior. The aim of this presentation is to seek an explanation of these disorders in hopes of contributing to their alleviation and eventual prevention.

Explanation and Understanding

The observation of a puzzling phenomenon, such as a boy who repeatedly bangs his head against the wall to the point where he sustains large swellings and lacerated skin, leads layman and psychologist alike to seek an explanation. The kind of explanation one finds greatly depends on the kind of question one asks. If the question is "What makes that boy behave like this?," the answer is likely to be in terms of something that *makes* the child bang his head, something that impells, motivates, or forces him to act this way. What is more, the search for an answer is likely to focus on antecedent events, on looking for an entity that is present inside the boy and pushes him to do what he does. Over the years, a variety of such causes have been invented to explain the puzzling behavior. These causes have ranged from inherent evil, through malevolent spirits, to inherited wickedness and unconscious conflicts. Each of these "explanatory fictions" (Skinner, 1953) has, in its time, served to give people the sense of understanding puzzling behavior, but the science of psychology cannot be satisfied with pseudoexplanations that do not lend themselves to experimental manipulations and have no referent, independent of the phenomenon they seek to explain. What is more, these pseudoexplanations have done little in the way of helping the children whose behavior they purport to explain, and such help is the most important reason for seeking an explanation. From that standpoint, more recent explanations in terms of such constructs as personality and character traits have also done little to improve the approaches used to modify changeworthy behavior (Mischel, 1973).

If the "what" question leads one to invent spirits and other mysterious forces, the "why" question ("Why does the child engage in head banging?") is likely to produce equally fallacious answers. The focus is now shifted from an impelling force to an attracting goal; children bang their heads in order to satisfy some need, urge, or impulse. To solve the "why" question, this need must then be identified, and people have again turned to inventions for an answer. One of the most frequently encountered pseudoexplanations here is the explanatory label. The observed behavior is given a label—the more esoteric, the better—and this label then comes to serve as an explanation. In the case of the head-banging boy, the behavior might be called *masochistic*, and the question "Why does the boy bang his head?" then receives the answer, "Because he's masochistic," or "Because it satisfies his masochistic needs." When this explanation is challenged ("How do you know he has masochistic needs?"), the answer returns to the observation which was to be explained in the first place ("Because he bangs his head."). The circularity of this should be obvious, yet many of the explanatory constructs still in use in psychology are of that order.

Aside from encouraging the postulation of needs that have no external referent other than the phenomenon to be explained, the "why" question is also likely to trap one into teleological explanations. These explanations infer a purpose, an intention, or a plan that antedates the emission of the behavior; the boy bangs his head "in order to" gain some satisfying goal that he was able to envision beforehand. A behavioral approach to psychology does not deny that people make plans and engage in behavior that follows such a plan. The problem is that the presence or absence of such a plan cannot be directly studied, and it is risky to infer the presence of a plan from observed behavior because topographically similar behavior may appear in the presence as well as in the absence of a plan. A nonverbal, severely disturbed child who bangs his head is not likely to tell us the purpose of his behavior, and to postulate such a purpose is not the most parsimonious route to a satisfactory explanation.

To summarize what has been said so far, an analogy might be helpful. If one observes that the sun appears in the sky in the morning and asks, "What makes the sun rise?," the answer might be, "The sun-god Helios is driving his 4-horse chariot across the heavens." If one were to rephrase the question and ask, "Why does the sun rise?," the answer might be, "In order to make daylight." Neither the "what" nor the "why" question is appropriate for science. The only question science can effectively investigate takes the form, "Under what conditions does this phenomenon occur?"

Returning to the head-banging boy, we can now ask, "Under what conditions does this boy bang his head?," and the psychologist can proceed to observe the phenomenon in question and to gather data on the events immediately preceding and immediately following the behavior. This will lead to the discovery that the behavior is a function of environmental conditions and that, when these conditions are modified, the behavior can be changed. When the full answer to the question about the conditions surrounding a given behavior is available, the behavior can be predicted and, under given circumstances, controlled—that is, created, changed, or prevented. These are the goals of science—prediction and control. When these goals are reached, one can say that an observed phenomenon is explained or, if one likes, "understood." Understanding in any other sense is scientifically meaningless, although philosophers, theologians, and artists—in laudable pursuits of their endeavors—will and should seek an understanding of the world in other terms. A discussion of behavior disorders must seek a scientific understanding because such understanding alone permits us to modify and, ultimately, to prevent problems of this kind.

Determinants of Behavior

The question about the conditions under which a given phenomenon takes place leads the behavioral psychologist to study the external environment. This is not to deny that there are also conditions of the internal environment that deserve study, and the biologically oriented psychologist, the physiologist, and the biochemist can study these conditions to great advantage. It is fallacious to assume, however, that an "ultimate" explanation of behavior can be found on the molecular, physiological level. Any specific behavior, taking place at any one time, represents the end point of the interaction of genetic-constitutional factors, the current physiological state of the person, current environmental conditions, and past learning which, in turn, was a function of a similar interaction. Each of these factors will reflect the developmental level of the person whose behavior one seeks to explain and in the case of a child, consideration of this level is particularly crucial. All of these interacting factors must be explored; to assume that any one alone will provide a necessary and sufficient explanation is to ignore the complexity of the phenomenon that is human behavior.

Genetic-Constitutional Factors   Each individual possesses unique attributes of a biological order. Some of these attributes people have in common with other members of the species, and they probably evolved and became a part of the human behavioral repertoire because of their survival value. Simple reflexes, the avoidance of noxious stimulation, and the escape from danger are examples of genotypical behavior that is largely a function of innate, genetic endowment. Other attributes, such as pain threshold, autonomic reactivity, and behavioral style, seem to be aspects of the individual's phenotypical uniqueness. An individual's attributes are probably present at the time of birth and may be viewed as hereditary in the sense that they represent the interplay of his or her parents' genes. With the exception of identical twins, every individual differs from every other individual in terms of the exact combination of genetic attributes, and any study of behavior must take these individual differences into consideration. While the science of genetics has made much progress in recent years, we do not, at this time, have enough knowledge to permit a clear differentiation between genotypical and phenotypical factors, and this lack of knowledge leads us to refer to those behavioral aspects with which a child appears to be born as *constitutional*. At this point, too, we are unable to influence these constitutional factors before they emerge, although, within limits, they can later be modified and brought under voluntary control. Thus, an individual can learn to make approach responses in the face of danger or noxious stimuli, to increase pain tolerance, or to modify such autonomic responses as heart rate or blood pressure (Shapiro & Surwit, 1976).

Past Learning   Another factor influencing present behavior is the person's past learning with respect to similar situations. All behavior, with the possible exception of the simple reflex, is either developed by or modified through learning. When we observe a specific response, we see the end result of a long history of learning; thus, behavior will be predictable to the extent that this past learning and its conditions can be known. In real life, it is next to impossible to reconstruct the conditions under which a person has learned and to know the nature of this learning; hence, human behavior is difficult to predict, but the best predictor is knowledge of past behavior under similar circumstances. This is the case because behavior depends on the prevailing environmental conditions and is specific to these conditions. When a person behaves predictably in different situations, it is because that person has learned to construe these situations as somehow similar or has acquired personal constructs (Kelly, 1955) that call for a similar response to different situations. People who behave adaptively carry few such response dispositions around with them from place to place; therefore, they do not often respond in the same way regardless of where they are. People who behave maladaptively often act in one place in a manner that would be appropriate for another place. In that sense, lack of situational specificity in behavior may be a characteristic of psychological disorders. At any rate, attempts to assess such response dispositions as character traits or personality states in hopes of facilitating the prediction of behavior have been singularly unsuccessful (Mischel, 1968, 1973).

From the standpoint of helping people with psychological disorders, past learning, by definition, is *past* and thus not subject to cancellation; that is, it cannot be made to have not happened. Past learning potently influences present behavior, yet we cannot hope to change present behavior by merely exploring past learning. We can, however, modify the effects of past learning by introducing new learning, and thereby have an influence on future behavior when the individual encounters similar circumstances.

Current Physiological States   At the moment people emit a specific behavior, a physiological state plays a role in that behavior. Physiological states may be constitutional and thus of relative permanence, as blood pressure, for example, or they may be temporary states, such as level of food deprivation or degree of autonomic arousal. These physiological factors affect the person's behavior. For example, to a person who is not to some extent deprived of food the opportunity for eating is not a reinforcing event, similarly, a person who is not at least mildly aroused may not respond to the presentation of a given signal that, at other times, would serve as a stimulus. Although physiological factors are thus preconditions or setting events for behavior, they themselves have their antecedents in environmental circumstances. Food deprivation (hunger) is a function of something going on in the environment, and arousal states are responses to a variety of conditions, such as sleep deprivation, threat, or stress. Since the environmental antecedents of an individual's physiological state are thus subject to modification, it is possible to modify the physiological state if one desires to modify the individual's behavior.

Current Environmental Conditions   The fourth interacting influence on current behavior, and of greatest interest to the behaviorally oriented psychologist, is the condition under which current behavior takes place. The immediate antecedents and the immediate consequences of a given action are present in the here and now; they can be observed, recorded, measured, counted, and otherwise made the subject matter of the science of behavior. What is more, current environmental conditions, unlike genetic factors or past learning, can be modified to influence not only behavior but also the physiological states that affect behavior.

The focus on behavior and the environment in which the behavior takes place lends itself not only to providing an understanding of behavior and behavior disorders, it also furnishes guidelines to those who seek to modify behavior disorders in a therapeutic endeavor. A study of behavior disorders that does not logically lead to their treatment would be no more than abstract theorizing, and there is too much human suffering involved to permit one the luxury of such esoteric pursuits.

The main principles we shall invoke in discussing the acquisition and change of behavior are the principles of respondent conditioning, operant learning, and observational learning. These principles find their most immediate application in the treatment of psychological disorders, but it is important to keep in mind that while they have been shown to have utility when they are applied in the *treatment* of disordered behavior, this is no proof that these principles are necessarily involved in the *development* of such behavior. One can assume that disordered behavior is the result of learning and that principles of learning operate there as they do in treatment, but support for this assumption cannot be adduced by pointing to the data from behavior therapy.

Because of obvious ethical constraints, one cannot produce behavior disorders for the purpose of demonstrating how they develop; laboratory analogues occasionally lend some support, but, ultimately, only painstaking longitudinal studies tracing the development of behavior disorders and recording all contributing conditions will permit us to be confident about statements on the genesis of psychological disorders.

Private Events

In the behavioral approach to psychological phenomena, one prefers to study that which can be observed or made observable. Overt behavior—what people do, what they say, and how they look—thus provides the primary data; in addition, physiological events that can be objectively recorded, such as changes in heart rate, skin conductance, or respiration, provide information about functions that are not visible to the observer without the aid of specialized equipment. Observed overt behavior as well as recorded physiological events can be described in objective terms; they can be seen by any number of observers who can agree on what they are seeing, and they can be communicated to others who can repeat the observations, given similar circumstances. Objectivity, communicability, and repeatability are the requisites of a science, and the data gathered by a behavioral approach thus permit the development of scientific knowledge about psychological phenomena. As information thus obtained accumulates, one can discover that certain discrete behavioral events coincide, with great predictability, with certain discrete physiological events, and at this point communication among investigators can be facilitated if, instead of continuing to list the discrete observations, they agree on a linguistic convention whereby this cluster of events is given a label. One can observe, for example, that many people when prevented from the completion of a goal-oriented response chain will increase the magnitude of certain motor responses; show a characteristic facial grimace; emit verbal expletives and statements like "I am angry"; develop a flushing of the facial skin; and have concomitant changes in heart rate, blood pressure, skin conductance, or breathing pattern, which can be displayed on specialized equipment. This cluster of observed phenomena can be called "anger," and such a term can then be used in discussions of behavior, provided one recalls that it stands not for a postulated internal state but for a series of observable phenomena and that it is these observations (operations) which define the term. Such operational definitions can be worked out for anxiety, joy, sadness, hunger, and other internal responses, but unless these have observable referents, the terms alone have no scientific standing.

Words like anger, sadness, or hunger are a part of the general English vocabulary. This creates some confusion because people describe their own sensations with these words, thereby giving the impression that, when used in the technical language of psychology, the terms also refer directly to internal states and are not merely convenient semantic conventions describing a defined set of observations. This confusion might have been avoided had psychologists decided to designate observed clusters of behavior by some arcane term especially invented for the purpose; but this would have prevented one confusion by creating another. At any rate, when a woman tells us that she is angry, she tells us something about a private experience. But to psychologists this verbal statement is merely one of many defining characteristics of the behavior cluster they have agreed to call anger, and unless at least some of the remaining characteristics can also be demonstrated, psychologists in their role as scientists must guard against accepting the verbal statement alone as a reliable index of the presence of the behavior cluster. This caveat is particularly important when we come to discuss the behavior of children, because young or severely disturbed children may not have words to describe their sensations or may be using such words in highly idiosyncratic ways.

The words with which we describe perceived internal states are learned in the course of language acquisition. Children learn the verbal labels for concrete external referents with relative ease. The object called "horse" can be pointed to by a parent who says "horse," and when the girl eventually repeats this word, she can be rewarded or, if on occasion, she calls it "cow," she can be corrected. It is far more difficult to teach verbal labels for internal events because parent and child do not have a common referent, and the parent is unable to provide the child with feedback as to the accuracy of a statement. For this reason, the language dealing with subjective states is far more unreliable than the language about the objective world. Some people describe as anger what others might label anxiety; others say they are embarrassed when someone else might report feeling guilty; and, as we have said, children very often have no words at all to describe their internal sensations. Thus, while an inquiry into how a person "feels" may be useful in eliciting one of the observable behaviors (the verbal statement), by itself the answer is of little value in the study of disordered behavior.

Behaviorally oriented psychologists do not deny that people experience internal sensations; they merely consider the verbal reports of such sensations highly suspect data, and hesitate to make inferences about internal states, preferring instead to deal with what can be observed. The same is true about the private events called *thoughts, fantasies, ideas, wishes, plans, memories*, etc. There is no doubt that people engage in these *cognitive processes*, but the only way in which a psychologist can study them is by observing the behavior (including verbal behavior) that accompanies these processes. Again, it is necessary to have more than a verbal self-report before a private event can furnish useful data. Self-reports may be inaccurate, withheld, distorted, or falsified, and the nonverbal or preverbal child has no way of giving such a report. From the point of view of psychology, it is more useful to record the observation that a boy flaps his arms, makes chirping noises, and while doing so jumps off high places than to have him tell us that he thinks he is a bird; but if all of these events are observed, it may help communication to make the statement that this child has bird fantasies. A therapist would undoubtedly wish to change that child's deviant and dangerous behavior regardless of the nature of the fantasy; and, as we shall see, it is possible to bring about such change without inquiring into or making inferences about the fantasies that may or may not be present and about which we can have no direct knowledge unless the child is willing and able to give us a verbal statement with reference to them.

To summarize, behaviorally oriented psychologists do not deny the existence of such private events as thoughts and feelings; they merely maintain that self-reports about such private events provide unreliable data, insist that their reliability must be enhanced by concurrently observed behavior before they can be used in a scientific study of psychological phenomena, and prefer, as a matter of strategy, to focus their attention on what can be observed or made observable.

PSYCHOLOGICAL DISORDERS

There is no absolute definition of a psychological disorder. The definition is a function of the social environment and thus relative to the cultural, historical, and social setting in which an individual emits a given behavior. If the behavior conforms to the prevailing consensual norm, it is considered *normal*; if it deviates from this norm, it is considered *deviant*. In a given society, at any given time in its history, the members of that society have fairly explicit expectations for the role-appropriate behavior of a child. These expectations are a function of the child's age, and they vary depending on the sex of the child, position in birth order, and the social status of the family. Children whose behavior deviates from these expectations, whose behavior does not fit into the expected order of the lives of those with whom they live, and whose behavior is thus "disordered" find themselves exposed to sanctions imposed by their peers and elders. These sanctions will be brought to bear if the behavior is emitted under conditions where it is deemed "improper" (literally, "where it does not belong"), because a given action may be appropriate in one set of circumstances but inappropriate in another. What is more, a behavior may be deemed acceptable when it is performed at one level of frequency or magnitude but unacceptable at higher or lower levels. Thus, for example, a father may approve of his boy's hitting another boy only if he has been hit first and only if the other boy is at least his age. Furthermore, occasional hitting of another on the part of a 9-year-old boy is usually tolerated, but when this occurs very often, it is deemed a problem, particularly if his family is of middle-class status.

With these points in mind, it is possible to propose the following definition of psychological disorders:

> *A psychological disorder is said to be present when a child emits behavior that deviates from an arbitrary and relative social norm in that it occurs with a frequency or intensity that authoritative adults in the child's environment judge, under the circumstances, to be either too high or too low.*

Peers, parents, and other adults in the child's environment will impose sanctions for deviant behavior; they withhold rewards or deliver punishments. Yet in the face of these negative consequences, the disordered behavior persists in the child's repertoire, giving such behavior its characteristic maladaptive, paradoxical nature. Despite repeated failure, frequent punishment, loss of friends, and absence of apparent rewards, the child persists to engage in the acts that have these consequences, and this paradox leads most observers to wonder what it is that "makes" the child behave in this manner. They seek to understand and explain the paradox, and this search leads, as we have seen, to a variety of formulations.

At present, the most direct approach to an understanding of disordered behavior is to view such behavior as acquired, performed, and modifiable according to the same principles of development and learning that apply to all other behavior. From this standpoint, one can attempt to resolve the paradox of maladaptive behavior by assuming that such behavior is maintained by indirect or delayed forms of reinforcement that are not mysterious but just not immediately apparent to the casual observer. The task of psychology then becomes the identification of these reinforcing conditions; for by changing these conditions one should be able to modify the disordered behavior. In addition to disordered behavior that is probably maintained by indirect or delayed reinforcement, there is a group of behavior disorders where children have never learned appropriate, expected response patterns. Such children, too, will encounter punitive consequences, and their behavior may therefore appear paradoxical, but because punishment can, at best, serve to suppress behavior and cannot teach new, appropriate responses, their persistence in the maladaptive patterns is not a mystery but a reflection of their deficient response repertoires. Here, the task of psychology is to find ways of teaching the children the skills they have thus far failed to acquire.

The Classification of Disorders

The real world, as it is called, does not come in neatly arranged classifications. The behavior we consider disordered is not very orderly and it does not lend itself to easy categorization. When an individual child comes to a psychological clinic, it is not too important to be able to classify that child's particular problem or set of problems. What is important is that the problems be recognized so that they can be alleviated. In clinical settings classification is done mostly for administrative, not for therapeutic purposes. Yet, in writing a book about the variety of problems with which children come for help it is unavoidable to introduce some kind of categorization and classification, to try and create some order in the realm of disorders. The moment one does this, one is forced to be arbitrary, for the classification of nature is, of necessity, arbitrary.

It has become customary to discuss psychological disorders under certain large rubrics that stem from the diagnostic categories developed by psychiatrists and child psychiatrists. As we shall see, these categories, such as early infantile autism or mental retardation, are not very satisfactory, and there are movements under way which are aimed at their revision or abolition (Hobbs, 1975). Much of the difficulty with these categories stems from the fact that rather than describing specific behavior, they represent theoretical abstractions that often bear little relationship to the behavior which is displayed by the children who are thus classified. Since our principal interest is in children's disordered behavior, a classification based on behavior would be far more useful.

Deficient and Excess Behavior   Behavior our present society chooses to define as disordered seems to fall into two major classes, depending on whether the behavior deviates from the norm by occurring too rarely or too frequently. In line with the definition we offered for psychological disorders, one can thus speak of *deficient behavior* and *excess behavior*. This dichotomy has been found useful in discussions of assessment (Hersen & Bellack, 1976) and treatment (Gelfand & Hartmann, 1975). By focusing on the distinction between deficient and excess behavior, a therapist can ascertain the goal of any treatment to be undertaken with a given child; for deficient behavior calls for an increase, excess behavior for a decrease in the relevant responses. A given child, classified under any of the traditional diagnostic rubrics, will usually display both deficient and excess behaviors. This is why the treatment focus must be on these latter and not on the diagnostic category. This is another way of saying that one must treat behavior, not diagnostic labels. Unfortunately, the traditional diagnostic labels are so widely used and well established that they must continue to be used as chapter headings for a book such as this, which deals with the psychological disorders of children.

RECAPITULATION

The science of psychology studies the subject of human behavior because behavior in its various manifestations and ramifications can be defined in an objective manner. In order to explain behavior one must examine the conditions under which it takes place. When this is done, one finds that behavior is determined by an interaction of genetic-constitutional factors, current physiological states, current environmental conditions, and past learning. While there are private events, such as thoughts and feelings, the only time a psychologist can study these and their influence on behavior is when they become manifest in what people do or say.

There is no absolute definition of a psychological disorder because what is considered disordered depends a great deal on people's judgment. This judgment usually revolves around whether the frequency or intensity of a given behavior is at the expected level; if it is not, the behavior is deemed disordered. One can therefore speak of excess and of deficient behavior, and children in the various diagnostic categories will usually be found to exhibit both of these kinds of behavior. The following chapter will be devoted to a review of studies by which investigators have attempted to establish patterns of disordered behavior in hopes of improving the classification of children's psychological disorders.

Chapter 2

The Classification of Psychological Disorders

Attempts to establish a taxonomy of psychological disorders would be an idle intellectual exercise were it not for the fact that there are several pragmatic questions, the answers to which await the development of a uniform system of classification. In order to study what kind of treatment works best with what kind of disorder, one must be able to define "kinds of disorders." If two investigators wish to compare data, they must be able to agree on the disorders they are discussing. If one wishes to ascertain the incidence of a particular disorder in a given population, one must have a taxonomic basis for conducting the survey.

These efforts are currently handicapped by the lack of a uniformly agreed upon system of classifying the psychological disorders of children. There are many reasons for this state of affairs, some of which will become apparent from the following pages; but the prime reason why we are still in the pre-Linnaean stage of our science is that there has been all manner of confusion about the nature of the phenomenon we wish to classify. Is a psychological disorder a disease, in which case one would want to follow the medical approach to classification and nomenclature? Are children's disorders analogous to adults' disorders, in which case the reasonably uniform nomenclature used there might be applied with only minor modifications? Should one base the classification on the manifestations of the problem, on its origins, on its effect on others, or on its probable outcome? Each of these possibilities and combinations of them have, at one time or another, served as the basis of attempts at classification, but none has proved satisfactory.

The phenomenon we wish to classify is, of course, not an object or an entity; it is the behavior and combinations of behaviors emitted by individual children whose social environment judges the behavior to be deviant. Attempts to reify behavior or to deal with it by analogy would seem to be the main reason why the classification of behavior disorders—and with it, the study of such disorders—has failed to progress.

LABELS AND THEIR CONSEQUENCES

Before we can proceed with a discussion of classification, it is important to recognize that we are dealing with more than an intellectual exercise of interest only to scholars and professional practitioners. Ultimately, we are dealing with the lives of children. We must therefore be aware of the impact our efforts to classify psychological disorders will have on the children who manifest these disorders.

A child behaves in a certain manner, and the people with whom that child interacts consider that behavior to be a problem. There are other children who behave in the same or similar manner, and eventually such a group of children comes to the attention of a specialized profession, say psychologists. These psychologists, in order to be able to communicate with one another, decide to give the problematic behavior of that group of children a distinctive label. Let us say they call it *odium* (a word of Latin origin which describes behavior that arouses disapproval and condemnation). There is, of course, no such psychological disorder; we use it as a fictitious example of what can happen after a label has been invented out of the need for a convenient description of some children's behavior.

Before long, people tend to forget that originally the word was meant to identify behavior and the children whose behavior occasioned the invention of the label will now be said to *have* odium. The word has become a thing; the concept has been reified. What usually happens next is that what started out as a label becomes an explanation. People who ask why these children behave that way will be told, "Because they have odium." Obviously, nothing has been explained. After this, it will not be long before the noun, which has been used as a label for a cluster of behaviors, comes to be used as an adjective in describing children who engage in these behaviors. One now speaks of an odious child, and children, thus labeled, will see themselves in that, usually uncomplimentary light. In fact, such children will now explain their own behavior in terms of the label: "I can't help behaving that way, for I am an odious child." Furthermore, since people expect odious children to behave in a certain characteristic fashion, children so labeled often live up to these expectations, especially if "odious children" are segregated in schools and institutions where people expect them to behave the way odious children do and where the only models which are available are other children who have been given that label. This circularity has been called "the self-fulling prophecy." It also goes without saying that there is a stigma attached to being an odious child or to "have" odium, and the end result of this process of labeling is rarely one that benefits the children whose puzzling or annoying behavior was given that label in the first place.

The consequences of categorizing and labeling children were discussed in considerable detail in an influential report by Nicholas Hobbs (1975), who points to the harmful effects of the present system of classifying troubled children. This system is gross and inadequate in that it obscures both the uniqueness of individual children and the similarities of children who are assigned to different categories. Hobbs (1975) points out that "the way a problem is defined will determine the way it is solved. It is thus a matter of utmost importance that there be made available an adequate system for . . . classifying with precision children loosely called handicapped, disadvantaged, or delinquent" (p. 233).

A system for classifying psychological disorders must be based on "meaningful and discernible behaviors" (Zigler & Phillips, 1961). The classificatory principle must be consistently organized around observable behavior; references to etiology, prognosis, social conformity, developmental stage, etc., must be explicitly stated as correlates of the particular behavior or class of behaviors.

When psychological disorders are defined in terms of a judgment made by the people in the child's environment, as these disorders invariably are, such judgments become central to any system of classification. In fact, one might say that we must classify not behavior but people's judgments about behavior. For when it is recognized that the definition of disordered behavior depends on the expectations of those in a child's environment, it becomes clear that one must consider not only the demands thus made of the child but also the tolerance level of this environment for behavior in its various forms. The data for classifying psychological disorders of children should therefore be the reports of those who, like parents and teachers, are in daily contact with the child. We are thus lead to a consideration of what, in child behavior, parents and teachers will judge to be disordered, and what they judge to be normal behavior of children.

WHAT IS NORMAL?

As a first approximation of a differentiation between disordered and normal behavior, one might assume that behavior which causes a child to be brought to the attention of a relevant professional is abnormal, while the behavior of children in the nonclinic population is normal. It should be immediately apparent that this is a poor basis on which to make the differentiation. The arbitrary and relative nature of what people consider to be a behavior disorder should lead one to suspect that the same behavior can be found on either side of the clinic door.

The children who come to professional attention represent a highly selected, biased sample of those who manifest a given behavior, and any studies based on these children must be viewed with this fact clearly in mind. The prevalence of the kind of behavior that brings children to the attention of relevant clinics and agencies has been shown to be remarkably high in unselected samples of the so-called normal population (Conners, 1970; Lapouse & Monk, 1959, 1964; Tuddenham, Brooks & Milkovich, 1974; Werry & Quay, 1971).

In a survey of all children attending kindergarten through second grade in the public schools of a town in Illinois, Werry and Quay (1971) used a 55-item checklist containing problems found among children brought to child guidance clinics. These problems, ranged from shyness to disruptiveness, from temper tantrums to bizarre behavior. The children's teachers were asked to check those behaviors they recognized in a given child, and the authors report that the mean number of such problems was 11.4 for the 926 boys and 7.6 for the 827 girls in the sample. The significantly higher incidence of problems among boys is a finding reported with great consistency by most investigators. In the Illinois study, thirty-six of the problems occurred with significantly greater frequency among boys; only five problems were more frequent among girls: shyness, seriousness, jealousy, sensitivity and physical complaints.

Conners (1970) conducted a comparison of 316 children, aged 5 to 16, who were attending a psychiatric clinic and 365 presumably normal children whose parents were attending a PTA meeting. He used a list of seventy-three problem behaviors on which the parents of the children checked the problems displayed by their child. While, as expected, the prevalence of problems was higher among the clinic patients than among the normal sample, some difficulties had a surprisingly high prevalence among the so-called normal children. Thus, their parents checked "restlessness" for 65 percent of the children; bed-wetting for 15 percent; nightmares for 24 percent; overeating for 11 percent; and biting, sucking, or chewing objects for 20 percent. While parents who attend PTA meetings represent a select sample of the general population of parents and may be somewhat more interested in and concerned about their child's welfare, Conners' data are remarkably consistent with those reported by Lapouse and Monk (1959). They found that in a sample of 482 children between the ages of 6 and 12—carefully selected to represent the general population of a city in New York State—17 percent wet their beds, 28 percent had nightmares, 27 percent bit their nails, and 43 percent experienced seven or more fears and worries out of thirty about which their mothers had been questioned.

The Louisville Behavior Check List (Miller, 1967a, 1967b) contains 163 statements describing both deviant and prosocial behavior in nontechnical language. When parents or teachers are asked to check the items that are descriptive of a given child, this instrument yields scores on eight scales in the areas of aggression, withdrawal, and learning disabilities as well as an overall "total disability" score which is based on ninety-three items that have been found to contribute to the other eight scales. Miller, Hampe, Barrett, and Noble (1971) mailed the Louisville Behavior Check List to a random sample of 500 parents of children between the ages of 7 and 12, drawn from the rolls of the city and county public school systems in and around Louisville. With mail and telephone follow-up they secured a 47 percent return, yielding 236 protocols. The analysis of the responses from this random sample of the general population revealed that "the average child within the general population manifests between 11 and 13 deviant behaviors" (p. 18), deviant behavior items occurring in at least 25 percent of the population. The scales were only minimally affected by such demographic variables as race, socioeconomic status, and age, and there were no significant differences between the total disability means for boys and girls, although the scores for boys had a higher variance. That is to say that boys manifested more extreme behavior than girls, particularly on the aggressive and learning disability dimensions. The scales reflecting academic disability and immaturity, scales Miller and his associates classify as learning disability, did show significantly higher means for boys than for girls. This finding, together with the negative correlation between intelligence and disability scores, led the authors to speculate that much disturbed behavior in childhood "may be linked to scholastic failures resulting from an incompatibility between children of lower intelligence and the modern educational system" (p. 21). A similar point was made by Hobbs (1975) who suggested that among the criteria members of our society use for deciding what is normal, good, and acceptable are to be rational and efficient in the use of one's time and energy; to value work over play; and to be "intellectually superior" (p. 29). Anyone who fails to live up to these and similar ideals risks being labeled abnormal and to experience pressure to conform to the ideal.

The most significant finding of the Louisville study would seem to be that scores for boys and girls were similar except in the area of learning disorders. Miller et al. (1971) point out that this finding stands in sharp contrast to the sex ratios among children referred to clinics which, in study after study, has shown an excess of boys over girls of the order of 3 to 1. Similarly, both informal reports and systematic studies (Peterson, 1961; Werry & Quay, 1971) have shown that teachers have more trouble with boys than with girls. A possible explanation for this discrepancy, offered by Miller et al. (1971), is in line with the thinking underlying this chapter: It is the tolerance of significant adults in the child's environment and not some absolute standard of normality that provides the basis for a definition of behavior disorders. Recalling that the boys in their sample were more extreme in their behavior and that they also had greater difficulty with formal learning, the authors suggest that the basic problem is in failure to learn. When failure occurs in boys, their reaction is more likely to find expression in aggression, hyperactivity, and antisocial behavior. When failure occurs in girls, their reaction is more likely to be manifested in social withdrawal, sensitivity, and fear. "Since children are often referred when they become problems to adults, and since agression is more likely to become a problem to adults, boys are more likely to be referred for treatment" (p. 21). The fact that a high incidence of learning disorders is found in treatment clinics that also have a high male/female ratio would seem to lend support to this speculation. The strong interaction between learning disorders and problem behaviors may also explain the discrepancy between the results reported by Werry and Quay (1971) and those of Miller and his associates. Werry and Quay, it will be recalled, used teachers as respondents and found a higher incidence of problems among boys while the latter, having gathered their data from checklists filled out by parents, failed to find such a difference. Assuming that the responses of parents and of teachers are equally valid, it may be that compared to girls, boys, who have more difficulty with learning, find school a more aversive situation and respond to that situation with behaviors viewed by their teachers as aggressive, hyperactive, or antisocial. Since behavior is largely situation-specific and not carried from situation to situation in the form of a trait (Wahler, 1975), these same boys may behave differently under the stimulus conditions prevalent in their homes, where their parents would rate their behavior as being no more problematic than that of girls.

The normative information provided by their random sample of the general population together with data from an earlier study based on a clinic population, permitted Miller et al. (1971) to set statistical cutoff scores at one and two standard deviations above the mean, respectively. A disability score of 25 (1σ above the mean) classified 85 percent of the general population as nondisturbed, while a disability score of 37 (2σ above the mean) accounted for 98 percent of the general population. This, in turn, permitted an estimate of the number of children in the total child population who might be expected to obtain scores in the disturbed range. Assuming that there were, at the time, 26 million children in the United States between the ages of 6 and 12, Miller et al. (1971) made the projection that there were one-half million children with a disability score of 25 in this age group. Put in another way, 15 out of every 100 parents in the community will reflect their judgment of their child in a disability score of at least 25.

Who Needs Treatment?

Since most of these children do not find their way to a clinical facility, one wonders what becomes of a behavior that a parent deems noteworthy enough to check off on a behavior inventory but for which the child receives no treatment because such treatment is either not sought or not available. As with most questions that are phrased in such a general fashion, the answer is "it depends." It depends on the specific nature of the problematic behavior and on the age of the child when this behavior is noticed. A follow-up study, spanning a 5-year period, conducted by Gersten, Langner, Eisenberg, Simcha-Fagan, and McCarthy (1976), revealed the following relations. When a child exhibits antisocial, delinquent behavior before age 10, such behavior will not necessarily still be a source of complaint when that child enters adolescence. On the other hand, when antisocial, delinquent behavior is present during adolescence it appears to be highly predictive of similar behavior in later years. A similar trend was found for problems of the anxious-withdrawn variety. This type of problem may well be outgrown if it appears in the years before middle adolescence but when it is found after that period, it may be predictive of a fairly fixed pattern of troubled behavior.

Gersten et al. (1976) conclude from their work that treatment or other intervention would have a different impact on a young person's later life, depending on the age the treatment was administered. When a child exhibits so-called neurotic, anxious-withdrawn difficulties somewhere between about age 8 and 12, treatment should produce little change other than that to be expected for untreated children. In other words, what benefit one might attribute to treatment may well be due to normal developmental changes. Similar conclusions about treatment effectiveness have been drawn from reviews of published studies (Levitt, 1957, 1963; Lewis, 1965). These reveal that between two-thirds and three-quarters of all children with problems typically seen in treatment facilities will improve within 2 years whether or not they receive the traditional kind of treatment which has been available in such clinics. The work of Gersten et al. (1976) adds two qualifiers to this information. One is that treatment for delinquent-antisocial behavior becomes particularly important after preadolescence. The other is that when a child exhibits aggression toward family members or peers or shows disturbances in speech, thought, or intellectual functions, treatment should be undertaken before the age of 6. These speculations, of course, are based on longitudinal comparisons, and not on a study of treatment effectiveness. Whether they are valid must be tested in future research, but their presentation stands as a reminder that the behavior of children, whether normal or problematic, must be seen in the context of developmental considerations.

The issue of normality and its converse, the question of when a behavior is a problem, has a number of other ramifications (Ross, 1963), not the least of which is the validity of the judgment made by the people in the child's environment about any particular aspect of that child's behavior. One must be concerned not only with the question "When is a behavior a problem?" but also with "When is a problem not a child's behavior disorder?" When the tolerance level of a child's environment is an important factor in the definition of a behavior disorder, then this tolerance level can also be too high or too low. If it is too low, parents may seek help around a behavior of their child that few others in their community would deem problematic, and the professional person to whom they come for help must thus exercise a judgment that will involve his or her norms, standards, and values. There are times when the parents' tolerance level and not the child's behavior may have to be changed.

One must also remember that some behaviors that a child's adult environment deems problematic is, in fact, an adaptive response to a problematic environment. Thus, in the survey by Werry and Quay (1971), half of the boys (49.7 percent) in the presumably normal kindergarten, first, and second grade classes in the public school system were reported as displaying "restlessness, inability to sit still"; "distractibility" was checked for 48.2 percent of the boys; and 46.3 percent of the boys were charged with "disruptiveness, tendency to annoy others." It makes little sense to speak of behavior problems when nearly half of an unselected population engages in that form of behavior. If one uses normal in the statistical sense, the restless, distractible, and disruptive behavior of the children in this school system would have to be viewed as normal behavior; yet the teachers check it off on a problem ("symptom") checklist. Whose problem is it? Could it be that classrooms in elementary school are so structured and teacher behavior so programmed that the "normal," to be expected behavior of male children is to emit responses the teacher identifies as restlessness and distractibility? If this is the case, the modification called for is situational-environmental and should not have its focus on changing the behavior of the boys so that they "adjust" to what may be an intolerable situation.

With the arbitrary and relative nature of the definition of psychological disorders clearly in mind, we turn now to a review of studies which represent attempts to contribute to a taxonomy of behavior disorders and use descriptions of behavior as basic data.

TOWARD A TAXONOMY OF BEHAVIOR DISORDERS

A number of investigators have taken the observations of parents or teachers as the basis for classifying psychological disorders of children. These observations can be recorded as responses on behavior checklists, or they can be the complaints around which children are presented to clinics specializing in work with psychological disorders. While none of the studies to be reviewed has led to a comprehensive system of classification, the results of studies of this nature may contribute to the eventual development of such a system.

Factor Analysis

The observations or complaints that parents and teachers report regarding the behavior of children can take a great many forms, and the words that might be used, including synonyms and euphemisms, probably number in the thousands. It is therefore necessary to reduce these descriptive statements to manageable size and to attempt to order them along some logical dimension. The statistical method of factor analysis permits the ordering of large numbers of discrete observations by identifying the nature of their interrelationship.

There are, for example, 163 statements in the Louisville Behavior Check List (Miller, 1967b), each describing a specific behavior that a child might be observed to emit. When parents are asked to indicate on this checklist which behaviors are descriptive of their child, they might pick as many as forty, some identifying deviant, some prosocial, behavior. When an investigator has collected many such checklists from a large sample of parents, it will be found that certain items on the list tend to be checked together; that is, they tend to correlate. For instance, on a checklist developed by Ross, Lacey, and Parton (1965), such items as "He teases other children," "He hits and pushes other children," and "He boasts about how tough he is" were usually checked together—when one item applied to a given boy, the others would usually also apply. On the other hand, such items as "He becomes frightened easily," "He is afraid of making mistakes," and "He is easily upset by changes in things around him" were rarely checked with the earlier items, but were, in turn, often checked together with each other and similar items.

A factor analysis identifies such intercorrelated clusters of items (factors), and the investigator can then give these factors a descriptive label and derive scales that make up the instrument. In the example given above, the first set of items belongs to the aggressive-behavior scale, the second set to the withdrawn-behavior scale of the checklist.

While factor analysis is a formidable statistical technique that makes use of complex computer programs, it is not free of the influence of fallible human decisions that an investigator must make at several crucial points of a factor-analytic study. Mention has just been made of the investigator's assigning descriptive labels to the statistically derived item clusters. This labeling entails a judgment and, as a result, similar clusters may be given different labels by different investigators. Other decisions an investigator is required to make and that affect the outcome of a factor-analytic study have to do with the selection of items to be included in the original data-gathering device, with the population to be studied, and with who the respondents are to be. After the basic data have been gathered, certain technical decisions arise, such as which of several available computer programs to use and how many factors to extract—decisions that are more often guided by what program happens to be at hand or from whom the investigator had learned statistics than by more rational considerations.

The Direction of Behavior

Because investigators differ in the decisions they make at these various choice-points, their studies are difficult to compare and their results are sometimes contradictory. Despite this, two general categories of maladaptive, excess behavior appear with an impressive frequency in diverse empirical studies (Achenbach, 1966; Conners, 1970; Dreger et al., 1964; Patterson, 1964; Peterson, 1961; Ross et al., 1965) as well as in deductive discussions (Ackerson, 1931; Ross, 1959). These categories differentiate excess approach behavior (aggression) and excess avoidance behavior (withdrawal). Different investigators give different labels to these categories, but they invariably revolve around the direction of the maladaptive responses, toward or away from the environment. The terms used to describe this dichotomy often reflect the writer's theoretical orientation. Kessler (1966) speaks of the effect of the disturbance and asks, "Who suffers?," the child or other people; Peterson (1961) writes, "In one case, impulses are expressed and society suffers; in the other case impulses are evidently inhibited and the child suffers" (p. 206) and speaks of these two classes as "conduct problems" and "personality problems." Achenbach (1966) labeled his bipolar factor interalizing versus externalizing so as to describe "conflict with the environment" as against "problems within the self" (p. 10). Studies that resulted in a more complex factor structure (Patterson, 1964; Dreger et al., 1964) include behavior clusters that can be recognized as subsuming children whose maladaptive behavior is expressed toward the environment (aggression) and those who retreat from social interaction (withdrawal). Scales developed to measure these two dimensions (Ross et al., 1965) have been shown to be reliable (Stover & Giebink, 1967) and capable of replication (Miller, 1977). There is thus considerable support for Peterson's (1961) conclusion that "the generality of these factors appears to be enormous" (p. 206).

One of the earliest attempts to find systematic interrelationships among the psychological problems of children was the work of Luton Ackerson (1931, 1942). Using the case records of children who had been examined at the Illinois Institute for Juvenile Research between 1923 and 1927, he intercorrelated 162 descriptive characteristics for his sample of 2,113 boys and 1,181 girls. These characteristics ranged from such objective statements as "police arrest" to such inferences as "mental conflict." The examination of his intercorrelations led Ackerson to postulate the dichotomy of "personality problems" and "conduct problems," and he described the former as resulting primarily in suffering for the child, the latter in suffering for others. Lacking the statistical techniques that might have permitted a sophisticated analysis of his data, Ackerson was unable to substantiate his assertion that child behavior problems can be ordered by this dichotomous classification, but later studies tended to bear him out.

Lorr and Jenkins (1953) selected 94 of Ackerson's 162 descriptive characteristics and subjected them to a factor analysis. This resulted in the isolation of five primary factors, which they labeled "socialized delinquency," "internal conflict," "unsocialized aggressiveness," "brain injury," and "schizoid pattern." These labels reflect the heterogeneity of the original Ackerson items in which several principles of classification had been confounded. Thus, "brain injury" relates to etiology, "schizoid pattern" to a severity dimension, "internal conflict" to a theoretical inference, and "socialized delinquency" to value differences between the child's immediate environment and the larger community. The only factor with a clear behavioral referent is "unsocialized aggressiveness." Since "internal conflict" is derived from such items as crying spells, sensitivity, worry, and attitudes of discouragement, this factor might have been labeled more appropriately with the term "over-inhibited child," which Jenkins and Hewitt (1944) had used in an earlier publication and that would identify withdrawn behavior. Ackerson's postulated dichotomy thus seems to have some merit.

Another study in which the original Ackerson data were subjected to a factor analysis is one by Himmelweit, which is cited by Eysenck (1960). Again, not all 162 items were used but, guided by theoretical assumptions about the structure of personality, only 50 were selected for study. This time three factors emerged from a factor analysis. The first, a general factor of abnormality, would seem to reflect that the data came from a disturbed population. The third factor is, according to Eysenck, "somewhat difficult to identify," but it seems to be based on items having to do with cognitive functions and work habits, items which Lorr and Jenkins (1953) had found in the factor they labeled "schizoid pattern." Of greatest interest is the bipolar second factor, which distributes items along the aggression-withdrawal dimension, thus lending further support to the "personality problem-conduct problem" dichotomy originally postulated by Ackerson (1931).

Dimensions of Behavior Disorders

Unlike earlier investigators, Peterson (1961) used data uniformly gathered specifically for the purposes of his research. He thus avoided many of the problems investigators invariably encounter when they attempt ex post facto research on information contained in old case records. Peterson made no theoretical assumptions about the structural organization of children's behavior disorders, but the two directions that the effect of maladaptive excess behavior can take—toward the child or toward the environment—again clearly emerged.

Peterson's initial pool of problems came from the cases of a child guidance clinic and consisted of 427 items. After discarding synonymous and redundant items, he chose the fifty-eight most frequent problems for a rating scale. This scale was submitted to twenty-eight teachers of 831 kindergarten and elementary school children in six different schools. His subjects were thus not clinic cases but unselected school children, a decision which was based on the assumption that the problem behaviors seen at a clinic are continuous with general child behavior. The teachers were to rate each problem on a 3-point scale of severity, but judgments of "mild" and "severe" were later pooled for the statistical analysis. Subsequent factor analysis revealed that a 2-factor solution described the intercorrelations. Factor one was labeled "conduct problems." The items with the highest loadings on this factor, across the four age levels, were disobedience, disruptiveness, boisterousness, fighting, attention-seeking, and restlessness. The second factor was labeled "personality problems." Here the heaviest loadings were found on items describing feelings of inferiority, lack of self-confidence, social withdrawal, proneness to become flustered, self-consciousness, shyness, and anxiety.

Peterson (1961) compared mean factor scores for boys and girls across age groups and found that boys consistently displayed more "conduct problems" than girls. Younger boys also had more "personality problems," but a reversal seemed to occur around the third and fourth grade, after which the scores for girls exceeded those for boys. The factor scores also showed some age-related changes in that "conduct problem" scores for both boys and girls were lower for the third and fourth grade age group than for the other three age groups. The same was true for the "personality problem" scores of boys, but the scores of girls showed a general rise. The respective relationships are shown in Figures 1 and 2.

The age-related changes in children's behavior problems are somewhat puzzling since there is no apparent reason why children in third and fourth grade should manifest fewer problems than children in lower or higher grades. Ross et al. (1965) analyzed the data from the standardization of their behavior checklist from this point of view, but found no changes related to grade level beyond those to be expected by chance. Miller (1968) confirmed these findings in his replication study. In the absence of further research, one must assume that Peterson's results were

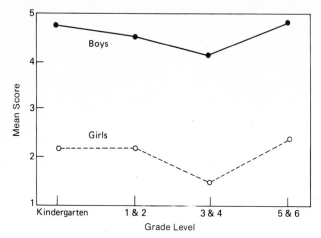

Figure 1 Age-related changes in mean "conduct problem" scores. (*After Peterson, 1961,* copyright 1961 by the American Psychological Association and reproduced by permission.)

related to the small number of teachers used in his study. Systematic differences in teachers may well be correlated with the grade level at which they are teaching so that in responding to checklists they may be working with what Miller has called "a built-in age-correction factor." Since the environment's tolerance is part of the definition of a behavior problem, it may be that this tolerance finds expression in the way a teacher rates the behaviors found in the classroom.

The dichotomous classification of behavior disorders received further support in the research reported by Achenbach (1966). This investigator compiled a list of

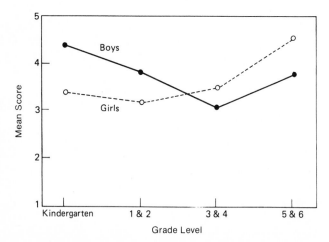

Figure 2 Age-related changes in mean "personality problem" scores. (*After Peterson, 1961,* copyright 1961 by the American Psychological Association and reproduced by permission.)

ninety-one problems and complaints (symptoms) and had raters review the case records of 300 male and 300 female children who had been referred to the child psychiatry unit of a large university hospital. Wherever a given problem was mentioned in the record, it was checked. Problems that occurred less than five times in the sample of 300 children were excluded, resulting in a final list of seventy-four problems. The mean number of problems recorded per case was 8.28, but this figure is biased by the fact that cases with fewer than three recordable problems had been excluded from the sample. Achenbach thus worked only with children who had multiple complaints and who had been referred to a treatment clinic. Certain other selection criteria that he used to compose the sample and that may have affected the outcome of the study should also be mentioned. There were no children with intelligence test scores of less than 75; nor were there any with serious physical illness, severe chronic physical handicap, or "good evidence for organic involvement" (p. 7). The ages ranged from 4 to 16 years; all children were white, and none had been institutionalized for more than 2 years.

The data thus obtained were subjected to a factor analysis. The first principal factor that emerged for both males and females in five different analyses, and as a highly reliable dimension, was bipolar. Achenbach chose to label this factor internalizing versus externalizing and states that the problems at the externalizing pole describe "conflict with the environment," while those at the other pole describe "problems within the self" (p. 10). The nature of the problems subsumed under these two categories makes it clear that they are analogous to the "conduct problem-personality problem" dichotomy found by Peterson (1961), which, in turn, corresponded to the Hewitt and Jenkins (1946) terms of "unsocialized aggression" and "over-inhibited behavior," describing, in other words, aggression and withdrawal.

The second principal factor isolated in Achenbach's study was somewhat less reliable and not as readily labeled as the first. Bizarre behavior and fantastic, delusionary, or hallucinatory thinking were the two most heavily weighted problems. "Descriptively, it seemed to include symptoms both of severe mental disturbance and of excessive belligerence. The label 'Severe and Diffuse Psychopathology' was finally chosen" (p. 10). This factor bears a striking similarity to the third factor isolated by Himmelweit in the work cited by Eysenck (1960), who pointed out that it may be similar to the psychoticism factor he had identified in studies dealing with adults. The severity or intensity of a given maladaptive behavior is clearly a dimension along which psychological problems can be ordered, and factor-analytic studies help us recognize that severity is a different dimension that should not be confounded with the dimension of the direction in which excess behavior is expressed.

In discussing the research on the behavior of children in an unselected, nonclinic population conducted by Miller et al. (1971), we mentioned that these investigators had failed to find differences between the behaviors of boys and girls, as reported by their parents. This result stands in contrast to that of Peterson

(1961), whose responding teachers did record sex differences and of Achenbach (1966), whose clinic population showed sex-related differences in factor structure.

Since the basic data used for this study were difficulties that eventuated in clinic contact, the most straightforward explanation for this difference is that parents will bring boys to a mental health clinic for reasons that are different from those for which they will bring girls. Thus, "breathing difficulty," "excessive talking, chattering," "fainting," "inappropriate indifference, e.g., to physical complaints," "over-eating," and "picking" had been reported only for girls, while only the records of boys contained "cruelty, bullying, meanness," "fire-setting," "loudness," "sexual perversion, exposing self," "showing off," "sleepwalking," and "vandalism." These differences, which reflect differential tolerance levels on the part of society, as well as differential sex-role expectations, are the most likely reasons for the differences in factor structure. These data should not be interpreted as reflecting genetic, sex-linked differences in behavior or in susceptibility to psychological disorders.

The two directions that the immediate effect of maladaptive behavior can take, toward or away from the environment, have thus been identified as principal dimensions in a series of studies using different populations, different data sources, and different methods of analysis. They again appear in the studies still to be discussed, but here these dimensions are to be found among a number of other factors that emerged from the data analysis. The conclusion that the dimensions of aggression and withdrawal have enormous generality (Peterson, 1961) when used in classifying child behavior, received further strong support from the work of Kohn and Rosman (1972a, 1973), who found these dimensions not only to have generality but also predictive power. Kohn and Rosman (1973) administered a 90-item Social Competence Scale and a 58-item Symptom Checklist to 407 children, ranging in age from 3 to 6, who attended day-care centers operated by the welfare department of a large Northeastern city. The Symptom Checklist included such items as, "Keeps to himself, remains aloof and distant" and "Gets angry or annoyed when addressed by an adult, even in friendly manner (not reprimand)." The Social Competence Scale consisted of items designed to assess the child's mastery of major areas of functioning in a preschool setting, such as "Cooperates with rules and regulations" and "Can be independent of adult in having ideas about or planning activities." This scale was so constructed that the child's functioning in five areas was covered; namely, relationship to teachers, relationship to peers, involvement in activities, self-care activities, and behavior during transitional periods. In addition to items describing high competence, such as those cited, there were items describing low competence, as, for example, "Seeks adult attention by crying" or "Dawdles when required to do something."

Each child was rated by two teachers whose ratings were pooled for purposes of the factor analysis. Two bipolar factors emerged from the analysis of the Social Competence Scale. They were labeled *interest-participation* versus *apathy-withdrawal* and *cooperation-compliance* versus *anger-defiance*. The factor analysis of the Symptom Checklist also revealed two major factors that accounted for a little over 50 percent of the communal variance of a 9-factor solution. They were labeled *apathy-withdrawal* and *anger-defiance*.

Model Building

It will be noted that the two symptom factors in the Kohn and Rosman (1972*a*) study have the same label as the negative poles of the two social-competence factors. In fact, the respective symptom factors and social-competence factors had high linear correlations, reflecting that behaviors defined as low in social competence and behaviors defined as "indications of emotional disturbance" are closely related, if not identical. An item such as "Child is bossed and dominated by other children," which appears on the Social Competence Scale, is clearly another version of "Withdraws or accepts it when others shove, hit, accuse or criticize him," which appears on the Symptom Checklist. It would seem that an assessment of social competence permits one to classify children into four major groupings, as indicated in the quadrants of Figure 3. The left column identifies children whose behavior is considered adaptive, while the right column identifies those whose behavior is considered maladaptive—society having defined defiance of norms and withdrawal from social interaction as negative or deviant behaviors. A look at Figure 3 also reveals that the diagonals represent bipolar dimensions. That is, interest-participation is the positive opposite of apathy-withdrawal, while anger-defiance is the negative counterpart to cooperation-compliance.

Such a fourfold classification of behavior had been suggested by Schaefer (1961) when he advanced his hypothetical "circumplex model" for social and emotional behavior, which was arranged around the orthogonal axes of extraversion-introversion and hostility-love. Schaefer (1961) identified the resulting four combinations of these dimensions as "friendliness—outgoing, positive behavior; conformity—compliant, controlled positive behavior; withdrawal—hostile, fearful avoidance of interaction; and aggressiveness—hostile attack with little impulse control" (p. 139). The results of Kohn's (1969) large-scale study would seem to support these four combinations, if not to confirm Schaefer's hypothetical model.

Interest-Participation	Anger-Defiance
Cooperation-Compliance	Apathy-Withdrawal

Figure 3   A fourfold classification of social competence. (*Based on Kohn, 1969.*)

Kohn's work (1977) is of particular interest because it extends the classification of behavior to a younger age group and into the adaptive realm, whereas earlier work had dealt almost exclusively with maladaptive behavior of older children. Kohn and Rosman (1972*b*) also report a highly important follow-up study that revealed that the factors have stability and predictive power. One hundred of the children who had been rated in preschool for the original study were reevaluated in their first year in public school, using the Metropolitan Achievement Test and Peterson's problem checklist. It was found that children who had been high on apathy-withdrawal in preschool tended to score high on Peterson's analogous "personality problem" factor, while children who had scored high on anger-defiance scored high on Peterson's analogous "conduct problem" factor.

Aggression and withdrawal appear to be behavioral characteristics that permit a reliable and predictively valid mode of classifying the behavior of children whether they are found in special treatment clinics or in the general population. This, in turn, confirms that the behavior of disturbed children is not qualitatively different from the behavior of so-called normal children; the behavior lies on the same continuum, and only a judgment of magnitude (too much or too little), which is a function of the tolerance level of the people who make the judgment, separates the child in the clinic from the child in the school. This conclusion was also reached by Miller et al. (1971) in their survey of children's deviant behavior within the general population. If maladaptive behavior is simply that behavior which society has labeled maladaptive and is thus behavior that follows the same principles of development and change as any other form of behavior, a meaningful classificatory system must reflect this continuity.

Based on this logic, Becker and Krug (1964) proposed a circumplex model for the social behavior of children. Working, in part, with data from an earlier study (Becker, Peterson, Luria, Shoemaker, & Hellmer, 1962), which were derived from behavior ratings on 5-year-old children, Becker and Krug (1964) graphically plotted the positions of five bipolar variables, generating the model shown in Figure 4. The generality of this approach was tested by assigning the results of studies by six different investigators to this circumplex. High concordance was demonstrated in this manner, reflecting the meaningfulness of the approach and its utility in ordering data on child behavior. As can be seen from the accompanying figure, the model incorporates the stability-instability and introversion-extraversion factors, and it also identifies the location of the "personality problem" and "conduct problem" sectors previously identified by Peterson (1961).

The fact that descriptions of child behavior lend themselves to categorizations that can be represented in two-dimensional drawings should not lead one to lose sight of the fact that these dimensions are not dimensions of child behavior but dimensions of adults' reports of child behavior. This distinction was stressed by Novick, Rosenfeld, Bloch, and Dawson (1966), who very correctly point out that one must distinguish between reports on behavior and the behavior actually emitted by the child. This becomes particularly crucial when the reports use categories requiring the respondent to draw inferences and make generalizations.

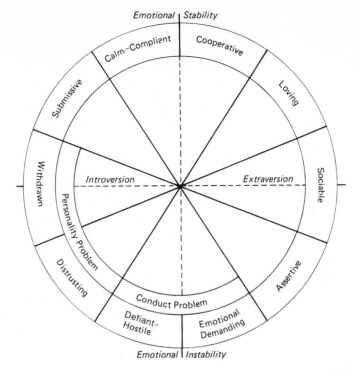

Figure 4 A circumplex model of child behavior. (*After Becker and Krug, 1964*, copyright 1964 by The Society for Research in Child Development and reproduced by permission.)

If, as was the case in the study by Becker et al. (1962), the parent or teacher is required to rate children on such dimensions as "dominant-submissive" or "soft-hearted—hard-hearted," the rating may say more about the respondent's perception than the child's behavior. Even where one can get high interobserver reliability on a rating of "dominant" for a given child, it would seem likely that the child is dominant in some situations and vis-à-vis certain peers but submissive under different conditions.

What emerges is the importance of maintaining a focus on objectively observable behavior while spelling out the stimulus conditions under which this behavior is observed. When this is done, as was the case in the work of Kohn and Rosman (1973), for example, a model like the one proposed by Becker and Krug (1964) can serve the useful function of ordering the data and conceptualizing the relationship between response classes.

RECAPITULATION

Psychological disorders of children are difficult to classify and their classification raises many questions. The very act of classifying has important consequences that must be kept in mind if the welfare of the child is to be protected. Not only is there the question of what is normal but even where behavior is seen as deviant, the need for treatment is not necessarily self-evident. Factor analysis is a statistical method that has been used in order to identify child behaviors that frequently occur together. Directions and dimensions of behavior have been identified and terms like conduct problems, personality problems, externalizer, and internalizer have been used to describe these characteristics. Such work has led to the building of conceptual models of child behavior, but thus far these have not found much use in practical application.

A presentation of psychological disorders from a behavioral point of view places a great deal of emphasis on the environmental variables which influence behavior. Since this emphasis might give the impression that the child is passively molded by these environmental influences, that the environment is solely responsible for determining behavior, it is well to remember that child and environment stand in a dynamic interaction to which the child makes his or her own important contribution. It is to an examination of this interaction that we turn in the next chapter.

Chapter 3

The Interaction between Constitution and Environment

Careful students of child behavior (Irwin, 1930; Shirley, 1933) have long ago reported striking individual differences in the behavioral style of very young children. Activity level, motility, frequency of crying, amount of food intake, and the sleep-wake cycle are among the many characteristics in which differences seem to be present from the time of birth. Lately, it has come to be recognized that these early individual differences contribute importantly to the organism-environment interaction which eventuates in that complex behavioral repertoire of the individual that we sometimes call personality. More specifically, it would seem to be a reasonable hypothesis that individual differences in behavioral style, interacting with the social environment, are an important factor in the development of behavior disorders.

> From the infant's first day of life on, a mother and her child are each unique individuals. Their responses to each other are based on their respective reaction patterns (personalities) within the matrix of the total environmental situation obtaining at the time. . . . Any particular mother will react to a child with a high activity level in a different manner than to a child with a low activity level [Ross, 1959, p. 76].

The potential stress resulting from a mismatch between the mother's expectations or tolerances and the child's behavioral style may well set the stage for discord and conflict.

In terms of Cattell's (1950) "three modalities of behavior traits," the largely constitutional behavioral style is the quality in which behavior finds expression; it is the *how* of behavior, as opposed to the *why* (motivation) and the *what* (abilities and content). Like other constitutional *anlagan* (predispositions), behavioral style can be modified within limits by environmental influences; it is not an immutable characteristic, but it is well to keep in mind that the ultimate behavioral outcome is the consequence of influences on an already existing style, not the result of the environment shaping a tabula rasa child. Strong support for this formulation was presented by Schaefer and Bayley (1963), who analyzed the extensive collection of longitudinal data from the Berkeley Growth Study and found that the child dimension of activity-passivity was relatively independent of parent-child relationships. They viewed this finding as supporting the hypothesis that the human infant is not completely plastic but responds to the environment in accordance with innate tendencies.

BEHAVIORAL INDIVIDUALITY IN EARLY CHILDHOOD

The most systematic approach to the question of behavioral style and its contribution to child development is the work of Thomas, Chess, and Birch (1968), whose New York Longitudinal Study of 136 children focused on behavioral individuality in early childhood (Thomas, Chess, Birch, Hertzig, & Korn, 1963). Without claiming that their sample is representative of the general population (the mean Stanford-Binet IQ of the children was 127), these investigators present a framework for the discussion of behavioral style that has far-reaching implications for the student of psychological disorders of children.

The study extended over a 10-year period, during which data gathering entailed parental interviews, teacher interviews, school observations, and observations of the child in the course of individual intelligence testing. The mean age of the children at the time of the first parental interview was 3.3 months, 50 percent of them being less than 2.5 months old. Parental interviews were repeated at 3-month intervals during the first 18 months; they were then held at intervals of 6 months until the child was 5 years old; thereafter, interviews were held on a yearly basis. School observations of 1 hour and teacher interviews began when the child entered nursery school and were repeated each year. The Stanford-Binet, Form L was administered at ages 3 and 6. In addition to the regular parental interviews, a special structured interview was held with each parent separately when the child was 3 years old. Validity of the information elicited from the parents was checked by independent observers who went to the homes of 23 of the 136 children. Throughout the study, the investigators used reasonable safeguards against confounding the data by using interviewers and observers who had no knowledge of the child's previous history or behavior. The reliability of interview and observation scoring is adequate for purposes of an investigation of this type (Thomas et al., 1963).

Throughout the interviews with parents and teachers the focus was on factual descriptions of actual behavior, and inferences as to the "meaning" of the behavior were not accepted. Thus, when a parent reported that the child "loved his cereal," the interviewer had been instructed to inquire what specific aspect of the child's behavior caused the parent to reach this conclusion. Individual patterns of behavioral style seemed to emerge, particularly around the child's reaction to new stimuli, demands, or situations—whether these were as simple as the first bath, or complex, such as entry into nursery school. For this reason, special attention was paid to the child's first response to a new stimulus and to subsequent reactions when the same stimulus was again presented.

Temperamental Characteristics

An inductive content analysis of the parental interviews for the first twenty-two children studied led the investigators to establish the following nine categories of behavioral style, called *temperamental characteristics* by the authors (Thomas et al., 1963).

Activity Level   This refers to the level, tempo, and frequency of general motility. A child with a high activity level is described as wriggling, kicking, moving, squirming, and running around a great deal. Parents would make such comments as: "She crawls all over the house," "He runs around so, that whenever we come in from the park I'm exhausted," or "She moves a great deal in her sleep." Low activity level, on the other hand, was described as: "In the bath he lies quietly and doesn't kick" or "In the morning she's still in the same place she was when she fell asleep." The characteristic of activity level was rated on a 3-point scale, could be reliably identified, and showed consistency over time. The same was true of all temperamental characteristics.

Rhythmicity   This category reflects the degree of regularity of such repetitive biological functions as sleeping and waking, rest and activity, as well as the food intake and elimination cycles. Scoring was based on the regularity or irregularity of these events.

Approach or Withdrawal   The initial reaction of the child to any new stimulus, such as food, toys, people, places, or procedures, can be categorized along this dimension on the basis of parental report and observations. "She always smiles at a stranger" is an example of the approach reaction, while "Whenever he sees a stranger he cries" describes a child whose preponderant style is to withdraw.

Adaptability   While the preceding category referred to the initial response, adaptability deals with the modifiability of the initial pattern; that is, with the sequential course of responses to new situations. Inasmuch as parents tend to view initial withdrawal or negative responses as changeworthy, adaptive behavior to the demands of the social environment is likely to be required. Thus, the child who spat out the cereal when it was first offered but who later came to accept it with little protest is considered adaptable, while the one who continues to reject the food manifests nonadaptive behavior. Thomas et al. (1968) present excerpts from parental interviews to illustrate this behavioral characteristic. Thus, "Now when we go to the doctor's he doesn't start to cry till we undress him, and he even stops then if he can hold a toy." As an example of nonadaptive behavior they reproduce the following statement: "Whenever I put her snowsuit and hat on she screams and struggles, and she doesn't stop crying till we're outside."

Intensity of Reaction   Whether a response is negative or positive, it can be emitted with high or low intensity, and each child has a dominant characteristic on this dimension that tends to run across modalities and situations. Intensity was scored in relation to responses to external stimuli as well as to deprivation and satiation. An example of high-intensity reaction is "She cries loud and long whenever the sun shines in her eyes"; of low intensity, "He squints at a bright light but doesn't cry."

Threshold of Responsiveness   This category deals with the intensity of the stimulus that is required in order to elicit an observable response. Threshold may differ for different sensory systems; thus, a child can have a high threshold for visual but a low threshold for auditory stimuli. Subsumed under this category is the concept of difference in limen; i.e., the magnitude of difference between stimuli necessary before the child shows evidence of discrimination. For example, "She notices any little change."

Quality of Mood   This category differentiates between the child whose pervasive mood is friendly, pleasant, and joyful ("He always smiles at a stranger."), and the child who tends to behave in a generally unfriendly, unpleasant manner ("She cries at almost every stranger, and those that she doesn't cry at she hits."). Positive mood tends to manifest itself in smiling and laughing, while negative mood is characterized by frowning and crying. As with all other categories, scoring is based on observable behavior, not on inferred states of unhappiness or happiness.

Distractibility   This category was used to indicate the ease or difficulty with which ongoing behavior can be interrupted by extraneous environmental stimuli. These stimuli may be introduced by a parent who desires to distract a child from an undesirable activity, or they may be chance stimuli in the environment that draw the child's attention from an ongoing activity.

Attention Span and Persistence   Attention span refers to the length of time a given activity is pursued, while persistence involves the question whether an activity is maintained despite interruptions and other obstacles. Although distractibility and persistence would seem to be reciprocal, it is necessary to treat them as separate categories because it is possible for a child to be both highly distractible and highly persistent. Such a child would return to a given task again and again, no matter how often distracted or diverted.

As might be expected, these nine categories of behavioral style are interrelated. This interrelationship is reflected in correlations ranging from −.49 to +.48. The largest number of significant correlations with other categories was found for intensity, adaptability, and mood quality; the interrelations among the other categories were low and generally insignificant. A factor analysis of the nine categories for each of the first 5 years of the subject's life revealed a clustering of mood, intensity, approach-withdrawal, and adaptability on the first factor of a varimax solution. The loadings on this factor range from .34 to .77; the loadings on the other two factors that emerged were considerably lower, and the clusters made little theoretical sense. The first factor, labeled Factor A, was thus selected for further use, to be discussed below.

Behavioral Style and Psychological Disorders

Of the 136 children in the study, 42 were identified as manifesting psychological disorders in the course of the 10-year contact with the research team. Children with psychological disorders thus represented 31 percent of the total study population. This figure denotes the prevalence of disorders over a 10-year span and is thus higher than the usually reported incidence data, which are based on cross-sectional surveys at one point in time. Nonetheless, it is likely that the families' ongoing contact with the research team, the availability of a child psychiatrist on the team, the recurrent interviews which were focused on child behavior, and the general level of sophistication of these parents resulted in their seeking help with problem behaviors more readily and earlier than might be expected of parents in the general population.

To be included in the so-called clinical sample, a child had to manifest disordered behavior that the team's child psychiatrist judged as representing a significant behavioral disturbance. Most (86 percent) of the children in the clinical sample were designated as manifesting mild or moderate reactive behavior disorders, such as sleep problems, peer difficulties, tantrums, or learning difficulties—complaints quite similar to those usually encountered by child guidance clinics. For all of these cases parental guidance was the recommended form of treatment, reflecting, as we shall see, the orientation of the study team.

Since in all but one of the forty-two cases it was the parents' complaint about the child's behavior that was instrumental in initiating the psychiatric study, it is of interest to examine the kind of behaviors the parents considered problematic. As Thomas et al. (1968) point out, these closely reflect then current child-care practices, expressing standards and attitudes prevalent among the total study sample. The parents were relatively tolerant of difficulties in the areas of eating, elimination, and masturbation which, though they reported them in the interviews, they did not define as problems. They tended to complain more about disturbances in the areas of sleep, discipline, and mood; but the greatest frequency of complaints occurred in the areas of speech difficulties, peer relationships, and school learning. Thus, it appears that the more readily a difficulty is visible to the outside world, the more readily the parents in this group defined it as a problem and sought help. Whatever functions are high in the value hierarchy of parents will become important considerations affecting the parent-child interaction by defining the focus of parental concern with selected aspects of the child's behavior. The presenting complaints encountered by the clinician may thus reflect contemporary parental values and attitudes at least as much as the adaptive difficulties prevalent in the child population at any given time.

The availability of the independently assessed data on behavioral style enabled the research team to make various comparisons between the temperamental characteristics of their clinical and nonclinical samples. The forty-two clinical cases had been further subdivided into children with "active" disturbances (n = 34) and children with "passive" disturbances (n = 8). The characteristic behavior of the children in the passive group was their nonparticipation in peer group activities. Children who displayed any behavior, such as crying or running away, or if they had physical complaints, such as nausea or stomach pains, were regarded as children with active disturbances.

Comparison between the nonclinical group and the children with active disturbances revealed that the latter had received significantly higher scores on activity level in their first year of life. Other variables of behavioral style, such as intensity, adaptability, threshold, distractibility, and persistence, were significantly different at later ages. The comparison between children with passive problems and the nonclinical group did not reveal early differences; but by the fourth and fifth year of life the children with passive problems were significantly more negative in mood, less active, more persistent, and more withdrawing in response to new stimuli than the nonclinical contrast group.

It should be recalled that a factor analysis based on the intercorrelations of the nine categories of behavioral style had identified a factor, labeled Factor A, that had high loadings on mood, intensity, approach-withdrawal, and adaptability and showed relative consistency over the first 5-year period. Comparison between the clinical group (active and passive) and the nonclinical group revealed that over the 5-year period and starting around the third year the clinical group came to deviate markedly from the nonclinical group in the direction of negative mood, marked intensity, and tendency to withdraw and to be nonadaptive.

Taking only those children who had been referred because of active problem behaviors before age 5 and comparing these on the nine categories and on Factor A with children in the nonclinical group, Thomas and his coworkers (1968) found that for each of the comparisons and for at least 4 of the 5 years, the children with behavior disorders deviated in temperament in the direction signifying greater adaptational difficulty. Particularly for Factor A, the clinical group differed from the nonclinical group in the nonadaptive direction in every one of the 5 years, becoming increasingly deviant over time. These findings suggest that children who come to be referred to a clinic *before they are 5 years old* tend to differ from children who, over a 10-year period, are never referred in the characteristics of mood, intensity, approach-withdrawal, and adaptability. The investigators took pains to point out that a given combination of behavioral styles in a specific child does not in and of itself lead to behavior problems, but that it is the interaction between these stylistic characteristics and the child's environment that can eventuate in clinical referral.

It is important to recognize that behavioral style and environment not only interact but that they also modify each other, and that children's behavior has as much of an effect on parents' actions as parents' behavior has on the children's (Yarrow, Waxler, & Scott, 1971). The child's behavioral style clearly represents a stimulus constellation to which the parents respond and that response, in turn, may be a function of the parents' behavioral style. On the basis of their observations, Thomas et al. (1963) conclude that life experiences can modify a child's behavioral style. Repeatedly faced with their parents' impossible demands, children who are initially very adaptable can become increasingly less adaptable over time. As with other behavioral styles, children with high scores on adaptability are children who are predominantly but not universally adaptive. Repeated negative experiences can result in a change in the ratio of adaptive to maladaptive response patterns. It is further possible that as children get older, they come to recognize that certain aspects of their behavioral style tend to have negative consequences so that they may learn to modify or control some of their reactions under certain circumstances.

Difficult Children

The interaction between behavioral style and environment is most readily illustrated by tracing the experiences of some of the children with a behavioral style marked by irregularity, nonadaptability, withdrawal responses, and predominantly negative moods of high intensity—a constellation which characterizes what Thomas and his colleagues (1968) chose to call "difficult children." Irregularity of biological functions may find expression in the areas of sleeping, eating, and elimination. As infants, these children will wake up at unpredictable intervals and seem to require less sleep than the average child of the same age. Since they do not develop regular sleep cycles, these infants' parents are awakened several times a night, and no matter what techniques they might try, they will find it impossible to get the child to sleep through the night. Similar unpredictability can be found in the irregularity with which hunger is expressed. The amount of food consumed at any given time and the intervals between eating can vary greatly, making it impossible for the mother to work out a self-demand schedule. Unpredictable preferences for specific foods, which may undergo abrupt changes, can also characterize these children, much to the exasperation of their parents. With similar unpredictability of elimination cycles, toilet-training procedures that are based on the parent's ability to anticipate the child's eliminations are doomed to failure.

The temperamental tendency of these children to withdraw in the face of new stimuli is particularly obvious in early infancy when new experiences are constantly impinging on the child. These children are described as crying when bathed for the first time, crying whenever a new food is introduced, and crying whenever a new person enters the room. Leaving the house may result in crying, protesting, clinging, and withdrawing, with the same reactions being evoked when returning to the house at the end of an excursion. The predominance of a high-intensity negative mood is manifested by relatively more crying than laughing, more fussing than expressions of pleasure.

It should by now be apparent why Thomas et al. (1968) labeled these as "difficult children." Children with these temperamental characteristics place special demands on their parents, whose reactions will play a major role in determining the course of their child's behavioral development.

The longitudinal data available to Thomas and his coworkers enable one to contrast the development of two of these "difficult children," thereby demonstrating the crucial role of parental reaction patterns. Both children, one a girl, the other a boy, displayed similar behavioral characteristics in the early years of life. They had irregular sleep patterns, difficulty with bowel movements, slow acceptance of new foods, lengthy periods of adjustment to new routines, and frequent periods of loud crying. The girl's father reacted to her behavior with anger, seemed to dislike the child, and spent little or no time with her. The mother, on the other hand, was more understanding and permissive but quite inconsistent. The only rules that were consistently enforced were those involving the child's safety. Both the father and the mother of the boy, on the other hand, were unusually tolerant and consistent. They accepted his lengthy periods of adaptation patiently and calmly and reacted to his negative moods without anger. They viewed his troublesome behavior as an expression of his individual characteristics and not as indications of a behavioral disturbance. By age 5½, the boy was functioning smoothly in peer relations and nursery school activity. By this time, the girl manifested explosive outbursts of anger, soiling, thumbsucking, fear of the dark, protective lying, negativism, poor peer relationships, and an insatiable demand for toys and candy.

It may well be that casual acceptance of temperamental characteristics permits a child to adapt to the demands of the environment at his or her own pace. On the other hand, the reaction that makes each incident into a conflict is likely to focus attention on that particular behavioral characteristic, thus reinforcing and perpetuating it.

Compared to the children with easier temperamental characteristics, the "difficult children" were far less likely to grow up without behavior problems. Approximately 70 percent of the temperamentally difficult children were reported as having developed such problems. Difficult children represented 23 percent of the total clinical group of forty-two, but only 4 percent of the nonclinical sample. It is a challenging research question whether the incidence of behavior disorders among "difficult children" can be reduced by educating parents to accept their children's individuality and helping them to adapt to their behavioral style so that the children, in turn, can adapt to the successive demands of socialization.

The orientation of the clinical and research group working with Thomas and his coworkers permitted them to focus on manifest behavior in working with the cases in the clinical group. In the majority of these cases, the choice of treatment was parent guidance focused on environmental changes and modification of parental functioning in dealing with the child. The interviews concentrated on the need for the parents to recognize and accept their child's individual pattern of behavioral style. The parents were advised to desist from unrealistic attempts to change the child's characteristic reaction patterns. With older children it was sometimes possible to acquaint them with their own temperamental characteristics and to teach them ways of arranging situations so as to minimize the negative consequences of their behavioral characteristics. When a girl knows, for example, that she characteristically has intense negative reactions to new situations, she can learn to introduce herself into such situations gradually, thereby reducing her negative reactions that may otherwise give her trouble. Thomas et al. (1968) view the reality of individual behavioral style not as an inevitability that must be fatalistically accepted but as a condition which, once recognized, gives both parent and child logical means of coping with individual differences.

THE CONTINUUM OF CARETAKING CASUALTY

It should by now be apparent that there is no point in asking who is to blame if a child develops a psychological disorder. It may well be that the combination of the same child with different parents or the same parents with a different child would have led to a different outcome. It is what Thomas and Chess (1977) have come to call the "goodness of fit." If one wanted to look for a cause, one would have to look at the interaction between child and parents, and if one were to attempt a prevention of psychological problems, one would have to address oneself to modifying this interaction.

The importance of the interaction between child and environment was not always recognized because retrospective studies of children with psychological problems tend to obscure this phenomenon. In retrospective studies, a group of children with problems is identified, say 8-year-olds with low intelligence and severe academic difficulties. The backgrounds of these children are then traced as far as possible, often to the period before their birth. When this is done, it is often discovered that the mothers of these children had a high incidence of pregnancy complications and difficulties during labor. From this history (and often without further data) early investigators often concluded that the children had sustained some injury to their brains and this was then cited in explanation of the problems seen in the 8-year-olds. What such a study fails to investigate is whether all children with histories of prenatal or birth complications end up with similar problems when they are 8-years old. If this were not the case, some other factor or factors would have to be involved. In other words, what is needed in order to answer a question about the cause of a problem is a longitudinal, so-called prospective study which traces the development of children from before birth through childhood. When this is done, a very interesting phenomenon is uncovered.

Sameroff and Chandler (1974) reviewed several longitudinal studies and arrived at the conclusion that the later development of children who had suffered a prenatal or birth complication *depends on the caretaking environment in which they are reared.* Those who are raised in economically deprived families or by mothers who had poor education or psychological disorders tend to be intellectually retarded when they are tested at school age. On the other hand, children with similar prenatal or birth complications who are raised in an advantaged environment apparently overcome whatever difficulties may be associated with their birth history, so that by school age they are intellectually no different from children whose prenatal and birth experience had been uneventful.

Earlier writers who had held the effects of pregnancy and delivery complications to be irreversible had spoken of a "continuum of reproductive casualty" (Pasamanick & Knobloch, 1966). For this phrase Sameroff and Chandler (1974) prefer to substitute the expression "continuum of caretaking casualty" in order to underscore their conclusion that difficulties surrounding birth do not necessarily lead to later problems, but that it depends on who suffers these difficulties and what experiences he or she has during infancy and childhood. If these experiences are favorable, reproductive complications need not have later consequences, but given unfavorable circumstances these "children at risk" may well turn out to be impaired. In other words, it is not so much the nature of a child but the interaction this child has with the environment that determines the child's later status. This interaction, however, appears influenced by the child's own state. Sameroff and Chandler (1974) point out that children with difficult reproductive histories tend to have more disrupting behavioral styles than those with good histories. In turn, not unlike some of the "difficult children" of whom we spoke earlier, they tend to elicit poor caretaking responses from their parents, and this may contribute to the development of psychological problems or disorders. Attempts at preventing such an unfavorable outcome must therefore address themselves to helping the child's caretakers to adapt to the special needs of an infant who may be difficult to raise because of his or her unfavorable birth experiences.

It should, of course, go without saying that complications of pregnancy and delivery should also be reduced to a minimum. It is here that socioeconomic considerations come to play a crucial role. It is a well-established fact (Birch & Gussow, 1970) that pregnant women in the low-income group receive less adequate prenatal health care than do women from the middle- and upper-income groups. The poor thus contribute a disproportionate share to the number of pregnancy complications and difficult deliveries. When this information is viewed in the light of the conclusion by Sameroff and Chandler (1974) that children with reproductive complications are more likely to develop disorders when they are raised in economically deprived families, it is not surprising that the poor contribute more than their share to the number of children who experience intellectual and psychological difficulties.

RECAPITULATION

In discussing the determinants of behavior in the Introduction, we stressed that one of the four interacting factors that enter into any specific behavioral outcome are the genetic-constitutional characteristics of the child. Among these characteristics are the behavioral-style variables which Thomas et al. (1968) isolated and examined with reference to their role in the development of behavior disorders. Although their study has its limitations, particularly in terms of sampling, it serves as a reminder that children make important contributions to the interaction with their environment. Their contribution consists, among other things, of such behavioral-style characteristics as activity level, rhythmicity of biological functions, approach or withdrawal reactions to new stimuli, adaptability, intensity of reaction, theshold of responsiveness, mood quality, distractibility, attention span, and persistence. Depending on the particular combination of these characteristics, parents may find the child easy or difficult to take care of, and "difficult children" may be contributing more than their share to those who display behavior that is considered disordered.

Other longitudinal studies have highlighted the fact that a child who has experienced complications before, during, or shortly after birth may exhibit behavior during infancy that makes special demands on the caretaking environment. If this environment responds favorably (and this may be easier in socio-economically advantaged than in disadvantaged families), no undue consequences need develop, but psychological casualties may result when the caretaking environment is unfavorable.

Having thus discussed the child's contributions to the interaction and the environment's reaction to that contribution, we come to focus again on what one can do in order to influence the child's environment; for this is the segment of the child × environment interaction that lends itself most readily to intervention, whether its goal is the prevention or the treatment of psychological disorders. Our next look will therefore be at the premises and principles which underlie a behavioral approach to these disorders.

Chapter 4

The Premises and Principles
of Behavior Therapy

Our presentation of the various forms of psychological disorders will be accompanied by a review of treatment approaches that behaviorally oriented therapists use in attempts to alleviate these disorders. These treatment approaches are subsumed under the term *behavior therapy*. In order to examine this form of therapy, we must first look at the basic premises of behavior therapists and at the psychological principles they are applying in their work.

The modern origins of behavior therapy with children can be traced to 1924, the year Mary Cover Jones published the case of Peter whose generalized fear of furry objects she had treated by the application of the principles of respondent conditioning. A few years later, Krasnogorski (1925), Ivanov-Smolenski (1927), and Gesell (1938) pointed to the relevance of Pavlovian conditioning to the treatment of psychological disorders. But it seems that the time was not ripe for this obvious suggestion, for although Mowrer and Mowrer (1938) described the treatment of bed-wetting by conditioning techniques in the intervening years, it was not until Salter (1949), Skinner (1953), Eysenck (1957), Wolpe (1958), and Bandura (1961) pointed out that laboratory-derived and laboratory-tested methods could be applied to the modification of psychological disorders that behavior therapy became more widely used.

Although the prototype of this form of treatment had been a 3-year-old boy (Jones, 1924*a*), early application of behavior therapy was almost entirely limited to adults, and 20 years after Jones had treated little Peter, only occasional reports dealing with the treatment of children had appeared in the literature (Ross, 1964*a*). While some publications in South Africa (Lazarus, 1959) and Great Britain (Jones, 1960) dealt with child cases, it was not until approaches based on the principles of operant conditioning were used in work with institutionalized children (Ferster & DeMyer, 1962) that behavior therapy became more widely applied in the treatment of children. By the time Gelfand and Hartmann prepared a review published in 1968, they were able to cite some seventy references. Between then and 1975 one count yielded more than 900 articles dealing with child behavior therapy (Graziano, 1975). It seems that the time was ripe!

THE PREMISES OF THE BEHAVIOR THERAPIST

Behavior therapy is an approach to the alleviation of psychological problems that rests on the premise that these problems represent learned maladaptive behavior or a failure to have learned adaptive behavior. The focus is on behavior as it occurs in the present, and the aim of the behavior therapist is to change that behavior in the adaptive direction. This premise leads the behavior therapist to seek behavior change through the application of various psychological principles that derive from research in the laboratory where learning has long been the object of systematic study. In the application of these principles various methods may come to be used, and behavior therapy cannot be viewed as synonymous with any one method or technique.

As we pointed out earlier, behavior that is observed at any point in time represents the end point of the interaction of four variables: genetic-constitutional endowment, past learning, the individual's current physiological state, and the current environmental conditions. Of these four, only two are subject to manipulation by a therapist wishing to induce behavior change; these are the current environmental conditions and the individual's physiological state. Since the physiological state is, in turn, changeable only by changing environmental conditions, the focus of behavior therapy falls on the environment in which the individual currently lives. This emphasis on the current situation is one of the defining characteristics of behavior therapy. Whether the problem be one of excess or of deficient behavior, the behavior therapist intensively studies what is going on in the here and now and makes remedial plans on the basis of information thus obtained. While the learning orientation logically implies the recognition of the fact that past events contributed to the development of present difficulties, the behavior therapist considers a detailed knowledge of the person's history unessential for planning or conducting therapy.

If it were possible to obtain a factual account of the conditions under which maladaptive behavior was acquired together with an accurate statement of the child's reinforcement history, such knowledge might aid a therapist in deciding on the most suitable approach to treatment. Unfortunately, information of this kind is not available. Several studies (e.g., Wenar, 1961; Robbins, 1963) have shown that the developmental "histories" obtained from mothers are neither reliable nor valid, and for this reason it would seem that a therapist's efforts can be put to better advantage than to try to gather such materials.

The focus of behavior therapy is on current behavior and its current circumstances, and this focus guides the work of the behavior therapist from the beginning of the contact with the client. As Kanfer and Phillips (1966) have pointed out, a behavioral approach must entail more than the application of learning principles to treatment as such; the behavioral approach must be reflected in all aspects of the clinical contact. This means that the expectations with which parents and child enter the contact must be relevant to the orientation on which the helping process is to be based. Members of the general public often have stereotyped notions about the nature of psychotherapy which are based on the much-publicized traditional approaches. This often means that the behavior therapist must correct these notions before much else can be done. Parents must be convinced that the therapist is interested in what is happening now, not in what happened years ago; that they are to relate what they saw the child do, not what they thought the child was feeling. Observed behaviors, not inferences about inner states, are the data with which the behavior therapist seeks to deal.

THEORETICAL BACKGROUND

The behavior therapist seeks to apply known psychological principles in the treatment of behavior disorders. In the case of deficient behavior, the therapeutic task is to establish missing responses; in the case of excess behavior, the child must learn to modify these responses so as to make the behavior more adaptive to the demands of the environment. In either case, treatment involves learning, unlearning, and relearning. The principles of learning which behavior therapists bring to bear on the analysis and modification of behavior disorders can be discussed under three headings—respondent conditioning, operant learning, and observational learning—although the three may well represent different aspects of the same basic process, and they assuredly interact whenever human learning takes place in a natural environment.

Respondent Conditioning

At times called *Pavlovian* or *classical conditioning*, this kind of learning involves the modification of a response that the organism is innately capable of making by substituting a *conditioned stimulus* for the natural or *unconditioned stimulus*. A well-known example is the case of little Albert (Watson & Rayner, 1920) who was conditioned to make a fear response to the stimulus of a white rat by having the rat repeatedly paired with a loud noise—a stimulus that elicits fear, apparently innately. Prior to this conditioning, the rat had been an object of curiosity to the child who was thus shown to have learned to fear the animal. It is a distinctive aspect of respondent conditioning that an innate response is elicited by a stimulus that precedes it and that the organism is passively responding to potent environmental events or external stimuli. The *conditioned responses* thus established usually involve the autonomic nervous system, and respondent conditioning is probably always involved when emotional responses, such as fear, come to be attached to previously neutral stimuli.

The following phenomena have been extensively studied in the psychological laboratory and are of particular relevance to the behavior therapist. *Stimulus generalization* is present when a response, at first elicited by one specific stimulus, comes also to be made when stimuli are presented that are similar in some respect to the original one. Because the response is the stronger, or the more likely to occur, the more similar the new stimulus is to the original one, it is possible to order this similarity along a continuum and to speak of a *generalization gradient*. The word *extinction* is used to describe the gradual diminution and eventual disappearance of a conditioned response when the stimulus to which it had been originally learned is repeatedly presented in the absence of the unconditioned stimulus. Using the classical case of the salivating dog as an example, when one repeatedly presents the sound of a bell, unpaired with food, the conditioned salivation response originally established through such pairing, will gradually cease to take place. From time to time, however, the old response will momentarily reappear when the conditioned stimulus is presented; this phenomenon has been called *spontaneous recovery*. This shows that a response that had undergone extinction did not get wiped out but was actively held back in what has been termed *conditioned inhibition*. When conditioning is selective in that a response is elicited by one stimulus but inhibited in the presence of a stimulus that is similar, one speaks of *differential* inhibition and the personal or animal is said to be engaged in *discrimination learning*.

Thus far, we have spoken of one conditioned response that has been attached to one conditioned stimulus; the salivation response attached to the ringing of the bell. Once such conditioning has taken place, it is possible to establish so-called *higher order conditioning*. In the example, the bell can now be paired with a light and eventually the salivation response will come to be elicited by the light alone and one would speak of *second-order conditioning*. Wolpe (1969) and others treat maladaptive emotional responses by what they variously call *counterconditioning* or *reciprocal inhibition*. Also referred to as *systematic desensitization*, this type of behavior therapy is derived from Pavlovian principles and presumably operates by substituting an incompatible response, such as relaxation, for the maladaptive one, usually anxiety, which had come to be attached to a particular set of stimuli. Whether this is indeed how systematic desensitization works is open to question (Davison & Wilson, 1973). At the very least, it is likely that other processes also enter into the treatment and we shall touch on these as we examine some of the applications of this form of treatment and its derivatives.

Operant Learning

In respondent conditioning, the environment elicits a response from a person who is a relatively passive participant in the process. The situation is reversed in the case of operant learning because here the person actively "operates" on the environment. It is the person who emits an action to which the environment reacts. That is to say that the response is instrumental in bringing about an environmental event; hence, the process has also been referred to as *instrumental conditioning*. The reason why it is important to stress this sequence is that it is the *consequence* of the response that serves to determine the probability of that response's recurrence under a similar condition at a later time. The condition which was present when the individual encountered certain response consequences is called the *discriminative stimulus*. Often called *stimulus* for short, it will now come to *control* that response, not in the sense of eliciting it, as is the case in respondent conditioning, but in the sense that the response is likely to occur with greater probability when this stimulus is present than when it is absent. One can conceive of the discriminative stimulus as a signal which indicates that the previously encountered consequence is likely to be forthcoming if the person were now to emit the response. Similarly, the consequence is not likely to be forthcoming if the response is made in the absence of the discriminative stimulus. The consequence is thus said to be *contingent* upon the response taking place under these stimulus conditions. Behavior learned under the operation of such contingencies, *operant behavior*, is a function of its consequences. If one wishes to change such behavior one must seek to change these consequences or the discriminative stimuli with which they have become associated.

The principle that behavior is a function of its consequences lies at the core of operant learning (Skinner, 1938). This being the case, it is essential that one examines the various kinds of consequences that can follow a response and to see what effect they have on the preceding behavior. Conversely, one must study behavior that is of interest in terms of the consequences it usually evokes from the environment, for this information is needed if one wishes to change the behavior. The systematic study of the relationship between the situation, the response, and the consequences has become known as a *functional analysis of behavior* for it asks what function a given response serves in its interaction with the environment.

The consequence of a particular response is classified in terms of the fate of the response on future occasions. If the response is more likely to occur after it had been followed by a particular consequence, that is, if the response has been strengthened, the consequence is viewed as a *reinforcement*. If the response is less likely to occur after it had been followed by a particular consequence, that is, if the response has been weakened, the consequence is viewed as *punishment*. It is important to stress that the definition of reinforcement and of punishment depends on the effect of a response consequence when that is observed at a later occasion. One therefore cannot speak of universal reinforcers or punishers but must, on each occasion and with every child, determine the effect a given consequence has on specific behavior. Nor must one make a priori assumptions about a particular consequence being either a reward or a punishment because, often in quite paradoxical fashion, a presumed reward turns out to be a punisher and what was thought to be a punishment turns out to strengthen a response, thus being a reinforcement.

Reinforcement and punishment can be subdivided on the basis of whether they entail the response-contingent application or removal of an event. This event, inasmuch as it is something the person notices, is again called a stimulus (a *reinforcing stimulus* or a *punishing stimulus*). Coming after the response has been emitted, it must be differentiated from the discriminative stimulus, which appears before the response is made. When reinforcement involves the application of a stimulus (as in the case of a child receiving a reward), we speak of it as *positive reinforcement*. When it involves the removal of a stimulus (as in the cessation of an irritation), we speak of *negative reinforcement*. Note that negative reinforcement is not the same as punishment!

Punishment can also take two forms. One involves the delivery of a stimulus (such as pain), in which case we call it *punishment by application* in order to differentiate it from the situation where a stimulus is removed (as in the case of deprivation of a privilege), which we call *punishment by removal*. The latter is usually referred to as *time-out from positive reinforcement*, but since this has the effect of reducing the frequency of the behavior for which it is a consequence, it is more appropriately viewed as a form of punishment.

There are thus four possible consequences to any given act or response: positive reinforcement and negative reinforcement, which strengthen the response; and punishment by application and punishment by removal, which weaken the response. A fifth possibility must also be mentioned. It is when nothing happens as a consequence of a response, as is the case when a child's behavior is totally ignored. In that event, the response will also be weakened; we speak of this process as *extinction*.

In order to put some of these terms into context, let us review the sequence of events that transpires in the learning of a response. This sequence involves the presence of a *discriminative stimulus* (the person notices something), and the emmission of the *operant response* (the person does something), whereupon a *reinforcing stimulus* is forthcoming (the person gets something), which is usually followed by a *consummatory response* (the person uses the reinforcing stimulus in a presumably satisfying manner).

Just as a reinforcer can only be defined by observing its effect on the response it had followed, so a stimulus can only be defined in terms of its function in the operant sequence. The ringing of the dinner bell is followed by a running to the dining hall only if the children can hear the bell and have not eaten for several hours. Whether a signal serves as a stimulus and thus has an effect on the person depends on that person's then current state, which is a function of such *setting events* as prior deprivation or satiation for the particular reinforcer.

The *schedule of reinforcement* expresses the reinforcement contingencies in qualitative and quantitative terms. The quality of a response may, for example, entail whether the word "please" was included in the request for a cookie, so that the child receives reinforcement (the cookie) only if this response quality was attained. Quantitative variations can entail how many responses are required before a reinforcement is delivered; viz., the *ratio of reinforcement*. For example, a child might have to complete three pages in a workbook or do 2 hours of homework before earning the privilege of watching television for half an hour. Reinforcement can be continuous or intermittent. When a new response is being learned, continuous reinforcement in the form of one reinforcement for every response, can be highly effective, but intermittent reinforcement (where not every response is reinforced) is desirable if one wants to make sure that this newly learned response will be maintained in situations where reinforcement is not always available. The time that elapses between the emission of the response and the delivery of reinforcement is yet another important variable. In general, the effectiveness of the consequence—whether reinforcement or punishment—is the greater the sooner the consequence is forthcoming. Delayed reinforcement or delayed punishment tend to be less effective.

Since a response, such as saying please, cannot be reinforced until it has been emitted, it must be a response that is already in the child's repertoire. Where this is not the case, someone—parent, teacher, or therapist—must select a similar, already established response and, by selectively reinforcing *successive approximations* of the criterion response, *shape* the desired behavior. If one wishes to substitute a desired for an undesired response ("Please give me a cookie" for "Gimme a cookie"), one must systematically omit reinforcement for the response one has defined as incorrect; that is, one places it on an extinction schedule, while delivering the reinforcer only when the correct response has been made. This is known as *differential reinforcement* of other behavior, the DRO procedure. Closely related to this is *discrimination training* where a child is to learn that a given response receives reinforcement under one set of circumstances but is not reinforced (or punished) under others. The appropriate stimulus conditions are usually identified by the symbol $S+$, the inappropriate ones by $S-$.

To complete this by no means exhaustive summary of procedures used in operant learning, a few important aspects remain to be mentioned. One is the phenomenon of *stimulus generalization* which, as in respondent conditioning, describes the fact that not only the original discriminative stimulus but also a range of similar stimuli can become capable of controlling a response. The more similar these stimuli are to the original, the greater will be the probability that the learned response will occur. Of course, since the reinforcer is also a stimulus (recall that it is technically called the reinforcing stimulus), generalization can also occur at that end of the sequence. Where the reinforcing cookie for "please" was at first chocolate chip, gingersnaps or brownies may also come to serve.

Another phenomenon to be touched on here is related to this issue. This phenomenon permits a wide range of stimuli to come to serve as reinforcers by deriving their reinforcing potential from their association with an effective reinforcing stimulus. We are speaking here of what is variously called *conditioned*, *secondary*, or *acquired reinforcers*, which prevail where a previously neutral event (one that had no reinforcing properties) that repeatedly precedes a reinforcing stimulus takes on reinforcing properties in its own right. This makes it possible to reinforce a child's response not only with such *primary reinforcers* as food but also by such secondary, *social reinforcers* as approval, attention, praise, or smiles or by such intrinsically worthless objects as coins, tokens, or grades on report cards. The principle underlying secondary reinforcement also holds in the case of punishment where one can speak of an *acquired punisher*. For example, when verbal reprimands, frowns, or threats have in the past been paired with the administration of more direct, physical punishment or deprivation of privileges, these more symbolic, social stimuli can acquire punishing properties in their own right.

Lastly, it is possible to have one response serve as a reinforcer for another response if the two responses have a different probability of being emitted. Where that is the case, the response of higher probability can reinforce the response of lower probability, a principle first described by Premack (1959) and known as the *Premack Principle*. Since children are often more likely to play than do homework, play can be used to reinforce homework if the opportunity to play is made contingent on completion of homework.

Punishment   The use of punishment, particularly punishment by application of physical pain, is deservedly controversial and therefore calls for a discussion of its implications. Hitting children in an attempt to reduce behavior that is annoying to their elders is no doubt as old a device as humanity itself. In fact, various forms of snapping, biting, or slapping an offspring can be observed among other animals, and it may be this primitive quality that makes civilized people wonder whether physical punishment is not an animalistic savagery that had best be eliminated from child-rearing methods.

One reason why physical punishment of children is so ubiquitous is that, of all the methods for influencing the behavior of others, it is the most readily available. Positive reinforcement, as we have said, requires for its effectiveness that the child be, in some fashion, in a state of deprivation for (that is, to want) the object or event one wishes to use as a reinforcer. To withdraw positive reinforcement, as in time-out, such reinforcement must already be available to the child and have been correctly identified. The same is true for negative reinforcement where an aversive condition must already be present. Doing absolutely nothing in consequence of a behavior, as one would have to do if one sought to use extinction, is often difficult or actually impossible because parents might decide to ignore a behavior to which siblings provide reinforcing consequences. This then leaves the delivery of aversive stimulation, particularly the infliction of pain, as the only manipulation that can be presented without preparation and regardless of the condition in which the child is

at the moment. Put more bluntly, a parent's hand is always at the ready and its sting on a handy part of the child's body is almost always an effective stimulus which, at least temporarily, disrupts the ongoing annoying behavior. It is this latter phenomenon that leads us to the second reason why the infliction of pain is such a ubiquitous child-rearing device which persists, often in the face of the parent's own humane values, despite the fact that, in the long run, it is often counterproductive.

When a child engages in behavior that is irritating to a parent, the child's behavior represents an aversive stimulus for that parent. When that parent shouts at and hits the child, that is very likely to disrupt the child's behavior, thus terminating the aversive stimulation the parent had been experiencing. Ongoing aversive stimulation that is terminated contingent on the emission of a response represents negative reinforcement; it reinforces the preceding response which, in this case, was the parent's delivery of punishment. Since immediate and consistent reinforcement greatly strengthens a response, this circumstance probably accounts for the fact that punishment is the most frequent mode used by adults to influence the behavior of children.

Punishment is thus readily available and reinforces the punisher, yet its effect in the person being punished, in this case the child, is complex and the current theoretical status of punishment in research on human learning is unsettled (Johnston, 1972; Parke, 1975). Among the effects of punishment appears to be a physiological arousal state that can become conditioned to the stimuli present when punishment is delivered. While these stimuli may be relevant to the particular behavior being punished so that this behavior will come to be avoided or suppressed by incompatible responses, the stimuli may also be relevant to the person delivering the noxious stimulation so that this person will come to elicit fear and hence avoidance or escape responses.

In addition to these emotional and interpersonal aspects of punishment, there is the consideration that it does not actually eliminate the punished behavior but simply leads to a suppression of the behavior because of the arousal of incompatible emotional responses and their consequences. Punished behavior will only remain suppressed as long as the conditioned aversive stimuli are present; once these are absent, the punished behavior is likely to reappear, particularly where it carries its own natural reinforcer, as in the case of taking cookies out of the cookie jar. For this reason, it is important that punishment, when used in treatment or child rearing, be paired with positive reinforcement of desirable responses that are incompatible with the responses to be weakened (Lichstein & Schreibman, 1977).

Observational Learning

When a response is not in an individual's repertoire, the principle of operant conditioning demands that the desired response be "shaped" by reinforcing successive approximations. Bandura (1969) has pointed out that the painstaking process of successive approximations is so inefficient that it lacks survival value in natural settings and is thus likely to work best under contrived laboratory conditions. Bandura has been instrumental in calling attention to a learning process that seems to play a major role in socialization, the process of observational learning.

When an *observer* watches a *model* engage in a given behavior, three effects can be observed. The observer may acquire new response patterns, previously not in his or her behavior repertoire; the consequences of the modeled action to the performer may strengthen or weaken the observer's inhibitory responses; and the observer's previously learned behavior in the same general class as that displayed by the model may be facilitated. Bandura (1969, 1971) stresses that the *acquisition* of the response does not require reinforcement of the observer at the time of observing but that the *performance* of the vicariously learned response may depend on reinforcement contingencies. At the same time, observational learning requires more than exposing an individual to modeling stimuli, and the absence of appropriate matching responses following such exposure may result from a variety of factors such as the observer's failure to have attended to the relevant stimuli, failure to retain what was learned, a motor deficit that makes it impossible to perform the response, or unfavorable conditions of reinforcement.

There are several factors which, when present, tend to enhance performance based on observational learning (Bandura, 1977). Observers are more likely to perform behavior when the model they had observed received reinforcement rather than punishment as a consequence of the modeled behavior. Similarity of model to observer is another variable that favors later performance. When the observer is a child, for example, it is better to have another child rather than an adult serve as a model (Kornhaber & Schroeder, 1975). The effect will be even greater if the model is high in status, prestige, power, or expertise. Lastly, the modeling effect is greater after observation of several models than after watching a single model.

Inasmuch as not only overt motor responses but also cognitive, attitudinal, and emotional responses can be acquired through observational learning, its role in socialization is immense (Bandura, 1977) and its contribution to therapy accordingly is very important (Rachman, 1972).

Cognitive Processes

As we stressed in an earlier chapter, behavior therapists do not deny the existence of cognitive processes. They recognize that people think, have fantasies, ideas, expectations, and memories and that they make plans, hold beliefs, and pay attention. The term "behavior" in behavior therapy should not lead anyone to conclude that the behavior therapist's sole focus is on the motor behavior of people with psychological problems. To approach the study of psychological disorders and their alleviation with such a narrow definition would be as limiting as it is unrealistic. Remembering that a behavioral orientation requires that all terms and concepts must ultimately have a referent in observable behavior, it is quite legitimate to examine cognitive processes and to apply to solutions of clinical problems the findings of psychologists who study these processes in the laboratory.

In the study of observational learning, for example, it has been found that children's performances can be enhanced if they are taught to encode the model's behavior (Bandura, 1971). That is to say that a child who describes what the model is doing in his or her own words is more likely to perform the modeled behavior correctly in a later test session. We can infer that these verbal statements influenced the child's thoughts and memories, but such an inference is not needed as long as we can observe the child first verbalize the statements and later demonstrate improved performance. Both of these "anchors" are behavior.

Verbal self-statements in the form of self instructions have been shown to improve the performance of hyperactive, impulsive children (Meichenbaum & Goodman,1971), and this has led to a fairly large body of literature dealing with behavioral self-control (Thoreson & Mahoney, 1974). Examples of the application of this approach will be encountered in later discussions of such topics as juvenile delinquency, learning disability, and hyperactivity where it will be apparent that cognitive factors play an important role in behavior. In some respects, however, the clinical application of cognitive methods (Meichenbaum, 1977) has advanced more rapidly than the laboratory studies on this topic. It is therefore not possible to present the principles of cognitive processes in as explicit a manner as can be done with respect to respondent conditioning and operant learning, which have been explored in the psychological laboratory for a far longer period of time. Yet, as dedicated and creative investigators continue their study of the role of verbal self-statements on a person's own behavior, one can hope that both a conceptual framework and a firm empirical basis for what has come to be known as *cognitive behavior therapy* will eventually be forthcoming.

IMPLICATIONS FOR TREATMENT

As this cursory summary of theoretical principles and pragmatic statements suggests, a variety of approaches are available to the therapist wishing to modify the problematic behavior of a child. When the problem takes the form of a behavioral deficit, the responses missing from the child's repertoire must be established; while in the case of excess behavior, the responses in question can be modified, reduced, or eliminated and replaced by more adaptive behavior. Often, as in the case of the autistic child, some behavior (e.g., speech) must be established while other behavior (e.g., head banging) has to be reduced, but no matter how complex, the necessary modifications of behavior invariably entail learning.

The various approaches available to the behavior therapist can be used alone or in combination and the choice depends, in part, on the specific needs of the case and the conditions under which treatment can be carried out. In the most general sense, the respondent conditioning paradigm can be viewed as best suited for the treatment of problems in the vascular-visceral-autonomic realm (e.g., fears), while the operant approach lends itself best to problems involving skeletal-muscular-motor functions (e.g., hitting or speech). This distinction follows the logic of a 2-

factor theory of learning (Mowrer, 1951; Rescorla & Solomon, 1967), but recent research has demonstrated that visceral responses can be modified through operant conditioning so that it is probably overly simplistic to assign autonomic responses to the respondent and voluntary responses to the operant conditioning realm (Kimmel, 1974). Furthermore, with the explication of observational learning by Bandura (1969), who has shown that emotional responses, motor skills, and complex social behavior can be learned vicariously, it has become apparent that behavior therapy is never purely respondent, purely operant, purely observational nor, for that matter, purely cognitive. Therapists may wish to focus their activities on one or the other of these paradigms, but all four will undoubtedly enter into the situation, no matter what they are, ostensibly, doing.

The therapist's choice of which paradigm to use as a focus will often be guided by the degree of cooperation that can be expected from the child client. In respondent conditioning, where the therapist presents stimuli to the child, it would appear that the child is a passive recipient of therapy, who merely reacts with elicited responses. Despite this apparent passivity of the child, it would be wrong to conclude that the therapist manipulates an unwilling or unwitting "victim," for unlike the animal in the classical conditioning experiment, the child is not in a restraining harness. The child is quite able not to attend to the stimuli the therapist presents, not to remain in the room, or to emit responses that are incompatible with those the therapist is trying to elicit. These circumstances make respondent conditioning treatment best suited to situations where children are motivated for getting help with a problem they recognize as troubling them. Cooperation in treatment is essential, and since this is more likely to be found with less severely impaired and older children in nonresidential clinic settings, it is there that this form of treatment has most often been found to be successful.

Where the operant conditioning paradigm guides the treatment approach, the child is a very active participant who engages in an operation—does something to the environment. The therapist arranges the environment in such a way as to assure that the child's operant responses occur under particular conditions and are followed by planned consequences. This contingency management requires that the therapist have some control over the stimulus and reinforcement conditions that the child will encounter, and the level of possible control will largely determine the effectiveness with which treatment can be conducted. Inasmuch as a therapist's opportunity for such control is greatest in a home or institutional setting where, with the help of parents or institutional personnel, the delivery of primary and secondary reinforcers can be influenced, most reports of treatment using operant methods have come from such settings.

In order to use observational learning as the principal focus of treatment, a therapist would need an appropriate and potent model or models and a child client who can be induced to observe these models engage in the behavior the child is expected to acquire and perform. This, again, requires cooperation on the part of the child client and a setting, such as a normal nursery school, where other children model age-appropriate behavior. An institutional setting where other children tend to model inappropriate behavior is thus not the place to attempt treatment by vicarious learning. In fact, as Estes (1970) has suggested, one source of the behavioral deterioration found in children who are institutionalized for long periods of time, such as mental defectives, may be the presence of inappropriate peer models whose influence is countertherapeutic.

Lastly, if a therapist wishes to make cognitive methods the focus of treatment, the instructions the child is expected to learn must be amenable to being phrased in clear, short statements using words already in the child's active vocabulary. The child must have the motivation to use the self-instructional sentences, and the task to which they are to be applied must be such that the child can quickly see positive results. By and large, such an approach seems to work best with fairly verbal, older children who recognize a problem with which they want help.

It should be obvious that a therapist who applies cognitive method will also be making use of the principles of reinforcement, as in rewarding the child initially for repeating the sentence. Furthermore, a therapist who teaches self-instructional sentences to a child is using observational learning and if the child should be making emotional responses, such as fear, to the task he or she is to master, principles of respondent conditioning may also find application. It can thus be seen that, as in any complex human behavior, every one of the principles and methods we have discussed will enter into the treatment of psychological disorders, and a behavior therapist will not hesitate to use any or all of them.

A Case Study

The case of Dicky, reported by Wolf, Risley, and Mees (1964) and Wolf, Risley, Johnston, Harris, and Allen (1967), serves to illustrate the use of a combination of methods, including the manipulation of a variety of contingencies in conditioning and extinction procedures and the introduction of a form of aversive control in order to reduce the frequency of grossly maladaptive behavior. Dicky was 3½ years old and had been diagnosed as a case of childhood schizophrenia. He engaged in such self-injurious behaviors as head banging, hair pulling, face slapping, and scratching. He lacked adaptive social and verbal repertories, refused to sleep alone, and did not eat in an age-appropriate fashion. His case became critical because he was in danger of losing his eyesight. Because of cataracts in both eyes, he had to have surgical removal of the lenses, and since he refused to wear glasses and habitually threw them on the floor, permanent retinal damage was very likely.

The therapists first attacked the boy's refusal to wear his eyeglasses because that seemed the most serious, immediate problem. Glasses wearing was gradually established by reinforcing it with food and later on with opportunities to take walks, go on rides, or play. Because the child's glasses-throwing behavior was incompatible with glasses wearing, a mild form of punishment was made contingent on glasses throwing. Following each glasses-throw, Dicky was put in his room for 10 minutes, a form of time-out from positive reinforcement (TO), if one views being in the company of others as a positively reinforcing condition. The same TO method was used to eliminate tantrums, self-slapping, and the pinching of teachers and other children in the nursery school. The effectiveness of this technique was demonstrated by experimental reversal (Wolf et al., 1964). Glasses throwing had taken place at the rate of approximately two times per day before treatment was initiated. Within 5 days of instituting the TO procedure, the rate of this behavior had decreased to zero, but when Dicky was no longer put in his room for throwing the glasses, thus reversing the contingencies, the rate of glasses throwing returned to its original high level after about 3 weeks. When Dicky was once again put in his room whenever this behavior occurred, it quickly decreased in frequency and virtually disappeared within 6 days.

Reversal can only be carried out if the target behavior is carefully defined and objectively measured, but the need for such measurement goes beyond the requirements of behavior analysis, because without it, treatment becomes unsystematic and the outcome impossible to define. This is illustrated in further work with Dicky, as reported by Wolf et al. (1967). After some of his more bizarre behavior had been modified during hospitalization, Dicky was enrolled in a nursery school where he emitted a high rate of pinching teachers and other children. At first, an attempt was made to put this behavior on an extinction schedule by ignoring it, but when this failed to change the pinching rate, Dicky was sent to a specially set aside small room whenever pinching occurred. After the first use of this time-out contingency, the rate of pinching decreased drastically, only 4 more instances of it being recorded over the next 74 class sessions. Prior to the introduction of the TO procedure, a teacher had attempted to modify the pinching by reinforcing patting, which was seen as an incompatible alternate response. Patting behavior stabilized at a moderate rate within a few sessions when Dicky was encouraged and praised for emitting this response. At this point, the teachers reported that they were succeeding in replacing pinching by patting. However, the observer's record on which instances of both patting and pinching had been entered for every 10-second interval clearly showed that contrary to the teachers' impression, the pinching rate had not decreased and that it did not decline until the TO procedure was instituted some 13 sessions later. Without the quantitative observer record, the teachers would have been under the mistaken impression that the development of a substitute response had been responsible for the decrease in the objectionable behavior. Inasmuch as Dicky's parents were to be instructed in the use of behavior modification techniques so that they could supplement the treatment at home, such an erroneous conclusion might have contributed to treatment failure and disappointment. With the variety of approaches used in Dicky's case over a period of 3 years, the boy was eventually able to attend a special education class in public school, where he made a good adjustment and learned to read at the primary level. By the time Dicky was 13 years old he was able to function well in a regular sixth grade class (Nedelman & Sulzbacher, 1972); a remarkable success of early application of operant procedures, given the fact that this boy had been viewed as a case of childhood schizophrenia.

Treatment Conducted by Auxiliary Therapists

As will be seen in the chapters which follow, much of the effectiveness of behavior therapy with children depends on the active participation in the treatment by parents, teachers, and other caretakers of the disturbed children, at times, on that of their peers, and in many instances, on that of the children themselves. The reason for this is that behavior is situation-specific so that changes in behavior must be brought about in the settings and with the people where the child spends the major portion of his or her life. Using these auxiliary therapists thus has a sound theoretical basis, but there is another reason why their help is necessary. It is that with the large number of disturbed children and the limited number of professional therapists, rather few children could receive help were it not for the extension of therapeutic effectiveness that has become possible through the involvement of so-called nonprofessional and paraprofessional people in the therapeutic enterprise.

Treatment methods based on operant principles, in particular, can be described in relatively simple terms and made available to a wide audience (e.g., Krumboltz & Krumboltz, 1972; Morris, 1976). For specific problems, such as bed-wetting, parents can be trained as effective therapists in as little as 2 hours (Paschalis, Kimmel, & Kimmel, 1972), teachers can learn to implement programs designed to reduce such intractable problems as the seizures of an epileptic child (Balaschak, 1976), a child's own siblings can serve as therapists (Colletti & Harris, 1977; Lavigueur, 1976), and in one case (Drabman & Spitalnik, 1973), a retarded child with an IQ score of 42 was employed as contingency manager to reduce the disruptive behavior of two peers.

In some instances, children with psychological problems have been taught to control their own behavior by self-monitoring (Broden, Hall, & Mitts, 1971; Flowers, 1972), self-instruction (Meichenbaum, 1977), and self-administration of reinforcers (Drabman, Spitalnik, & O'Leary, 1973). The success of any of these approaches does, of course, depend not only on the quality of the training these auxiliary therapists have received but also on their interest, enthusiasm, personal qualities (James & Foreman, 1973) and relationship skills (Alexander, Barton, Schiavo, & Parsons, 1976). When Kent and O'Leary (1977) selected four therapists who had no more than B.A. degrees but social skill, enthusiasm, and experience in working with children, they found that these women, after a single, one-semester training course, were as effective as four clinical psychologists with Ph.D. degrees in treating children with conduct problems.

Because so many problems of children manifest themselves in the home, parents have been the most frequently used surrogates for the professional therapist (Bernal, 1972; Glogower & Sloop, 1976). Several reviews have been devoted to this topic (Berkowitz & Graziano, 1972; Johnson & Katz, 1973; O'Dell, 1974; Patterson, 1974; Reisinger, Ora, & Frangia, 1976). Like the outcome study conducted by O'Leary,

Turkewitz, and Taffel (1973), which reported improvement in 90 percent of the cases, these reviews generally attest to the effectiveness of this approach. Having parents act as therapists is, however, not without its dangers. In a study by Herbert, Pinkston, Hayden, Sajwaj, Pinkston, Cordua, and Jackson (1973) mothers of children with psychological problems were taught to attend to their children's appropriate behavior and to ignore their deviant responses. While such differential attention usually results in marked improvements in the child's behavior (Hawkins, Peterson, Schweid, & Bijou, 1966; Rinn, Vernon, & Wise, 1975), Herbert et al. (1973) found that for four of the children in their study there was a substantial increase in deviant behavior, leading the writers to the conclusion that parent training programs of this kind must be carefully evaluated in order to make certain that the intervention has the desired effect.

A Cautionary Note

Many behavioral principles are basically rather straightforward and almost self-evident. The principle of reinforcement, for example, is a formal expression of the age-old folk wisdom found in the adage, "You can catch more flies with honey than with vinegar." Those who advocate that if one falls off a horse one should get back on it right away lest one develop a fear of horses, are saying something about the conditioning of emotional responses. Similar examples could be given with respect to observational learning and the operation of cognitive processes. This, of course, is not surprising for, after all, the maxims we hand down from generation to generation are based on long experiences with practices used in daily life that have proved their worth. The laboratory scientist has merely taken these practices and subjected them to more rigorous tests to see whether they really work and under what conditions they work best. When the scientist now goes back to the public and speaks of contingencies of reinforcement, stimulus generalization, or extinction, these concepts make sense to lay people who learn them readily and are able to apply them with relative ease. Unlike the more esoteric ideas the public gets from other branches of psychology and other sciences, information about the principles of learning as they apply to behavior change lends itself to application by those with very little training. The ethical implications of this will be discussed in the next chapter. Here a somewhat different point must be made.

The self-evident nature and apparent simplicity of the principles underlying behavior therapy should not lead anyone to believe that such therapy can be planned and directed by untrained or poorly trained individuals. As was just pointed out, parents, teachers, institutional workers, and others can often serve as valuable therapeutic agents after relatively little technical training, but the treatment program itself should always be designed in consultation with a qualified professional person who is thoroughly familiar with child behavior therapy. Treatment is never without its risks. Jones (1924b), whose pioneering work was cited at the beginning of this chapter, recognized this years ago.

Having helped a little boy over his fears of furry objects by judicious pairing of a favored food with the feared object, Jones wrote:

> This method obviously requires delicate handling. Two response systems are being dealt with: food leading to a positive reaction, and fear-object leading to a negative reaction. The desired conditioning should result in transforming the fear-object into a source of positive response (substitute stimulus). But a careless manipulator could readily produce the reverse result, attaching a fear reaction to the sight of food [1924b, p. 388].

RECAPITULATION

Behavior therapy is based on the premise that the behavior of children with psychological disorders follows the same principles as all other behavior and that the most efficient approach to the treatment of such disorders is to focus on observable responses which take place in the child's current life situation. Principles of respondent conditioning, operant learning, observational learning, and cognitive processes find application in behavior therapy. Details of these principles were presented and many of the relevant terms were defined. Punishment was singled out for special discussion because of its frequent use and abuse. A case of a severely disturbed boy was used to illustrate the fact that the treatment of complex behavior calls for a complex interplay of many different but interrelated psychological principles. The relative simplicity of many treatment methods has made it possible for so-called lay people to act as auxiliary and surrogate therapists. While this is a welcome and necessary development, it occasions a cautionary note lest it be forgotten that no treatment is without its risks and dangers. This touches on ethical implications which call for the detailed examination to which the following chapter will be devoted.

Chapter 5

Ethics, Values, and the Rights of Children

A presentation of psychological disorders of children and of the treatment of these disorders demands a discussion of the ethical implications of these topics. The very use of the term "disorder" raises the question of who is to say what is and what is not a disorder. In presenting a definition of the term psychological disorder, we emphasized that this label is based on an arbitrary and relative judgment made by other people. Once behavior has been judged to be disordered, attempts to intervene, to set the behavior in order, almost invariably follow. Whether these attempts are called teaching, training, rehabilitation, correction, or therapy they inevitably involve one person doing something to another person. Intervention is always intrusive. One person is the agent of change, the other the object of that change agent's ministrations. Whenever one person seeks to do something to another person, even if it is presumably helpful, one must ask whether that help is wanted. What about the right to refuse help? With a person's right at stake, this becomes an ethical issue and when that person is a child the issue can be quite complicated.

At least since the days of Hippocrates it has been appreciated that when one person undertakes to treat another a very special situation exists that has sensitive ethical implications. When behavior therapy first came upon the scene its early pioneers (Kanfer, 1965; Krasner, 1964) quickly recognized that they too had to be concerned with the ethics of their attempts to influence the behavior of those who came to them for help. More recently, therapists of diverse orientations have begun discussions of ethical issues (Koocher, 1976; Van Hoose & Kottler, 1977), for these are not unique to behavioral approaches. Yet there are two reasons why these issues are particularly critical for the behavior therapist. One is that behavior therapy is a very effective method of bringing about behavior change. The other is that the rudiments of behavior therapy are relatively easy to learn so that people other than well-trained behavior therapists can use, hence, misuse them. Furthermore, behavior therapists have become sensitized to the ethical implications of what they do because some of the words they use, like control, manipulation, technique, influence, modify, stimulus, and punishment have a tendency to arouse public antagonism, fear, suspicion, and—not infrequently—to occasion distortions in newspapers, magazines, films, and television programs. Krasner (1976), who once contributed to this public relations problem by unwisely speaking of the therapist as a "social reinforcement machine" (Krasner, 1962), now recognizes how much public acceptance of an endeavor depends on the terms which are used to describe it.

ETHICAL ISSUES

The ethical implications of treating an individual's psychological problems increase in magnitude as an inverse function of that individual's freedom of choice. In the case of an adult who voluntarily seeks professional help one should be able to assume that this person is able to leave treatment as freely as it was entered. This is not to say that there are no ethical issues here; for the therapist's activities may still range from the scrupulously proper to the outrageously immoral. There are questions of privacy and confidentiality, appropriate fees, responsible referral, and timely termination of treatment that must always be considered. But the moment the person is in treatment under conditions that are other than voluntary, the picture changes dramatically; for where the voluntary client can simply walk out when there is something about the therapy or the therapist he or she does not like, this option is greatly reduced or unavailable for those who are in treatment under some kind of duress. Such duress can take many forms, from the pressure exerted by a spouse who threatens separation unless the partner enters treatment, to the social stigma that is attached to alternate lifestyles or sexual preferences, to a court-imposed condition of probation which requires therapy, to the prisoner who must enter treatment as a condition of parole, and finally to the patient who has been committed to a psychiatric hospital where treatment is prescribed by the staff. Where does the child fall on this continuum of volition?

The issue of the right of children to make decisions about their own lives, to shape their own destinies, is one of enormous complexity. As Hobbs (1975) has observed, at an early age the child is totally dependent on others. Some time later on, exactly when depends on the child's state of residence, the young person is presumed to be responsible and legally accountable for his or her actions. "Somewhere in between, he becomes in fact the best judge of how his life should be lived" (Hobbs, 1975, p. 118). Where that point lies has never been defined and the child thus dwells in a state of limbo. Most people consider the child to hold an inferior status compared to adults. Adults are seen as being responsible for the child and therefore as entitled to make decisions on the child's behalf. "Father (or mother) knows best" is generalized to other adults in the society and not even the courts regard the child as a full member of society; as a citizen whose rights are protected by the Constitution.

Where children, in general, are presumed to be incapable of making their own decisions in matters affecting their lives, children with a psychological problem are, if anything, viewed as being even less competent to make these decisions. Not only are they minor, they are also disturbed. It is therefore not surprising that very little has been written or said about the rights of children in the realm of psychotherapy.

THE RIGHTS OF CHILDREN AS THERAPY CLIENTS

What are the rights of children with respect to psychotherapy? There are, of course, the obvious civil rights which are protected by statute such as the right not to be killed, maimed, sexually molested, kidnapped, or imprisoned by someone claiming to be a therapist. Left out of this list is the right not to be hurt, either physically or psychologically; for the issue of punishment has not been adequately settled when it comes to children. Leaving that for later discussion, we can say that none of the civil rights listed are really germane to the questions about children's rights as clients in psychotherapy. What we are, or should be concerned with here, are the less specific, more abstract human rights such as those having to do with integrity as a person, privacy, and self-determination. To these, child therapists and others have given very little thought (Koocher, 1976).

The Joint Commission on Mental Health of Children (1970), a prestigious body which had been convened by an Act of Congress, published a list of what they viewed as the "inalienable rights of children." While their manifesto spoke of the right of a child to receive psychological care and treatment, no mention was made of the rights of a child who is receiving such treatment. Nor, for that matter, of the rights of children to refuse such treatment. The members of the Joint Commission, most of whom came from the mental health professions, thought they knew what is best for children.

Therapists, like other adults such as teachers, parents, and judges, see themselves as working for the child's best interest. This may be a more sophisticated version of the protestations of the father who, while spanking this son, intones that it is for the boy's own good. Our society is beginning to question the assumption that parents always know what is best for their child. Witness the increasing frequency of prosecutions of parents who injure or maim their children in the course of "disciplining" them. It may be time to look at child therapy and to ask whether the therapist can always be trusted to protect the child's rights and to work in the child's best interest (Ross, 1974).

The Involuntary Status of the Child Client

The issue of a child's rights emerges even before treatment begins. Unlike an adult who ordinarily *comes* to treatment as a free agent, the child is *brought* to treatment by the parents who have decided that the child needs help. It is rare for a child to have agreed with his or her parents that outside help is necessary and most children are reluctant if not opposed to enter treatment. Child therapists thus begin much of their work with involuntary clients and this places a special obligation on them to consider the ethical implications of their professional activities.

Although the important decision about entering treatment is usually made by adults acting on behalf of the child, most children come to appreciate the help they are getting once treatment begins. But even there, crucial differences between child clients and adult clients remain. Once an adult has entered treatment voluntarily, he or she retains a very crucial right, the right to terminate treatment by the simple device of not returning for the next appointment. Children have no such right. They are brought back to the therapist, protestations notwithstanding. The adults, having decided that the child needs treatment, insist that their plan be carried out. This leaves the child only one recourse: to refuse cooperation with the treatment procedure. Such refusal, however, will nearly always be viewed by both therapist and parent as "a part of the child's problem," a problem that must be resolved as a part of treatment. The refusal is rarely seen as a rightful assertion of a child's prerogative to autonomy in decision making. If one were to view the child as a person and not as chattel, one might wonder whether this attitude does not involve a violation of the child's right to refuse treatment.

Refusal to cooperate with a treatment plan is relatively easy when the approach takes the form of verbal or play therapy. Here the child need merely remain silent or decline to participate in play activities. Repeated "I don't knows" and "becauses" can stymie the most skilled psychotherapist. It is in this respect that behavior therapy can be more insidious. When, under a therapist's directions, parents or other adults who are in control of the reinforcers carry out a systematic plan of arranging reinforcement contingencies so as to strengthen behavior they deem desirable and weaken behavior they deem undesirable, the child may literally not know that a treatment program is in effect and certainly has no way of rejecting it, short of running away. We shall return to the ethical implications of behavior therapy after exploring yet another aspect of the involuntary status of the child client.

Children not only lack rights regarding participation in treatment, they also lack the right to decide what the goal of treatment should be. Adults usually decide for themselves that they have a problem and seek help with that problem. In the case of children, adults decide what is wrong and they make plans to set things right. They assume that the child would be better off if he or she had more friends, were better able to tolerate criticism, were more assertive, less moody, more industrious, more productive. In most instances, in fact, what the child is to be treated for are the things that bother the parents. Whether they bother the child is rarely taken into consideration. A child's assurance of satisfaction with the way things are and insistence that there is no problem, are usually shrugged off as indicating that the child does not know what is needed because he or she is too young or too disturbed. If not that, these assurances set in motion a campaign to convince the child of the wisdom of the adults' decision which, when successful, represents an enterprise in attitude change which, though less direct, may also be seen as constituting an invasion of the child's rights.

Just as there are problems involving the child's rights when it comes to entering treatment, deciding on the treatment goal, and continuing in therapy, so there is a potential problem related to ending therapy. Clinicians encounter occasions where a child is in treatment and the parents suddenly decide, for reasons of their own, that treatment should be terminated. When this happens, and unless the therapist can persuade the parents to reconsider their decision, the child will be pulled out of treatment regardless of whether it is in the child's best interest and whether or not the child agrees with the decision or was even consulted when the decision was made. The involuntary status of the child client may thus play a role at every stage of treatment, from beginning to end.

THE THERAPIST'S DILEMMA

Behavior therapists pride themselves on having their clients set the treatment goal. They do not presume to tell people what is best for them. Yet when it comes to children, they share with therapists of other orientations the problem of having to decide who is their client, the parent or the child. An example may help to highlight this issue.

A 7-year-old boy is brought to a therapist by a mother who complains that her child "won't ever obey, won't hang up his clothes, won't straighten up his room, and has atrocious table manners." The boy talks back when she asks him to do something and invariably asks her to explain and justify her demands. This leads to frequent altercations between mother and child and these, in turn, result in her getting into conflict with her husband who wants things to be quiet when he is home.

In the course of assessment, the therapist discovers that this family's value system is one where children are to be "seen but not heard." Tentative attempts to seek modification of these expectations result in objection and refusal on the part of the parents. Interviews with the child elicit the typical 7-year-old's denial of problems with assurances that, as far as the boy is concerned, "everything is all right." Asked specifically whether he would like to get help so that he would have fewer altercations with his mother, the boy responds with, "I don't need any help."

If the therapist were to view the child as having a right to self-determination, a withdrawal from the case would be indicated at this point. Yet the question immediately arises whether this decision can really be left to the judgment of a 7-year-old. Put another way, does a 7-year-old really have the right to refuse treatment? Are we not entitled, maybe indeed required, to have mature adult judgment override the immature judgment of a child? But at what point does a child's judgment cease to be immature? At ten, thirteen, sixteen, eighteen? It was not long ago when one was a minor until age twenty-one. Now one is an adult at eighteen. Is the line between maturity and immaturity an arbitrary line? And is it really to be determined by chronological age?

Like most ethical issues, the matter of a child's human rights is not easily settled. In fact, and again like most ethical issues, it entails a conflict between values; for if one respects the right of the child to self-determination, one almost invariably violates the right of the parent who is seeking help about a child's problems. In the example just cited, should the therapist refuse to help the parents who have come because they are troubled by their child's behavior? Alternatively, should the therapist substitute his or her own judgment for that of parents and child alike and enter the case with the aim of modifying the parents' behavior so as to provide the child with an environment more in line with the therapist's own values?

Parents, one could argue, are able to look out for themselves. As we have said, adults simply terminate treatment when they deem the therapist's activities inimical to their interests. Who is to look out for the interests of the child? The usual answer to this question is that the child therapist works on behalf of the child's interests. But what, in our example, are the child's interests? Is it in the boy's best interest to let him struggle through a stressful childhood because we want to respect his right to refuse help? One could rationalize this by hoping that the boy might grow up to be a questioner of authority, but the chances for his doing so are slim and the price is high—and the desirability of questioning of authority is no more than value judgment. Conversely, is it in the boy's best interest to learn to live in his authoritarian home with a minimum of stress and conflict; a possibility he might be offered if one helped him adapt to the reality he has to face? It is again a value judgment to say that stress and conflict are bad, while serenity and harmony are good qualities for a child's environment.

Even if there were an easy answer to the question of what is in the child's best interest, one would still be faced by the therapist's dual obligation, which complicates matters still further. The therapist is charged with helping the child; but at the same time the therapist is an agent of the parents who are paying for the service and have, by law, the right to make decisions on behalf of the child. Gelfand and Hartmann (1975) point out that by law the child is the ward of his or her parents and that, under ordinary circumstances, decisions about modifying the child's behavior are made by them. Yet these writers recognize that the matter is not always simple; for there are some unwise or even unfit parents who fail to act in the child's best interests. Parents or other legal guardians therefore cannot and should not be solely responsible for decisions about treatment. Gelfand and Hartmann (1975) posit the case of a boy who is brought for treatment because he refuses to shoplift in order to help support the family. In this case, the therapist's decision is easy. He or she cannot facilitate the commission of a crime and must therefore refuse the parents' request. The therapist may, in fact, be obligated to protect the child through legal channels because the case involves child abuse. The therapist, say Gelfand and Hartmann (1975), is not simply an agent of the parents or of the child but must determine how best to serve all concerned. They recommend consultation with experienced therapists when one is faced with difficult decisions about whether or not and how to intervene.

The Child Advocate

Several other suggestions besides consultation with a colleague have been advanced as solutions for the dilemma in which therapists may find themselves when they are called upon to be both helper of the child and agent of the parents (Ross, 1974). One of these is to introduce an independent child advocate into the treatment setting. This would be someone who is neither paid by the parents nor a colleague of the therapist and who should thus be in a position to make certain that the treatment planned and undertaken is serving the child's best interests. Such an advocate would have no obligation but to see to it that the child's human rights are protected. In the realm of research we now have institutional committees charged with protecting the rights of human subjects. Why not a similar tribunal in the realm of therapy when the intended recipient is a child or some other involuntary patient who is deemed incapable of making important decisions? In reviewing the suggestion for a child advocate Koocher (1976) thought it unrealistic to expect such an advocate to be readily available or even always to know the child's best interests, yet he agrees that some circumstances, particularly those involving aversive methods of treatment, should require a mandatory outside evaluation of the plans for treating a child.

The Joint Commission on Mental Health for Children (1970) made child advocacy its foremost recommendation. The commission recognized that someone had to be charged with looking after the interests of children when adults make legislative, judicial, or administrative decisions. Interestingly enough, the commission did not mention the need for such an advocate in the area of child therapy. It was as if these mental health professionals felt that children did not need anyone to protect them from psychotherapists! It is, admittedly, difficult to decide who would be an appropriate advocate and, as Koocher (1976) stressed, we must guard "lest the wolves be sent to watch over the sheep" (p. 27), but the issue is too important to avoid facing simply because it is complex. Some solution to the therapist's dilemma must be found.

A "BILL OF RIGHTS"

Until a meaningful system of child advocacy or another mechanism to protect the rights of children becomes established, or even in preparation for such a development, it is well to try and make the rights of children in psychotherapy explicit. Following a proposal advanced earlier (Ross, 1974), such as a "Bill of Rights" (Koocher, 1976) should cover at least four basic principles: the right to be told the truth, the right to be treated as a person, the right to be taken seriously, and the right to meaningful participation in the making of decisions involving the child's life. When these rights are honored, a child will be able to develop as an individual who, being respected, will learn to respect the rights of others. Let us examine each of these principles and see what they imply in terms of the child as a client in therapy.

The Right to be Told the Truth

The foremost principle of any interaction between people in the context of therapy as elsewhere is the principle of honesty (Ross, 1964). Deception has no place in a therapeutic relationship. This is no less true when one is treating children than when one is treating adults. When children are old enough to be talked to, they are old enough to be told the truth. People will say, "He's too young" or "She wouldn't understand," but such statements reflect the person's inability to communicate with the child, not the child's inability to comprehend a statement that is phrased in an appropriate way for the child's developmental level. In talking to a child one may have to simplify the content of one's message, but simplification is quite different from equivocation. To equivocate is to lie. Telling a child the truth may require skill and patience: skill in using words the child will understand and patience in perservering until the child has understood. Unless a therapist has such skill and such patience, he or she had better not work with children.

The Right to be Treated as a Person

This principle deals with the respect that should be accorded to any human being, no matter how young, how impaired, or how disturbed. Human rights cannot be abridged because the law defines a person as a minor or a label identifies the person as incompetent. No person, and especially not a child who is particularly vulnerable vis-a-vis adults, should be treated as a thing, an object. No data need be cited in support of this assertion. We are here dealing with basic, a priori values of our culture to which anyone who wishes to work with children had better be committed.

   In clinical practice, the child's right to be treated as a person often revolves around issues of confidentiality and privacy. When a client is an adult, the confidentiality of the therapeutic relationship and the right to privacy are taken for granted. When the client is a child, confidentiality and privacy are often violated. They should be respected. A child's therapy session should not be observed by someone else without the child's knowledge and what the child communicates to the therapist should not be divulged without the child's permission. The child's parents should not be viewed as having a preeminent right to know what the child says and does during treatment. The principle of honesty also enters here, for if the child has been assured that his or her communications will be treated as confidential, then they must be. If the child has been led to believe that he or she is alone with the therapist, then one-way mirrors or closed-circuit television must not be used for observation.

The Right to be Taken Seriously

Here we are addressing the frequently encountered tendency of adults to view what a child says as something inconsequential and insignificant that can be shrugged off and ignored. Serious comments coming from a child are often considered cute or amusing and responded to in that vein. These attitudes are also found in discussions about problems and treatment plans. When a child is asked for an opinion, that opinion should be taken seriously. If a child's opinion about the need for treatment or the goal of treatment has been solicited, then the response should be respected and not ridiculed or ignored. It is better not to ask a child's opinion than to disregard it once it has been sought. A sham involvement of the child is worse than no involvement at all.

The Right to Participate in Decision Making

This is related to the point just made. In making plans that will involve the child's life, the child's participation should be elicited, and once elicited, the contribution made by the child should be respected. Participation in making plans obviously does not mean that the child's opinion will be the sole basis of the final decision. For that reason, children should not be asked whether or not they wish to get help with a problem, for if they say no we should be prepared to respect and therefore accept that decision. Presenting the child with a choice from among several available options (which need not include outright refusal) is one way of assuring involvement in decision making without giving the child a veto over the entire matter.

Some Qualifications This "Bill of Rights" has been presented without qualifications because the issue is so important that an unequivocal statement serves to alert one to its implications. In considering each of the principles we have outlined, it is obvious that some qualifications are needed when the principles are translated into practice. While the principle of honesty can probably be stated as an absolute in that one should never lie to a child, the issues of confidentiality and privacy, which were cited under the right to be treated as a person, may well have to be dealt with in relation to the particular circumstances. In order to establish a base line for a given behavior, for example, an observer may have to be introduced into a classroom without the knowledge of the child who is to be observed. In some parent-training situations, a hidden observer may have to watch the parent-child interaction in order to be able to provide the parent with feedback about his or her behavior with respect to the child. At issue here is not that surreptitious observations should never be conducted but that the child should not be told that there is no observer when, in fact, an observer is present.

In the area of making decisions affecting the child's life it may at times be necessary for adults to make important decisions in which the child has no opportunity to participate. One must presume that adults, by virtue of their greater experience and wider knowledge, are sometimes able to make judgments on behalf of the child that are more adequate than those the child would be able to make. What is involved here are considerations involving the child's maturity with respect to the complexity of the matter being decided. Parents are, in the final analysis, responsible for the welfare of their children and one aspect of this responsibility involves making decisions. What is often overlooked, however, is that this responsibility also entails accountability, and our courts and legislatures are only now beginning to make it clear that parents are accountable to society for the decisions they make and the actions they take regarding their children. In matters of child abuse, parents are being held accountable, and it is here that the notion of child advocacy is beginning to find implementation.

ETHICAL CONSIDERATIONS IN BEHAVIOR THERAPY

It should by now be apparent that ethical issues pervade all forms of therapy with children; in fact, all relationships involving children. Behavior therapists have neither a monopoly on awareness of these issues nor are they the only ones who need to be concerned about them. At the same time, there are certain aspects to the use of behavioral principles in conducting therapy that require that the behavior therapist be especially alert regarding ethical considerations.

One reason for this is that in many instances behavioral methods appear to be more potent than other psychological approaches for bringing about behavior change. As Gelfand and Hartmann (1975) pointed out, greater power entails greater responsibility. Another reason for the need to be ethically sensitive, touched on earlier, is that where the agent of behavior change has control over the reinforcement contingencies it is possible to change behavior without the consent and possibly even without the knowledge of the person whose behavior is being changed. This matter has been grossly exaggerated by those who oppose behavior therapy for philosophical reasons, but it requires consideration in the case of children who depend on the adults in their environment for food, comfort, and privileges. These adults are therefore in the position to decide in what direction they want to change the child's behavior. This decision entails value judgments, an issue to which we shall shortly return.

Another aspect of behavior therapy that contributes to the importance of ethical awareness on the part of behavior therapists is the variety of methods that are available for inducing behavior change. Variety permits choice, but who is to make that choice? Again, with adults one can outline the options which are available and have the client participate in the decision. When the client is a young child, it may be impossible to explain the options in such a manner that the child is in a position to make a truly informed choice. Therapist and parent may have to make the decision, and this places an extra burden of responsibility on these adults. In line with the rights of children, however, every effort must be made to involve the child as much as possible in the decisions and to secure his or her informed consent to the procedure to be used. Remembering the point that usually children are not in the position to terminate treatment on their own, provision should also be made for ensuring that the child has a way of indicating the desire to discontinue the process.

The Use of Punishment

The aspect of behavior therapy that demands ethical considerations more than any other is that some methods involve aversive procedures. These include such negative consequences for excess or undesirable behavior as deprivations of privileges, reprimands, criticism, response cost, isolation, and noxious stimulation. As response consequences that weaken the response on which they are contingent, these procedures all share the technical name *punishment*, and no matter what euphemism the therapist may choose, the child no doubt views all of them as just that. So let us talk about these procedures as punishment, purposely focusing on a word with unpleasant connotations so that we may be reminded to use aversive procedures with great circumspection.

Prior to the decision to use an aversive procedure to reduce an excess behavior, the therapist must consider whether the same goal can be accomplished by other methods, such as reinforcing an incompatible response or changing the stimulus conditions that control the excess behavior. One is justified in introducing punishing consequences only when available positive alternatives have been tried and have failed to bring the desired result. Even then punishment contingencies must be accompanied by positive consequences designed to strengthen desired alternative behavior. Whenever aversive procedures are to be used, the therapist must be prepared to provide assurance that if the undesirable behavior were to continue unchanged, the ultimate outcome would be more damaging to the child than the effect of the aversive procedure. Such justification is required particularly if the aversive procedure involves the infliction of physical pain or discomfort. In fact, physical pain must be used as a treatment procedure only in those extreme cases where the alternative would be serious injury to the child or to others, as is the case in self-injurious or assaultive behavior. That it is essential that the child's parents give their fully informed consent to such procedures should go without saying. In view of the profound nature of the disorders we are considering here, it is likely that the child is not in a position to participate in the choice of procedures. This is an instance where an infringement of the child's right to be involved in decision making is unavoidable.

VALUES AND VALUE JUDGMENTS

Closely related to ethical considerations are issues involving the values of parents, of therapists, and of the society in which we live. Because the goal of therapy is to change behavior, this goal supposedly represents a state that is better than the state in which the client is found when therapy is initiated; viz., the present state is deemed undesirable, the state to be sought is presumably desirable. Good and bad, desirable and undesirable are value terms. Somebody is making a judgment. Whose judgment is it to be and how can we know that it is correct? Is it necessarily better to be obedient than rebellious; conformist than individualistic; peaceful than aggressive; orderly than untidy; realistic than visionary; organized than spontaneous? The answers to these questions may be obvious to some while others may wish to qualify them by a "that depends." As a therapist one is often faced with questions like these because parents' concerns and teachers' complaints are frequently based on the fact that a child exhibits one rather than the other of these bipolar characteristics.

We have previously cited the example of the parents who complained because their child refused to engage in shoplifting. There the answer seemed easy because the law could be used as a guide. Aside from the fact that compliance with the law entails yet another value judgment, it can be recognized that this fictitious example represents a highly unlikely situation. More likely are instances where parents complain about disobedience or teachers complain about excessive motility and noisemaking.

It is in the area of modifying children's classroom behavior that the question of values comes clearly into focus. What kind of a classroom do we want? One where all children sit quietly at their desks and do not speak unless they are called upon? Or one where children move about from place to place and freely talk to each other and to the teacher? The issue was highlighted in somewhat exaggerated form by Winett and Winkler (1972) in a paper with a subtitle "Be Still, Be Quiet, Be Docile," which expresses their belief that this is the unwholesome goal of behavioral interventions in classrooms. That paper elicited a rejoinder by O'Leary (1972), who felt that its authors had set up a "straw-man" and that their criticism was unjustified. This exchange underscores the fact that treatment goals entail value judgments for which there are no absolute standards of right or wrong.

The principles on which behavior therapy is based can be used to many ends. Especially with young children, where significant adults often have control over the contingencies of reinforcement, is it possible to apply these principles to whatever end one selects. It must be recognized that psychological knowledge about how to influence and change behavior can be used by those who would put it to use for what many others would consider to be selfish or nefarious ends. Although the basic principles of reinforcement and hence of behavior change are relatively easy to learn—in fact, behavior therapists often explicitly teach them to parents and other intermediaries—there is no guarantee that they will always be used in desirable ways. It would be futile to try guarding against this danger by having psychologists keep their knowledge to themselves. Knowledge is a tool and like all other tools, whether knives or nuclear energy, it can be used for good as well as for evil. Psychology is no exception. Once one knows how to change a child's behavior one can, like Fagin, train children to steal or one can help them acquire skills that are more in keeping with the values of the larger society. Psychology can tell us how to get to a goal; it cannot help us decide what that goal should be. That decision depends on our values. For this reason, all who would seek to use psychological knowledge, whether as a therapist, as a teacher, or as a parent, should examine their values and make them public so that others who hold different values can have the opportunity to voice their opinions. To pretend that behavior therapy has nothing to do with values and that the values of behavior therapists have no impact on their activities is to ignore a crucial dimension of our interaction with the people who come to us for help. If the help these people want is in a direction that runs counter to our values, behavior therapists have the ethical responsibility to refuse rendering their service.

RECAPITULATION

Before proceeding with the topic of psychological disorders of children and their treatment, a discussion of its ethical implications seemed imperative. Children are particularly vulnerable when judgments are passed that involve their behavior and when decisions are made that entail changing their behavior. Adults who are responsible for these children therefore have a special obligation to consider the ethical implications of their activities. In therapy, children are usually involuntary participants. The therapist who works with children is often in a dilemma because the interests of the child and the interests of the parents do not necessarily coincide. The therapist must then determine whom to consider the client. It may be necessary to develop a system of child advocacy so that somebody who is objective can look after the interests of the child and ensure that the child's rights are respected. These rights include the right to be told the truth, the right to be treated as a person, the right to be taken seriously, and the right to participate in decision making. There are aspects to behavior therapy that bring ethical consideration into sharp focus; this is particularly true when some form of punishment is to be used as part of the treatment procedure. Throughout this chapter questions were raised to which no answers were given. This should not be surprising in view of the topic of this chapter. In the realm of ethics there are no answers, only questions—questions to which each of us must continuously seek his or her own answer.

Chapter 6

Behavioral Assessment

Before one can attempt to initiate a therapeutic intervention in a child's behavior—in fact, before one can know whether such an intervention is necessary—one must undertake a careful study of the behavior that has occasioned the clinical referral. Such a study should include attention to the child's developmental level, past learning, and response capacity. These can usually be most expeditiously ascertained by using standardized tests for which norms are well established (Nelson, 1975). Because discussion of such tests is available in such works as that by Sattler (1974), we shall not cover them here. Instead, we shall concentrate in the following on the assessment of the environmental variables, the antecedents and consequences, which control and maintain the child's current behavior. When these variables are correctly identified by means of a behavioral assessment, their modification enables one to change the child's behavior if such a change seems indicated.

ASSESSMENT OF CHILD DISORDERS

The purpose of assessment in a clinical context is to find out the answers to four related questions: (1) What, if anything, is wrong? (2) What kind of help, if any, is needed? (3) What should be the goal of intervention? and (4) How can that goal best be reached? It is worth noting that it should not be taken for granted that simply because a child is brought to the attention of a clinician something is necessarily wrong with that child. Nor should one assume that even if there is a problem that this necessarily requires a clinician's intervention with the child. The first step in any assessment thus revolves around defining the problem. Unlike adults who seek clinical help in their own right, children almost never appear in a clinician's office by themselves. They are invariably brought there by an adult, usually by a parent or, when the clinician works in an institutional setting, by a teacher or houseparent. Unlike adults, who state their own complaints, children's problems are stated in complaints voiced by the referring adult. The clinician must thus decide whether the adult's complaints are valid reflections of the child's behavior or whether they represent more the adult's problems than the child's difficulties.

The Validity of Parental Complaints

When we ask whether the complaints presented by the adult who brings the child to the clinician are valid, we are, in effect, asking whether the child in question differs from a normal child of the same age. We know from our discussion in Chapter 2 that there is a great deal of overlap between the behavior of children who are considered normal and the behavior of those who are referred to clinics or who are classified as deviant. In any specific case, we may be dealing with excessive sensitivity or even distortion on the part of the adult and not with anything but normal, age-appropriate behavior on the part of the child.

Questionnaires on child behavior which are filled out by parents are often used in clinical settings in order to obtain a quick overview of the parents' complaints. Some of these instruments have been used in research (e.g., Miller, Hampe, Barrett, & Noble, 1971; Sines, Pauker, Sines, & Owen, 1969), but their validity has rarely been checked against direct observation of the child's behavior. For example, in the study of Miller et al. (1971) parents of presumably normal children were asked to respond to a behavior checklist of 163 items in order to establish a norm against which to compare the responses of parents of children referred to a clinic. This work revealed that the average child sampled from the general population was described by his or her parents as manifesting between 11 and 13 deviant, but usually unrelated, behaviors. Miller et al. (1971) presented a statistically determined cutoff score of 25 deviant behaviors, which provided a dividing line between "normal" and "deviant" children, and led to the estimate that deviant children represent 16 percent of the general population. Useful as such information can be, it must be remembered that it is based not on the actual behavior of children but on the responses of parents to a checklist on which they report their perception of their children's behavior. The crucial question is the validity of this and similar checklists: do parental reports truthfully reflect child behavior?

It is here that work by Lobitz and Johnson (1975) makes an important contribution, for it permits a comparison between parents' questionnaire responses and two different direct observations of behavior. These investigators studied two groups of children and their families. One group of twenty-eight families had children between the ages of 4 and 8 who had been referred to a clinic for such behavioral excesses as aggressiveness, destructiveness, temper tantrums, and disobedience. The second group served as a control. They consisted of families who had been recruited from the community through the use of school rosters or advertisements and whose children had never been treated for behavior problems nor was any member of their families currently under psychiatric care. These groups were studied with three different measures: a 47-item parent questionnaire developed by Becker (1960), an observation conducted in the clinic, and a home observation.

The observation in the clinic involved six 5-minute, structured situations. They consisted of the parents playing cards with each other after having asked the child to play quietly alone; the parents leaving the child alone in the room to play with a toy; each parent playing alone with the child; and each parent being alone with the child and giving him or her a series of twenty-two commands. The behavior taking place in these situations was coded by an observer who sat behind a one-way mirror.

The observations that took place in the family's home entailed five consecutive daily visits by an observer who spent 45 minutes watching the family just before dinner. While there were some constraints placed on the family (such as no television), an attempt was made to obtain as natural and spontaneous a picture as possible, considering the fact that there was an observer in the house.

In view of the fact that parental complaints are the principal basis for the referral of children, it is noteworthy that Lobitz and Johnson (1975) found that the correlations between the child-behavior variables and the scores from the parent questionnaire were negligible. Similar results have been reported by Peed, Roberts, and Forehand (1977), thus supporting the speculation advanced by Novick, Rosenfeld, Bloch, and Dawson (1966) that what parents report on child-behavior rating scales and similar instruments bears little relationship to child behavior when it is observed by others. Of course, one cannot tell which set of data—the report of the parents or the report of the outside observers—represents "the truth." It might be that both the observers and the parents distort reality in different directions or that both sources report what is actually going on, except that parents' questionnaire responses reflect their experience with single, dramatic events or with behavior that occurs with relatively low frequency, while observers can report only on events that take place while they are present.

When Lobitz and Johnson (1975) analyzed whether the home and clinic observer data could be used to differentiate between the clinic and the nonclinic children they found considerable overlap between the two groups. The parent questionnaire scores, on the other hand, differentiated the two groups very effectively. In other words, when parents judge their own children it is possible to tell which child is referred to a clinic and which child is not, but when outside observers look at these children, they have trouble telling them apart. This strongly suggests that factors besides actual child behavior contribute to whether parents label a child as deviant and seek help from a clinic. Among these factors Lobitz and Johnson (1975) identify marital distress between parents, other difficulties in the family, low parental tolerance, or high expectation for child behavior. It would seem valuable to heed the stress these authors place on the importance of going beyond parental complaints about their child before child therapy is instituted, of investigating the parents' perceptions, labeling, and attributions, and of studying the family interaction pattern as Snyder (1977) has done. At the same time, it would be a mistake to assume that a child's behavior problems necessarily reflect marital discord between his or her parents. When Oltmanns, Broderick, and O'Leary (1977) compared the marital adjustments of parents of children who had been referred to a psychological clinic with those of presumably normal controls, they found much overlap in these adjustments. Furthermore, their data show that the degree of improvement in the child's behavior as a result of treatment is unrelated to the level of their parents' marital adjustment. That is to say that it is possible to undertake successful treatment of children even when their parents' marital adjustment leaves much to be desired.

Interviewing the Parents

An interview with the parents is the best available method of ascertaining whether the complaints with which they bring a child to a clinic are indeed valid targets of intervention or whether the parents' perceptions or expectations are distorted. Best because when used by a skilled clinician, the interview can range over a wide array of topics that might not be covered by a standard questionnaire or checklist. While there is no assurance that the information obtained through an interview is a more valid reflection of reality than parents' written responses to printed questions, the interviewer is in a position to note hesitations, discomfort, revealing inflections and stresses, and nonverbal interactions between parents from which the validity of the answers can be estimated. It may, indeed, also be true that how parents perceive the events in their home, how they talk about their child's behavior, and the extent to which they agree or disagree about these topics is at least as important from the standpoint of planning an effective intervention as obtaining a complete and veridical report of actual events.

In some clinical settings parents are asked to complete a checklist or questionnaire before coming for their first interview. While this serves to provide the interviewer with some clues as to the areas of parental concern, eliciting such pre-interview responses may give the parents a set of expectations about what the interviewer is likely to consider important, thus potentially excluding from discussion topics that might be critical for understanding the problem. For example,

Wahler and Cormier (1970) describe the use of preinterview checklists which cover the child's behavior in the home, at the school, and in the community. Parents who have responded to such checklists may well appear for their interview with the assumption that they are expected to report only on the things the child does. They would not be prepared to discuss what they do with respect to the child's problem behavior, how they and the child's siblings react to it, and whether they agree or disagree on how the problem should be handled. Important issues related to these family interaction patterns which the parents had not been prepared to discuss would then have to be elicited during the interview.

Wahler and Cormier (1970), who speak of the assessment interview with parents as an ecological interview, point out that it serves two functions. One is to acquaint the parents with the orientation of the therapist; viz., the ground rules or language system. This includes the stress on observable, operationally defined events as opposed to inferences, assumptions, and abstract summary terms, such as jealousy, unhappiness, or shyness. By repeatedly asking the parents how they know that their child is, for example, jealous, the interviewer teaches them a different way of talking about their experiences, a way that is more appropriate for a behavioral approach to treatment. The second purpose of the ecological interview is to identify the relevant behavior, the settings in which it occurs, its antecedents, and its consequences. We shall have more to say about these in a later section.

As an aid in conducting an interview with a child's parents, Holland (1970) presented an interview guide covering twenty-one steps or points that should be covered. Built around a functional analysis of behavior and designed for use in an operant framework, this interview guide facilitates the investigation of the child's behavior, but makes no explicit effort to ascertain the nature of the family interaction pattern. An alert interviewer, however, should be able to get hints about these aspects from the way the parents respond to the topics broached by the interview guide. For example, in the first step the parents are to be asked to state their general goals for the child and their present complaints about him or her. Subtle disagreements often emerge at this point, as when one of the parents defines the problem in a way that differs from the way the other has stated it. Similarly, when the parents are asked to rank the list of problems in order to identify the one on which intervention efforts are to be concentrated, it may develop that what the mother deems most important is, to the father, but a minor issue. The way such disagreements are handled, whether they occasion a heated argument or a rational discussion, whether a compromise is reached, who defers to whom, and whether the interviewer is asked to serve as arbitrator should again throw light on parental interaction and facilitate discussion of this topic. Without such flexibility and alertness on the part of the interviewer, Holland's (1970) guide can become a mechanical list of questions dealing with child behavior and with the various positive and negative consequences that the parents might bring to bear in order to modify the behavior.

Interviewing the Child

How much useful information one can obtain by talking to the child is a function of his or her age, level of cooperation, and degree of disturbance. Even though an interview with the young client may not be very fruitful, seeing the child is an important part of pretreatment assessment. Not only will the parents expect that the clinician meet the child but in any discussions with the parents about the child, it is necessary that the clinician have firsthand knowledge of the person they are talking about.

There are few guidelines that can be offered for interviewing children, and the literature on behavioral assessment is singularly silent on this point. In talking to a child one must avoid being condescending or patronizing, while phrasing one's questions and statements in a way that the child can understand. While the interviewer should seek information about relevant issues, including those about which the parents are concerned, topics should not be pursued to the point where the child finds the experience aversive.

Among the topics to be covered in an assessment interview with a child are how the child perceives the problem about which the parents have expressed concern, the things the child likes and dislikes, relations to parents, siblings, and peers, and his or her hopes, wishes, and expectations. By asking what the child knows about the reason why he or she is seeing the clinician, one can sometimes obtain reflections on how well child and parents communicate.

Young children often find it difficult to sit in a chair and talk to an adult. With them, some clinicians find it helpful to engage in a child-appropriate activity, like going for a walk or playing with a toy. Play activity, however, should serve only as a means for obtaining information, not as an end in itself. The so-called play interview used by traditional child therapists in which dolls are utilized as surrogates for the child is too indirect and requires too many inferences to be appropriate for a behavioral assessment.

Inquiries about Private Events

In the course of interviews with the parents and with the child, the clinician seeks to elicit information of relevance to the problem behavior. Such information deals with what the child and the parents have observed, the events which take place in the home or at school, the frequency or intensity of specific behaviors, and similar objective reports. This, however, is not the only purpose of assessment interviews; for these should also seek to elicit verbal reports from the parents and from the child on what they think and feel about—how they construe—the events surrounding the problem behavior. It is here that the behavioral psychologist is interested in statements about private events, fully cognizant that the validity of such statements is unknown so that the information thus obtained can be used only in the context of other, more objective data.

In theory, it is possible to conduct a behavioral assessment by relying solely on observations of the child's behavior and its functional relationship to his or her environment. In practice, however, this procedure can be greatly expedited by the judicious use of questions directed at the people in whose behavior one is interested. The potential effectiveness of a reinforcer, for example, can be more quickly ascertained by asking a verbal child what he or she would like than by trying out various consequences and observing their effect on the behavior. Knowing that a child regularly runs and hides whenever the father comes home, we can ask questions designed to elicit information about what the child expects the father to do. Seeing a girl who never volunteers to speak in class, we can ask how she perceives school and herself in relation to school. If she replies, "I'm so stupid and always say the wrong thing," she has provided important information about a personal construct that bears on the nature of the stimulus situation as she perceives it.

A person's subjective perceptions, what Kelly (1955) called personal constructs, play a critical role in determining behavior. In fact, these constructs may often account for the inappropriateness of the behavior of psychologically disturbed persons who, construing widely different situations as if they were the same, act in a very stereotyped fashion. If a boy construes himself in such words as, "I am a shy child," he may behave in a hesitant, passive, timid, and diffident manner in a wide variety of situations, even when such behavior fails to result in positive consequences. Because it is difficult to know what constitutes a stimulus for an individual unless one finds out how that person perceives the situation, what meaning it has for him or her, inquiries aimed at eliciting personal constructs form a legitimate part of a behavioral assessment.

THE OBSERVATION OF BEHAVIOR

Even the best interview with parents can provide only a secondhand report of what the child is doing, and the child's verbal reports may contribute little to one's understanding. Important as it is to ascertain how parents and child view and evaluate the situation, the therapist will have to have a more direct basis for assessing the child. There is no substitute for firsthand observations, but while "seeing for oneself" might seem to provide an objective picture, this approach too has its deficiencies.

Ideally, a child's behavior should be observed in the setting where it is deemed to be a problem. Thus, if the complaints come from the school, observations should be conducted in the classroom or the playground. If the complaints revolve around the child's behavior in the home, that is where observations ought to take place. In clinical practice, such on-site observations raise logistical problems having to do with therapists' time and the expense of visiting the child's own environment. Research institutes and university clinics, which can use students and other research assistants as observers, are often able to afford sending observers to the child's home or school. It is from such occasions that we have information about the problems in the use of naturalistic observation as a means of behavioral assessment (Lipinski & Nelson, 1974*a*). These problems have to do with the accuracy of the observations, the reactions of the person to being under observation, and such procedural issues as what to observe, when to observe, and how to record the observations (Mash & Terdal, 1976).

Observational Procedures

Before one can hope to observe behavior a decision must be made about what is to be observed. The problems around which children are brought for professional help are often stated in vague descriptive forms, such as unhappiness, lack of friends, jealousy of a younger sibling, or disobedience. Complaints emanating from the school are often phrased as misbehavior, disruptive behavior, or discipline problem. All of these must be restated in an objective form so that they become observable, measurable entities. Once this is done, and before observation can take place, it is necessary to have an objective observational code. The multitude of events which take place in even a two-person interaction is so great that without some guideline for what is to be the focus of the observers' attention, the resulting record would be so diffuse as to be of little or no use. Observational codes have been developed for various purposes, depending on where the observations are to take place. Patterson (1977) described a code for use in observing the interactions between parents and children, while O'Leary and Becker (1967) developed a coding system for use in observing behavior of children in a classroom.

An Observational Code   When O'Leary, Kaufman, Kass, and Drabman (1970) sought to study disruptive classroom behavior they established nine categories, each of which was defined in such a way that observers could agree on whether a given event had or had not taken place. A look at these categories and their definitions will illustrate the refinement necessary in order to approach observation in an objective manner.

The first of the O'Leary et al. (1970) categories is labeled "out-of-chair." It is defined as any movement of the child from his or her chair when such movement is not permitted or requested by the teacher. To be scored as having taken place, such movement must leave no part of the child's body in contact with the chair. If some part of the body is still touching the chair, other than the child sitting on his or her feet, the movement falls into the second category, called "modified out-of-chair." The third category is called "touching others' property." This is defined as the child coming into contact with the property of another without permission to do so. It includes grabbing, rearranging, or damaging the property or touching the desk of another child.

"Vocalization" is the fourth observation category in this scheme. This category includes any proscribed sound made with the mouth, whether it be a verbalization or a noise. (Any other audible noise that is not permitted by the teacher is scored in category 7, which is labeled "noise.") The fifth category is entitled "playing," and is defined as the child using his or her hands to play with an object

in a manner which is incompatible with learning. It is noteworthy that even this highly objective set of definitions here contains a qualification which calls for an inference on the part of the observer, inasmuch as it is difficult to decide whether twirling a pencil, for example, is or is not compatible with learning. This dilemma, of course, stems from the fact that learning is a construct and not a behavior.

The next category (number six) is called "orienting." Here an observer would score any turning around, provided the child is seated and the turn entails more than 90 degrees, using the desk as the reference point. Category 7, "noise," has already been mentioned. Category 8, "aggression," is scored when the child makes a movement toward another person that results in coming into contact with that person (excluding brushing against another). Note that this definition of aggression says nothing about the intensity of the response, the child's intentions, or the reaction of the other. While this is a somewhat idiosyncratic definition of aggression, it does permit very objective scoring. The last category in this series is "time off task." It is scored when the child does not engage in the assigned work during the entire observational interval.

After it has been decided what behavior is to be observed, and after objective definitions of that behavior have been established, it is necessary to select a measurement procedure from among several available alternatives. This selection must be based on such considerations as the nature of the behavior in question, the place and time available for the observations, who is to do the observing, plus various economic and logistic considerations.

Measures of Frequency and Duration

Evidence Recording   The simplest form of measuring is to count evidence from which it can be inferred that the target behavior has taken place. Such recording can be used when the behavior in question occurs relatively infrequently and leaves, when it occurs, some readily observable and unequivocal evidence. When these conditions are met, it is not necessary for an observer to monitor the child's behavior continuously because all one needs to do is to check the appropriate surroundings for the trace or result of the behavior. When such is found, an entry is made in an appropriate log, showing the date and time the event was discovered.

An example of a target behavior which lends itself to evidence recording is bed-wetting. A wet sheet in the morning is evidence that at least one wetting has taken place during the night. Or, conversely, a dry sheet in the morning permits one to record that the child has slept through the night without wetting. This information can be accumulated so that it can be expressed in terms of the number of dry nights per week or the number of dry nights in succession, depending on the contingencies to be employed in the treatment plan.

Because evidence recording does not permit the observation of the actual behavior, it is important that the artifacts with which one deals are valid indicators that the behavior has or has not taken place. In the case of bed-wetting, one might find a dry sheet on the bed and erroneously record a dry night when, in fact, the child has surreptitiously changed the sheets during the night or slept on the floor in order to keep the bed dry. Similar cautions must be kept in mind when evidence recording is used to measure clothes hung up, homework delivered, or money missing from a purse, since a sibling might have removed the clothes from the hanger, the homework could have been copied from someone else, or the money been taken by a spouse.

Event Recording   This form of measurement entails a predetermined unit of time, during which an observer records every instance of the target behavior's occurrence. Because the observer must watch the child's behavior during the entire time unit, logistical considerations often determine the length of this unit. If the observer is in the child's presence anyway and the target behavior is relatively infrequent, the observation period can be quite long. For example, if the target behavior is calling out the answer to a question without being asked and the classroom teacher serves as the observer, the entire class period or even the whole school day might be an appropriate unit. Behavior that occurs with greater frequency might be observed during a specially designated observation period. To measure the frequency of a child's stuttering, for example, one might designate a half hour or an hour as an observation period and count the number of times this problem appears.

The actual recording of events can be done in various ways, ranging from tally marks on a piece of paper to the use of mechanical devices, such as wrist or hand counters. The total count can then be expressed in terms of frequency per unit time, and the results of several observation periods can be stated in terms of an average. Depending on the nature of the problem, an observation period might be at the same time every day, as in the case of playing with food during dinner, or it might vary systematically or randomly if one is interested in a more pervasive problem behavior, such as hitting other children.

During the initial assessment interview with the parents, it is sometimes possible to obtain hints about the circumstances surrounding the problem behavior. On the basis of these hints, the observer can be instructed to note not only the instances when the behavior takes place but also to record what happened just before and just after that point. An initial approximation of that can sometimes be obtained by simply requesting a parent to maintain a narrative record. From this, variables that appear crucial can then be identified and the observer instructed to note on the record when they occur. For example, a mother may report that her child's temper tantrums seem to take place when the older sibling returns home from school or that stuttering increases when the father talks about his work at the dinner table. These antecedents can be indicated on the record or graph that serves as a tabulation of the behavior itself. Similarly, consequences to behavior which are suspected to occur with regularity, such as father stops talking when daughter stutters or mother comes to her side when child has tantrum, can be entered on the record by a checkmark following the symbol or code identifying the event.

Interval Recording In using event recording, every instance of the target behavior which occurs during the observation period is counted. This method does not lend itself for use with behaviors that have a high frequency and it is limited to the observation of one or a very limited number of target problems. These difficulties are not encountered in the use of a more sophisticated method, that of interval recording. Here the period during which observation is to take place is divided into equal units of time and a target behavior is counted if it takes place during such a unit. In the study by O'Leary et al. (1970), from which we cited the observation categories, the 20-minute arithmetic lesson was divided into 30-second units. During each unit the observer would watch a specific child for 20 seconds and then take 10 seconds to record on a tally sheet which of the nine behavior categories had occurred during that interval. This arrangement is necessary when an observer seeks to keep track of several different categories of behavior. When only one behavior is of interest, continuous recording of, say, 10-second intervals can be maintained. Since it is difficult to keep an eye both on a stopwatch and on a child, various mechanical devices, such as a beep transmitted to an earphone or a moving paper tape that exposes the writing surface at predetermined intervals, can facilitate event recording.

Event recording requires the use of a specially trained observer who does nothing during the session except record. It is therefore an expensive way of gathering data but, at the same time, it is a highly sensitive form of measuring behavior. Because the record will show exactly what took place at any given moment, it is easy to compare the records of more than one observer to establish their reliability. Furthermore, the record will reflect not only the presence or absence of a given behavior but, particularly when the recording intervals are very brief, it will also show for how long (over how many recording intervals) the behavior lasted. When the interval is longer than a brief moment, however, interval recording introduces a measurement error because frequency and duration become confounded (Powell, Martindale, Kulp, Martindale, & Bauman, 1977). In a 20-second observe, 10-second record system, for example, an entry which shows that a given response took place in both the first and the second 20-second interval may mean that the response was sustained for more than 30 seconds or that there were two discrete emissions of the response 30 seconds apart. If the response of interest is screaming, for example, it may make a difference to know whether it is sustained or intermittent.

Duration Recording If one is primarily interested in how long a response lasts, interval recording, though it can reveal duration, may be too cumbersome. In fact, interval recording may be inappropriate if the behavior in question has a relatively low frequency so that an observer would spend many observation periods without recording anything. Temper tantrums or bedtime crying are examples of the kinds of behavior where duration recording is applicable. Here the observer starts a timing device when the behavior begins, stops it when it ends, and records the length of time which has transpired. It is obvious that this method requires that the behavior have a clearly observable beginning and end and that the observer must be present when the behavior takes place.

Measures of Other Dimensions of Behavior

Interresponse Time   Thus far we have discussed measures of behavior that concern frequency or duration, answering the questions "how often?" and "how long?" Another question might be, "How much time elapses between instances of the behavior?" Where these instances come relatively infrequently, interval recording would be a very wasteful procedure, even though the tally sheet, in addition to showing when a response took place, would reflect during how many intervals the response did not take place. Recording of interresponse time is the obverse of duration recording. One notes when the behavior occurs and then records the time which elapses until the next instance. Information about interresponse time can be useful in behavior problems where a therapist might wish to lengthen or shorten the intervals between target responses. Examples of this can be found in such psychophysiological reactions as asthma where the treatment goal might be to lengthen the time between attacks. In the case of children who manifest lengthy pauses in their speech, on the other hand, the treatment goal might be a reduction of these intervals. In either case, a measure of response frequency or duration would not provide the necessary information.

Response Latency   A related measure is one that answers the question, "How long before the response takes place?" This is a question about response latency and it, too, can be made the object of observation and recording. Here the observer obtains the time it takes the child to initiate a response after the relevant stimulus has been presented. Parents sometimes complain that their child does not respond promptly enough to their requests or instructions. Should this be perceived as a problem worthy of intervention, a response latency measure would be appropriate because the goal of intervention would be to reduce this latency.

Response Magnitude   Yet another dimension of behavior that might be made the object of observation and recording is the magnitude or intensity of the response. Here we are no longer able to rely on counting or timing but should, ideally, rely on an instrument that measures weight, pressure, or volume. How hard does the child press on the pencil? How gently does she touch the baby? How loudly does he yell? How softly does she talk? are questions along lines of this dimension. When the use of a measuring instrument is not feasible, intensity might be quantified in such terms as whether the child's speech can be heard by someone a specified distance away or whether the pencil rips the paper on which the child is supposed to write.

Distance   Lastly, there is the dimension of length or distance that would have to be measured and recorded in appropriate units, such as inches, yards, or city blocks. In working with a child who is afraid of going to school, for example, the focus of measurement might be how close that child is able to approach the school on successive days of treatment.

Combinations of Recording Methods

The various methods of recording we have discussed are, of course, not mutually exclusive. With any given child one may at one time wish to use the highly accurate interval recording, while at a later stage event recording may be sufficient. Further, it is possible to combine several methods. Event recording plus duration recording are an obvious combination. Here the focus of interest would be not only on the frequency of a given behavior but also on its duration. How often do temper tantrums take place and how long does each one last? Changes in the course of treatment may be reflected in either or both of these dimensions and a good record should reveal them.

A procedure that can be combined with any of the methods mentioned is time sampling. Depending on the nature of the behavior that is of interest, observations might be conducted at varying times of the day or on different days. In the case of classroom behavior, a child might be observed not only during an arithmetic lesson but also during reading; not only in the classroom of one teacher but also in that of another. It is one of the many advantages of behavior observations that they can be tailored to fit the needs of the individual case.

The Training of Observers

Observing behavior in such a way as to produce an accurate record is a skill that must be learned. Various methods of training observers have been developed. The most efficient of these is the use of a film showing interactions either in a classroom or in a home situation which observers-in-training are asked to score, using an observational code devised for this purpose. The goal of such training is to bring the observers to a high level of accuracy so that they will consistently record the events which actually take place. The record of their observations, in other words, should be both reliable and valid. We shall return to this psychometric issue a little later. For the moment, we shall assume that observer accuracy exists when the records produced by two or more observers show a high level of agreement. On this basis, the training of observers is conducted by having them observe and score situations depicted in the training film until they reach a criterion of agreement either with each other or with an experienced observer. What actually happened, reality, is thus defined in terms of what several people agree to have observed. Consensus is, in the final analysis, how our culture defines reality.

Training observers until they reach a high level of accuracy is, unfortunately, no guarantee that the records such observers produce will continue to be accurate. There are various sources of observer bias; thus, initially high interobserver reliabilities may be misleading (Kent, Kanowitz, O'Leary, & Cheiken, 1977). One of these sources is observer drift; viz., changes in observer agreement over time.

Another is due to expectations the observers might have about the purpose of the study for which their records are to be used (Kent, O'Leary, Diament, & Dietz, 1974). The results of spot checks on observer agreement may also be spurious. It has been demonstrated that two observers will show increased agreement when they know that their accuracy is being assessed (Romanczyk, Kent, Diament, & O'Leary, 1973). To guard against these sources of observer bias, Kent et al. (1977) recommend continuous assessment of observer accuracy or intermittent spot checks made in a covert manner.

Reactions to Being Observed

As is true in any assessment where the person whose behavior is under scrutiny is aware of being tested or observed, there is the question to what extent this awareness affects the person's behavior. This matter of the reactive nature of observations is difficult to study because it requires a comparison between two conditions of observation. In one condition, the presence of the observer is known to everyone involved; in the other, the observer is surreptitiously introduced into the setting so that people do not know that they are being observed. Such deception is ethically unacceptable; consequently, we know very little about this issue. It seems that when observers are placed into the classroom of a campus laboratory school their presence has little systematic effect on the behavior of the children or of their teacher (Dubey, Kent, O'Leary, Broderick, & O'Leary, 1977). When an observer comes into a home, however, family interaction patterns appear to change (Lipinski & Nelson, 1974a). In order to eliminate whatever reactive effect an outside observer might introduce, alternate methods for obtaining a record of behavior have been tried; among these are self-observations and observations conducted by the child's parents.

Self-Observations With children who are able to cooperate, it is possible to have them record their own behavior. Such self-monitoring has been used to obtain a record on children's study behavior (Broden, Hall, & Mitts, 1971). Here too, however, a reactive effect has been reported (Lipinski & Nelson, 1974b). It seems that when a person begins to monitor and record some aspect of his or her own behavior, this behavior tends to change in the direction of improvement. Self-recording might thus be used as a therapeutic device, but the effect is not always present. Self-reporting by boys in a group home who monitored their own room-cleaning behavior, for example, produced no systematic effects (Fixsen, Phillips, & Wolf, 1972).

Inasmuch as assessment in behavior therapy is not merely a procedure used prior to treatment but a process that continues throughout and often beyond treatment, self-observation is also used as a means of monitoring treatment progress. Plachetta (1976), for example, had a 6-year-old boy maintain a chart showing his progress in controlling his fecal soiling, while Hutzell, Platzek, and Logue (1974) reported on a case of an 11-year-old boy whom they taught to monitor his motor tics (the head jerking and "barking" of the Gilles de la Tourette syndrome) as part of a successful treatment program. Research conducted by Spates and Kanfer (1977) suggests that the therapeutic effect of self-monitoring may depend on whether the child participates in establishing the criteria by which the adequacy of his or her behavior is to be judged.

Observations by Parents   Another source of information on child behavior which obviates an outsider coming into the home to observe is to use reports based on observations carried out by the child's parents. While this approach provides data on behavior in the child's natural setting, it too has its drawbacks. Foremost among these is the questionable validity and reliability of records provided by parents. Since a parent is so intimately involved in the child's life and has such a great investment in having the problem behavior reorganized and changed, the records kept by a parent may be subject to many distortions. Where the target behavior is a clearly definable event, such as a dry bed, a parent can be a very reliable record keeper, but when treatment is to focus on complex interpersonal problems, such as fighting with a sibling or complying with parental requests, the observational record may leave much to be desired. Here, the record may reflect not only the presence or absence of the child's response but also the parents' changing tolerance level, the parents' motivation for obtaining help, and the presence of the parent when the child's behavior takes place. Like other observers, parents require training and external monitoring if their records are to be useful in the assessment and treatment of their child's behavior. But unlike observers who are paid by a clinic to do a job or students who are working for course credit, parents are not under the therapist's contingency control and their motivation to participate in the observational process may have to be maintained by frequent personal or telephone contacts.

The validity of observations by parents   We have previously touched on the question of the validity of the complaints with which parents bring a child to a clinic, referring in that connection to a study by Lobitz and Johnson (1975). From the same research group comes a study (Eyberg & Johnson, 1974) that deals with the question of the validity of the reports parents present regarding the progress and outcome of treatment. Eyberg and Johnson (1974) studied families who had a child in treatment for a behavior problem in the area of aggressiveness, disobedience, hyperactivity, and temper tantrums. Five different measures of treatment progress and outcome were used. These were observation data gathered by the parents, observations conducted by trained observers in the home and in a laboratory situation, and two questionnaires filled out by the parents. Since all of these measures dealt with the problem behavior of the identified child in each family, one might expect that they would all reflect the same changes in the course of treatment. This, however, was not the case. A fairly high degree of treatment success was indicated by the observational data gathered by the parents, by their responses to the attitude questionnaires, and by their reports concerning the outcome of treatment. However, on the basis of the observations in the home and in the standard laboratory situation conducted by trained outside observers, which one might presume to be more objective than the reports by the parents, only a modest degree of success was evident. Which data are we to trust? What the parents observe and report or what is seen by the therapists and their trained assistants?

Several answers are possible. One is that the behavior observed by the outsiders was not representative of the child's typical conduct. Eyberg and Johnson (1974) suspect that when the observers initially entered the home and when the family first came to the laboratory to be observed, the child's behavior was subdued so that fewer of the aggressive-negativistic responses were manifested. On the other hand, when these observations were repeated after completion of treatment, parents and children may have been more comfortable being observed so that relatively more spontaneous negativistic behavior emerged, thus masking the effect of treatment.

Another explanation, also entertained by Eyberg and Johnson (1974), is that child behavior did not really change dramatically but that the parents' tolerance level changed in the more liberal direction in the course of contact with the clinic. Changes might thus have been brought about in parents' attitudes rather than in child behavior. Given the importance of parental perceptions in defining children's problem behavior, such an effect of clinic intervention should not be belittled. Since parental tolerance levels are especially crucial in such child behaviors as aggression, disobedience, and temper tantrums, it would be interesting to find out whether a result such as that reported by Eyberg and Johnson (1974) would also be found when the target behavior is something like school phobia, bedwetting, or a learning disability. This also relates to the third explanation offered by these investigators, who suggest that home observations may not always directly assess the problems treated because the observations take place at times when the behavior is not in evidence. If a child's negativism or aggression occurs primarily around bedtime, for example, an observer coming to the home during daylight hours would never record such behavior and no difference between pre- and postreatment observations could be reflected in the data analysis. The conclusion to be drawn from a recognition of the problems highlighted in the Eyberg and Johnson (1974) study is that assessment for behavior therapy, and particularly for outcome studies, should take several forms because each method may be sampling a somewhat different aspect of child and parent behavior.

MULTIPLE METHODS OF ASSESSMENT

When a child's behavior has been assessed by multiple methods, such as parent interviews and ratings, direct observations in the home or school, and observations in a standard situation, such as a clinic analogue of a real-life interaction between parents and child, it should not be surprising if each of these sources contribute different but complementary information. Simply because the behavior of which the parents complain is not seen during a home visit by an observer or does not emerge in the clinic setting, one should not conclude that the parental report is invalid. Such discrepant findings are, in fact, to be expected by behavior therapists who, after all, base their work on the assumption that behavior is situation-specific and not a function of underlying personality traits. In line with the social learning conceptualization advanced by Mischel (1973), marked differences in child behavior in different settings should be viewed as reflecting relatively good adaptive capacities. It is an indication that a child is profoundly disturbed when his or her bizarre mannerisms and stereotyped behavior are seen time and time again and in vastly different settings.

Assessment is never an end in itself. Unless it has a purpose and function related to the life of the child who is being assessed, it is an idle exercise. One of the purposes of assessment is to decide what intervention, if any, should be undertaken in order to help the child. With that in mind, different and even discrepant information from different sources does not become a cause for consternation and for asking which is right and which is wrong, but an occasion for making constructive plans. Among these plans is setting treatment goals and specifying the criterion by which treatment outcome is to be evaluated. Assessment is not something that is undertaken only at the beginning of treatment; it is an ongoing process that provides the basis for deciding when the goal of treatment has been reached and permits vital follow-up evaluations after treatment has been completed.

VALIDITY AND RELIABILITY

The question about the validity of a test asks whether the test measures what it was designed to measure. The question about the reliability of a test asks whether the test provides its information with consistency. To be useful a test must be both valid and reliable, but when one is dealing with observations of behavior, these twin questions of psychometrics take on a special meaning. With the typical psychological test—an achievement test, for example—the question of validity revolves around whether the score a person attains on that test accurately predicts how well he or she will perform "in real life." The criterion by which test validity is ascertained is direct observation of the behavior the test is supposed to predict. When the measuring instrument is not a specially contrived test but the direct observation of behavior itself, what is to be the criterion by which validity is to be evaluated? Or is there no question of validity when behavior is being observed?

The answer is obvious in the case of evidence recording; for here the record is based not on the behavior itself but on the traces the behavior leaves behind. Those traces might be spurious; the evidence misleading, hence, invalid. This point was touched on in the discussion of evidence recording where we indicated that the artifacts from which one infers the occurrence of a given behavior must be valid indicators that the behavior has, indeed, taken place. When one observes a coat lying on the floor and concludes that the child has failed to hang this garment in the closet, this conclusion may be wrong if the child had, in fact, hung up the coat but a sibling has come along and thrown it down. The validity of evidence recording is unknown and can only be ascertained if one combines evidence recording with direct observations; from time to time watching the child hang up the coat—that is, doing some event recording. If, on the occasions of these spot checks the child is seen hanging up the coat, one may assume that when one finds the coat on the floor it is proof that the child has failed to hang it up. Yet this will always remain an assumption for, on occasion, the coat on the floor may have a different cause. This then becomes an issue of reliability. Is the evidence consistently valid or is it sometimes misleading? If misleading, what percentage of the time is it so? Questions of validity and reliability are thus just as pertinent in the case of evidence recording as in the case of any other test.

Is there less of a question of validity in the case of event, duration, and interval recording? When an observer records the number of times a child is "out-of-chair," can there by any doubt that this record validly reflects what has indeed happened? Of course, there can be doubt. Recall that "out-of-chair," as used as an observation category by O'Leary et al. (1970), was defined as movement out of the chair when such movement is not permitted and when it entails no part of the child's body remaining in contact with the chair. Clearly, an observer might record an instance of "out-of-chair" when a part of the child's body is still in contact with the chair or when the teacher had requested the child to get up but the observer had failed to hear that request. In that case, the record would be invalid with respect to that entry; for it would show an event that had not actually taken place, a so-called Type II error. Conversely, it is possible that an event had taken place, but the observer failed to notice it. Thus, the record would lack validity because it would not reflect an event that had, in fact, occurred—a Type I error. As with any other form of measurement, observational records are subject to both types of errors.

Interval recording can have a combination of these errors by virtue of a misplaced entry. It is the task of the observer to note for each time interval whether a given behavior has taken place. If the observer is careless, fatigued, or over-burdened by too many categories, an entry could be made in the wrong cell, thus showing the behavior to have taken place during a time interval when it had actually not taken place. The record would thus wrongly indicate that the event had not taken place during one time unit and equally wrongly show it to have taken place during another (earlier or later) time unit. Note that the total count of how many times during the entire observation period the behavior had occurred would be correct. This would be satisfactory for event recording; it is unacceptable for interval recording.

In order to guard against records with low validity or, at least, to know to what extent a record can be trusted, investigators who use behavior observations as their measurement usually compare the data gathered by two or more observers. If it can be established that different observers agree on what they have seen and if they make identical entries in their records, it is assumed that the event has actually taken place at that time. It is assumed, in other words, that the recorded observations are valid. Strictly speaking, this method tells us something of interobserver reliability, and the question of validity becomes obscured in a philosophical haze concerning the question whether reality is what two or more honest people agree it to be. We have already touched on the problems of observer expectations, observer drift, and observers' reactions to being themselves observed when we discussed the training of observers. Let us turn to how interobserver reliability is computed.

Interobserver Reliability

When interval recording is used, the reliability is computed by comparing the records of two or more observers, interval by interval, for instances where the occurrence of an event was recorded by at least one of the observers. Agreements and disagreements on such occurrences are counted and the number of agreements is divided by the sum of agreements plus disagreements; i.e., the total number of observation units. This quotient is then multiplied by 100, which yields a percentage of agreements. To be acceptable, interobserver reliability should be 90 percent or higher. If it fails to reach this level, the response definitions may have to be refined, the observers may need more training, the duration of the observation interval may have to be lengthened, or the observation period as a whole may have to be reduced. High interobserver reliability can be spuriously inflated, however, and there are a number of pitfalls against which one must guard. It is possible, for example, to obtain impressive reliability indexes by selecting for observation behaviors that occur with high frequency, in which case even random recording would result in agreement between two observers on the basis of chance alone. Other sources of inflated reliabilities, such as observer drift or a small number of observational categories, have been discussed by Kent and Foster (1977) in their review of methodological issues in observational procedures.

For methods of observation other than interval recording, reliability is computed by dividing the count provided by the observer who has the higher number into the count of the observer with the lower number and multiplying this fraction by 100 for a percentage of agreements. Just as evidence, event, and duration recording are less refined than interval recording, so is the manner in which their reliability is computed.

Reliability data for several sessions can, of course, be combined to provide an average expressing the level of agreement between observers. In practice, however, the use of more than one observer over an extended period of time becomes prohibitive. What is then done is to establish interobserver reliability at the beginning of a study, particularly in the course of observer training, and then to use spot checks by introducing a reliability recorder only intermittently and, ideally, in a covert manner (Kent, Kanowitz, O'Leary, & Cheiken, 1977).

Tests of Validity

Thus far, the discussion has dealt with direct observations of behavior in its natural setting, such as the classroom. The issue of validity becomes more complex if the observations are conducted in contrived laboratory situations where a family might be asked to engage in various structured activities or when observations are conducted in the home but only during specific times, such as the dinner hour. Now the question arises whether the samples of behavior being observed are representative of the behavior that takes place in the family's home and at other times of the day. This is another version of the question of validity. It can be addressed by comparing the results obtained from behavior observations with other measures of the behavior which is of interest. In this matter, the *concurrent validity* of the observations can be examined. To assess the concurrent validity of the Behavioral Coding System developed by Patterson (1977), for example, measures obtained with that system on the basis of laboratory observations were compared with mothers' ratings of the behavior of their children and with daily reports of child behavior submitted by their parents. The significant correlations of the coding system with these measures can be considered to be a reflection of its validity.

If one is willing to assume that the judgments that lead to clinic referrals are valid criteria for differentiating adaptive from maladaptive behavior, another test of the validity of a behavior coding system is possible. This test provides a form of *criterion validity*, though it must be remembered that the criterion itself is of questionable validity. The test would consist of comparing the scores that the coding system provides for a group of children referred to a psychological clinic with the scores of a group of nonreferred, presumably normal children in a public school. On a valid coding system, the scores of the clinic children should be significantly different from the scores of the school children.

It will be recognized that both concurrent validity and this form of criterion validity beg several questions. If two different tests correlate with one another, it could mean that they both lack validity. If a measuring system varies with a criterion, there is no guarantee that the criterion itself is valid. Because of these uncertainties, a measuring instrument based on the observations of behavior should be required to satisfy not one but several different tests of validity.

VISUAL PRESENTATION OF OBSERVATIONAL DATA

Observational assessment almost invariably consists of measures obtained over a period of time. Whether this be a sampling of a given behavior over a week in order to ascertain its stability, whether it entails several observations during the course of treatment in order to track changes, or whether it involves taking a measurement before and after treatment and a follow-up measure some months after conclusion of treatment, one needs some way of comparing the measures obtained at these different points. Such comparisons are most readily made when the points to be compared are presented in visual form. Unlike most static forms of assessment where a single score represents a child's status, behavioral assessment should reflect the dynamics of change over time. Furthermore, unlike research involving comparisons between groups of subjects where measures of central tendency and of variance represent aggregates of data, therapeutically oriented behavioral assessment focuses on the behavior of an individual child. In this sense, the assessment is essentially a study of a single subject, and it is to the analyses used in single-subject research that behavioral assessment turns for its format for displaying results. It is the format of the graph that provides a readily available visual record of the stabilities and changes of the behavior under scrutiny.

The information contained in such a graph and the data on which it is based can tell us only what the child does, i.e., the behavior, how much of it occurs, the frequency of the action, and when during the period of observations the activity took place. What is lacking is the important information about the conditions which control this behavior—its antecedents and consequences. Since it is these conditions that will have to be manipulated if the child's behavior is to be changed, it is important that an assessment provide information about the controlling variables.

THE IDENTIFICATION OF EFFECTIVE REINFORCERS

Before a behavior can be changed, whether in the direction of increasing deficient behavior or decreasing excess behavior, the reinforcers which maintain that behavior must be identified. They will have to be presented in order to strengthen new, desirable behavior and they will have to be withdrawn in order to weaken undesirable, problematic behavior. It cannot be stressed sufficiently that there are no universal reinforcers. What is reinforcing for one child may be a neutral or even a punishing event for another. For this reason, the effective reinforcers must be ascertained for each individual child and, since reinforcers may lose their potency over time, their effectiveness must be monitored continually during the course of a treatment program.

It is well to recall that the technical definition of a reinforcer is any stimulus that, when presented following a response, will raise or maintain the probability that this response will recur on a subsequent, similar occasion. A reinforcer can thus be identified only after its effectiveness has been observed. Prior to that, one can speak only of *potential* reinforcers. Viewed in this manner, just about anything might be a reinforcer; a fact that can be readily confirmed from everyone's experience with people who engage in behavior for any of a vast array of reasons or motivations. If one wishes to modify a child's behavior by changing the reinforcing consequences of that behavior, one must narrow down this vast list of potential reinforcers to those which have a likelihood of being effective. This narrowing process is relatively easy when the goal of intervention is the reduction of excess behavior; for here one need only observe the actual consequences of that

behavior in order to arrive at a hypothesis of what it is that maintains that behavior. This hypothesis is tested by removing that consequence and observing
the effect of this intervention on the target behavior. A functional analysis of behavior based on appropriate recording, to be discussed in the following section,
should provide a ready answer to whether the correct contingencies have been
identified. The problem is more complicated when one seeks to establish or
strengthen behavior that is deficient in the child's repertoire and where a reinforcer
has to be introduced contingent on the behavior having been emitted.

Verbal Inquiry

A first approximation of a circumscribed list of potential reinforcers, which can
then be tested for their effectiveness, is compiled by questioning the people most
likely to know what events the child deems to be attractive, that is, reinforcing.
Obviously, one can ask the child a simple question such as, "Tell me some of the
things you like," for things a child likes may well turn out to be effective reinforcers. Again, however, one should not designate these items as reinforcers until
they have stood the empirical test of application. In addition to asking the child,
the child's parents can be useful sources of information regarding potential reinforcers. Questions about the child's favorite foods, toys, activities, experiences,
hobbies, or television programs should lead to a helpful list.

A somewhat more structured approach to an interview-based list of reinforcers is made possible by a printed list of questions to which the child's parents are
asked to respond. One of these is the Children's Reinforcement Schedule (Phillips,
Fischer, & Singh, 1977), a printed list of questions to which the child's parents
are asked to respond; another, the Children's Reinforcement Survey developed
by Clement and Richard (1976). Such a list includes questions about people with
whom the child likes to spend time, places the child likes to frequent, things with
which the child likes to play, and activities the child likes to undertake. Whether
the child likes to do something is put in terms of the amount of time he or she
spends on it. The question about places, for example, is phrased, "List below the
10 places where your child spends the most time each week." It should be obvious
that the answers to such a question must be further evaluated before one can assume that the place where a child spends most of his or her time has a reinforcing
quality. Children spend a great deal of time in the classroom, but that does not
necessarily mean they like being there. A more helpful way of phrasing these
questions would be, "Given a free choice, where would the child be spending most
of his or her time?"

The idea that children, given a free choice, will seek out activities that are
reinforcing for them has been formalized in Premack's (1959) Differential Probability Principle, which states that for any set of responses the most probable response in a free-choice situation will serve to reinforce the less probable response
when it is presented in a contingency relationship. What that means in practice is
that if a boy, left to his own devices, is more likely to play ball than to do home-

work, the opportunity to play ball when the homework is completed will reinforce working on homework. Arranging such a contingency, "If you do the homework, you may play ball," should thus result in greater homework production.

Direct Observation

In view of the Premack Principle, it is possible to identify potential reinforcers by observing what the child does when alone or in a free-choice situation. The greater the variety of activities available to the child in such a situation, the larger the number of potential reinforcers that can be identified. It is possible to set up a playroom in a clinic where the child can be observed but once the apparently preferred activities are discovered, it is still necessary to test whether they will indeed serve to reinforce the behavior which is to be changed. The observations can only provide suggestions, they cannot ensure that the effective reinforcer has been determined.

There are several reasons for this uncertainty. One is that an activity may be attractive to a child when he or she is alone but when that activity is presented by a therapist or a parent in consequence of a response, it may have an entirely different value. Another reason lies in the little understood relationship between the response and the reinforcing stimulus. It is easy to see that the opportunity to run around on the playground can reinforce sitting and studying in the classroom, while being given a chance to run around the playground is not a reinforcer for having followed the rules while in the swimming pool. Other relationships are not so easy to understand and because there seem to be response-specific reinforcers, it is again necessary to stress that nothing should be assumed about the effectiveness of a reinforcer until that effectiveness has been tested.

The Use of Tokens

The availability of a wide choice of potential reinforcers from which the child can freely choose the one that is most attractive (reinforcing) for him or her at any given time is best implemented in a "token" program. Here the child is taught that the token dispensed in immediate consequence of the desired behavior can later be traded for any of a variety of prizes, privileges, or activities which represent the backup reinforcers. The token, whether it is a poker chip, a checkmark, or a bead, serves as a generalized conditioned reinforcer which, having no intrinsic value, derives its reinforcing value from the fact that it can be traded for something that is valuable to the child. Since what is valuable may change from time to time as the child gets bored with an activity or satiated with candy, the token reinforcer retains its potency over considerable periods of time. From the point of view of assessment, the use of tokens requires only that a wide range of backup reinforcers be available. What to include among these can often be determined by an interview with the parents or the child, but the range can also be extended at a later stage of treatment as the child indicates what additional item he or she would like to "purchase" with the earned tokens.

Generalized conditioned reinforcers also include the so-called social reinforcers, such as smiles, praise, and similar positive attention. Many children have learned that these are pleasant consequences for their behavior, but it is again important to remember that one cannot assume the reinforcing potency of these events and that only a systematic test with careful observations and recordings can ascertain whether a child will indeed be reinforced by an adult's praise or show of pleasure.

Qualities of a Good Reinforcer

An assessment effort aimed at identifying effective reinforcers may reveal a fairly large number of objects and activities that might be reinforcing for a particular child. Therefore, it is sometimes necessary to select from among this list those reinforcers which lend themselves particularly well to the purposes of a treatment program. A series of characteristics of a useful reinforcer is listed by Gelfand and Hartmann (1975).

To be useful, a reinforcer must maintain its reinforcing capacity over a long period of time; that is, it must resist satiation. For example, when food is used as a reinforcer, the child may become satiated within the first 15 minutes of an hour's training session. To combat this, one can either keep the individual reinforcer units small or the training session brief. Better still, one can use several different reinforcers or, ideally, rely on generalized conditioned reinforcers (tokens) as discussed above.

Since reinforcement is most effective when it is delivered immediately after the response has been emitted, a good reinforcer should be capable of being readily dispensed. A meal that must first be cooked, an outing that cannot be held until the following weekend, or a party that must be arranged weeks in advance are examples of cumbersome reinforcers. Again, the token recommends itself as a reinforcer that can be quickly delivered and permits a bridging between the behavior to be reinforced and the eventual production of the backup reward.

Another desirable characteristic of a good reinforcer is that the child have no access to it except in consequence of the behavior the therapist, parent, or teacher wishes to strengthen. This means that the delivery of the reinforcer must be under the exclusive control of the person seeking to use it. If the reinforcer is a favorite dessert or a small amount of money, the effectiveness of that reinforcer will be undercut if the child can get the dessert without working for it by going to a neighbor's house or can obtain the money as a gift from grandmother. Providing a reinforcer when the child has not satisfied the agreed-upon contingencies or conditions, giving a noncontingent reinforcer, destroys the effectiveness of that reinforcer and may reward instead such activities as sneaking off to the neighbor's or putting the touch on grandma.

It stands to reason that the selected reinforcer should be compatible with the goals of the treatment program, that it should be readily available, and that it fit into the value system and economic reality of the child's family. One would not want to use food as a reinforcer for weight loss nor dispense caramel candy in the course of a session devoted to speech training. One should avoid using a reinforcer, even in the context of a program using tokens, that may not be available when it is needed as, for example, a sled in the middle of summer. Lastly, where a family objects to the use of toy guns or the reading of comic books, a therapist would be ill-advised to place these objects among a child's backup reinforcers, just as monetary reinforcers should not be introduced in amounts the family cannot afford or deems excessive. A therapeutic program should not be the cause of family conflict.

FUNCTIONAL ANALYSIS OF BEHAVIOR

When the conditions which seem to surround the behavior in question, especially the reinforcing consequences, have been tentatively identified through interview and observation, the assessment turns to a testing of the hypotheses thus formulated. Inasmuch as the assessment now becomes an experiment which deals with a single subject, the within-subject design provides the method for this approach. What we wish to know is whether the child's behavior is indeed a function of the antecedents and consequences we believe to have identified; viz., whether the behavior will change when these conditions are changed. Such a functional analysis of behavior can use one of several experimental designs. We shall here present only the two most widely used approaches: the reversal design and the multiple baseline design.

The Baseline

Before it can be ascertained whether an intervention such as changing the consequences of a behavior has an effect, it is necessary to have a basis for identifying that effect. To talk about a change, one must know how to answer the question, "A change from what?" This answer requires a baseline against which change is to be evaluated. To obtain a baseline it is necessary to measure and record aspects of the problem behavior before any intervention has taken place. If the complaint has to do with bed-wetting, for example, a baseline would consist of a count of the number of dry nights before any attempt is made to do something about this problem. For what duration of time should this counting be continued before the baseline period can be terminated and intervention begun? Unfortunately, there is no ready answer for this question. The aim is to obtain a stable, reliable baseline, one from which changes due to an intervention will be readily apparent. This calls for a baseline showing a clear trend or pattern from which it is possible to project with reasonable confidence how this pattern would look if nothing were done to change it. In the case of bed-wetting, the length of the baseline period would depend on the fluctuations of dry and wet nights. If there were no dry nights at all (and the parents reported that this has always been the case), a one-week baseline would provide an adequate record. On the other hand, if there were occasional dry nights, say once or twice per week, it would be necessary to maintain the baseline condition for 2 or 3 weeks so that the record could clearly reflect that pattern. The greater the fluctuations in the frequency of the target behavior, the longer it will take for a trend to emerge; the smaller the fluctuations, the more quickly will the necessary projection become possible.

The Reversal Design

Once a stable baseline has been established and it is possible to say with a fair degree of assurance that the starting point is known, the planned intervention can be introduced and its effect on the behavior recorded. If the intervention has an effect on the behavior, a change in the frequency of the target behavior should very quickly be reflected on a graphic record. If there is no change, it means that the intervention is ineffective. In that case, the problem may have been incorrectly analyzed and further assessment may be required.

For the purpose of an illustration, let us assume that the problem we are working on is two siblings' low rate of appropriate interaction with one another. (Note that this may be the obverse of frequent fighting or that it may represent no interaction at all. In either case, we are interested in increasing appropriate interaction that would, correspondingly, reduce the changeworthy problem.) After baseline observations over a 5-day period, during which the frequency of the desired behavior hovered around one per day, the parent initiated a systematic regime of attending to positive sibling interactions by praising the children and expressing her pleasure while, at the same time, ignoring them when they had a fight. Let us turn to the following graph (Figure 5) to see what happened. Panel I of this graph displays the baseline data.

After the first day of the intervention phase, the number of times the children engaged in positive interactions rose to four per day, continued to increase for the next 6 days, and then seemed to stabilize around a frequency of eight. This information is shown in Panel II of the graph. Thus far we have a so-called baseline—treatment, or AB design, where A stands for the baseline and B for the treatment. With this alone, however, we cannot be certain that the introduction of the change in the mother's handling of the situation was indeed responsible for the improvement. Some other factor, which fortuitously entered the picture at about the same time and which we had not identified, might have brought about the increase in the children's positive interaction. Additional information is needed before one can assume that the intervention that was introduced had indeed been responsible for the observed change. Such additional information is provided by a reversal design.

A reversal, or ABAB design, serves to increase one's confidence that the intervention was indeed responsible for the change. What it involves is a return (reversal) to the conditions that existed during the baseline phase. In our example, this return entails having the mother once again scold the children for fighting and ignoring them when they played quietly with one another as she had been

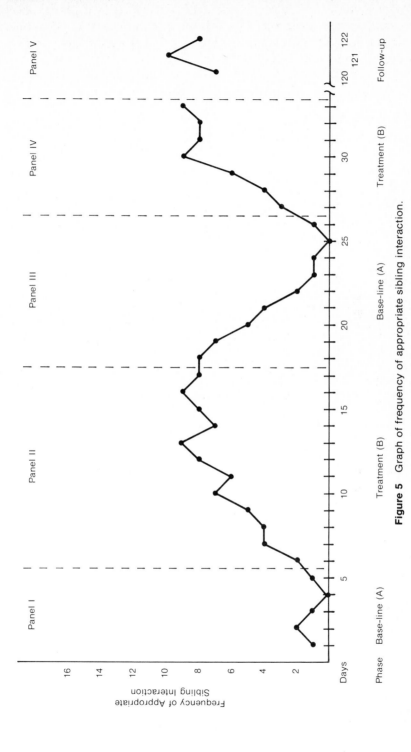

Figure 5 Graph of frequency of appropriate sibling interaction.

doing in the past. Panel III of Figure 5 shows what might have happened if this were a real case. The desirable behavior drops rather precipitously back to where it had been during the baseline period. This phase, again identified as A because it reinstates the preintervention condition, is obviously not the point at which to stop. Satisfied that the intervention was indeed effective, treatment is once again returned to condition B; hence, the designation ABAB design. If, with reinstating the treatment condition, the behavior once again returns to the desired level (see Panel IV), it is reasonably certain that an effective reinforcement contingency has been identified. There remains the important test of whether the improvement brought about by the intervention will be of lasting benefit. For this reason, a responsible therapist conducts a follow-up after termination of treatment. During this phase, the behavior is once again observed and recorded. Panel V in Figure 5 shows that in our fictitious example the children continued their constructive interaction several months after the systematic manipulation of the contingencies had been stopped.

The Multiple Baseline Design

In order to establish whether the intervention was indeed responsible for the change in the child's behavior, the reversal design required that the mother resume her pretreatment behavior toward the children. As a result, the children's behavior quickly returned to the baseline level. This means that for about 7 days the problem for which the mother had sought help was once again in evidence. Only after the treatment conditions had been reinstated for about 4 days was the positive effect once more recaptured. There are obviously many problem behaviors that one would not wish to reinstate after once having succeeded in changing them in the desired direction. Similarly, many parents or teachers are loath to live through another period of difficulty with the child merely in order to know whether the effective variables had been identified, even though that knowledge might contribute to more effectively helping the child. For that matter, there are behaviors such as newly acquired skills, like stair-climbing or speech components, a therapist would not want to risk losing with a reversal and that might not readily return to baseline level with a reversal of contingencies because reinforcers other than those controlled by the therapist have come to maintain them. When for one or more of these reasons a reversal design cannot be used, the multiple baseline design offers a good alternative for assessing the variables that control a child's behavior.

In order to use a multiple baseline design several changeworthy behaviors or responses must be identified. Examples of these might be a variety of household duties a boy is expected to perform, homework in different subject matters, the various categories of classroom behavior that are considered disruptive, correct pronunciation of different consonants, or constructive interaction with different members of the family. Each of these behaviors must be separately observed, measured, and recorded, first during baseline and later during treatment.

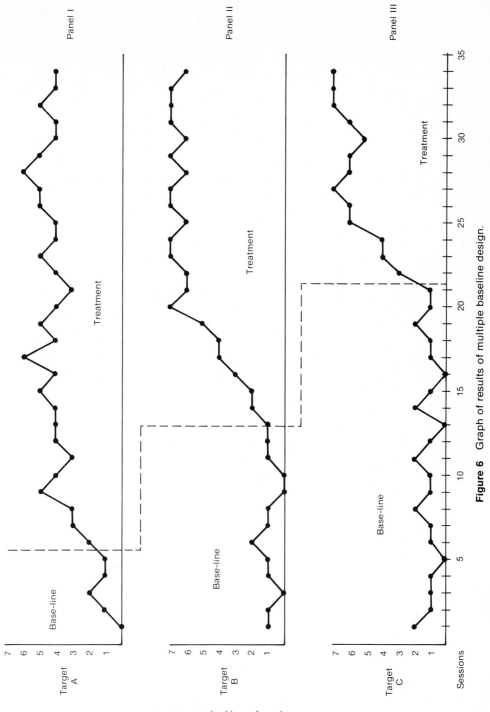

Figure 6 Graph of results of multiple baseline design.

Baseline recording begins at the same time for all target behaviors. After a stable baseline has been reached for one of the targets, the treatment intervention is initiated for that target while the other behaviors continue in baseline. The next target is subjected to the treatment after its effect is reflected in the record of the previous target behavior. Meanwhile, the other target(s) continue in baseline, to be treated only after the earlier target behaviors have changed. In other words, treatment is introduced sequentially and repeated measures of all target behaviors are continued throughout. Figure 6 illustrates how the results of such a procedure would be plotted on a graph.

The three panels in Figure 6 display the records of three target behaviors. Each data point reflects the frequency of the behavior during the session identified below Panel III. The panels are thus comparable in the vertical dimension and the dotted, steplike line shows how the baseline ends at different, sequential points in time. The effectiveness of the treatment is demonstrated by the fact that the target behaviors did not show a change until after the treatment had been instituted. As with the reversal design, it is assumed that the behavior would have continued at baseline level if the intervention had not taken place. This assumption is given a test in a multiple baseline design where the behaviors treated later in the sequence remain in baseline for considerably longer than is usually the case in a reversal design. This fact, of course, also represents one of the disadvantages of this design, because it requires that the problems represented by the targets held for later treatment continue when an effective intervention may already be at hand. For this reason, a therapist may wish to order the behaviors to be treated in terms of the severity of the problem, leaving those that are relatively less important to the last.

Because the assessment methods we have described here are essentially experimental designs which were originally developed in the psychological laboratory, it is easy to receive the impression that the results one obtains are primarily of interest to the therapist; that the data are being gathered in order to satisfy the therapist's scientific curiosity. In clinical situations, faced with pressing problems of troubled children, the temptation is great to short-cut these assessment methods or to omit them altogether. It is therefore well to remember that the evidence for the effectiveness of an intervention is as important to the therapist as it is to the child and the child's parents or teachers. There are many things that can influence a child's behavior, but they often do so only temporarily. Unless one has clearly identified the variables which effect a permanent improvement, little will have been gained and these variables can only be identified by employing a systematic method of assessment. What is more, once the variables are identified and thus known, this knowledge can be used later if some other behavior of the child should come to be viewed as changeworthy. The mother who has learned that her differential attention to the child's activities can serve to increase or decrease behavior will be able to use this knowledge in many situations without having to seek professional help. Whereas a therapist's instructions or explanations might have little effect, the graphic demonstration provided by a record of measured behavior often serves to convince parents or teachers that they are doing something that is effective.

RECAPITULATION

Assessment is an essential first step whenever intervention in a child's life is under consideration. Once such preliminary assessment has led to the decision to intervene, assessment continues throughout the treatment so that progress can be substantiated and, failing such progress, that the approach can be changed until success is assured. Even after the treatment goal has been reached, periodic follow-up assessment should be conducted in order to make certain that the treatment effect is being maintained. Assessment is thus an integral part of the treatment process.

While interviews with the family and checklists or questionnaires can provide valuable information, no assessment is complete unless it includes direct observations of behavior and written or graphic records of these observations. Various methods of observation are available, and the choice among these depends on the nature of the problem and the place or places where it occurs. Similarly, the measures to be used in these observations must be adapted to the given case. The training of observers and issues related to the child's reaction to being observed require consideration in the light of the important questions of the validity and reliability of data based on observations.

Because many approaches to child therapy involve the manipulation of the consequences which maintain the target behavior, the identification of effective reinforcers is a central aspect of assessment. Reinforcer effectiveness and other contingencies controlling the behavior are best explored by a functional analysis for which several designs are available. The graphic record reflecting such an analysis provides not only information about the baseline or pretreatment behavior but also evidence for change and knowledge about the variables responsible for that change. Without such a record, therapy is based on hunches, impressions, and inferences, and progress may be more wishful thinking than reality.

Chapter 7

Aggression

In the socialization of the child no response pattern has more important implications, both from the point of view of the child's own adaptation and of its effect on society, than that involving aggression. The failure to teach children to restrain aggressive behavior or at least to express it in ways and under circumstances deemed appropriate by society can have serious long-term consequences. Robins (1966) studied the status of a group of adults who had been referred to a child guidance clinic for a variety of problems 30 years earlier. She found that those individuals who, as children, had been referred for aggression and other antisocial behavior were more likely to have serious psychological problems as adults than those who had been referred for other problems, such as fears and phobias. Further, the more severe the antisocial behavior had been during childhood, the more likely it was that serious problems would be present in adulthood. These findings suggest that both the individual and society could be spared much suffering if effective procedures were applied to modify aggressive behavior during childhood.

In order to understand the problem of aggression so as to be able to deal with it from a therapeutic and preventative point of view, it is necessary to arrive at a meaningful formulation of this complex issue.

AGGRESSION IS A RESPONSE

Aggression is best viewed as an overt response. Of the many different responses a person directs at other people, only some are labeled aggressive responses. This labeling is a reflection of a social judgment that is influenced by several factors. As analyzed by Bandura (1973), these include the characteristics of the behavior itself, the characteristics of the person doing the labeling, and the characteristics of the person whose behavior is being labeled. Likely to be judged as aggressive are behaviors such as physical assault or destruction of property, which result in aversive consequences for others. Responses labeled as aggressive are usually of high magnitude or intensity and they are often followed by expressions of pain and injury on the part of the victim. The characteristics of the person doing the labeling enter the picture when it is that person's values and expectations that determine whether a response is or is not labeled as aggressive. Depending on the labeler's social background, the activities of a group of boys might be labeled "horseplay" or "aggression." The characteristics of the person whose behavior is being labeled are also often related to social background. Various stereotypes come into play, according to which behavior is seen as aggression if it is emitted by a member of one ethnic group but as sport if participated in by a person from a different social milieu.

When aggression is viewed as an overt response, it is necessary to differentiate it from a motivational factor that is often correlated with aggression but is neither synonymous with nor does it invariably accompany aggression. This motivational (emotional) factor is a physiological arousal state generally called *anger* or *rage*. It appears to be elicited by certain stimuli, particularly those involving attack (aggression directed against the individual) and frustration (blocking of a response sequence before the consummatory response is reached).

THE LEARNING OF AGGRESSION

Once aggression is defined as a response, it becomes possible to study the conditions under which it is learned, and when these conditions are known, it should be possible to modify and ultimately control this socially disruptive behavior.

Reinforcement of Aggression

Like any other instrumental response, aggression is strengthened by reinforcement. This may take the form of positive reinforcement, as when a child's aggressive response obtains for him or her a desired object, or of negative reinforcement, as would be encountered when an aggressive response terminates an aversive state like being attacked by another child. Additional negative reinforcement may be involved if the aggressive response is also followed by a reduction of a noxious tension state, such as the one we call anger. It is not at all unlikely that the apparent universality of aggression and the obdurate nature of the response in the face of attempts to modify it are a function of the many ways in which it can be reinforced.

A formulation of some of the conditions under which aggression can be learned was presented and tested by Patterson, Littman, and Bricker (1967). They view aggressive behavior as relatively rare high-amplitude responses that represent a special case of a broader class of assertive behaviors. Assertive behaviors, these writers point out, have two characteristics: they demand an immediate reaction and carry the implied threat of increasingly assertive behavior in case of noncompliance. The reaction demanded from the environment very often provides reinforcing consequences, thus aiding the acquisition of these behaviors in the course of a child's socialization.

Patterson et al. (1967) maintain that all children who emit aggressive behavior must previously have acquired the more general class of assertive behavior, which they view as necessary, though not sufficient conditions for aggression. If assertive responses were always met by the demanded response on the part of the person to whom it is addressed, this response class would be limited to assertive behavior; that is, aggressive behavior would not develop. However, since the vagaries of human interaction do not always operate to give immediate gratification of every request, the request will often be repeated at higher intensity and, if it is then met, that higher intensity response will be the one that is strengthened and learned.

Most of the assertive behavior of young children is of relatively low amplitude and short duration because, typically, the responses are not accompanied by emotional arousal. Patterson et al. (1967) state that *two* conditions must be met before a child is labeled as aggressive: his or her assertive responses must be emitted at high magnitude and frequency *and* these responses must be under the control of aversive emotional states which, when terminated contingent on the aggressive response, further strengthen this behavior through negative reinforcement. In this formulation, the aversive emotional state may take one of several forms, including hunger, fear, or anger, the last of which may or may not be related to prior experiences with frustrating conditions.

Of the two major factors which are involved in the acquisition of aggressive behavior, according to Patterson and his colleagues, the first entails the shaping of relevant responses into the child's repertoire. The initial training in assertive behavior is probably accomplished by the parents, but younger siblings and peers will later contribute to the development of these responses. While a parent may, at least at times, insist that a shouted demand be repeated in the form of a polite request before it is granted, siblings and peers are more likely to give in when pushed, hit, or yelled at by an older sibling or stronger playmate. A younger sibling can also receive training in aggressive behavior when his or her occasional counterassertions are reinforced, particularly in families where such behavior is encouraged or permitted by parents.

The second major factor involved in this formulation of the acquisition of aggressive behavior is the high-intensity, emotional state which, when accompanying assertive responses, makes this behavior a social problem. Patterson et al. (1967) suggest that in order for a child to be labeled an aggressive child, he or she must have received massive social reinforcement for aggressive behavior and have been exposed to frequent aversive emotional stimulation from the environment.

In order to test the hypothesis derived from their formulation about the acquisition of assertive-aggressive responses, Patterson et al. (1967) conducted a painstaking observational study of 36 nursery school children that covered a 9-month period. During this time they recorded 2,583 aggressive responses and their consequences. Each aggressive event was coded as belonging to one of four categories: bodily attack, attack with an object, verbal or symbolic attack, and infringement of property or invasion of territory. The consequences were categorized in one of seven classes in terms of the response made by the victim of the aggression. These response consequences were passive (no response, withdrawing, or giving in), crying, assuming defensive posture, telling the teacher, recovering property, and retaliation. The seventh category, a relatively infrequent one, was teacher intervention.

On the basis of reinforcement principles it was assumed that the consequences arbitrarily labeled *positive* (passive, crying, or defensive responses on the part of the victim) would strengthen the aggressive behavior directed at that particular victim, while those consequences arbitrarily labeled *negative* (telling the teacher, recovering the property, retaliation, and teacher intervention) would weaken the aggressive behavior directed at that particular victim. In other words, it was predicted that when an assertive response was followed by a positive consequence, the aggressor would, on the next occasion, select the same aggressive response and the same victim. On the other hand, if the behavior had been followed by a negative consequence, it was predicted that the aggressor would, on the next occasion, change either the nature of the aggressive response or the victim or both.

The data supported these predictions at a high level of significance, leading to the conclusion that the typical nursery school provides social interactions that serve to maintain assertive-aggressive behavior in children. What is more, this social setting also provides an extremely efficient program for the acquisition of assertive behaviors by children who are initially passive and unassertive. These children were frequently victimized; but when they eventually counterattacked, they were reinforced by positive consequences, and after that the frequency of their initiating aggressive responses tended to increase, with this behavior showing a typical acquisition pattern.

Contrary to the investigators' expectations, the proportion of positive reinforcements a given child would provide for the aggressive behaviors of others was unrelated to the frequency with which he or she was victimized. Victimization did not reveal a stable pattern, but the amount of social interaction that a given child engaged in seemed to be a major factor in determining the amount and kind of reinforcement he or she would get for this behavior. The data reported by Patterson et al. (1967) suggest that the child who interacts with peers at a high frequency is the one most likely to be reinforced for aggressive behavior. The highly aggressive child was found to have a high rate of peer interaction, and the passive child with a high rate of interaction was the most likely to acquire aggressive behaviors. While peer interaction seems to be partly a function of general activity level, the investigators believe that the child who interacts at a high rate is the child for whom peer-dispensed social reinforcers have acquired high potency. This complex interrelationship between activity level, social reinforcement, and social interaction requires further research before the relative contributions and possible causal relations of these and other factors can be known.

While the Patterson et al. (1967) data lend strong support to the reinforcement formulation of the acquisition process for assertive-aggressive behavior, they recognize that not all of the subjects behaved in accordance with their theoretical predictions. Thus, there were two highly aggressive children whose behavior seems to have been maintained by other than the positive consequences dispensed by their victims, and there was one passive subject whose counterattacks were never successful, but who nonetheless began to acquire aggressive responses. It appears, as the authors point out, that there are individual differences in the kind of reinforcing stimuli that control assertive responses and that no single set of generalized reinforcers for these responses applies to all children.

The pioneering study by Patterson et al. (1967) demonstrated the roles positive and negative reinforcement play in the acquisition of aggressive behavior. Others have shown that, like other learned responses, aggression undergoes extinction when reinforcement is withdrawn (Cowan & Walters, 1963), that both stimulus generalization and response generalization can take place (Horton, 1970; Walters & Brown, 1963), and that it is possible to change the stimuli controlling aggressive responses by using a discrimination-learning procedure (Bandura & Walters, 1963).

Modeling of Aggression

Observational learning appears to be another important aspect contributing to the learning of aggression. Bandura, Ross, and Ross (1963) had children observe an adult model who engaged in a variety of novel aggressive behaviors toward a large balloon doll ("Bobo" doll). Those children who had observed this were more likely to display these novel behaviors on a subsequent occasion than those who had watched the model behave in a calm, nonaggressive manner. New forms of aggressive responses can thus be acquired through observational learning. However, the children who had observed the aggressive model later also displayed a higher overall level of aggression than the other children. This included aggressive responses that had not been part of the model-displayed behavior, thus demonstrating that exposure to aggressive models may also facilitate the performance of aggressive behaviors that had already been in the child's repertoire, a phenomenon known as disinhibition of aggression.

In recent years a great deal of interest has centered on the question whether children's extensive viewing of television has an effect on their behavior, especially with respect to violent program content and its relation to child aggression. A review of available research (Liebert & Schwartzberg, 1977) leads to the conclusion that aggression modeled by characters on television, whether these be cartoon figures or live actors, does affect the viewer; thus, the principles of observational learning also apply in this realm. Not only does exposure to violence modeled on television lead to disinhibition of aggression on the part of the viewer, but there is also evidence that it can result in the direct imitation of the violence and in lowered sensitivity to, that is increased tolerance for, aggression.

The role of observational learning in the acquisition of aggression may well be an explanation for the apparent paradox that parents who use physical punishment in their attempt to control the aggressive behavior of their children tend to raise highly aggressive children (Bandura & Walters, 1959; Hollenberg & Sperry, 1951). Physical assault, whether or not committed by a parent under the guise of discipline, is a prime form of aggression, and the parent thus models aggressive behavior by a larger and stronger on a smaller and weaker person. Since this usually occurs when the parent also shows evidence of being emotionally aroused, the child may well learn to make aggressive responses under these conditions and against such victims. The punishment situation may, in fact, be a particularly potent condition for such learning because the child is also likely to be emotionally aroused, and a certain amount of emotional arousal seems to facilitate learning (Schachter & Singer, 1962). Parents who resort to physical punishment not only model aggressive behavior, they are also likely to find that the aggressive behavior they hope thereby to eliminate will not go away. This is because the punishment usually occurs with some delay and thus at an inefficient point in time in terms of learning-theory principles, which state that a consequence is most effective when it follows the relevant response almost immediately.

The High-Magnitude Theory of Aggression

Bandura and Walters (1963) proposed a theory of aggression that holds that the cultural definition of aggression is in part a function of the intensity or magnitude with which the response in question is emitted. Response intensity, they state, can be increased by exposure to such conditions of frustration as delay in anticipated reinforcement or an interrupted goal-directed behavior. Their theory also maintains that a given high-magnitude response may be learned under conditions where it is not judged to be aggressive but that when the same response is emitted under different circumstances, it can be regarded as an instance of aggression.

The above assertion was put to experimental test in a study conducted by Walters and Brown (1964), who trained boys from kindergarten, first, and second grades to emit high-magnitude or low-magnitude responses in doll-punching or lever-pressing tasks on which they were differently reinforced. Following each training session every subject was paired with another boy of the same age, and the two were invited to engage in competitive games requiring a good deal of body contact. The behavior of the experimental child in each pair was observed and scored for such responses as butting, kneeing, elbowing, kicking, punching, pulling, pushing, etc. The results were clearly in line with the hypothesis; for the children trained under high-intensity conditions emitted significantly more aggression responses during testing than did those who had been trained under low-intensity conditions. It will be recalled that the responses used during the training sessions were hitting and lever-pressing, while the behaviors scored as "aggression" in the testing sessions did not include hitting and certainly not lever-pressing. The generalization from training to testing involved not only the nature of the response but also the characteristic of intensity.

While the games used by Walters and Brown (1964) in the testing procedure were highly competitive, they did not entail frustration in the sense of either delayed reinforcement or interrupted goal-directed behavior. The pretraining alone seemed sufficient to bring about differential degrees of aggression depending on whether a particular child had been given high-intensity or low-intensity training preceding his participation in the games. A study by Davitz (1952) had used two of these very games for aggression training, suggesting the demand characteristics of these games; yet, even in the face of these characteristics, the children with low-intensity training emitted significantly fewer aggressive responses while engaged in these games.

The Davitz games are "cover that spot," "scalp," and "break the ball." Their respective goals are to cover a small "x" on the floor with some part of one's body when the game is terminated, to tear a cloth bandage ("scalp") from the opponent's arm while protecting one's own "scalp," and to break the other players' Ping-Pong balls while protecting one's own ball. Using these games, Davitz (1952) trained 20 boys and girls between the ages of 7 and 9 to be aggressive, while a comparison group received "constructive training" involving the drawing of murals and the completion of jigsaw puzzles. Prior to the seven 30-minute training sessions, the children had been observed during 18 minutes of free play that were recorded on motion-picture film. A similar period of free play followed a "frustration session." In this session the children were led to believe that they would be shown a series of five films. After the first reel had been shown, each subject was given a bar of candy, but the second reel was interrupted at a climactic point and the candy taken away. During the filmed free-play session following this frustration situation, the children who had been trained to behave aggressively in the competitive games behaved significantly more aggressively than did those trained in constructive activities. What is more, the subjects who had been trained to engage in constructive behavior behaved more constructively after the frustration than did the subjects who had been trained for aggression. This study strongly suggests that frustration does not automatically lead to aggression but that the stimuli involved in a frustration situation tends to elicit whatever response pattern happens to be dominant in a given subject's response hierarchy. Since the children in the Davitz experiment were exposed to the frustration and then tested in the same small group of 4 with whom they had been previously in their training sessions, it can be assumed that they provided the stimulus complex for each other that controlled the response pattern elicited by the frustration situation. Inasmuch as constructive play is by and large incompatible with aggressive behavior, constructive activity may well serve as the response pattern which, when sufficiently strengthened, can take the place of aggressive behavior, provided aggression is simultaneously weakened by nonreinforcement.

Conditions Favoring Aggression

Frustration is a stimulus configuration that often controls aggressive responses. In fact, in our culture it is so often observed that frustration precedes aggression that for several decades the frustration-aggression hypothesis of the Yale group (Dollard, Doob, Miller, Mowrer, & Sears, 1939), who held that aggression is always the consequence of frustration, was viewed as defining the necessary and sufficient conditions for aggression. Note that this formulation does not state that frustration is *always* followed by aggression, but the frustration-aggression hypothesis was often interpreted as if it proposed this causal sequence.

The word *frustration*, as used in everyday language, carries connotations of a state in an individual who has been thwarted in some action—one says "I feel frustrated." From a behavioral point of view it is best to limit the use of "frustration" to designating a stimulus configuration represented by external events surrounding the blocking of a response sequence. When frustration is used in this way, aggression can be viewed as one of many responses that an individual might learn to emit when this stimulus configuration is present. Conversely, the response labeled as aggression can be learned to a great variety of external stimuli, such as the command, "fight!" or the sound of a gong in a boxing ring.

The blocking of a response sequence before the goal is reached ("frustration," for short) has two characteristics that raise the probability that it will come to control responses that are likely to be labeled as aggressive. One characteristic is that the blocked goal can often be reached—the frustration removed—when a high-intensity response, such as pushing, is emitted. The other characteristic is that response blocking tends to elicit an arousal state that increases the probability that any response emitted under these circumstances will have relatively high intensity. If, in the child's reinforcement history, such high-intensity responses (pushing, hitting, kicking, etc.) are repeatedly followed by attaining the blocked goal or other reinforcement, such responses are strengthened and likely to be emitted whenever the child encounters a similar stimulus configuration ("frustration"). Inasmuch as our culture defines high-intensity pushing, hitting, and kicking as "aggression," the frustration-aggression sequence can be observed with great frequency. This does not mean, however, that aggression is the innate or inevitable consequence of frustration. It can, in fact, be demonstrated (e.g., Block

& Martin, 1955) that some children consistently respond to frustration in a manner our culture defines as "constructive," and it would seem to follow from the work of Davitz (1952) that careful discrimination teaching can develop a child who behaves in a prosocial fashion whenever he encounters frustration.

We know that some learning is facilitated when the learner is in a state of emotional arousal. This not only enhances the likelihood of the acquisition of the frustration-aggression sequence but it also has bearing on the aggressive behavior of disturbed children who may be seen as more frequently aroused or more highly aroused, or both, than those in the general population. A study by Cowan and Walters (1963) bears on this issue. They compared thirty boys, residents in an institution for "emotionally disturbed children" and ranging in age from 8 to 13 years, with an equal number of noninstitutionalized controls from public school. The subjects were reinforced with colored glass marbles for making hitting responses aimed at the stomach of an automated Bobo clown. One group received reinforcement on a continuous schedule, another on a 1 to 3 fixed-ratio schedule, and a third group was on a 1 to 6 fixed-ratio schedule. After a subject had made eighteen responses, reinforcement was discontinued and he was allowed to continue responding until he desired to stop. During this extinction period, the institutionalized children gave significantly more responses and continued to respond for a longer time than the noninstitutionalized children.

Under two of the three reinforcement conditions, the institutionalized children responded more rapidly than the noninstitutionalized children. During both acquisition and extinction, the institutionalized children performed in a manner that suggests a greater effectiveness of reinforcement procedures for this group. Cowan and Walters point out that the institutionalized subjects became highly excited when placed in the experimental situation and that this excitement frequently lasted throughout the experimental sessions. The authors suggest that the greater effectiveness of reinforcers under conditions of arousal is due to the fact that arousal restricts attention and thus places a subject's behavior more under control of salient environmental cues.

While this formulation is consonant with other studies, particularly those from the area of vicarious learning (Bandura & Rosenthal, 1966), there is an alternate explanation to the Cowan and Walters findings than one that focuses on the effectiveness of reinforcers that were dispensed during the training trials. The institutionalized subjects were described as having been referred to the hospital because they presented behavior problems to the community. These behavior problems presumably included a high proportion of aggressive behaviors; in other words, aggressive responses have a high probability of occurrence in the repertoire of these institutionalized children. Such responses, as Premack (1959) has suggested, are reinforcing in their own right so that the institutionalized subjects may well have received two reinforcers: the hitting response *and* the glass marble. This would account for both the higher response rate and the resistance to extinction without invoking the hypothesis about arousal level. To test the latter it would be necessary to teach disturbed children a response that is not likely to be high in their hierarchy. It would also be necessary to control for the differential consequences to stopping the clown-hitting response (extinction) inasmuch as institutionalized children are then taken back to the ward, while the school child is returned to his or her classroom. If returning to the ward is a negative consequence, sustained activity on the experimental apparatus in the absence of reinforcement might be avoidance behavior and not resistance to extinction.

The reinforcing capacity of hitting responses aimed at a plastic clown is highlighted in a paper by Hops and Walters (1963), who point out that during the operant phase of their study, that is, before reinforcement was introduced, many children reached a level of response that may have been near their physiological limit. This study also suggests that the rate of hitting responses in a Bobo clown situation is an aspect of the child's general activity level. It may be that a child who has a characteristically high activity level has a greater likelihood of being called *aggressive*. The Hops and Walters results may bear on this point. They show that there is a wide range of individual differences among children's activity level and that there are high correlations between response rates that reflect considerable intraindividual consistency under different reinforcement conditions. Children who have a high activity level emit a high rate of responses under many different conditions, and when response possibilities are restricted, as in an experimental Bobo clown situation, these children emit a high rate of hitting responses. It would be fallacious to conclude from observing the behavior of such children that they are "aggressive." Before one can draw conclusions about a child's generalized aggressive response tendency, one would have to demonstrate that he or she emits a higher rate of aggressive responses than of other responses that are equally possible in a given situation.

An experiment in which the child subjects were able to choose between an aggressive and a nonaggressive response was conducted by Lovaas (1961a). The aggressive response involved a bar press that activated a ball-game apparatus in that one boy doll would hit another boy doll on the head with a stick. The nonaggressive response involved a bar press that activated a ball game apparatus in such a way that a ball would be thrown to the top of a cage from where it would return through obstacles to its original position. The experimental manipulation took the form of showing the subjects two films—one was depicting humanlike cartoon figures in highly aggressive interaction, while the other was a peaceful scene showing a bear family in humanlike play. The children who had been shown the aggressive film engaged in significantly more play behavior with the hitting dolls than did those children who had been shown the nonaggressive film. The results thus give evidence for an increase in aggressive responses as a function of exposure to film-mediated aggression, suggesting that the viewing of aggressive films is likely to make children more aggressive.

While doll-play aggression is only an analogue of interpersonal aggression, a second study by Lovaas (1961b), using the apparatus previously described, lends further support to the utility of doll play as a device for studying aggression responses. This study demonstrated the generalization of aggressive responses from the verbal to the nonverbal mode. Two groups of children were differentially reinforced for making aggressive or nonaggressive verbal responses in the presence of a "bad" and a "good" doll. Seven subjects were reinforced with trinkets for emitting such responses as "bad doll" and "dirty doll," while the other seven subjects were similarly reinforced for emitting nonaggressive verbal statements. When these children were then given the choice of playing with the aforementioned hitting-dolls or bouncing-ball equipment, those who had been reinforced for verbal aggression showed a significant preference for playing with the hitting-dolls apparatus.

"Catharsis" and Aggression

Taken together, the two studies by Lovaas (1961a, 1961b) would seem to argue strongly against the validity of the catharsis hypothesis, which holds that a child can "get aggressive impulses out of his system" by either giving these presumed impulses verbal expression or by the vicarious experience of observing aggression depicted in the form of a film or television program. Children who had been reinforced for aggressive verbal statements made more, rather than fewer, aggressive motor responses, compared to their base-rate performance, and the same was true of children who had watched an aggressive film.

Three related studies, conducted by Mallick and McCandless (1966), were specifically designed to test the hypothesis that aggressive play has no cathartic effect. The three studies were similar in design. A total of 168 children in the third grade were asked to engage in a moderately simple block-construction task. They were told that they could earn 5 cents for each of five tasks, provided each was completed within a time limit. A child of the same sex as the subject, attending the sixth grade, served as the experimenters' confederate and had the task of interfering with the subject's activities in such a way that the subject was frustrated in completing his or her tasks on time. Sarcastic remarks were interspersed with this interference. In the nonfrustration condition, the confederate helped the subjects complete their tasks, but no monetary reward was either promised or given.

Following the block-construction task, which lasted for 5 minutes, all subjects entered one of three interpolated tasks, which lasted for 8 minutes. Depending on the condition to which a particular subject had been assigned, the interpolated task consisted of shooting at a target on which a picture of a child of the same age and sex as the confederate had been placed, engaging in social talk with the experimenter, or being given a "reasonable interpretation of the frustrator's behavior." This interpretation consisted of indicating to the subject "that the frustrator was sleepy, upset, and would probably have been more cooperative if the subject had offered him two of the five nickles." The third phase of the study consisted of a behavioral measure of aggression. All subjects were given the opportunity to "punish" the confederate, either by pushing a button that presumably administered a mild shock to him or her or by pushing one of two buttons that would either help or hinder the confederate in a task he or she was presumably attempting to complete. The "shock" situation prevailed in one of the three studies, while the other measure was used in the remaining two. For the second and third study, Mallick and McCandless also administered a "like-dislike" scale on which the subject was asked to indicate his or her attitude toward the confederate. This scale was administered both before and after the interpolated 8-minute task.

Analysis of the like-dislike ratings revealed that the frustration treatment (interference with assigned task) had a highly significant effect in that the children in the frustration groups disliked the experimenters' confederate much more than did those in the nonfrustration groups. For those whose interpolated phase entailed either social talk or aggressive play, the dislike rating was not reduced, while those who had received the "interpretation" showed a significant change in the direction of more positive attitudes. The behavioral measures of aggression (pushing the "shocking" or "hindering" button) showed that frustrated subjects had significantly higher mean aggression scores than comparable treatment groups of nonfrustrated subjects. Again, as on the attitude scale, the group that had been given the "interpretation" showed significantly fewer aggression responses than the subjects in the other two frustration groups; in fact, they did not differ in their responses from the subjects in the nonfrustration groups.

The catharsis hypothesis would predict that a child made angry by the frustration situation and given a chance to express aggression in the target-shooting session would show less residual aggression on a subsequent measure than a child who had no opportunity at "catharsis." Contrary to this prediction, the interpolated aggressive play did not reduce aggression as measured by the button pressing. In fact, for those subjects who had not been frustrated, aggressive play actually increased subsequent aggression toward the nonfrustrating playmate.

The findings thus suggest that aggressive play not only fails to have a "cathartic" effect but that, as reinforcement theory would predict, aggressive play in the presence of a permissive adult actually leads to increased aggression and that the verbal expression of hostility, as facilitated by the like-dislike ratings, also increases subsequent behavioral aggression.

Mallick and McCandless view the results from their interpretation condition as showing the cathartic, aggression-reducing effect of a "reasonable interpretation." The reduction of aggression on both the attitude and the behavioral measures is difficult to conceive as "catharsis" in the traditional pressure-releasing sense. The subjects under this condition could not express or act out their anger; instead, they listened to some explanatory statements from the experimenter. Since the statements entailed apologies for the confederate's behavior, coupled with placing blame on the subject for not having offered the confederate a portion of his potential monetary gain, they may well have carried the implication "Don't be angry at him, it's really your fault." Rather than having cathartic value, this message was more likely to indicate the adult experimenters' nonpermissive, potentially punitive attitude toward expressing aggression against the confederate, Inasmuch as the experimenters' permissive presence during the aggressive play seemed to have increased subsequent aggression, it would seem reasonable to assume that the nonpermissive attitude implied in the so-called interpretation served to increase suppression of aggressive responses, a development that can hardly be viewed as "catharsis." This conclusion is all the more plausible because the subjects in this study are described as coming principally from the middle and upper class; that is, they were the children for whom the kind of statements made by the experimenter about the confederate's behavior probably represent well-established discriminative stimuli for suppressing aggressive responses.

IMPLICATIONS FOR PREVENTION AND TREATMENT

On the basis of the various studies just reviewed, we can draw a number of conclusions about the learning of aggressive behavior which, in turn, should permit us to speculate about how such learning might be avoided and to discuss how aggressive behavior might be reduced when it has already been acquired.

Four Conditions for Learning Aggression

There seem to be four conditions under which aggressive responses can be learned. The first is when aggression is positively reinforced by the fact that the aggressor attains his or her goal, as when a child pushes another child off a playground swing, thereby obtaining access to that swing. The second condition entails parental permissiveness regarding aggressive behavior. When parents, particularly those who are usually critical, stand and do nothing when their child displays aggression, their failure to intervene may well be viewed by the child as implicit approval, hence reinforcement (Crandall, 1963). Such implicit reinforcement may, of course, accompany the more direct reinforcement of goal attainment and thus be particularly potent. Parental approval of aggression may also be involved in the third condition for the learning of aggression, the modeling of aggression. Here, the parent may either be modeling aggression directly by engaging in aggressive behavior, as in meting out physical punishment, or indirectly by showing approval of aggression being displayed by someone else. A parent who cheers enthusiastically at a boxing match is obviously indicating to an observing child that hitting another is all right, at least when the occasion is labeled as a sport. Finally, the fourth condition under which aggressive responses can be strengthened is when such responses are negatively reinforced by the contingent reduction of aversive stimulation. This may be an attack by another where fighting back can lead to reinforcement or it may involved emotional arousal of the kind we label fear or anger.

The Prevention of Aggression   It seems to follow from the above that if parents desire to raise a child who does not behave in an aggressive manner, they should seek to arrange reinforcement contingencies in such a way that aggressive responses are not reinforced while nonaggressive alternatives are established and strengthened by reinforcement. It is, after all, possible to be able to play on a swing by expressing a polite request, waiting one's turn, or sharing. Furthermore, parents should refrain from modeling aggression themselves and consistently indicate disapproval whenever and wherever aggression on the part of others is observed by their child. There are, of course, many situations in a child's life where parents are unable to control what happens so that even if they wanted to, they may be unable to raise a totally nonaggressive child. Ultimately, what is needed in order to live compatibly with other people is for the individual to acquire internalized controls over aggressive responses when these have been unavoidably learned in the course of growing up.

Such internalized controls might be mediated by negative self-evaluations in consequence of an aggressive act. Since such negative self-evaluations are aversive, the individual should seek to avoid them by desisting from aggressive behavior. A study by Perry and Perry (1974) showed that highly aggressive boys actively seek out indications of suffering on the part of their victims. These investigators concluded from this result that these children had failed to internalize culturally accepted standards, possibly because they had experienced direct reinforcement for aggression and exposure to aggressive models in the course of their socialization. The observation that highly aggressive children do not inhibit their aggression in the face of a victim's suffering was also reported on the basis of a study by Perry and Bussey (1977). Here, 24 fifth-grade boys who had been identified by their peers as frequently displaying hostile, belligerent, bullying behavior (high-aggressive) were compared to an equal number of boys for whom the same peer nomination inventory had resulted in their being designated as low-aggressive. These children participated in an experiment where they were first annoyed by another child who was a confederate of the experimenters. Following this, they were placed into a situation where their ostensible task was to let the confederate know when he made a mistake on the arithmetic problems on which he was working in an adjoining room. The signal for this was a noisy sound whose loudness could be controlled by pushing one of 10 buttons. The child was told that these buttons would produce a noxious noise of increasing intensity, depending on which of them they pushed. In addition, there was a "pain indicator" on which the confederate could signal how much the sound had hurt him. This pain ranged from "not at all" to "my whole head aches." (All of this was, of course, a sham since, unknown to the subject, nothing happened to the confederate whose supposed responses had been programmed by the experimenters.)

Following the "teaching session" described above, each boy was invited to reward himself by picking as many tokens as he thought he deserved for what he had done to the other boy. The tokens were exchangeable for prizes and the more tokens a boy took, the better the prize he could obtain. It was on this self-reinforce-ment test that the low-aggressive boys took many fewer tokens when they thought they had injured their partner than when they had been led to believe that his discomfort had been relatively slight. The high-aggressive boys' self-reinforcement, on the other hand, was relatively unaffected by the suffering they thought they had caused to their "victim." Perry and Bussey concluded from this that high-aggressive boys do not experience the negative self-reactions following aggressive behavior that are experienced by boys who generally express less aggression. While this study does not permit the conclusion that low-aggressive children are such *because* they experience negative self-reactions following aggression, the data are at least highly suggestive that such may be the case.

Reducing Aggressive Behavior

In the discussion of their monograph, Patterson et al. (1967) had pointed to the implications of their study for the clinical treatment of aggressive children. Tradi-tional treatment approaches for such children have primarily focused on the removal of frustrations, often by placing the child into a protective institutional environment. This is done largely on the no-longer tenable assumption that frus-tration is the prime antecedent to aggression. Since aggression has been shown to be a response maintained by its consequences, modifying the antecedent con-ditions will reduce the frequency of the aggression response only for as long as these antecedent conditions are kept out of the child's environment; that is, only for as long as the child remains in the highly protective institutional surrounding. As soon as such a child returns to the unprotected life of the community where the old contingencies continue to be in effect, the aggression responses will return to the pretreatment rate. This is particularly due to the influence of the peer group, which tends to provide immediate and powerful social reinforcers that maintain aggressive behavior. The strength of this behavior can thus not be changed by tem-porary removal of the discriminative stimulus (frustration), which will reduce the frequency of the undesirable response only for as long as this artificial condi-tion can be maintained.

To produce more permanent changes in aggressive behavior it is necessary to use a dual approach aimed at weakening aggressive responses while strengthen-ing socially desirable responses that can take their place. If aggressive responses are reinforced by the reactions of the peer group, one way of assuring that this reinforcement is withheld and the aggression response thus placed on an extinc-tion schedule is to remove the aggressor from the peer group as soon as an aggres-sion response has been emitted. Such a time-out procedure has been shown to be effective in cases ranging from nursery school children (Firestone, 1976) to in-stitutionalized delinquents (Burchard & Barerra, 1972).

The time-out principle was used by Tyler and Brown (1967) who isolated an offending boy for 15 minutes immediately following a behavior that had been defined as aggression. In this manner, they were able to reduce the antisocial behavior of a 13-year-old institutionalized delinquent boy who, prior to their study, had spent a total of 200 days in an individual isolation room and whose behavior had become increasingly unmanageable during those months. When the frequency of aggressive responses is reduced in this manner, it is, of course, essential that defined acceptable behavior, such as academic performance or, at least, specified units of time during which no disruption occurred, be strengthened by positive reinforcement.

Differential reinforcement of other behavior (DRO), combined with a 30-second time-out procedure was used by Repp and Deitz (1974) to reduce both aggressive and self-injurious behavior of institutionalized retarded children. Another way of reducing the frequency of aggressive behavior is to ascertain its reinforcing consequences and to remove these, where this is possible. (Where this is not possible, removing the child—as in time-out—is, of course, the alternative.) An analysis of the consequences maintaining the aggressive behavior of a nursery school child was reported by Pinkston, Reese, LeBlanc, and Baer (1973) who, like Brown and Elliot (1965) before them, found that contingent teacher attention was the critical variable. As would be usual in a preschool and similar setting, whenever the child emitted an aggressive act, the teacher would turn to the child in order to intervene, thus "paying" attention and reinforcing the very behavior she was hoping to stop. The aggressive behavior was thereby maintained, impeding the development of the child's peer interactions. When the teacher was instructed to ignore the child's aggressive behavior as much as possible and to attend instead to the child who was being attacked, the target child's aggressive behavior declined. At the same time, having the teacher attend to him when he was interacting with peers in a nonaggressive fashion resulted in an increase of this socially desirable behavior.

It stands to reason that the contingencies operating in nursery schools are also in effect in a child's home. For this reason, intervention for aggressive behavior logically takes the form of involving parents in the treatment of their own children (Patterson, 1974). This point will be touched on in the next chapter, which deals with juvenile delinquency; for when the behavior we label as aggressive is displayed under circumstances where law enforcement agencies become involved, the label juvenile delinquent may easily become attached to the child whose problem was discussed in the present chapter. Similarly, where high-magnitude responses take the form of excessive physical activity which disrupts classroom decorum, the child may be labeled a discipline problem, a disruptive child, or a hyperactive child. As a result, some studies related to the issue of aggression, for example, those of O'Leary and Becker (1967) and Patterson, Jones, Whittier, and Wright (1965), will be discussed in the chapter on hyperactivity.

RECAPITULATION

Aggression represents a serious problem both for the child who emits it and for those who are its victims. Best viewed as a response which is reinforced by its consequences and thus learned, aggression can be acquired in many situations. These range from the nursery school where teachers and other children reinforce aggression, to the home where parents may model it in the context of meting out punishment. The high-magnitude theory of aggression has been a fruitful basis for research that has contributed to a better understanding of the variables involved. One of these variables is frustration, here defined as a situation where a response received not only this positive reinforcement but also the negative reinforcement which results from the reduction in the noxious arousal state we call anger and which often accompanies aggression.

Aggression seems to be learned when it is reinforced, either directly through goal attainment or the reduction of noxious arousal, or indirectly by adult approval, permissiveness, or modeling. Once the conditions under which aggression is acquired have been identified, it is possible to propose ways for preventing its development. These ways include the teaching of socially acceptable alternative modes of behavior and the development of internalized controls.

With children whose aggressive behavior requires modification, a change in the reinforcing consequences is highly effective. Since consequences, such as peer approval, are often readily available and difficult to withhold, time-out procedures serve to remove the child from exposure to the opportunity to receive these consequences. Considerable work along this line has been done with aggressive behavior emitted by children who are labeled juvenile delinquent. We turn to that topic in the following chapter.

Chapter 8

Juvenile Delinquency

A LABEL SELECTIVELY USED

Juvenile delinquency is not a psychological term. It is a label the judicial system of society applies to children and adolescents who engage in behavior that the statutes define as illegal. Such behavior may range from curfew violations and loitering to theft, arson, assault, and murder, and the young people who engage in such behavior may be doing so for a variety of reasons and under many different circumstances. It should therefore be obvious that the term *juvenile delinquent* designates a widely heterogeneous group of offenders (Jurkovic & Prentice, 1977) and that any statement purporting to apply to all people who carry the label juvenile delinquent is likely to be a gross overgeneralization.

It must also be pointed out that the label juvenile delinquent is applied to only a segment of those individuals who violate statutory norms. Technically, a person does not become a juvenile delinquent until so adjudged by a court. Between the performance of the delinquent act and this adjudication there operates a selective process that results in the labeling as juvenile delinquent of only an unknown proportion of the actual offenders. This selection is based not so much on the behavior of the youthful offenders as on the behavior of others in relation to them and their offenses. Someone must, first of all, discover the offense and bring the offender to the attention of an appropriate authority. If an individual police officer is involved, he may decide to do no more than issue a stern reprimand, to send the youngster home, or to take him to the police station. Only some of those taken to the station are actually "booked," and not all whose act is thus recorded are then referred to the court. A variety of options are available to the court, ranging from an informal hearing, warning, and release to the parents, to probation, adjudication, parole, and commitment. Only the case that has been adjudicated delinquent enters official statistics on delinquency. Thus, data based on these statistics grossly distort any conclusions regarding incidence or prevalence. This is particularly true as far as conclusions regarding social class, neighborhoods, or ethnic background are concerned, since the various decisions made by the police officer and others regarding the disposition of the offender are influenced far more by who he is than by what he has done. When one attempts to gather delinquency statistics not from arrest records or court statistics but from anonymous self-reports of high school students (Nye, Short, & Olson, 1958), it emerges that norm-violating behavior, in general, has relatively little relationship to socioeconomic class.

DEFICIENT BEHAVIORAL CONTROLS

The norm violations committed by juvenile delinquents rarely involve complex skills that would have to be learned before the act could take place. Unlike such adult crimes as forgery, counterfeiting, or safecracking, most juvenile offenses, such as shoplifting, vandalism, or auto theft do not require a delinquency-specific skill. (Driving an automobile is a general skill; stealing a car with keys in the dashboard represents the application of this skill under unauthorized circumstances.) From this point of view it seems incorrect to speak of delinquency as learned behavior; it seems more productive to conceive of delinquency as behavior that reflects the offender's *failure to have learned* essential controls that most other young people in our society have acquired in the course of growing up. Most children learn what is and what is not acceptable behavior, and most acquire controls over their own behavior that keep them from engaging in the unacceptable. The juvenile delinquent would thus be one who has either not learned to discriminate between acceptable and unacceptable behavior or who, having learned the discrimination, has not acquired adequate controls so that his or her behavior is not guided by this discrimination. This formulation places the emphasis in a study of delinquency on deficient discrimination or deficient behavioral controls. The prevention and treatment of delinquency would therefore have to focus on the teaching of these controls. What is more, most juvenile delinquents lack the socially approved skills with which they might achieve the gratification they obtain through their norm-violating behavior. The teaching of such skills and providing opportunities for using them must therefore be another goal of prevention and treatment programs.

Formulating juvenile delinquency in terms of behavioral deficits shifts the treatment of these individuals away from an approach based on punishment. New skills can never be taught by using punishment which, by definition, is a consequence that weakens rather than strengthens behavior. The emphasis falls instead on establishing new, socially approved behavior for young people who have been apprehended and adjudicated delinquent (Cohen & Filipczak, 1971). Similarly, in order to prevent youngsters from ending up as juvenile delinquents, one would want to teach the necessary prosocial skills to children who are seen as being at risk of becoming delinquent, the so-called predelinquents (Reid & Hendricks, 1973).

Delay of Gratification

It is not unreasonable to assume that such delinquency-incompatible behaviors as remaining in school, holding a job, saving one's earnings, and similar norm-abiding acts require that one be able to maintain a response under conditions of delayed reinforcement. Delinquent behavior can thus be viewed as partly a function of an absence or weakness in the ability to delay gratification, to inhibit behavior for the sake of later reinforcement. The ability to defer gratification has been found to relate positively to a laboratory index of resistance to temptation (Mischel & Gilligan, 1964) and to questionnaire data on social responsibility (Mischel, 1961).

Roberts and Erikson (1968) explored the relationship between measures of delay of gratification and ratings of adjustment in a school for delinquent adolescent males. A group of fifty subjects were asked to write an essay in answer to the following instruction: "A boy won $1,000 as first prize in a contest. What do you think he will do with it?" The responses were scored for delay of gratification on the basis of whether the boy saved the money or spent it immediately. Nine days before the subjects were scheduled for discharge, they were presented with a coupon that gave them the option of trading it for one cigarette or of holding it until their discharge at which point the coupon would be worth one package of cigarettes. The study revealed that those boys who were able to delay gratification on both the verbal (essay) and the behavioral measure, received higher adjustment ratings from their supervisors. Since the subjects were already delinquents at the time this study was undertaken, it does not, of course, answer the question whether low impulse control led to the boys' delinquency in the first place. On the other hand, since the institutional supervisors can be viewed as representative of the norm-setting segment of society, their ratings suggest that the youngster who can delay gratification is more likely to be considered the "good guy" who obeys the rules and regulations than his impulsive peer who tends to be judged a "general nuisance."

The ability to delay gratification is acquired during childhood and can be shown to increase with age (Mischel & Metzner, 1962). In fact, one of the defining characteristics of social maturity is the ability to function under conditions of delayed reinforcement. The conditions under which this ability is acquired are not fully known, but laboratory studies suggest that opportunity to observe a model forgo immediate gratification for the sake of greater gratification later on is one means of inducing a child to behave similarly. Bandura and Mischel (1965); Mischel (1966); and Liebert and Ora (1968), have conducted a series of experiments in which a child is given the opportunity to observe another child or an adult who, given a choice between a small prize that can be obtained immediately and a larger prize for which one has to wait, selects the latter. When the observing child is later placed into a similar choice situation, he, too, will select the delayed reward even if the delay is for as much as 6 weeks.

Self-imposed Standards

The temporal delay of gratification is one expression of self-control; the self-imposition of reward standards is another. In the course of socialization children must acquire the ability to evaluate their own performance and to develop standards for the self-administration of praise and tangible reinforcements. Self-reward is often considered as one aspect of "resistance to temptation." In experimental self-reward situations (Liebert & Ora, 1968), a girl would have material rewards available to her, and to the extent that she adheres to a norm requiring that these be taken sparingly, she is exercising self-control. Exposing a child to a model who exemplifies self-reward behavior has been demonstrated to be a potent means of teaching this form of self-control (Liebert, Hanratty, & Hill, 1969; Allen & Liebert, 1969a, 1969b; Mischel & Liebert, 1967).

One dimension affecting the effectiveness of vicarious learning of self-reward standards is the model's consistency. Parents who demand a stringent level of achievement standards of their child while displaying self-indulgence in their own behavior may be particularly ineffective models. The consequence of such discrepant training was studied by Mischel and Liebert (1967), who asked children to participate with an adult model in a bowling game that seemingly required skill but on which scores were experimentally controlled. A plentiful supply of tokens, which could be exchanged for prizes, was available to both the model and the child. In one experimental group the model rewarded herself only for high levels of performance, but told the child to reward himself for lower achievements; in a second condition the model rewarded herself for low performance, but let the child reward himself only for higher achievement; while in a third group the model rewarded herself for high performance and told the child to reward himself only for equally high achievement. Following these procedures, measures were taken of the child's self-reward criteria while performing the task in the absence of the model or any other social agent. Children who had been permitted to reward themselves for relatively low performances during training by a self-stringent model showed no conflict about rewarding themselves for mediocre performance in the model's absence, and they did so uniformly. Children who had been instructed to reward themselves for only high performance levels by a model who also exhibited adherence to this stringent standard subsequently maintained the high criterion when left to perform entirely alone. In contrast to these two groups, children who had stringency imposed upon them but observed the model behave self-indulgently did not behave in a consistent fashion. Approximately half of the children in this group continued to adhere to the more stringent standard on which they had been directly trained, while the other half adopted the more lenient standards which they had observed. This investigation strongly suggests the importance for effective socialization of consistency between direct instruction and the performance modeled by the socializing agent.

It thus appears that delay of gratification and the self-imposition of reward standards can be learned by the vicarious mode of observing a model. Other controls and other modes of learning are no doubt relevant to the study of norm-violating behavior, and a variety of investigators have approached this issue from several different points of view.

THE LEARNING OF NORM-ABIDING BEHAVIOR

The process by which a child acquires delinquency-incompatible, norm-abiding behaviors and behavioral controls is frequently called *moral development*. Morality can be viewed as behavior regulated by the goals and norms of the group in which an individual lives. Such regulation requires that the individual has accepted these goals and norms as his own, an acceptance usually construed as *internalization*. This construct has been extensively studied by Kohlberg (1964), who approached it from the standpoint of moral judgment and found remarkable consistency in the different types of statements about moral situations obtained from individuals at different levels of "moral thinking." While judgments expressed in answer to verbal questions may well play a role in guiding behavior, it is of greater relevance to the topic here under discussion to examine research in which actual behavior along "moral" lines can be observed. Such studies, however, require an extrapolation from often highly artificial laboratory situations to conditions found in the daily life of individuals.

A sophisticated instance of such studies is the work of Aronfreed and Reber (1965), who investigated the development of internalized behavioral suppression. For purposes of their study, Aronfreed and Reber considered internalization to have taken place when a behavior, originally acquired under the control of an external agent, can be reliably elicited in the absence of such an agent. The children in this study had the task of picking up one of two toys and describing its use to the experimenter. When they picked up the more attractive of two toys, they were punished by mild social disapproval, while mild approval was contingent on their picking up the less attractive object. After nine such training trials, the experimenter left the child alone with a pair of toys and monitored his or her behavior to assess "transgression," defined as picking up the more attractive toy. The experimental variable of greatest interest was the timing of punishment, since members of one group had been reprimanded as they reached for the more attractive toy, while members of the other were censured after they had held it for a few moments. The results showed that transgression was effectively prevented by punishment, with punishment at initiation more potent than punishment upon completion of the proscribed act.

On the basis of a review of this and similar research, Hoffman (1970) concluded that moral development is a complex phenomenon that ultimately leads to behavioral conformity, perception of authority as rational, impulse inhibition, and consideration for others. He suggests that four processes, which may take place simultaneously and independently, interact to bring about socialization in the moral realm. The first of these processes consists of experiences involving differential reinforcement through reward and punishment of specific acts defined as "good" or "bad" by the agents of socialization. The behavior thus learned will generalize to similar situations, and if the reinforcement contingencies remain essentially unchanged, the behavioral standards learned in childhood will be maintained throughout life. This form of behavior control has its locus in the external environment and does not involve any internalization. The second process postulated by Hoffman moves behavior control beyond the mere avoidance of punishment and involves the child's perception of rules and authority as no longer arbitrary but as objective and rational. Experiences with rational authority figures who give reasons or explanations for demands that the child change his or her behavior and opportunities for him or her to assume the role of authority (as in participation in decision making) appear important requisites for this process.

The third process postulated in Hoffman's (1970) formulation of moral development may well be the most crucial in establishing internal controls over behavior. It entails the formation of what is generally known as conscience, traditionally called *superego*. Norm-abiding behavior ultimately depends not merely on avoidance of externally imposed consequences but, more importantly, on the avoidance of noxious stimulation, which has its source within the individual ("guilt"). It appears that this step requires experiences with important adults who use "love withdrawal" (as opposed to "power assertion") as a technique of child rearing. Love-withdrawal techniques take the form of parents expressing disapproval for undesirable behavior by contingent removal of such social reinforcers as attention, company, verbal exchange, and other forms of social interaction. It is essentially a form of suspension from social reinforcement ("time out") or, if one prefers, from "love." Hoffman points out that love-withdrawal has a highly punitive quality since it entails the threat of abandonment or separation. Since the parent's absence is likely to have been associated with painful or noxious stimulation sometime in the child's previous history (as when an infant is hungry but the mother is not immediately available for feeding), one can speculate that love-withdrawal has stimulus qualities that elicit noxious arousal (anxiety). When the stimulus qualities, elicited by love-withdrawal, are repeatedly paired with undesirable behavior, it is reasonable to assume that these behaviors and the cues associated with the immediate antecedents of these behaviors ("impulses") come to elicit the noxious arousal state, which should then lead to avoidance of the undesirable behavior, even in the absence of the parental figure. It is this arousal state, elicited by violations of norms or by the anticipation of such violations, that is usually referred to as guilt and seen as an important factor in maintaining norm-abiding behavior.

The fourth process of moral development postulated by Hoffman involves the capacity of individuals to control their behavior by considering its effect on the experiences of others, particularly the potential victims of proscribed behavior. This capacity for "empathy" presumably has its antecedents in parental statements involving explanations of the effects of one's behavior on others. The capacity for empathy requires considerable abstract ability and represents a rather advanced state in the development of moral behavior.

TYPES AND SOURCES OF DELINQUENCY

Failure to adhere to the conduct codes of society so that proscribed behavior comes to be emitted may be related to the temporary lapse of poorly established learned controls, to the failure to have learned these controls, or to the fact that the behavioral norms a child has learned do not coincide with the norms of that segment of society which writes and enforces the rules. These three conditions, under which delinquent behavior may be observed, permit one to speak of three forms of delinquency: the *impulsive delinquent*, the *unsocialized delinquent*, and the *socially delinquent*.

The *impulsive delinquent*, sometimes called the *neurotic delinquent* because anxiety, insecurity, and unhappiness often accompany the delinquent behavior, has learned that stealing is punishable behavior. On occasion, however, and sometimes only once in this child's entire youth, the attractiveness of a given object, combined with a stimulus configuration that provides opportunity and a low probability of being detected, overwhelms his or her controls so that the antisocial act is performed. As with any other behavior, its future course will be a function of its consequences. If they are negative—the child is caught and punished or experiences subjective discomfort in anticipation of potential punishment (guilt)—the probability of repetition is lowered. If the consequences are positive—the child is not punished, experiences minimal subjective discomfort, and the stolen object serves as a reinforcer—the probability is increased that the action will be repeated when similar circumstances again present themselves. When treatment of this type of delinquent is focused on the child's family interactions (Stuart, 1971), the outcome is often very promising. For example, Stumphauzer (1976) reported the case of a 12-year-old girl who had been stealing for 5 years. When a family contract was established so that the child could obtain privileges and other reinforcers in return for defined contributions to family harmony, and after the girl had been taught to reinforce herself for behavior that is incompatible with stealing, this problem stopped within 6 weeks and remained under control during an 18 months follow-up period.

The *unsocialized delinquent* is at times referred to as the *psychopathic delinquent* or the *sociopathic delinquent*. This is an individual whose behavior has developed under conditions of learning that failed to establish the internal controls that keep most people in the culture from committing antisocial acts. It is a fair assumption that these conditions of learning are found in the child's family during the formative years, and several well-known studies (e.g., Glueck & Glueck, 1950, 1959, 1962; McCord & McCord, 1959) have focused on the family structure and parent-child relationship of juvenile delinquents. There is, of course, no one-to-one relationship between background variables and delinquency, and it is fallacious to assume that all delinquents have a common background or that background factors found with relatively high frequency among delinquents will differentiate delinquents from nondelinquents. Studies always show that a large percentage of delinquents have the background commonly found among nondelinquents and, conversely, that there are nondelinquents with backgrounds commonly found among delinquents.

Glueck and Glueck (1959) have identified a series of family factors that permit one to predict delinquent behavior with reasonable accuracy when one studies *groups* of children; for any *specific* child predictions are hazardous. The Glueck Social Prediction Table associates the following with potential delinquency: *overstrict or erratic paternal discipline, unsuitable maternal supervision, paternal indifference or hostility, maternal indifference or hostility, and lack of family cohesiveness (weak affectional ties and few shared interests)*. When these factors were assigned weighted scores based on the frequency with which they were found among a sample of delinquents, lack of family cohesiveness and maternal indifference or hostility to the boy were the most heavily weighted factors. While such a finding is highly suggestive, about one-third of a group of 890 delinquent and nondelinquent children fell in a midrange of scores where predictive validity is very low.

The Cambridge-Somerville Youth Study (Powers & Witmer, 1951) was a large-scale project in which 253 boys were intensively studied, and those among them who became delinquent were followed up 20 years later. When McCord and McCord (1959) evaluated the results of this work, they found that the environmental factors most likely to lead to delinquent behavior were a combination of absence of maternal warmth and a criminal paternal role model. Similarly, Bandura and Walters (1959) reported that the aggressive delinquent boys they had studied came from families marked by parental inconsistency in child rearing and rejection by fathers who used physically punitive methods of discipline.

The acquisition of behavior controls that seem weak or absent in the unsocialized delinquent would seem to require the following: consistency in the consequences parents bring to bear on the child's behavior; clear guidelines as to what is acceptable behavior; positively regarded, good role models; and conditions under which social approval can acquire secondary reinforcement potential. When these conditions are absent, the probability that a boy raised in such a family will come to be identified as a delinquent appears greatly increased.

The *socially delinquent* is a label used to describe the youngster whose behavior conforms to the standards of his or her immediate social environment (like a youth gang) but violates the norm established by the members of the dominant culture who write and enforce the laws. This type of delinquency is also known as *subcultural* or *gang delinquency*, and it is frequently associated with membership in the lower socioeconomic class.

It has often been reported that there is a higher probability for delinquent behavior among lower-class than middle- or upper-class children (Short & Strodtbeck, 1965). This relationship holds for urban areas; but when urban and rural communities are compared (Clark & Wenninger, 1962; Erickson & Empey, 1965), it can be shown that delinquency rate is not a function of social class per se but of factors associated with social class, such as neighborhood, family structure, and peer associations. The environmental conditions in the urban lower-class neighborhood would seem to be more likely to favor the development of delinquent behavior than would the conditions found in other areas. Parental preoccupations with day-to-day survival questions, father absence, and limited family resources around which to develop shared interests may conspire to produce the conditions that were so predictive of delinquency in the Glueck and Glueck (1959) studies. It stands to reason that delinquency is a function of a complex interaction of factors and that any one condition—be it father absence, the "broken home," poverty, or erratic discipline—is not likely to be a direct cause.

One-parent households are found more frequently among delinquents than among nondelinquents. This has led to theories about the role of the "female-based household" in the development of delinquency (Miller, 1958). Such a household may exist for a variety of reasons and have a great many implications in terms of the child's socialization. Absence of the father may be due to death, separation, desertion, or divorce. In each instance, a good deal of interpersonal conflict or trauma may have preceded the actual time the father left the household, and assumptions about the effect of the "broken home" on the child must take these facts into consideration. Nye (1958), for example, has pointed out that broken but happy homes produce less delinquency than intact but unhappy homes. A second condition leading to a "female-based household" involves the absence from birth onward of a legal or stable union between the child's mother and father. Since such a family does not represent a breakdown of a marriage but is often an accepted pattern in certain subcultures, there is no reason to assume that the child will have experienced conflict between father and mother or the trauma involved in a father's death or departure. At the same time, poverty, social disintegration, lack of recreational and educational opportunities, and easy access to delinquent role models are often correlated with this subcultural family pattern, so it is extremely difficult to ascertain which factor or combinations of factors contribute to delinquency.

Father absence is usually seen as representing the absence of the stricter disciplinarian and the lack of a masculine role model. While these generalizations may have some merit, one should not lose sight of other implications the one-parent home has for the child's socialization. Among these are the greater demands on the mother's time and energy which are likely to strain her relations with the child. Her demands for compliance may increase, while, at the same time, her consistency in enforcing them may be low. In the two-parent household, reinforcements are dispensed by both parents and when one parent is nonreinforcing because of preoccupation or anger at the child, the other parent may be available to provide succor. Under conditions of father absence, the peer group may early become an important source of reinforcements, social support, and role models.

The availability of unsupervised, unoccupied groups of same-sex peers tends to be greater in the lower-class than in the middle-class neighborhood, giving rise to a class-related phenomenon of *gang delinquency* where the peer group, operating within its own value system, supports and reinforces the delinquent behavior of its members. It is here that the individual youngster may learn a set of behavioral norms that are approved by those who are important sources of reinforcement but that happen to run counter to the norms of behavior approved and enforced by the modal group in society. Such individuals may acquire controls over their own behavior, but these controls tend to lead them to conform to the delinquent standards of their social reference group; hence, the term *socially delinquent*.

Conditions of Learning in the Lower-Class Culture

The norms, values, and "focal concerns" of the lower-class culture have been discussed by Miller (1958) who sees them as the generating milieu of gang delinquency. The observations of this cultural anthropologist are based on extensive work by seven trained social workers who maintained contact with twenty-one street-corner groups in a slum district for a period of 3 years. Miller (1958) lists, roughly in order of importance, six focal concerns (values) of people in the lower-class culture. They are trouble, toughness, smartness, excitement, fate, and autonomy. Since the reinforcement contingencies of the lower-class peer group are largely guided by these focal concerns, which thus represent important conditions of social learning for its members, these focal concerns bear some elaboration.

TROUBLE   Getting into and staying out of trouble is a dominant feature of lower-class culture, and the alternatives are generally between "law-abiding" and "non-law-abiding" behavior. According to Miller (1958) individuals are judged in relation to these behavioral alternatives, and status is gauged along this dimension. Thus, a mother will assess the suitability of a given boy as a companion for her daughter less on the basis of his achievement potential, as she would in the middle class, but on the basis of the likelihood of his getting into trouble. With limited opportunities for skill attainment and educational achievement, "getting into trouble" is one of the few ways by which individuals can obtain attention and recognition from their peers; hence, behavior that is likely to get one into trouble may be reinforced. In fact, as Miller points out, in certain situations, "getting into trouble" is a source of prestige, and some adolescent groups (gangs) make membership contingent on a demonstration of law-violating behavior.

TOUGHNESS   This concern has its focus on behaviors that are considered signs of "masculinity," such as physical prowess, bravery in the face of physical threat, lack of sentimentality, and an exploitative attitude toward women. Some of these qualities, such as strength and endurance, have a good deal of survival value in a street-corner culture of the inner city; others are modeled and reinforced by the peer group as conforming to the defined masculine role. Behavior which is incompatible with that role, including interest in the literature or art of the middle class and "soft" and sentimental behavior, elicits negative reactions from the peer group, which evaluates such behavior as role-inappropriate and derides it with terms associated with homosexuality.

SMARTNESS   In this focal concern, value is placed on the ability to attain a goal, such as material goods or personal status, through mental agility. It involves the ability to outwit, outsmart, and outfox others while avoiding having others "take," "con," or dupe you. The peer group not only provides the training ground for this ability through mutual teasing, kidding, razzing, and "ranking" but it also rewards smartness by assigning leadership roles and high prestige to the individual with demonstrated skill in this area. Miller (1958) points out that the street-corner group allocates leadership roles to both the tough and the smart, with the ideal leader combining both capacities. In a choice between smartness and toughness, the former tends to be the more prestigious quality—reflecting, according to Miller, a general lower-class respect for "brain" in the sense of shrewdness, wit, and adroitness in verbal repartee.

EXCITEMENT   Like the other focal concerns of the lower-class culture, this one represents a bipolar continuum ranging from thrill to boredom. Life fluctuates between these extremes, with brief periods of thrill and emotional stimulation alternating with longer periods of boredom and routine. Excitement—involving elements of risk and danger—is actively sought and accompanied by the use of alcohol, gambling, sexual adventuring, and music. Fights are not infrequent aspects of excitement in view of this volatile mixture of activities. The breaks in routine characterizing excitement clearly involve the "focal concerns" previously mentioned, since toughness and smartness are brought into play and trouble frequently follows. In this connection, it is interesting to note that in a study by Whitehill, DeMyer-Gapin, and Scott (1976) antisocial, preadolescent children worked harder for change and variety than did children in a control group.

FATE   Largely as a function of the conditions under which they are raised and live, lower-class individuals tend to view the locus of control over their lives as outside themselves. A set of poorly comprehended forces over which they have relatively little control tend to determine the experiences of lower-class individuals. Positive experiences are thus attributed to fate, luck, or fortune, while negative events are similarly explained as a function of unlucky destiny. Miller (1958) points out that the pervasive gambling in the lower class is a reflection of this orientation, though gambling also involves smartness and excitement.

AUTONOMY   This involves a concern with independence and freedom from external constraints or superordinate authority. Concern with autonomy finds expression in such statements as "No one's gonna push *me* around" or "I don't need *nobody* to take care of me." Again it interrelates with other concerns, such as smartness, toughness, and trouble. Since getting into trouble often entails an encounter with restrictive, superordinate authority, there is a certain incompatibility of these two values, and a good deal of excitement can ensue when one has to use one's smartness to flirt with trouble and yet preserve one's autonomy.

We have mentioned in passing that the male adolescent peer group in lower-class society supports these focal concerns by making status and group membership contingent on the individual's adherence to these values. In Miller's (1958) formulation *belonging* and *status* become focal concerns specific to the street-corner group, but these are on a higher level of abstraction than the six concerns previously discussed inasmuch as they are the means by which belonging and status are attained.

At this point, it may be well to examine the implications of the focal concerns identified by Miller in terms of their possible contribution to delinquent behavior. If the peer group is an important, and, in some cases, an almost exclusive source of reinforcement, the values of this group will importantly shape the individual's behavior. It is apparent that the focal concerns of the lower-class ethos as postulated by Miller (1958) not only favor adolescent behavior that society-at-large has defined as delinquent but, in many respects, they also are incompatible with such norm-abiding activities as working or going to school which, were they engaged in, might provide the adolescent with an alternate source of reinforcement. If freedom from constraint, outwitting the other, physical prowess, skirting trouble with the law, and a reliance on luck instead of personal initiative and effort are the means of maintaining group membership and status, one is far more likely to engage in theft, assault, or destruction of property than to seek and hold gainful employment. These value-based behavioral tendencies interact with the social and economic conditions in which the lower-class child grows up. As Cloward and Ohlin (1960) have pointed out, it is far more likely that an individual seeks gratification through illegitimate means when the accessibility of gratification through legitimate means is limited or closed altogether. In an environment of this kind, the adolescent lacks access to adults who might present role models for socially constructive behavior; he has available to him models of socially disapproved behavior, and so fails to develop the skills necessary for success in society-at-large and by the means this society approves. It is this lack of skills, not only the academic skills taught in school but also such social skills as making a favorable impression in a job interview and coming to work regularly and on time, that become major blocks to success within the approved norms.

DELINQUENCY AND THE CONSEQUENCES OF BEHAVIOR

Reinforcement

Regardless of the type of delinquency, the behavior which leads a young person to be labeled a juvenile delinquent is a function of its consequences. Any attempt to change a delinquent's behavior must therefore begin by examining these consequences; that is, the contingencies of reinforcement maintaining that behavior.

The pioneering studies of Schwitzgebel (1964, 1967) approached delinquency from the point of view of such a functional analysis. This type of analysis not only permits one to study the conditions which maintain a given behavior, it also permits one to specify the desired end point of behavior change as concretely as possible and identifies the behavioral steps necessary for reaching this end point. Schwitzgebel (1964) worked with thirty white males with a mean age of 18 years who had been adjudged delinquent by the courts, twenty of them having spent 6 months or more in correctional institutions. Through successive approximations and positive reinforcement, these young men were taught such employment-compatible social skills as coming to work on time, being dressed appropriately, and limiting hostile statements in their conversation. In addition, they were taught to solder and other technical skills before they were helped to find jobs in the community. On follow-up 3 years later, the arrest and incarceration record of the first twenty subjects was about half of that of a matched control group whose names had been obtained from police records.

One of the investigations conducted by Schwitzgebel (1967) within the confines of the larger project dealt with the differential effectiveness of positive reinforcement (praise, cigarettes, candy, etc.) and mild punishment (interviewer's inattention and mild verbal disagreement). He reports that the positive consequences were effective in increasing positive statements, but that the negative consequences failed to decrease hostile statements. While this is in no way a conclusive test of the effectiveness of punishment, a study by Schlichter and Ratliff (1971) lends support to the conclusion that punishment is not as effective a means of facilitating learning in delinquents as it is with nondelinquents. These investigators matched forty-five delinquent males committed to a correctional institution with an equal number of students from a junior high school who had no record of delinquency. These subjects were observed in a two-choice discrimination task with either positive reinforcement for correct responses or punishment for in-correct responses, or a combination of both positive reinforcement for correct responses and punishment for incorrect responses, respectively. Reinforcement consisted of poker chips that could be exchanged for money; the punishment was a loud (98-Hz) tone which signified that the subject was "losing" on what was presented as a "learning problem." The results showed that the nondelinquents performed better in the punishment condition than the delinquents, whereas the delinquents performed better in the reward condition than the nondelinquents. Further, for the nondelinquent group the punishment condition was significantly more effective than the reward condition in producing correct responses.

Before one erroneously concludes from the studies of Schwitzgebel (1967) and Schlichter and Ratliff (1971) that delinquents become such because they are less responsive than normals to punishment and social disapproval, it is well to recall that these data were gathered *after* these young people had been labeled delinquent and, in most instances, had spent time in correctional institutions. It is therefore important to ask what possible effect these circumstances might have on the individual's performance under the conditions of (mild) punishment used in these studies. Schlichter and Ratliff (1971) conjecture about the effects of the probable reinforcement histories with authority figures of delinquents and non-delinquents. They assume that the experimenter was regarded as an authority figure because he was working with the approval of the people in charge of the institutions. They further assume "that delinquents have experienced fewer posi-tive reinforcements and nondelinquents, fewer punishments from authorities"; therefore,

> it follows that positive reinforcement for delinquents and punishment for normals may represent unusual events which are contrary to their expectancies and, therefore, serve to heighten attention to the task itself. Such heightened attention should serve to facilitate performance for delinquents in the reward condition and performance for nondelinquents in the punishment condition [p. 48].

Regardless of whether or not these speculations are correct, it stands to reason that one cannot assume a priori that any given consequence for behavior will have an effect with any given individual, be he delinquent or nondelinquent. As was done in the Schwitzgebel (1967) study, the effectiveness of a given conse-quence, be it reward or punishment, must be ascertained for each and every in-dividual whom one wishes to teach a new response. In that respect, a generalized reinforcer, such as a token or money that can be exchanged for an object of high attractiveness for the individual, clearly has a greater chance of being effective than a uniform consequence like a 98-Hz noise.

Punishment

The most frequently applied consequence of antisocial behavior (when it is de-tected) is punishment. The incarceration to which society resorts in dealing with delinquent behavior is punishment regardless of what it is called. This punishment is often ineffective partly, at least, because it is introduced long after the actual commission of the delinquent act on which it is supposed to be contingent. To be effective in reducing the frequency of a given behavior, punishment must follow that behavior as quickly as possible. Even then, the weakening of the undesirable behavior is not enough to assure that the person will henceforth behave in a socially approved manner. Explicit and systematic steps must be taken to establish and strengthen such approved behavior by the introduction of response-contingent positive consequences so that this behavior can take the place of the delinquent behavior being weakened. Unfortunately, those who use punishment often use it alone in the mistaken expectation that desired behavior will appear automatically to take the place of the hopefully reduced delinquent behavior.

Once a young delinquent has been placed in a correctional institution, aversive control usually continues to dominate attempts to enforce compliance with rules and regulations. Violations are dealt with by lengthy deprivations of various privileges or by more stringent measures, such as extended solitary confinement. Again, these are often ineffective. On the other hand, the negative consequences involved in brief social isolation, when judiciously used, appear sufficiently potent to weaken undesirable responses. Even such ordinarily intractable behavior as the antisocial acts of institutionalized adolescent delinquents can be modified by the use of a 15-minute period of isolation when it is introduced immediately and consistently as a consequence of every instance of specified unacceptable behaviors (Burchard & Tyler, 1965; Tyler & Brown, 1967).

There appears to be a paradox in the fact that such relatively mild punishment as having to spend 15 minutes in an empty room can effectively modify behavior of delinquents for whom far more severe punishments have usually been ineffective. Yet Burchard and Tyler (1965) succeeded in reducing the antisocial behavior of a 13-year-old, institutionalized delinquent boy through the use of isolation, combined with positive reinforcement for clearly defined periods that he did not have to spend in isolation. This same boy had spent a total of 200 days in an individual isolation room during the year prior to the onset of the reported study, and during that time his behavior had become increasingly unmanageable. The prime difference between the systematic and the unsystematic use of punishment would seem to explain this apparent paradox. In the systematic application of operant principles, negative consequences to unacceptable behavior are *immediately* and *consistently* introduced whenever unacceptable behavior occurs. When punishment is used unsystematically, unacceptable behavior usually has to reach a given magnitude before the adults in the environment intervene, and even then the punishment is usually introduced as a last resort. A great many interpersonal events take place between the incipient onset of the unacceptable behavior and the eventual introduction of the negative consequences, and these events tend to serve a reinforcing and not a suppressing function.

Burchard and Tyler (1965) describe the temporal sequence of staff behavior to the disruptive behavior of one of the boys as follows. When Donny first begins to "act up," staff members try to ignore this behavior for as long as possible. During this time, peer approval and attention tend to reinforce the behavior. As the behavior continues and increases in magnitude, attendants turn to attempts at supportive persuasion to desist. When this (reinforcement) is unsuccessful, the staff becomes angry and only at that point finally introduces punishment. But that is not all. Staff members now feel guilty, and this reaction manifests itself in sympathy visits to the child in the isolation room. With the contingencies structured in this fashion, it is not surprising that Donny's unacceptable behavior increased over time; for staff and peer attention occurred immediately after the response, while the punishment was delayed and ambivalently administered. The program instituted by Burchard and Tyler, on the other hand, had Donny immediately and perfunctorily placed in his isolation room as soon as he displayed any unacceptable behavior. The staff was instructed to approach this intervention in a matter-of-fact way and at the onset of carefully specified target behavior, that is, before they themselves had become emotionally aroused by the behavior. It was also stressed that isolation had to be on an all-or-none basis and that it should never be used as a threat. It is very likely that the systematic nature of punishment when used in the operant frame of reference is the principal factor in its efficiency. In everyday child rearing, punishment tends to be used in the unsystematic, arbitrary, last-resort fashion described by Burchard and Tyler, and this probably explains why it is rarely an effective technique for the suppression of undesirable behavior.

INTERVENTION IN FAMILY SETTINGS

The child's early learning in the context of the family is the prime source of socialization and conformity in what Hoffman (1970) and others call the moral realm. It is in the family where potent reinforcement by important models takes place and where both verbal and nonverbal communication exert a powerful influence on the development of the child's behavior. It should therefore not be surprising that the most effective programs designed to prevent or treat delinquency are those which intervene in the child's own family. Such intervention has taken a variety of forms. Some investigators approach it by teaching parents to be unambiguous in stating instructions and consistent in bringing appropriate consequences to bear on the child's behavior (Patterson & Reid, 1973). Others seek to increase the rate of exchanging positive reinforcers between parent and child (Reid & Hendricks, 1973), while Stuart, Tripodi, Jayaratne, and Camburn (1976) focus on improving communication and establishing equitable give and take among the family members.

Alexander and Parsons (1973) compared a combination of these family approaches with more traditional procedures (client-centered and psychodynamic treatments) in working with families where one child had been identified as delinquent. Compared with youngsters in the other treatment or control groups, those in the families who had received the behaviorally oriented form of treatment had significantly less recidivism. Recidivism is the repeating of delinquent behavior and represents the most common measure of the effectiveness of intervention with delinquents. Since recidivism is very frequent in delinquent populations, it must be shown to decrease for an intervention program to be considered effective. In addition to the recidivism measure, Alexander and Parsons (1973) evaluated the families' negotiating-communication skills. They found that those who had received the behavioral treatment displayed more equally shared verbal interaction, fewer silences, and more constructive interruptions of each other than did the families in the other groups.

The Achievement Place Model

Since it is not always possible to intervene in a delinquent child's own family, other investigators have shown that treatment in familylike community settings provides a constructive alternative to the institutions where juvenile delinquents are usually confined. Group homes for working with court-referred delinquent children were pioneered by Phillips (1968), whose original facility in Lawrence, Kansas—known as Achievement Place—has served as a model for numerous family style homes in various communities. The programs are based on the premise that delinquent behavior is the product of inadequate social-learning experiences; thus, the goal of intervention is the development of appropriate social and personal behavior. The home is under the direction of a trained staff who take the place of the parents in a typical family and who conduct a structured, systematic program, based largely on the principles of operant learning.

An Achievement Place program focuses on the teaching of such social skills as how to make an introduction; of providing academic skills, such as how to study and doing homework; of establishing self-care skills in such areas as meal preparation and personal hygiene; and of developing prevocational skills designed to permit a young person to find work in the community. The typical resident in such a group home is of junior high school age, about 3 to 4 years below grade level on academic achievement tests, whose trouble with the law has resulted in being adjudicated delinquent. The length of stay in such a home is 9 to 12 months.

The Achievement Place program employs a token economy approach to establishing constructive behavior (Phillips, Phillips, Fixsen, & Wolf, 1971). For specified desired actions the children receive points that serve as reinforcers. These points can later be converted into a great variety of privileges, such as the use of tools, telephoning, snacks, or an allowance. At the beginning, behavior is heavily reinforced by a daily point system. This system is later reduced to a weekly point system and, ultimately, the children progress to a merit system in which all privileges are free and reinforcement for desirable behavior takes the form of praise, approval, and affection. Behavior is carefully monitored throughout, and after four successful weeks on the merit system, a child is advanced to a "homeward bound" schedule. In this schedule the children return to their own homes while spending occasional nights at Achievement Place for discussions of any problems they might be having at home. This return to the child's own home, the ultimate aim of the program, is coordinated through regular meetings between the child's parents and the program staff. Once the child's behavior is problem-free, these meetings are discontinued.

The Achievement Place program in Lawrence, Kansas, has been the site of many studies which assessed the specific aspects of the endeavor, such as the reliability of the children when they are asked to monitor their own behavior (Fixsen, Phillips, & Wolf, 1972), or the efficacy of self-government by the children (Fixsen, Phillips, & Wolf, 1973). In addition, the overall effectiveness of the program has been assessed by various means (Fixsen, Phillips, Phillips, & Wolf, 1972). A comparison was conducted between sixteen boys whom the court had committed to Achievement Place, fifteen boys who had been sent to a state institution in which about 250 youths were housed, and thirteen boys who had been placed on probation. Though it must be stressed that the boys had not been assigned to these three groups on a random basis, measures such as school attendance, police and court contacts, and academic performance revealed the superiority of the Achievement Place program over the other two dispositions. The reduction in the recidivism rate was particularly impressive. Within the first 12 months, 6 percent of the Achievement Place boys, 13 percent of the state school boys, and 31 percent of the boys on probation had committed some delinquent act that had led to their being once again adjudicated delinquent and placed in an institution. By the end of 24 months following their release, the cumulative totals of readjudicated youths was 19 percent for Achievement Place, 53 percent for the state institution, and 54 percent for those on probation. There thus appears to be much merit in a family style approach to the treatment of delinquency, but not all delinquent or delinquency-prone youngsters are lucky enough to be exposed to this approach early in their delinquent careers.

INTERVENTION IN INSTITUTIONAL SETTINGS

By the time a juvenile delinquent is confined in a correctional institution, he or she will have lived many years in an environment where delinquent behavior was reinforced. Attempts at unlearning this strongly reinforced behavior and replacing it by newly learned, prosocial behavior must therefore be very intensive and as all-encompassing as possible. Consequences of behavior must be carefully controlled so as to ensure that they are conducive to the changes which are desired.

An institutional program, based on the principles of social learning, operated for a few years at the National Training School for Boys in Washington, D.C. (Cohen & Filipczak, 1971). This project was identified by the acronym CASE II, which stands for Contingencies Applicable to Special Education—Phase II, having followed an earlier—Phase I—demonstration. The project entailed a comprehensive token system in which the inmates who were enrolled in it could earn

points for studying and passing tests. These points functioned as the only means by which available backup reinforcers could be purchased. These included such privileges as a private room and private shower, better cafeteria food, access to a recreation lounge, or to a telephone. Anyone who chose not to work for the points or failed to earn them was given the standard institutional food and facilities.

At any one time, CASE II involved twenty-five 14- to 18-year-old inmates of the institution who had been selected as representative of the entire inmate population in terms of their offenses and other characteristics. The primary aim of the project was to raise the students' academic level so that they might reenter the public school system upon discharge, inasmuch as all of them had been high school dropouts. Cohen assumed that an improvement in basic academic skills will result in better adjustment once the student is returned to his community. The evaluation of the project was therefore based both on academic measures and on recidivism rate.

The average length of stay in the program was about 8 months. During that time, the CASE-II students improved an average of one to two grade levels and their intelligence test scores rose an average of 12.5 IQ points. These are impressive changes but in the absence of a control group, it is impossible to say how much of the increase was due to increased familiarity with the tests, to the fact that on the second administration of the intelligence test the students could earn points, and to the use of programmed instructional material in addition to the use of the token system.

For thirty-seven students who had spent at least 90 days in the program the recidivism rate was compared with the National Training School figure for previous years. That rate had been 76 percent within one year of discharge. For eleven CASE-II students who had been released directly into the community, this rate was 27 percent during the first year after discharge and 36.4 percent by the end of the third year. Sixteen other students had gone from the CASE-II program into another institutional program before their discharge. This meant that for them a different set of contingencies operated before they returned to the community. The effect of this is reflected in the fact that their recidivism rate was 62.5 percent during the first year and 68.8 percent over a total 3-year period. Again, the results are impressive but again we must temper them by pointing to some ambiguities. One source of ambiguity is that of the thirty-seven students who had spent at least 90 days in the CASE-II program, only twenty-seven could be located for follow-up. The other problem is that it is not clear why some students were discharged directly into the community, while others had additional institutional experiences. Yet, despite these questions, the work described by Cohen and Filipczak (1971) represents a landmark demonstration of constructive changes that can be introduced in the rehabilitation of juvenile delinquents when established principles of learning are put to use. Studies of more circumscribed efforts where tighter experimental controls are possible have repeatedly confirmed the effectiveness of behaviorally oriented programs for juvenile delinquents (Barkley, Hasting, Tousel, & Tousel, 1976; Burchard & Tyler, 1965; Hobbs & Holt, 1976; Staats & Butterfield, 1965; Tyler & Brown, 1968).

RECAPITULATION

The norm-violating behavior society labels *delinquent* can be construed as a function of deficient behavioral controls. Among these are the ability to respond under conditions of delayed reinforcement (delay of gratification) and the self-imposition of standards (resistance to temptation). These behavioral controls and delinquency-incompatible, norm-abiding behavior are learned, and the study of delinquency must therefore turn to a study of the conditions under which such learning takes place or fails to take place. Important among these conditions are experiences with differential reinforcement of acceptable and unacceptable behavior, encounters with rational authority figures, the establishment of internal controls, and the capacity to consider the effects of one's behavior on others. For many reasons, the circumstances conducive to these conditions are often absent in the lower-class culture where the value system, especially among the young, tends to be incompatible with the norms imposed by the middle class. As a result, the socially or subcultural type of delinquent frequently comes from that segment of society.

In seeking to prevent or treat delinquency it is important to attend to the consequences of such behavior. As usual, reinforcement is a more potent consequence than punishment, although most contemporary approaches seem to favor the latter. Effective methods of intervention which apply the principles of reinforcement have been demonstrated in families and familylike community settings as well as in selected institutions.

Chapter 9

Fears, Phobias, and Social Isolation

The problems to be discussed in this chapter represent avoidance responses to specific objects or situations that result in *withdrawn behavior* on the part of the child. Because such behavior interferes with children's interaction with their environment and thus prevents them from learning other adaptive responses, the difficulty is, at times, cumulative. As we shall see in the discussion of school phobias, a child who makes avoidance responses to the school situation will be unable to learn the things the school is supposed to teach, thus falling behind in the acquisition of academic subject matter, and the resulting fear of failure may further exacerbate such a child's difficulties. A similar sequence can be traced for children who avoid interacting with other children. This avoidance will result in their failure to acquire the skills involved in peer relations, making these relations even more difficult to establish and therefore even more strenuously avoided. Thus, what may have begun as excessive avoidance behavior comes to be complicated by skill deficits so that intervention, if too long delayed, will have to address not only the excessive avoidance, which must be reduced, but also the deficient skills, which must be increased.

FEARS AND PHOBIAS

Surveys of children's fears have shown that almost all children develop some specific fears sometime during their childhood (MacFarlane, Allen, & Honzik, 1954). Some fears are adaptive in that they keep children away from objectively dangerous situations, while other childhood fears dissipate over time and may be considered to be normal developmental phenomena (Miller, Barrett, Hampe, & Noble, 1972b). We are here not concerned with such normal fears but, instead, with those fears that are excessive and thereby prevent the child from following age-appropriate pursuits. When such disabling fears are specific to one situation or object, one speaks of them as a *phobia*, modifying the term by the object of the phobia, hence such terms as dog phobia, school phobia, water phobia, etc. Manifestations of fears and phobias take the form of an active avoidance of the feared object, which is often accompanied by verbal expressions of fear, changes in skin color, tremors, and gastrointestinal upset.

Anxiety: Some Theoretical Considerations

The avoidance and escape responses one observes in children whose behavior is marked by withdrawal are presumably learned under conditions where such responses reduce or eliminate aversive stimulation. An aversive stimulus, such as one associated with the sensation of pain, ordinarily elicits behavior that will result in the termination of such stimulation. Such escape behavior probably has a large innate, genetic component, its species-preserving characteristics having favored its evolution. From the standpoint of behavior economy, repeated exposure to and escape from the aversive object would be costly, and most of the time the individual, after a limited number of exposures, no longer comes face-to-face with the aversive object because one learns to avoid it. In order to explain avoidance behavior, it is necessary to postulate something that takes the place of the aversive object which, being avoided, is no longer an effective aversive stimulus. Some other aversive object or condition must mediate the avoidance behavior, something that will maintain this behavior by furnishing the reinforcing consequence otherwise rendered by the termination of the aversive stimulation of the (now avoided) object. This "something" that mediates avoidance behavior is the very useful hypothetical construct *anxiety*.

Used as a hypothetical construct, anxiety is viewed as a process that gives rise to observable phenomena, including phenomena "other than the observables that led to hypothesizing the construct" (Ruebush, 1963, p. 462). Observable phenomena, from which one can infer the presence of anxiety but which do not necessarily all occur together, are measurable physiological changes, including changes in heart rate, respiratory rate, and skin conductance; changes in motor behavior, such as muscular tremors, hyperactivity, motor disorganization, and a low threshold for motor responses ("jumpiness"); and verbal reports of subjective changes, such as feelings of apprehension, worry, anticipation of threat, and sensations of fear, particularly from unspecifiable sources of danger.

As used in the present context, anxiety is viewed as having physiological, motor, and cognitive components, but the identification of anxiety does not demand the demonstration of all three components in every case. It appears, in fact, that there are considerable individual differences in the way in which the three components correlate with one another (Martin, 1961). During treatment some individuals report subjective improvement and behave accordingly before changes in heart rate can be recorded, while others will show changes in heart rate before they report subjective improvement (Leitenberg, Agras, Butz, & Wincze, 1971).

The basis of most of the available knowledge about the relationship between physiological changes and other measures of anxiety comes from experimental work with adults. While most theorists make the assumption that a child's experience of anxiety is accompanied by physiological changes, particularly in the autonomic system, there is little direct evidence concerning the validity of this assumption. Patterson, Helper, and Wilcott (1960) studied the relationship between anxiety and verbal conditioning in children. They used the electrical resistance of the skin (GSR) as the measure of the physiological concomitant of the anxiety that was presumably aroused in the child by having been taken to the physiological laboratory, seeing the complicated electronic equipment, having to lie down in a dimly lit room, and having electrodes taped to forearms and palms. This study emphasizes the difficulties and complexities of this type of research, for while the environmental stimuli seem to have aroused anxiety, as reflected in the children's verbalizations, the relationship between verbal conditioning and skin conductance remained ambiguous. Children with very high or very low skin conductance tended to show little conditioning, but among the high-skin-conductance children, those who inhibited motor activity acquired the conditioned verbal response (verbs on a word-association task) more rapidly than those who expressed motor activity.

Recordings of physiological arousal states give the appearance of great objectivity because they can be represented in the form of mechanically produced tracing on paper tape. Unfortunately, the intercorrelation of various physiological measures is so low and the individual differences in reactivity are so high that these measures have little clinical utility in the present state of knowledge and technique. For this reason and because it is far easier to ask a child questions than to attach electrodes to his body, most research on anxiety in children has taken the form of questionnaire studies.

Most of these studies start from the premise that anxiety is a state, an enduring though fluctuating condition in which the anxious child is at all times and which can be measured without reference to environmental circumstances. If one construes anxiety as a response, learned to and elicited by specific situations and possibly generalized from these, the research literature on anxiety-as-a-state has limited relevance.

Research on anxiety-as-a-response requires that one present children with a stressful stimulus (or conduct one's study in a naturally occurring crisis situation) and measure their anxiety. The methodological and ethical difficulties in conducting such research are readily apparent. One cannot expose a child to truly stressful situations merely for the sake of studying the reactions. The moment one uses some attenuated stress one does not know whether the stimulus is anxiety-arousing, for to ascertain this one would need a measure that is independent of the one to be used in the study. Moreover, stressful stimuli are usually transitory, yet anxiety questionnaires take time to administer. For these reasons, negative results are impossible to interpret. They may mean that no anxiety was elicited because the stimulus was not anxiety-arousing. Or they may mean that the stimulus was anxiety-arousing but that the subject did not respond with anxiety. Or they may mean that the stimulus was anxiety-arousing and that the subject responded with anxiety but that the anxiety had dissipated by the time the questionnaire was administered. Then again, the questionnaire might not have been a valid measure of anxiety—or a combination of all these factors was at play. With all these problems, it is not surprising that experimental anxiety studies using verbal reports as a measure have failed to obtain significant results (Ruebush, 1963).

The current state of research-based knowledge about anxiety in children is thus one of considerable ignorance. We have a widely used hypothetical construct that can be defined in terms of observable phenomena. We know that changes in endocrine secretion are correlated with certain changes in physiological state (Funkenstein, King, & Drolette, 1957) but that verbal labels of these subjectively experienced changes are unreliable. Developmental issues are barely explored and a practical methodology for studying anxiety responses through self-report has yet to be developed. Despite all that, the hypothetical construct *anxiety* serves such an important heuristic function that a discussion of behavior disorders is virtually impossible without recourse to this construct.

From the standpoint of a discussion of psychological disorders, it is of little import to ask how anxiety originally came to be a part of a child's behavior repertoire. The facts appear to be the following: certain situations, different for different children, have the capacity to elicit the arousal response we call anxiety; this response (anxiety) has noxious qualities; and other responses that are followed by a reduction of anxiety tend to be strengthened. When these responses are maladaptive because they interfere with the child's expected life role, they and the anxiety that maintains them become problems calling for alleviation. The fact that procedures based on the principles of learning can be used to reduce the anxiety and, hence, the associated avoidance responses is strongly suggestive of the hypothesis that these principles were also operating when anxiety was acquired, but there is little evidence that this was indeed the case. The frequently cited demonstration of a learned fear response, reported by Watson and Rayner (1920) in the classical case of Albert, shows only that a fear response can be learned; but this study cannot be used to support the contention that all fear responses are learned nor that the fear responses of a specific child seen in a clinical situation were originally acquired through learning.

"**Emotional Disturbance**"   As will be seen in the following, some behavior disorders are maintained by the anxiety-reducing consequences of the child's maladaptive responses. Since the behavior can thus be construed as disturbed by the emotion of anxiety, the term *emotionally disturbed* might be used appropriately in these cases. This term has unfortunately been used so loosely that it has lost its original meaning and serves largely to confuse the issue. In fields such as special education the expression emotionally disturbed has come to cover every form of behavior disorder, including the most profound impairments. Since there is no evidence that an emotion is implicated in every form of disturbed behavior, it seems best to restrict the use of *emotional disturbance* to those cases where behavior problems can be demonstrated to be the direct consequence of an emotion, such as generalized fear. Even in those cases it should be kept in mind that the emotion is disturbing the behavior and that it is not the emotion that is disturbed, as the term emotionally disturbed tends to suggest.

SCHOOL PHOBIA AND OTHER FEARS

The list of possible fears is without limit because any neutral stimulus can theoretically acquire fear-eliciting characteristics. There thus are reports of fear of darkness (Kanfer, Karoly, & Newman, 1975; Leitenberg & Callahan, 1973), of dog phobias (MacDonald, 1975), and phobias of tall buildings (Croghan & Musante, 1975), among others. We shall here focus on the phobia that is both the most frequent and, potentially, the most disabling for children; the excessive fear of school, usually called *school phobia*. It must be noted, however, that not all children who refuse to go to school are school phobic. Some refuse to go to school because other activities are more reinforcing for them. They are usually called *truants* and their behavior is typically dealt with through administrative-judicial, rather than psychological or medical channels. Other children may fail to attend school, not because they are afraid of the school but because they are afraid of leaving home. Some of these children may be afraid of losing a parent by death or abandonment and they have discovered that they can reduce their fear by staying close to that parent, not letting him or her out of sight. These children are said to have *separation anxiety* and though the effect takes the form of not going to school (among other places where they refuse to go without the parent), this condition should not be confused with school phobia.

School Phobia

This problem is characterized by strong fears associated with attending school. The children verbalize vague dread and apprehension about disaster and frequently complain about such physical problems as headaches, stomach aches, or nausea. It is also not unusual for such children to express fears about a variety of other things, such as darkness or being left alone. It is usually difficult to tell how many of these complaints are actually associated with the fear that is elicited by stimuli associated with going to school and how many are operant in nature in that they are maintained by the reinforcement of not having to go to school when one pleads a headache.

Kennedy (1965) differentiated between two types of school phobia. Type 1 is characterized by an acute onset representing the first such episode in a child who is in his early years of school. The problem often occurs on a Monday, following brief illness and authorized absence from school the previous week. The child often expresses concern about death and about the mother's physical health. The parents' psychological state is usually unremarkable, and they are in good communication with one another. They share responsibility for family management and respond to efforts at helping their child with understanding and cooperation. Kennedy's Type 2, on the other hand, characterizes cases where school refusal has occurred several times before and where the original onset was gradual. It occurs mostly in the upper grades and can start on any day of the week. In these cases, the parents have poor communication and manifest psychological or behavior problems of their own. The father tends to show little interest in household or children, and the parents fail to cooperate in the treatment procedures aimed at getting their child back to school.

It is very likely that school phobia represents an overdetermined response pattern. Nearly all children, at one time or another, express a reluctance to go to school. If the parent deals with this reluctance in a matter-of-fact way and insists that school attendance is expected and required, nothing will come of the incident. On the other hand, if the parent begins to make lengthy inquiries into why the child does not want to go to school, eliciting more or less plausible and more or less factual rationalizations, and then agrees to let the child stay home, the basis of future school-avoiding behavior may well be laid. For other children, an event or series of events at school have a highly noxious quality, making school, in fact, a fear-arousing situation. Being teased or attacked by other children, losing in competition, fighting with a friend, or being embarrassed by the need for physical exposure in connection with undressing for gym may all initiate fear of school and school refusal. Some of the circumstances just listed may be more critical for girls than for boys, and this may account for the fact that school refusal is one of the few forms of psychological disorder for which boys do not outnumber girls; for here the incidence among girls is at least as great as among boys, some reports actually pointing to a higher incidence for girls (Talbot, 1957).

Once a child refuses to go to school, thus avoiding the fear-arousing conditions that would be encountered there, remaining at home and the reinforcing qualities this entails will lend secondary support to the avoidance behavior. Being allowed to watch television, being fed by mother, being fussed over because one is "sick" will all conspire to make it more difficult for the child to return to school. What is more, once several days of school have been missed, returning there becomes even more unpleasant to contemplate. The child will have missed instructional content and thus fallen behind the rest of the class with the aversive consequences this implies.

Also, returning after an absence often results in being singled out for curious attention and questions about the reason for the absence which, in this case, are embarrassing to answer. In fact, returning to school after a few days of absence due to physical illness is unpleasant for many children, and, as in Kennedy's Type 1, it is not unusual for school refusals to have their onset immediately after such legitimate absence, including, at times, a long weekend.

Because school refusal is strengthened by the reinforcing events encountered while away from school, it has been recognized that this behavior must be reversed as soon as possible after onset if intervention is to be successful. Giving a child spurious medical excuses and facilitating instruction at home "until he gets over his problem" are by now generally recognized as achieving exactly the opposite of what is intended—to get the child back to school. Kennedy (1965) stressed the need for immediate intervention, starting as soon as the child refuses to go to school.

While forced exposure to the feared situation, together with reinforcement of approach behavior, seems successful in overcoming acute school phobia problems that have had little opportunity to become confounded by various secondary gains, the chronic and complex Type 2 cases seem to call for treatment of more than school refusal. Kennedy's description of his Type 2 cases suggests, in fact, that for them school refusal was only one of a variety of other problems, including family disorganization, antisocial behavior, and profound psychological disorders requiring institutionalization. Kennedy, and others, find these cases very difficult to treat.

One of the reasons why immediate intervention and early return to school are so important in cases of school refusal is that missing instructional content makes resumption of studies more difficult, and hence, return to school more aversive. Whenever a child's schooling has been interrupted or learning ability impaired for any length of time, help calls for reducing the behavior that is incompatible with school attendance and learning, accompanied by simultaneous efforts to strengthen learning-appropriate behavior. In addition, and because of the cumulative nature of education, these children need the benefits of intensive remedial educational efforts, designed to help them catch up with all the basic skills they failed to acquire during the time their school refusal interfered with their acquisition of knowledge and skills. Unless such a child can be helped to reach the age-appropriate achievement level, the school experience will continue to be unrewarding, and avoidance responses to school and learning are likely to be repeated.

Treatment of Fears and Phobias

Conditioning methods have been used in the treatment of children's fears from the days Mary Cover Jones (1924a) reported her pioneering study with Peter. She reduced this child's fear of furry objects by gradually strengthening fear-incompatible responses, a method that has since come to be known as counterconditioning, systematic desensitization, or therapy by reciprocal inhibition. Relaxation is the fear-incompatible response most frequently used in work with adolescents (Hallsten, 1965) and adults (Wolpe, 1969), but this is only rarely applied in work with children (Tasto, 1969), possibly because training in deep muscle relaxation is difficult with young subjects. For this reason, Lazarus and Abramovitz (1965) explored the use of "emotive imagery," an approach that is based on the assumption that it is possible to inhibit anxiety by the induction of child-appropriate imagery with positive emotional content. Images that presumably serve an anxiety-inhibiting function are those that arouse such feelings as self-assertion, pride, affection, mirth, or fearlessness. The child is instructed to imagine a situation associated with such a feeling, and once such imagery is induced, the therapist presents anxiety-eliciting images, carefully graded from mildly to highly anxiety arousing. On each step on this previously established anxiety hierarchy, the pleasant imagery is paired with anxiety-arousing stimuli, and when treatment is successful, the child should be able to make his fear-incompatible emotional response when the previously anxiety-arousing situation is presented in imagery and, presumably, in real life.

School Phobia   Behavior as complex as refusal to attend school has components of both respondent and operant nature, for while the avoidance responses may have served fear-reducing functions at one time, it is likely that they are later maintained and complicated by the reinforcements available in the home for a child who is not going to school. Lazarus, Davison, and Polefka (1965) took cognizance of the multiple factors that maintain a school phobia by treating a 9-year-old boy using both respondent and operant procedures. They reduced the intense fear of school by exposing him to school-related stimuli in gradually more difficult steps that were accompanied by the presentation of anxiety-reducing stimuli. In the company of a therapist whom he seemed to like and who might thus be viewed as an elicitor of responses that were incompatible with anxiety, the boy first walked to school on a Sunday. The next day, he and his therapist walked together from the house to the schoolyard while the therapist sought to elicit from the boy anxiety-reducing, pleasant ideation. On subsequent days, the boy visited the empty classroom after school hours, then entered the classroom with the therapist for a brief chat with the teacher, and only after a week of such *in vivo desensitization* did the boy spend the entire morning in the classroom while the therapist waited outside. Throughout all this, approaching the school was actively reinforced while as many of the reinforcements for staying at home were removed. In effect, the contingencies were reversed. Where school-avoiding behavior had previously received reinforcing attention, such attention was now focused on its reciprocal—school-approaching behavior.

The treatment approach developed by Kennedy (1965) for cases of school phobia with recent onset (Type 1) is based on the consideration that secondary complications should be avoided. His procedure has the following six essential components.

1 Good communication with referral sources so that children can be referred on the second or third day after onset of school refusal.

2 A deemphasis of somatic complaints.

3 Decisive insistence on school attendance, including the use of force, where necessary.

4 A structured, success-focused interview with the parents, stressing the need for a matter-of-fact approach to the problem and the importance of complimenting the child for his going to school and staying there, no matter how brief or stormy that attendance.

5 A brief interview with the child, held after school hours in which the importance of going on in the face of fear and the transitory nature of a phobia are stressed.

6 An informal telephone follow-up.

Using this approach over a period of 8 years, Kennedy treated a total of fifty carefully selected cases, all of whom responded with complete remission. Follow-up failed to reveal evidence for the emergence of other problems, and the children continued to attend school.

The decisive insistence on school attendance emphasized in Kennedy's approach seeks to reduce the possibility of confounding and complicating the school refusal by such factors as the reinforcement involved in staying home, the added source of school avoidance stemming from the missed lessons, which might introduce fear of potential failure upon return to school, and the impossibility of having the fear undergo extinction when the usual condition for extinction—unreinforced exposure to the conditioned stimulus—cannot occur. This last point bears on the self-perpetuating aspects of avoidance responses that are maintained by fear reduction.

Theoretically, a fear response is acquired when a previously neutral stimulus, such as the school building, acquires fear-arousing properties through pairing with a stimulus that, innately or through prior conditioning, has the capacity to elicit fear. This respondent conditioning paradigm—the pairing of an unconditioned stimulus with a conditioned stimulus resulting in a conditioned response—would predict that without further pairing the conditioned response will undergo extinction. Contrary to this prediction, the fear continues and the avoidance response is maintained. What maintains it, as Baum (1966) and Solomon and Brush (1956) have pointed out, is the reinforcing effect of fear reduction contingent on the avoidance response. This protects the child from exposure to the conditioned stimulus, unpaired with the unconditioned stimulus, so that the fear does not undergo extinction. To bring about extinction of a fear response thus maintained, one has to prevent the avoidance response and thereby assure that the child is exposed to the conditioned stimulus but not to the unconditioned stimulus. Such prevention of the avoidance response leads to rapid extinction (Baum, 1966), and Kennedy's (1965) approach to school phobia may well entail aspects of this procedure.

The principles of forced exposure to fear-arousing conditioned stimuli have been incorporated in "implosive therapy" (Stampfl & Levis, 1967), which Smith and Sharpe (1970) used in the treatment of a school-phobic 13-year-old boy who had been absent from school for 7 weeks. In implosive therapy, the client is instructed to visualize a highly anxiety-arousing scene involving his or her phobia; a step intended to expose him or her in imagery to the conditioned stimulus, unpaired with the unconditioned stimulus. With this procedure, Smith and Sharpe were able to have the boy return to his most anxiety-arousing class after one treatment session and to have him in full school attendance after four sessions. They report that the boy continued to attend school thereafter and that his grades and peer relations improved.

Implosive therapy can only be used if a child is highly motivated for help since his or her cooperation in visualizing fear-arousing situations is absolutely essential. The more frequently used conditioning method for treating fears—counterconditioning as it is involved in systematic desensitization—is less stressful and thus probably more suitable and preferable in work with children.

Garvey and Hegrenes (1966) report the treatment of a school-phobic child by a modified form of desensitization. The therapist and the child approached the school together in a series of steps graded from the least anxiety-evoking situation (sitting in a car in front of the school) to the most anxiety-evoking condition (being in the classroom with the teacher and other students). The authors view this approach as similar to that used by Wolpe (1958, 1969) and formulate it in terms of the respondent conditioning paradigm. This, as Lazarus et al. (1965) have pointed out, overlooks the fact that both respondent and operant factors are at work. Clearly, the therapist's implicit and explicit approval of approach responses reinforces and strengthens such behavior and thus contributes to the treatment.

Methods based on conditioning principles seem capable of reducing children's fears and phobias, although, as Davison and Wilson (1973) have pointed out, it is not at all clear what actually is the critical ingredient of these treatments. What is fairly certain is that principles other than those derived from classical conditioning come into play when therapists threat these problems. Cognitive factors (what the child says to himself) and social reinforcement (the implicit or explicit approval by the therapist) are undoubtedly also involved. Different therapists have therefore stressed different aspects in their treatment approaches. Hersen (1970), for example, bases treatment for school phobia on differential reinforcement (DRO) of other than school-avoiding behavior. That is, he seeks to decrease the reinforcements available to the child for staying home, while arranging contingencies in such a way that successive approximations to returning to school and school attendance itself receive positive reinforcement. This approach takes a bit longer than Kennedy's rapid treatment, but it is obviously less stressful for all concerned. A follow-up on a DRO approach to school phobia over a 9-month period showed that it had lasting effects and no untoward consequences (Ayllon, Smith, & Rogers, 1970). With appropriate instructions, the child's parents can do most of the actual treatment by managing the necessary contingencies once these have been identified through careful assessment on the part of the professional therapist (Tahmasian & McReynolds, 1971).

Other Fears Fear of the dark, another common fear among young children, has been treated by teaching such children to make statements to themselves, such as "I am a brave boy; I can take care of myself in the dark" (Kanfer, Karoly, & Newman, 1975). Another method of treating fear of the dark involves reinforced practice (Leitenberg & Callahan, 1973). Here, fearful children are instructed to remain in a darkened room for initially brief, then gradually lengthening periods of time. Progress, as reflected in increasing periods of exposure, is reinforced, but exposure and positive reinforcement are not the only ingredients of this treatment. The children also receive instructions which are designed to arouse expectations of gradual success and their progress is depicted in graphic form. As usual with such treatment "packages," it is impossible to know which of these aspects is crucial to the success and whether all of them are indeed necessary.

In most of the treatment methods that have been applied to fears and phobias, the fearful child is exposed to the feared stimulus, either in imagery or in real life. When observational learning is the treatment of choice, exposure to the feared object is vicarious in that the child merely observes someone else who is making approach responses. A report by Bandura, Grusec, and Menlove (1967) showed that, after having observed a peer model fearlessly make progressively stronger approach responses toward a dog, children who had displayed fearful avoidance behavior toward dogs showed stable and generalized reduction in such behavior. It is possible to present fearless models by means of motion pictures, and the effect on the observer is enhanced if several models display the fearless behavior (Bandura & Menlove, 1968). Ritter (1968) has shown that it is possible to use modeling procedures with groups of children whose snake phobias were treated in this manner.

Since fearful children are constantly exposed to fearless peer models, one might expect that their fears should be reduced in the course of everyday life. While this may well happen with some children, research on modeling suggests why this is not the case in every instance. Observational learning is enhanced when the model resembles the observer. A fearless peer differs from a fearful observer along the dimension of fear. This lack of similarity between model and observer may well attenuate the effectiveness of the observation (Kornhaber & Schroeder, 1975). A study by Hill, Liebert, and Mott (1968) showed that fear reduction through modeling is made more likely if the model is shown as initially fearful, only gradually emitting fearless approach responses. These investigators produced a film showing an elementary school boy who fearlessly interacted with a dog during the opening scenes and an initially fearful boy of nursery school age who gradually learned to emulate the model's behavior. The sequence thus not only portrayed two models but it also modeled the act of imitation itself. The film was shown once to a group of nine nursery school boys who would not fully approach a harmless, caged dog during a pretest. After this single exposure to the film, eight of the children were willing to approach, feed, and pet the large dog, whereas only three of the nine boys in a matched control group were able to do so.

The Effectiveness of Treatment

Many forms of treatment for children's fears and phobias have been shown capable of reducing these problems but before we conclude that this proves the effectiveness of these interventions, we must look at a study conducted by Miller, Barrett, Hampe, and Noble (1972a), who investigated what happens when a child with a phobia receives no treatment at all. There were 67 children between the ages of 6 and 15 who were randomly assigned to one of three groups. The first group received traditional psychotherapy in which the children were encouraged to explore their feelings and conflicts. The second group received systematic desensitization, involving relaxation training and exposure to a graded hierarchy of imaginary fear-arousing situations. The group in which the children received no treatment was a so-called waiting-list control. After an initial evaluation, these families were told that the clinic could not offer them treatment right away and that they would be placed on a waiting list. Treatments were given three times per week for 8 weeks and the control group waited for the same length of time. All were reevaluated after the 8 weeks and again for follow-up at 14 weeks.

The results of this outcome study reveal that there was "a marked reduction of target phobia in all three groups from preevaluation to follow-up" (Miller et al., 1972a, p. 275) and that "neither behavior therapy nor the more standard psychotherapy to which it was compared was more effective than the control procedure" (ibid., p. 276). These findings are those for the group as a whole and are based on evaluations carried out by a member of the research team who used various checklists and behavioral measures. When the reports of the children's parents are used as a basis for evaluating the outcome, it turns out that they reported the phobias to be significantly less severe when their child had been in one of the treatment groups than when they were members of the no-treatment control group. Furthermore, when the children in the study are divided into a younger (6 to 10) and an older (11 to 15) group, within the younger group, where 96 percent showed marked improvement, therapy turned out to have been significantly more effective than being on the waiting list. For the older children, on the other hand, neither form of treatment succeeded in diminishing the phobia any better than no treatment at all.

One and two years later Miller and his colleagues (Hampe, Noble, Miller, & Barrett, 1973) reevaluated the condition of sixty-two of the children who had participated in their original study. By that time, many of the children who had been on the waiting list as well as those who had not improved originally had received some form of treatment. Eighty percent of the group was now either problem-free or significantly improved and only 7 percent continued to have a severe phobia. Overall, the investigators concluded that "time-limited therapy of two months duration is effective for about 60% of phobic children" and that "the lifespan of phobias in children appears to be somewhere between two weeks and two years, with most phobias dissipating within one year of onset" (Hampe et al., 1973, p. 452). Considering the fact that over the 2-year period 60 percent of the children who had still been phobic at the end of the treatment had received additional professional care and other guidance and counseling, it is somewhat difficult to agree with these authors' view that "phobias go away by themselves and therefore need not be treated" (ibid., p. 451). More to the point would be that "the justification for treatment comes from the fact that treatment greatly hastens recovery" (ibid., p. 451) and that "it is necessary to devise differentiated treatment procedures for different age groups" (ibid., p. 452).

SOCIAL ISOLATION

Children may fail to interact with other children for a variety of reasons. One of these may be related to fears, such as of being attacked, ignored, or ridiculed by others. Other reasons, however, have to do with the child's failure to have learned the social skills one needs in order to interact effectively with one's peers. Not knowing how to play with others, for example, may well lead a child to find interaction with other children to be aversive and thus anxiety arousing. Withdrawal from the group is then reinforced by anxiety reduction. Such a child, as Gottman (1977) has pointed out, usually "hovers" on the periphery of the social group, being neither accepted nor rejected, but simply ignored by the peers. As with fears, the effect of this behavior is usually a cumulative worsening of the condition because by not interacting with others, such a child is unable to acquire the needed social skills and thus becomes more and more isolated. This cycle can only be broken by explicit intervention aimed at teaching social skills to these isolated children (Gottman, Gonso, & Schuler, 1976).

   An example of a child whose social isolation was related to deficient skills is presented by Buell, Stoddard, Harris, and Baer (1968), who reported the case of a nursery school child who did not know how to use outdoor playground equipment. As a result, she interacted very little with the other children but when the investigators taught her how to use the equipment, the girl's physical and verbal contact and her cooperative play quickly increased. Unfortunately, social withdrawal is maintained not only through the negative reinforcement of anxiety reduction but also by the positive reinforcement that is often given in the form of increased adult attention for the "shy" child. A case of this nature was reported by Allen, Hart, Buell, Harris, and Wolf (1964). Here, a nursery school child received a great deal of attention from teachers who were concerned about her lack of interaction with peers. As long as the teachers attended to the girl's isolate behavior, she rarely played with other children, but when the teachers were instructed to attend to the child only when she was in contact with other children (but not when she played alone), her rate of peer interaction increased to a high level. To test whether adult attention had indeed been responsible for the change in behavior, these investigators reversed the contingencies, attending to isolation but not to interaction. As soon as the contingencies were reversed, the behavior also reversed: adult attention was indeed the independent variable controlling the child's social behavior. As is always the case in such an ABAB design, the contingencies were then again reversed so as to support the socially desirable behavior, which was then maintained over a period of many months of further observation.

The role played by adults (often quite unwittingly) in the development and maintenance of children's social problems is illustrated in a case reported by Straughan (1964). An 8-year-old girl was referred by her mother because the child "was not as happy as she should be." Vaguely worded, general complaints of this nature can usually be broken down into more discrete maladaptive response classes by asking such questions as "What does she *do* that makes you say that she is not happy?" This case was no exception. Further investigation revealed that the child was inhibiting much age-appropriate spontaneous emotional expression in the presence of her mother. Treatment was therefore directed at desensitizing the child to her mother, who had come to be an anxiety-eliciting stimulus. The method used was to have the child in the playroom and to introduce the mother into the girl's presence when she was happily and enthusiastically engaged in play. After five play sessions, the child had indeed learned to be relaxed in the mother's presence and the mother, in turn, had become able to interact with the child in a more natural and spontaneous manner.

Children who emit a high rate of avoidance responses to a wide variety of situations and who avoid social interactions will have few friends and limited interests. Their behavior is generally maintained on a very low rate of positive reinforcement, and they typically exhibit frequent crying spells, marked sensitivity to criticism, easy discouragement in the face of failure, extensive worry, lack of enthusiasm and interest, and a generalized sad and listless approach to tasks. These characteristics have led such children to be labeled *depressed*, but it is doubtful that this label contributes anything to the understanding of their problem. In fact, based on a review of the research literature, Lefkowitz and Burton (1978) have questioned whether it is meaningful to speak of childhood depression as a clinical entity. Like all other terms that involve an inference about a child's internal state, *depression* must be translated into operational terms that refer to observable behavior before one can hope to do something constructive for the child. When a child encounters few positive reinforcements, one would want to expose him or her to situations that provide opportunities for experiencing positive consequences for adaptive be-havior. Often that means that such children have to be taught age-appropriate skills, including social skills, before they can make use of such opportunities.

Treatment of Social Isolation

Since social isolation of children is usually not expressed by an avoidance of adults but by an avoidance of children, the goal of treatment must be increased peer interaction. A way of doing this was demonstrated by Strain, Shores, and Timm (1977), who employed other children as confederates to increase the social behavior of isolate children. They instructed these confederates to approach the isolates and invite and encourage their participation in play. By tailoring this intervention to the individual child as, for example, in carefully chosing the confederate, these investigators achieved the desired goal. In some respects, their approach is similar to the carefully graded series of approach steps to a feared object that is the basis of desensitization therapy. Once a child has acquired some of the social skills needed for successful interaction, other skills are often learned in the process of being exposed to other children. Such generalization was demonstrated in a study of four "unassertive" children who were taught specific assertive behaviors (Bornstein, Bellack, & Hersen, 1977). Here assertiveness generalized from training to untrained situations and was maintained over a 4-week follow-up period.

The use of modeling procedures has been demonstrated with socially withdrawn nursery school children (O'Connor, 1969, 1972). A film portraying eleven scenes of young children in progressively more active interaction was shown to a group of withdrawn children while a matched control group viewed a film about dolphins. On the modeling film, a female narrator talked about what the children were doing and of the fun they were having. Behavior observations carried out in the classroom immediately after the showing of the film revealed the effectiveness of the modeling film in that the children who had been exposed to it now displayed more social assertiveness than the children in the control group. In fact, on blind behavior ratings, the initially shy children were indistinguishable from their socially normal classmates. O'Connor (1972) was also able to show that the effects of the intervention lasted at least over a 3-week follow-up period, with the treated children's peer-interaction scores remaining at normal levels. On the other hand, Keller and Carlson (1974) report that the effect of film-mediated modeling for children with low levels of social responsiveness was maintained over a similar period of time for only some of the children in their treated group. It may be that maintenance of the positive effects of modeling depends on the child having opportunities to practice the newly facilitated response pattern under conditions where they receive positive reinforcement for interacting with other children, particularly from their peers. Conceivably, it is this factor which made the use of another child as "therapist" so effective in the study by Strain et al. (1977), which, incidentally, also contained a form of modeling in that the confederates demonstrated the game in which they tried to interest the withdrawn child.

Much of the work with socially isolated children has been done with relatively normal children attending nursery school, but social skill training can also be accomplished with severely disturbed children. A demonstration by Romanczyk, Diament, Goren, Trunell, and Harris (1975) speaks to this point. Using such reinforcers as food and adult attention, these investigators temporarily increased the play behavior of four psychotic children who had displayed little or no verbal and social interaction with either adults or peers. When the experimental reinforcers were withdrawn, social play remained above the original (baseline) frequency for a few sessions, but eventually isolate play returned to its prior level. The authors conclude from this demonstration that their procedure has potential use in clinical settings, but they found the deterioration of the social play when intervention was terminated "very distressing." Clearly, with such severely disturbed children more than ten sessions of training are needed if one wants to ensure lasting results.

Inappropriate Gender Behavior

Social isolation, as we pointed out, may be the result of a child's failure to have acquired the social skills needed for age-appropriate interaction with other children. In order to achieve satisfactory interaction with others, however, a child must have not only the skills appropriate to his or her age level, the skills must also be appropriate for the child's sex. A child who does not engage in gender-appropriate behavior will often be ridiculed and ostracized by other children and thus become socially isolated.

The learning of sex roles begins in the first two years of life and by the end of the preschool years boys and girls display distinctly different behaviors. Boys have generally learned to be more assertive and to prefer gross-motor activities, while girls have been taught to be less competitive and to seek quieter endeavors (Serbin, O'Leary, Kent, & Tonick, 1973). Despite the desirable trend on the part of enlightened adults to stress the equality of boys and girls and to minimize arbitrary sex-role differences, our society continues to maintain certain stereotyped expectations in terms of speech patterns, body movements, and activity preferences regarding what is "proper" for boys and for girls. These stereotypes are usually shared by the children who impose their own sanctions when a youngster does not conform to these expectations. By and large, there is somewhat greater tolerance for deviant sex-role behavior in girls than in boys (Fagot, 1977). Girls who display "tomboy" behavior are usually more readily accepted than boys who behave like "sissies." In that sense, cross-gender behavior is more of a problem when it occurs in boys than in girls.

Occasionally, cross-gender behavior in boys becomes so pronounced that parents seek professional help. These boys consistently display feminine mannerisms, gestures, and gait, often preferring to dress and speak in an exaggeratedly feminine way. Given society's continuing intolerance of even slightly effeminate behavior in males, boys who display such extreme cross-gender behavior are often the object of severe sanctions and ridicule from their peers, both male and female. This, in itself, would be reason for therapeutic intervention, but there are other reasons. As Rekers (1978) has pointed out, longitudinal data indicate that pronounced effeminate behavior in boys has been related to gender-identity problems when these children become adults. These problems are often accompanied by social and psychological difficulties and are, by and large, resistant to treatment. Thus, in order to prevent these later sexual orientation disturbances and associated adjustment problems, treatment of gender-identity difficulties should be instituted as early as possible.

Relatively little is known about the factors that enter into the development of gender-identity problems, but some of the factors that may be responsible have been identified in a study by Hetherington (1965). She found that in families characterized as "mother-dominant," boys were more likely to imitate their mothers' behavior than their fathers' and that they demonstrated less pronounced masculine sex-role preferences than boys in "father-dominant" families. This would be consistent with the literature on observational learning (Bandura, 1977), which shows that children are most likely to model themselves after those adults who have the greatest control over the dispensing of reinforcers. It would therefore seem that the mother and her behavior would have to assume a focal role in the treatment of boys with cross-gender problems.

Treatment of Gender Problems   For the purpose of treatment, inappropriate gender behavior is construed as representing a behavior deficit in the sense that these children do not possess gender-appropriate responses in their repertoires. Accordingly, the treatment approach taken is not aimed at simply suppressing or eliminating the cross-gender behavior. This would leave the child without gender-appropriate responses. Instead, gender-appropriate responses must be taught to the child so that these can replace the responses which the social environment deems inappropriate. This is the approach taken by Rekers and his colleagues, who have been among the most active clinical investigators in this area (Rekers, 1975; Rekers & Lovaas, 1974; Rekers, Lovaas, & Low, 1975; Rekers, Yates, Willis, Rosen, & Taubman, 1976).

A program designed to strengthen the gender-appropriate behavior of a boy, while concurrently weakening the inappropriate, effeminate responses, was described by Rekers et al. (1975). The child, identified as "Carl," was 8 years, 8 months old and displayed a full repertoire of feminine behaviors. He had a pronounced feminine inflection and content in his speech, made excessively female gestures, and often stated that he preferred to be considered a girl. In school he tended to be disruptive and to relate in a teasing manner to other children. His peers called him "sissy" and "queer," and their ostracization had led to increasing social isolation and chronic unhappiness. Treatment took several forms and was carefully controlled in order to demonstrate its effectiveness. The boy's sex-typed verbal behavior was made the target of intervention during work at the clinic. Using the method of differential social reinforcement of speech content, masculine or neutral topics received the therapist's interest and attention, while feminine topics were ignored. This resulted in a marked decrease in feminine topics, accompanied by a decrease in the boy's use of feminine inflections, although the latter had not been a specific target of the intervention. The changes, however, were limited to the clinic setting. The treatment focus was therefore shifted to the child's home where the mother was taught to implement a system of token reinforcements for masculine play, gestures, and speech patterns. All of these changed in the desired direction but, again, the effect was limited to the setting where the training had taken place. At school, Carl still behaved in his old, inappropriate way.

The focus of treatment was now shifted to the school, where the child's teacher was trained to apply a response-cost procedure to what was termed the boy's "brat" behavior. Carl would start each day with a supply of ten points, which he stood to lose for creating a class disturbance, bossing or teasing another child, or behaving rudely to the teacher. These problems were of particular importance to the teacher. Once these had decreased, the system was extended to cover the boy's feminine mannerisms. After a total of 15 months of this treatment program, Carl's feminine behaviors had become markedly reduced; he had developed a masculine interest pattern; and his overall social and emotional adjustment showed major improvement. When he was transferred to a different school in order to remove him from the children who had known him as a "sissy and queer" and among whom he still had that reputation, the new teacher considered him to be as well adjusted and well accepted as any other child in her class.

Because Carl had a severe lack of gender-appropriate social skills, there now ensued an additional 15-month period during which he was taught games and sports considered appropriate for boys of his age. A young man was provided with whom Carl formed a "buddy" relationship because, lacking a stable relationship with a new stepfather, Carl had only limited access to gender-appropriate role models. With all of these efforts, the therapeutic gains won during treatment were shown to have been maintained when the boy was evaluated a year later, when he was 12 years and 2 months old.

The Generalization of Treatment Effects

In the discussion of the case of Carl we noted that the changes in his behavior that had been brought about in the clinic failed to be manifested in his home or at school until he had also received treatment in those settings. From a theoretical standpoint, it is not surprising that responses learned under one set of stimulus conditions are not automatically emitted under other stimulus conditions. In fact, such assessment techniques as reversal and multiple baseline designs (see Chapter 6) are predicated on the assumption that responses are contingency specific. Generalization of treatment effects should not be expected to occur automatically. A child who has learned a new set of responses in the clinic will not necessarily demonstrate these at home or in school. This is why much of child behavior therapy has been moved out of the atypical setting of the consulting room into the typical settings where children spend most of their lives (Tharp & Wetzel, 1969). Where this is not possible, explicit plans must be made for generalization by building relevant procedures into the treatment program. As Stokes and Baer (1977) have pointed out, this can be done in a variety of ways. Among these are training different responses in different settings and at different points in time; transferring the management of contingencies from the therapist to persons in the child's natural environment (Miller & Sloane, 1976); using partial or, occasionally, noncontingent reinforcement; introducing mediating stimuli that can be verbal in nature and can be present in different situations. Such procedures will not only assure generalization of the treatment effect but they should also serve to maintain this effect over time. These are issues about which behavior therapists are showing increasing concern (Keeley, Shemberg, & Carbonell, 1976; Kent & O'Leary, 1976).

RECAPITULATION

Fears and phobias are best conceptualized as responses that are mediated by a complex set of reactions we label anxiety. While it is possible to demonstrate that a fear response can be acquired, it is not necessary to know how a specific fear was acquired in order to treat it. School phobia is one of the most common of these problems and because it interferes with a child's education, early treatment is very important. The sooner such treatment is instituted and the sooner the child is returned to school, the more likely it is that that problem can be reversed. Several kinds of treatment have been demonstrated to be effective with fears and phobias. These include those based on classical and operant conditioning principles, observational learning, and cognitive interventions. It is possible that many child phobias will dissipate in time, but their disabling characteristics and secondary consequences would seem to argue for early treatment.

One of the consequences of fears and phobias is social isolation, but this can also come about because the child lacks the social skills appropriate for his or her age and sex. Treatment is therefore usually directed at teaching these skills and this can be done both directly, by selectively reinforcing appropriate behaviors, and indirectly, by exposing the child to models who display such behavior.

Psychotic Behavior: Early Infantile Autism

The word *psychotic*, as we shall use it here, is meant to communicate only that the problem in question represents a profound disturbance of behavior. The word is far too vague to be used in any other fashion, and a reference to a child as psychotic says no more than that the child is very severely disturbed. Beyond that, we have to look for more specific terms in order to discuss profoundly disturbed children in a coherent fashion. *Early infantile autism* is one such term. Another, describing a distinctly different form of disorder, is *childhood schizophrenia*.

EARLY INFANTILE AUTISM

There is a great deal of confusion in the professional literature about the use of the word *autism*. In its original sense, autism refers to a distorted, self-centered form of thinking that is controlled by the thinker's needs or desires and bears little relation to external reality; the form of thinking which takes place in dreams, daydreams, and fantasy. As such, autism is a normal phenomenon, provided the person who engages in such thinking is able to differentiate between reality and fantasy and as long as autistic distortions of reality do not come to control the person's behavior.

When people act on the basis of their autistic productions—taking them, as it were, for perception of reality—they become unable to cope adaptively with the demands of the environment; their behavior would then be classified as *psychotic*. The profoundly disordered, psychotic child probably engages in autistic thinking; yet, the term *autistic child* is not synonymous with psychotic child. To reduce the possible confusion, the term autism, in the context of disturbed behavior, should be used only when it is intended to refer to that highly specific and quite rare form of profoundly disordered behavior whose full technical name is *early infantile autism*.

Early infantile autism was first described and named by Leo Kanner (1943), who, in his psychiatric practice, had encountered a small number of children who displayed a cluster of behaviors that made them appear to belong to a unique group. While Kanner's medical orientation led him to view this behavior cluster as a syndrome defining a disease entity, there is, at this point, no reliable psychometric evidence to support the existence of such an entity. As Masters and Miller (1970) have pointed out, there has, as yet, been no valid, empirical demonstration of early infantile autism as anything more than a construct based on a hypothesized inter-relationship among observable events. These observable events characterize the group of children who fall under the rubric of early infantile autism, and one can discuss these behavioral characteristics without assuming that they define a disease entity.

Characteristics of the Autistic Child

As its name implies, early infantile autism occurs in a child's early infancy. Parents usually report that their child displayed behavior deficits and was "different" from the moment of birth. They recall that the child failed to anticipate being picked up and reacted as if other people did not exist. As these children grow older, this *autistic aloneness* takes the form of an absence of interpersonal behavior. They do not emit the social smile, seem not to recognize members of the family, and do not engage in such social games as peek-a-boo or pat-a-cake. They will fail to develop appropriate language; a deficiency or gross distortion of speech for purposes of communication is one of the most frequently reported characteristics of autistic children. Another, is their pronounced insistence on sameness, coupled with a stereotyped preoccupation with a limited number of inanimate objects to which they often cling with great tenacity. Despite these marked behavior deviations, medical examinations reveal no gross neurological impairment, and the children's physical development usually proceeds normally.

When Ward (1970) reviewed the available literature, he found that the above characteristics are generally agreed upon as defining early infantile autism, al-though, as we shall see, there continues to be much disagreement regarding the etiology of this condition—if indeed it is *a* condition in the sense of being a unitary behavior disorder that can be reliably discriminated from other profound dis-turbances in child behavior.

Children who display all four of the defining characteristics just presented—

early onset of austistic aloneness, absence or distortion of language, stereotyped insistence on sameness, and lack of demonstrable physical defect—are exceedingly rare. It has been estimated that less than 1 percent of the clinic population in a large child psychiatric center meets the criteria for being appropriately called cases of early infantile autism (Kanner, 1958). Careless usage of this term has led to its application to children who manifest profound behavior deviations without meeting the necessary defining characteristics, and this has contributed to confounding the issue and complicating needed research. Until there is general agreement among clinicians and research investigators as to what children to include in a given category, little progress can be expected.

Despite its rarity, early infantile autism has attracted a great deal of clinical and scientific interest, largely because of the assumption that detailed study of grossly deviant development might lead to a better understanding of the principles underlying normal development. For example, the language peculiarity of autistic children raises the question how children, in general, acquire the appropriate use of pronouns. The few autistic children who develop language frequently manifest *pronominal reversal*; they will repeat personal pronouns the way they hear them, thus speaking of themselves as "you" and of the person addressed as "I." A moment's reflection on how difficult it is to correct a child who speaks in this manner ("No, you should not say you, you should say I") highlights the as yet unanswered question of how normal children master the correct usage of I and you. Whether the study of deviant development will indeed contribute to an understanding of normal development is, of course, a question only the future can answer. It would seem more logical to expect that the proper study of normal development is normal development and to assume that full understanding of normal processes will permit the prediction and control (understanding) of deviant processes. Be that as it may, infantile autism presents enough of a problem in its own right to warrant study for its own sake and for the sake of the children whose grossly deviant behavior gets them placed in this category.

Etiological Speculations

Early infantile autism has been attributed to a wide variety of causes, ranging from strictly environmental (Ferster, 1961) to purely constitutional (Rimland, 1964), with interactional formulations (Zaslow & Breger, 1969) taking the middle ground. Each of these positions points to a treatment approach that is logically consistent with the causal speculations, and positive results reported with the treatment approach are often taken as support for the causal speculation.

The logical fallacy in this reasoning should be recognized before we take a look at some representative theorizing. The fact that one can modify a given maladaptive behavior through the application of principles of operant conditioning, for example, does not provide proof that these principles were operating when the maladaptive behavior originally developed. The only way a casual sequence can ever become known is to trace the development of a disorder from its onset on the basis of careful and complete longitudinal observations of a large enough number of cases to permit the generalization that all cases of this nature develop in this way. Retrospective reconstruction, based on mothers' recalls of the events in their children's earliest days, has been shown to possess neither reliability (Wenar, 1961) nor validity (Robbins, 1963). Nor is the demonstration that isolated "autistic" behavior, such as head banging, can be shaped in monkeys through operant techniques (Schaefer, 1970) more than a provocative analogue.

Ultimately, speculations about etiology are by nature theoretical, and theories can never be proved, in the sense that they can be shown to be true or false. Theories are only as good as their capacity to order available facts and to permit the generation of testable hypotheses. It is by these criteria that the following formulations should be judged.

Environmental Formulations The most detailed statement of a purely environmentalist hypothesis about the development of early infantile autism is that presented by Ferster (1961), who uses infantile autism as synonymous with "childhood schizophrenia," which, in turn, he views as a prototype of adult schizophrenia. Despite this rather idiosyncratic terminology, Ferster's description of the children he discusses makes it clear that he is talking about early infantile autism, as usually defined.

Ferster examines the major characteristics of the autistic child's behavior from the standpoint of functional analysis, which leads him to ask what specific effects the child's behavior has on the environment and how these effects maintain autistic behavior. He observes that the behavioral repertoire of the autistic child is limited and that the absolute amount of activity is low. In fact, he believes that the principal difference between the autistic child and the normal child is in the relative frequency of behavior. The major performance deficit of autistic children, according to Ferster, lies in the degree to which their behavior is a function of the behavior of others. He points out that the limited speech of the autistic child is not maintained by its effect on the social environment; it does not benefit the listener (as would the communication of a descriptive statement) but results in immediate benefit to the speaker (as does a statement of a demand). When the child's behavior has an effect on the environment, it usually does so because the behavior is an aversive stimulus for others. This is the case with such atavisms as tantrums and self-destructive, self-mutilating behavior, which often occur at relatively high frequency. The rest of the autistic child's performance is of a simple sort, having only slight effect on the environment, such as finger flipping, twisting soft objects, or rubbing a smooth surface. The strongest reinforcing stimuli are food, candy, or ice cream, while secondary reinforcers are weak, and generalized social reinforcers, such as a smile or adult approval, seem to maintain little of the autistic child's behavior. The range of responses and of effective reinforcers is thus severely limited. Equally minimal appears to be the autistic child's perceptual repertoire. A limited set of stimuli control his or her behavior, and an increase in stimulus complexity disrupts this control.

Ferster proposes that all of the characteristics of autistic children can be viewed as having developed as the result of their reinforcement history, that is, the circumstances in the early life of these children. If the difference between the autistic child and the normal child is in the frequency with which given behavior occurs, a functional analysis will ask how the response frequency is affected by the effect responses have on the environment. The answer is that when behavior is not reinforced or is reinforced only intermittently, it will be emitted at low frequency, may fail to develop, or may become extinguished. This would be the case where parents fail to respond to the child or do so on an erratic schedule. Ferster speculates that parents who are preoccupied with behavior that is prepotent over caretaking activities or whose own repertoire is disrupted by somatic disturbances, diseases, or depression are parents who find dealing with a child aversive and less rewarding than alternative activities.

When parents fail to respond to a child's behavior when it is emitted at low magnitude, it may undergo extinction; but when they then selectively attend to such high-magnitude responses as tantrums, these come to be strengthened, resulting in the relatively low frequency of social behaviors and in the relatively high frequency of atavisms. At the same time, children who find their parents only occasionally presenting them with reinforcing stimuli will discover that their behavior has a consistent and predictable effect on the nonsocial, physical environment. The doorknob at the end of a string exerts a mild pull whenever the string is jerked, and while this pulling effect is a weak reinforcing stimulus, its durability and ready availability in the face of the absence of stronger, social reinforcers acts to maintain the string-jerking behavior. Furthermore, the parents are not likely to interfere with such noiseless, nonirritating behavior, while they may actively discourage behavior that would have a greater effect on the environment, such as handling household objects, playing with toys, or moving objects about the house. This, Ferster believes, accounts for the fact that a large part of the autistic child's repertoire consists of behaviors that have small, limited effects on the physical environment. By similar reasoning, he sees the child's reduced overall performance as interfering with the development and effectiveness of acquired conditioned and generalized reinforcers.

As Ferster (1961) points out, the range of responses and of effective reinforcers is severely limited in the case of autistic children. Equally limited is the range of stimuli that control these children's behavior. A somewhat different way of saying this is that much of the environment of autistic children lacks meaning for them. As Lovaas, Schreibman, and Koegel (1974) have stressed, the meaning that the world has for a person determines, among other things, what will be perceived as rewarding and what as punishing. Beyond such primary reinforcers as food and such primary punishers as pain, most of the consequences that affect our behavior are acquired, secondary reinforcers and punishers, such as smiles and frowns. It is easy to appreciate that a child for whom smiles and frowns do not have acquired stimulus value will have a very atypical development, particularly in terms of social interaction. Ferster's analysis, then, pinpoints as central to autistic children's pervasive behavioral deficits their failure to acquire secondary reinforcers and punishers. A series of experiments by Ferster and DeMyer (1962) and laboratory studies by Lovaas and his colleagues (1974) demonstrated that careful attention to the nature of stimuli and reinforcers permits one to teach new responses to autistic children. This has had important clinical implications to which we shall return later.

The limited number of stimuli that control the autistic child's behavior is, according to Ferster's formulations, the result of the narrow range of conditions under which the child's behavior is reinforced. Where this is the case, behavior would not be emitted under conditions that are dissimilar from those under which it was learned, and sudden shifts in stimuli are likely to elicit emotional responses that may interfere with established performance. Ferster cites a case where a child's behavior became disrupted when a previously constant companion, a babysitter, suddenly departed.

Ferster concludes his hypothetical analysis of the development of infantile autism by stressing the cumulative effects of behavioral deficits. During the first four years of a child's life, the parents can have such exclusive control over the conditions reinforcing the child's behavior that their atypical contingency management could produce the gross behavioral deficits seen in the autistic child. Once such children become exposed to the larger community after age 4, they are unlikely to develop normal behavioral repertoires because the community tends to reinforce only age-appropriate behavior. To make it possible for a parent to have exclusive control over a child's contingencies of reinforcement, Ferster has to postulate that the child's environment contains a limited number of such people as siblings, relatives, and neighbors, who could attenuate the social isolation where one parent might be the sole source of reinforcement. Accordingly, he expects that severely disturbed autistic children are, in general, firstborn children raised in physically or socially isolated families.

While available data (Wing, 1966) support the speculation that the majority (54 percent) of autistic children are firstborn, we have no information to support the contention that autistic children come from isolated homes or from families where one parent is largely absent. Nor does the available literature support the presence of the postulated parental characteristics which call for general disruption of the parental behavior repertoire and a prepotency of other than child-caring performances, resulting in a large amount of intermittent reinforcement of the child's day-to-day behavior. It must, furthermore, be recalled that children reared in understimulating, overcrowded institutions where behavior is likely to be reinforced on highly erratic, intermittent schedules have never been reported as developing early infantile autism, although they do display limited behavior repertoires and cognitive defects. Pending the accumulation of the kind of objective assessment and direct observations called for in Ferster's provocative paper, his formulations must be considered no more than challenging hypotheses that would, if confirmed, make parental behavior the sole factor causing the development of early infantile autism.

The Fallacy of Holding the Parents Culpable   Ferster's operant formulations, derived from Skinner's (1953) view of human behavior, bear a remarkable similarity to the theorizing of such traditional psychoanalysts as Bettelheim (1967) in that both consider infantile autism as primarily the result of parental behavior. Bettelheim views the parental environment as responsible for the fact that the child is not exposed to experiences that are vital for normal development. While Bettelheim invokes unconscious maternal wishes that the child did not exist and Ferster prefers to make no such motivational assumptions, both formulations lead to the conclusion that the parents are to blame for the fact that their child is autistic.

The parents of autistic children are often described as of better than average, frequently superior intelligence. There is said to be a high incidence of professionals with graduate degrees among them. They are frequently pictured as "emotionally cold," introspective, detached, and excessively objective. Their child-rearing practices are said to be characterized by a "mechanization" of parent-child relations. Rimland (1964) searched the available literature for support for these descriptions and found that the picture of the cold, reserved, efficient, and highly intelligent parent was present in most reports. While the descriptions of these parents tend to be consistent in many cases, one must not lose sight of the fact that these parental characteristics may be an artifact, especially since more careful assessment fails to confirm the hypothesis that parents of autistic children are intellectually brilliant and emotionally cold (Wolff & Morris, 1971). None of these parents are ever seen until *after* their child has been diagnosed as autistic, and by that time they have usually been living with the grossly atypical behavior of this child for several years. At that point, it is not surprising that they are found to be "disdainful of frivolity, humorless" (Rimland, 1964, p. 25) and that the interaction with their child is remarkably different from the expected norm. A study by Klebanoff (1959) strongly suggests that having a seriously disturbed child affects maternal attitudes to child-rearing and that a formulation that views these attitudes as contributing to the child's disturbance may be reversing the casual sequence.

Why should one find the repeated reports of the high intelligence and graduate education among parents of autistic children? Obviously, having an autistic child will not make the parents more intelligent or better educated. Here the direction of influence must be from parent to child—or must it? It is entirely possible that the high parental intelligence of autistic children represents a bias in selection. As we have said, true cases of early infantile autism are exceedingly rare. This means that most family physicians and pediatricians and few psychiatrists and psychologists will have had experience with such children. Many may thus be misdiagnosed as deaf, brain-injured, or mentally retarded, thus never coming to the notice of those who study and write about early infantile autism. Who, then , are the children who do come to the attention of those relatively few specialists who know about early infantile autism? Might it not be the children of parents who are sophisticated enough not to accept the first professional diagnosis, who read about other possibilities, who have the knowledge and the financial resources to seek professional advice at one of the major medical centers in this country where the specialists who study and write about early infantile autism are located? If this were the case, then these specialists would be getting to see primarily those autistic children whose parents are intelligent, educated, and reasonably well-to-do. One has to be extremely careful in drawing conclusions from correlations. If two phenomena are observed to occur together with some regularity, it does not necessarily mean that one causes the other, and one certainly cannot tell which causes which.

Any theoretical speculation about the basis of early infantile autism that seeks to find causation in the parental characteristics described must also deal with the following facts: where autistic children have siblings, these are almost invariably described as normal; autistic characteristics are present from the time of birth; and the sex ratio among autistic children is of the order of 3 or 4 boys to 1 girl. Finally, there is the fact that when sets of twins are autistic, these are almost invariably identical pairs. Rimland (1964), who reviewed all 200 or so "bonafide cases of autism referred to in the literature" (p. 57), identified eleven monozygotic twins—concordant for infantile autism. It all seems to suggest that in seeking *the* cause of early infantile autism (if, indeed, there is such an entity), one has to look beyond a strictly environmentalist answer.

Biological Formulations   At the pole opposite the environmentalist position of such theorists as Bettelheim and Ferster stands the neurophysiological speculation of Rimland (1964). That writer concluded from a thorough review of the available literature that infantile autism can be traced to one single critical deficiency in the child's cognitive function—an impaired ability to relate new stimuli to remembered experience. Children with such an impairment would be severely limited in deriving benefit from their experience, each event being, as it were, totally new and without relation to anything that transpired in the past. As a result, they would be unable to understand relationships or to think in terms of such abstractions as symbols, concepts, and analogies. Unable to integrate sensations into a comprehensible whole, they would perceive the world as vague, obscure, overwhelming, and frightening. Since there would be little or no carry-over of an experience with a given individual from one occasion to the next, people would fail to acquire meaning, and interpersonal relationships would be impossible.

The postulated basic deficit in relating perceptions to memory would also explain the language difficulties of autistic children and why many of them do no more than parrot words they have just heard, a phenomenon called *echolalia*. The characteristic insistence on sameness—near panic when even minor changes are made in their surroundings—and stereotyped preoccupation with inanimate objects can be viewed as attempts on the part of these children to minimize the confusing effects of their deficit. It is likely that even with their impairment, stimuli that are presented in identical fashion time and time again will eventually come to be associated with their consequences so that change or removal of these stimuli would elicit an emotional response.

In addition to postulating the cognitive defect that might mediate the behavior of autistic children, Rimland (1964) speculates on the nature of the physiological basis of this defect. He suggests that the reticular formation of the brainstem is the structure whose integrity is crucial for the integration of memory with current perceptions and assumes that damage to this structure manifests itself in the impairment shown by autistic children. On the basis of his reading of the available literature, Rimland further suggests that an excess of oxygen during early infancy might be responsible for the reticular damage. Since there are great individual differences in reactivity to oxygen, even the oxygen level naturally available in the atmosphere might exceed the tolerance level of some genetically predisposed infants.

Rimland thus goes further than most other theorists with biological orientations in speculating about the specific part of the brain that is impaired and about how this impairment came about. When one observes the grossly atypical behavior of autistic children, it is not too farfetched to assume that something is going on in their brains that results in this behavior. Memory, perception, language, and learning are obviously functions of the brain and when these are disturbed, something in the brain must not be functioning the way it should. Whether one wishes to speculate about this depends on one's choice of scientific strategy. A psychologist can legitimately concentrate on studies of memory, perception, learning, and language without being concerned about the physiological events that underlie these functions. Neurophysiologists, on the other hand, have a legitimate task in studying how the body produces behavior. Ultimately, the facts uncovered by the neurophysiologist and those established by the psychologist must be fit together in order to produce a comprehensive theory of human life. We are a long way from such a synthesis.

After some 15 years of studying autistic children and following their development, a group of investigators at Indiana University Medical Center (DeMyer, Barton, DeMyer, Norton, Allen, & Steele, 1973) concluded that their work, in conjunction with that of others, supports the "biological cause theory of autism, even though the exact nature of the cause is unknown" (p. 242). They would "locate the brain as the site of the abnormality" (ibid.) and "place the bulk of infantile autistic or psychotic cases with the neurologically handicapped who have severe learning disorders" (ibid.). They say that it is the learning disorder which interferes with the autistic child's acquisition of language and with other crucial learning. This is a very conservative formulation with which it is difficult to disagree. Rimland (1964) had gone considerably beyond this in his purely theoretical speculations.

The hypotheses advanced by Rimland, though plausible on the basis of available knowledge, require careful scientific investigation before they can be viewed as correct explanations for the development and nature of early infantile autism. The theory has the merit of accounting for the available facts, listed earlier, and, like other biological formulations, it has the advantage of not placing blame for the condition on the behavior of the child's parents.

In Rimland's formulation, early infantile autism stems from a basic cognitive defect, the inability to relate present sensory stimuli to past experience. This would explain the phenomenon of autistic aloneness on the basis that the child is unable to acquire interpersonal attachments because the stimulus constellation represented by the mother and other persons fails to become associated with pleasurable experiences. This, in turn, would explain the absence of the social smile (of recognition), anticipatory movements to being picked up, and the failure to enjoy simple interpersonal games. Failure in the development of such affective components of behavior as pleasure is thus seen as secondary to failure in the development of necessary associations. When Kanner (1943) first described autistic disturbances, he emphasized the affective component as central to the problem and, in fact, referred to it as an inborn affective disturbance. The issue whether infantile autism is an associational deficit *or* an affective deficit is resolved in a formation presented by DesLauriers and Carlson (1969), who reason that sensory *and* affective processes might be defective in the case of children in the category of early infantile autism.

To account for the combination of sensory and affective difficulties that they attribute to autistic children, DesLauriers and Carlson (1969) postulate a neurophysiological mechanism involving two arousal systems. One of these, presumably located in the brainstem reticular formation, is postulated as serving as the source of activation and energy, while the others, thought to be found in the limbic-midbrain system, is seen as mediating incentive, reward, and positive reinforcement functions. The formulation requires that these two arousal systems operate in reciprocal fashion in order for learning to occur. When this reciprocity is unbalanced, as the result of an inborn organic deficiency, such gross developmental disorders as are found in autistic children will result.

Their theoretical formulation led DesLauriers and Carlson (1969) to describe a treatment approach which is designed to overcome or compensate for the defective arousal mechanism. The approach centers on efforts to expose the autistic child to "high-impact, affective stimulation of a consistent, persistent, and well-structured nature" (p. 67) in order to overcome the postulated problem with the arousal system. The high-impact stimulation advocated by these authors is best obtained through the child's tactile, proprioceptive, and kinesthetic sense receptors; thus, their form of therapy entails a lot of close physical contact with the child.

The emphasis on near receptors (those involving direct contact with the body) as opposed to distance receptors (sight, hearing, and smell) derives from the conviction of DesLauriers and Carlson that the developmentally and phylogenetically more primitive near receptors play a vital role in helping the child differentiate and separate himself as an individual—to form what they call a "body image" which they describe "as the sum total of physical, sensory contacts between the child and the mother" and view as "the instrument of relationship and communication between these two" (pp. 13f.). For normal development to take place, there has to be a bodily interaction between mother and infant, with the infant seeking stimulation and the parent responding. These authors suggest that infantile autism develops because the child" not only does not reach out for human contacts, he is also unreachable by those around him who try to contact him" (p. 15). The autistic child does not take the initiative in seeking the stimulation that is necessary if adequate parental responding is to be elicited. Not only does the parent have no response to give "but the incentive to give a response progressively dies, and the parent eventually appears just as distant from the child as the child is from the parent" (p. 15). This formulation is similar to that of *attachment defect*, to be discussed below.

In their emphasis on near receptors, DesLauriers and Carlson are in agreement with a hypothesis advanced by Schopler (1965), who was also led to recommend a form of treatment aimed at stimulating near receptors through bodily contact. One of the most salutary consequences of this formulation is that treatment becomes not an arcane ritual performed in the secrecy of the playroom but an educational process in which the child's family and teachers are urged to participate. They are instructed to provide highly impactful, affective stimulation and to offer the child a wide variety of sensory experiences through tactile, kinesthetic, and proprioceptive contacts. Parents are encouraged to engage in the same playful interactions they would with a normal child, except that they are to do so more forcefully, more playfully, more persistently, "just more of everything" (p. 171). At the same time as this playful, joyful interaction is forced upon the child in a highly intrusive manner, the adult is expected to impose controls on the child's behavior; preventing disorganized, purposeless, and aimless activity.

DesLauriers and Carlson (1969) describe their work with five young autistic children with whose treatment they were remarkably successful. Such success, however, cannot be adduced as evidence for the validity of their theory, which thus remains no more than a provocative speculation. Another, even more speculative formulation of how autistic children come to be autistic was advanced by Moore and Shiek (1971). Taking their cue from the reputedly superior intelligence of the parents of autistic children, they assume that these children ought to have the genetic potential for being of very high intelligence themselves. Could it be, they ask, that these children are already so advanced in their intellectual development during the foetal stage that learning takes place in the intrauterine environment? If this were the case, they argue, what these yet-to-be born children would be learning would be related to the sameness, rhythmic movements, and limited stimulation which exist in the uterus. When they are then born, these children are already "imprinted" on the intrauterine environment and therefore unable to learn from the more complex world in which they now live. Such speculations are incapable of being put to test, and they therefore stand only as an example of theorizing at the biological end of the environmentalist-constitutionalist continuum.

An Interactionist Formulation   A theoretical speculation about the development of early infantile autism that bears a certain similarity to that advanced by

DesLauriers and Carlson (1969) is one offered by Zaslow and Breger (1969). Extrapolating from the observations of ethologists and other students of the early development of nonhuman species, these authors point out that an essential step in social development is the formation of the infant's attachment to the mother. They postulate that this formation of attachment does not take place in the case of the autistic child. Attachment, they suggest, is a function of the early infant-mother interaction to which the infant contributes as much as the mother. Autistic children, they speculate, are less "cuddly" than the average baby, the quality of "cuddlyness" presumably being a normally distributed, constitutional trait. When an infant who is low in cuddlyness happens to have a mother who redoubles her efforts at physical contact with her baby, the child's development may well be unremarkable. On the other hand, when the mother reacts to this constitutional quality of her child by reducing her physical contact—thus depriving the infant of the kinesthetic, tactual, visual, and auditory stimuli associated with being held— the child will be unable to form the crucial attachment which, in part, derives from being held while passing through periods of stress and rage.

This theoretical speculation of Zaslow and Breger thus points to a *mismatch* between infant and mother as the source of infantile autism. The child is low in cuddlyness, and the mother reduces her contact with the child, who, in turn, is deprived of the stimuli associated with being held which are particularly crucial for the formation of attachment during episodes of intense arousal. The failure to form attachment then leads to the characteristic autistic phenomena. The child will not learn the social smile, will fail to acquire language, and will be unable to relate to the social environment. Instead, humans will be actively avoided, and the child will attempt to master the nonhuman environment on his or her own terms. This formulation would thus account for the three foremost characteristics of the autistic child: absence of language, autistic aloneness, and preservation of sameness.

Their emphasis on the importance of being physically held during periods of rage and stress leads Zaslow and Breger to a therapeutic approach, the "rage reduction method," which emphasizes holding the child in close body contact until rage episodes subside. They view it as essential that the therapist establish the fact that the adult is "in charge," thus interrupting the child's so-called negativistic response system, which centers around self-initiated, self-maintained actions.

As far as the rage-reduction method of treating autistic children is concerned, we have a report by Saposnek (1972), who compared one session of this method with one session of more traditional therapeutic contact, using two matched samples of fifteen autistic children each. This investigator states that only the rage-reduction group showed significant positive change in terms of approaching the therapist and maintaining eye contact. In a more general sense, this form of treatment is reported to work for some children (Zaslow & Breger, 1969), but its long-range effectiveness has not been demonstrated. Even if it had, the effectiveness of treatment would again not be a test of the validity of the rather loose causal speculations on which it is based. It must also be stressed that inducing rage as a therapeutic stratagem would seem to be justifiable only if it could be shown that other, less drastic methods are ineffective and that rage-reduction is the only way of helping a child. As an example of an alternative, we cite the work of Marchant, Howling, Yule, and Rutter (1974), who report that they have increased the sociability and attachment to people of two autistic children by introducing slight and gradual changes in their environment aimed at reducing their attachment to objects.

Inductive or Deductive Logic?   The speculations about the etiology of early infantile autism discussed thus far were largely developed by observing the behavioral deficits of autistic children and trying to infer what might have caused their problem. This inductive process led Rimland to a strictly biological model and Ferster to a model that is purely environmental in nature. Other formulations fell somewhere between these extremes, some, like Zaslow and Breger proposing an interaction between biological and environmental factors. As is true of any product of inductive inference, the validity of these formulations cannot be put to a definitive test. Another approach to exploring the problems of autistic children takes the form of deductive reasoning. Here, one begins with facts about behavior, in general, which have already been established through laboratory research and then tests, by further laboratory studies, how these facts apply in the specific case of autistic children. This approach takes time because it entails a piecing together of relatively small bits of research findings. At any one point, conclusions about the nature of autism are at best tentative. No impressive theoretical edifice can be displayed in its complete form because, as is always the case in science, that edifice is continually "under construction." We turn, in the following, to one such project that begins and ends in the psychological laboratory and which, while possibly less satisfying than a complete theoretical model, has the advantage of empirical support.

Early Infantile Autism and the Development of Attention

If we are to respond to the world around us in an adaptive fashion, we must be capable of noticing the relevant aspects of that world. An object is not a stimulus unless it is noticed and a response consequence cannot function as a reinforcer unless we have noticed that it appeared as a result of our action. A model cannot teach us anything unless we notice what he or she is doing. One can interpret all this noticing as *attention*, which is a highly useful construct when one wishes to study human behavior (Berlyne, 1970).

It is well to distinguish two aspects of attention: *intensive* aspects and *selective* aspects. Each plays an important role in our ability to learn about the environment and thus to cope effectively with its demands.

The *intensive* aspects of attention are *arousal*, *attentiveness*, and *degree of concentration* (Berlyne, 1970). Arousal may be viewed as distributed along the continuum from sleep to wakefulness. It has physiological correlates in heart rate and electrical activity of the brain and can therefore be quantified and measured. Attentiveness has to do with a person's momentary readiness to receive and process stimuli. It is not the same thing as arousal; for in extreme states of arousal (as in high excitement) a person's attentiveness to minor variations in external stimuli is often very low. The third of the intensive aspects of attention, degree of concentration, has to do with whether a person attends to a wide or a narrow range of incoming stimuli. The intensive aspects of attention then tell us how much attention a person is giving to the stimulus field as a whole.

The *selective* aspects of attention, as identified by Berlyne (1970), deal with the question how the amount of attention a person is giving to the stimulus field comes to be distributed among the various aspects of that field. Here, it is useful to distinguish three processes: *exploratory behavior*, *abstraction*, and *selective attention*. The first of these, exploratory behavior, entails the physical act of directing the sense organ toward the sources of stimulation, as in moving the eyes in the direction of a visual event or bringing the nose to a flower one wishes to smell. The difference between looking and seeing should remind us that exploratory behavior is not the same as attention. Abstraction has to do with the process whereby a person attends to one dimension of an object while ignoring other dimensions of the same object. This would be involved when we attend to the color of a poker chip, while ignoring its size, shape, weight, and texture. Lastly, we come to selective attention itself which, according to Berlyne (1970), should be the only process we should be referring to when we speak of attention.

At any given moment a person is exposed to stimulation from a great many sources and through every sense receptor. Visual, auditory, tactual, kinesthetic, and proprioceptive nerve fibers are constantly carrying impulses which often demand conflicting, mutually incompatible responses. Behavioral chaos would result if we were not equipped with the capacity to select among these impulses and to attend—thus be prepared to respond—to one or a limited number at a time. To do this we use selective attention, which is therefore a highly adaptive capacity. A defect in this capacity should make learning very difficult, if not impossible (Ross, 1976).

The Development of Selective Attention   Studies of the development of normal children (Conroy & Weener, 1976; Hagen & Hale, 1973; Salapatek & Kessen, 1973; Stevenson, 1972) have demonstrated that a child's ability to attend selectively to specific aspects of the stimulus field develops over time and does not seem to reach its optimal level until just before adolescence. As with all other developmental phenomena, one finds individual differences; some children develop selective attention more quickly, others more slowly than the rest, and a few may remain at quite immature levels for a long time or throughout their lives.

The very young child is "captured" by one aspect of the stimulus field and attends to it to the relative exclusion of all others. But even in infancy one can discern individual differences, with some infants consistently orienting toward a single feature, while others alternate their gaze between single and multiple features (Salapatek & Kessen, 1973). Studies of eye movements have shown that until about age 6, children generally restrict their scanning of a stimulus to a limited area (Vurpillot, 1968). During these early years, children seem to attend to the world around them in an overexclusive manner and the nature of the simulus appears to be the major determinant of what aspect of it becomes the focus of their attention. There is probably little or no selectivity involved in this form of deploying attention, and we can refer to this mode as *overexclusive attention.*

In the next stage of their development, somewhere around age 4 or 5, children enter a period during which they seem to attend to many aspects of a stimulus situation; many more, in fact, than the minimum essential for efficient processing of the information available to them (Stevenson, 1972). We might call this *over-inclusive attention* and note that the child who uses this mode of attending well into school age might be viewed as distractible and would probably have trouble learning to read (Ross, 1976). True *selective attention* does not seem to become possible until around age 12. At that age, the normally developing person should be able to focus on those aspects of a stimulus complex that carry the information that is essential for responding to it in an adaptive manner. Irrelevant and incidental features can now be ignored but when the task changes and these features come to be defined as relevant, attention can be shifted to focus on them.

In line with this formulation, selective attention is the mature mode a person attains after having passed through earlier stages of overexclusive and over-inclusive attention. This development must be viewed as gradual; changes from one mode to the next are not abrupt steps—they occur slowly during periods where the modes overlap. Difficulties in the course of the development of selective attention would manifest themselves in various ways, depending on the level at which the difficulty occurs and the demands that the environment makes on the child at that level. Overinclusive attention, as we have said, would interfere with the acquisition of reading where the child is supposed to focus attention on the shape of the printed letter and not on the myriad of other stimuli that are also present in the situation. Remaining in the overexclusive mode beyond earliest infancy, on the other hand, would interfere with all kinds of learning in a most profound manner because such children would not be able to associate different stimuli with one another, focusing, as they do, on only one stimulus at a time. The effect of this difficulty would be an inability to learn the recognition of people, the use of language, the consequences of behaviors, and the meaning of secondary reinforcers. In other words, such failure to develop beyond the overexclusive mode of attention might well result in the profound behavioral deficit we call early infantile autism.

There is fairly substantial research support for the formulation that early infantile autism is related to difficulties in the area of attention. Most of this research comes from the laboratories of Ivar Lovaas and his students. They have shown that children with early infantile autism manifest the phenomenon of overexclusive attention, which these investigators have variously referred to as stimulus overselectivity (Lovaas & Schreibman, 1971), overselective responding (Schreibman & Lovaas, 1973), overselective attention (Newsom & Lovaas, 1973), and selective responding (Lovaas, Schreibman, Koegel, & Rehm, 1971). Because none of these terms convey the fact that the responses of these children are much more a function of the stimulus characteristics that "capture" the child's attention than of any (voluntary or intentional) selection on the part of the child, overexclusive attention would seem to be a more felicitous term.

Lovaas et al. (1971) trained groups of autistic, retarded, and normal children to respond by a simple bar-press to a stimulus complex consisting of simultaneously presented auditory, visual, and tactile cues. Once the child had learned to discriminate the stimulus complex, the investigators examined which of the stimuli within the complex controlled the response by introducing test trials on which only one of the three stimuli was presented. They found that the autistic children responded primarily to only one of the cues, while the normals responded uniformly to all three. The retarded group functioned between these two extremes. It was also shown that the problem of the autistic children was not that they were impaired in one or another sense modality; for with additional training they learned to respond to the individual cues to which they had previously not reacted. Since that original work, there have been additional studies that demonstrated the same phenomenon in a situation involving only two stimuli (Lovaas & Schreibman, 1971), and where all cues were in the visual (Koegel & Wilhelm, 1973) or auditory modality (Reynolds, Newsom, & Lovaas, 1974).

If one recognizes that learning involves the contiguous or near-contiguous pairing of two or more stimuli, failure to respond to one of these stimuli can be viewed as an important factor in the development of the difficulties manifested by the autistic child. As Lovaas and his colleagues (1971) point out, the acquisition of interpersonal and intellectual behavior is based on the prior acquisition of conditioned reinforcers, which involves their contiguous association with primary reinforcers. Furthermore, the establishment of appropriate affect may involve the contiguous presentation of two stimulus events so that the affect elicited by one of these events (the unconditioned stimulus) can come to be elicited by the other (the conditioned stimulus). Language acquisition, in terms of learning the meaning of words, again involves pairing of stimuli, as does the acquisition of new behavior through observational learning. If a child were to attend to only one of a complex of contiguously presented stimuli, a grossly impoverished behavioral repertoire, so typical of the autistic child, might be the expected outcome.

There are indications that the overexclusive attention of autistic children represents a developmental lag and not a permanent, irreversible defect in their cognitive abilities. Schover and Newsom (1976) demonstrated that autistic children respond to stimuli in the manner used by normal children at a younger age, while Schreibman, Koegel, and Craig (1977) succeeded in reducing overexclusion by continuing the testing of autistic children beyond the point where experimenters had usually stopped, thus providing these children with additional opportunities to learn. When Koegel and Schreibman (1977) used a differential reinforcement contingency, such that a child was reinforced only for responding to multiple cues but never for responding to a single cue, they were able to demonstrate that autistic children could learn to distinguish a multiple-cue complex from each of its two component parts. This suggests that we may eventually discover an efficient method for enhancing the development of attention. Until then, however, the treatment of autistic children should take their difficulty in attending to multiple stimuli into consideration. For instance, the usual practice of helping children learn by providing them with extra cues or prompts may be counterproductive with autistic children because they may attend exclusively to the prompt and not to the distinctive feature of the stimulus complex (Schreibman, 1975; Koegel & Rincover, 1976). Rincover and Koegel (1975) showed that a child who had apparently learned to respond to the request, "Touch your chin," had done so to the cue of the raising of the therapist's arm, meant to model chin-touching, and not to the verbal statement. When the verbal statement was later presented alone and in a different setting, the child failed to respond. These investigators point out that a therapist working with an autistic child must be sure that the child learns new behavior on the basis of the stimulus by which the therapist desires to achieve control, since otherwise the newly learned behavior may not generalize to other settings.

Attention and Treatment   It is of interest to note that DesLauriers and Carlson (1969) and Zaslow and Breger (1969) had arrived independently but simultaneously and by rather different theoretical routes at treatment approaches that have a great deal in common. Both groups emphasize stimulation of the near receptors, both stress the importance of high levels of stimulation (rage in one case, intense pleasure in the other), and both would have the therapist forcefully intrude in the children's autistic world and interrupt their stereotyped, repetitive behavior. Add to this the description of the operant learning approach used by Lovaas (1966), who has child and teacher sit with their heads about one foot apart and, when necessary, "the adult physically [prevents] the child from leaving the situation by holding the child's legs between his own legs" (p. 123). Near receptors are also stimulated in this approach when, in reinforcing a child for a correct response, the teacher places food directly into the child's mouth.

When different treatment methods all claim some degree of success, one would need to look at their common ingredient for a cue to what makes them effective. From the point of view of the formulation about the development of attention, it may well be that all of these methods in one way or another accommodate to the primitive mode of attention autistic children seem to be using. Near receptors, and particularly the sense of touch, represent far more focused stimulation than the distance receptors of vision and hearing. Near receptors also are developmentally more primitive; their development precedes that of the distance receptors both phylogenetically and ontogenetically. By intrusive insistence on tactile, kinesthetic, and proprioceptive stimulation under conditions of high affective excitation, these various forms of therapy may succeed in capturing the child's attention, which might otherwise be focused on something else.

Arousal Level   Several writers (e.g., DesLauriers & Carlson, 1969) see the need to expose the autistic child to high levels of stimulation as related to the child's arousal level. The construct *arousal* is, like many such constructs, rather vaguely defined. As used by Berlyne (1960), arousal motivates behavior in that the person seeks to maintain arousal at an optimal level. When arousal is below this optimal level, as in a state of boredom, the person will seek to increase stimulation and, hence, arousal; when arousal is above the optimal level, as in high excitement, the person will seek to reduce stimulation and, with it, arousal. It is further thought that learning is facilitated by high arousal, although extreme arousal disrupts the acquisition of new responses. If what is "optimal" varies from individual to individual, it would explain why some students of autistic children (e.g., Metz, 1967) report that these children seek higher-than-normal levels of stimulation, while others (e.g., Hutt, Hutt, Leed, & Ornsted, 1965) find that they are in a chronically high state of physiological arousal.

If one assumed that autistic children have a defective arousal system, it would suggest that some of them would require high-intensity stimulation for effective learning, while for others this would not be necessary. DesLauriers and Carlson recognized this when they differentiated between the hyposensitive and the hypersensitive autistic child. A study by Metz (1967) lends support to the assumption that some autistic children require a higher intensity of stimulation for effective learning than do normal children. He compared ten autistic, ten schizophrenic, and ten "outstandingly successful" children in a situation where they were able to control the volume of tape-recorded sound by operating a lever. The autistic children selected significantly higher volume settings than did the normal children, while the schizophrenic youngsters were more variable in their choice of settings.

It has been suggested that some of the atavistic, at times self-injurious behavior, such as rocking and head banging, represent a similar "turning up of input volume" on the part of the autistic child who is at a chronically low level of arousal and whose behavior is reinforced by the resulting high stimulation. While we know of no study, analogous to that of Metz, that demonstrates stimulus-reducing behavior on the part of autistic children, recollections about the early infancy of autistic children often include reports of such infants arching their body away from the people who attempted to hold them. This may represent the infants' avoidance responses to stimuli that are, to them, of too high an intensity, and thus aversive. Similarly, the frequent descriptions of autistic children who walk around covering their ears with their hands may tell of children trying to reduce stimulation to which they are hypersensitive.

Arousal, as Berlyne (1970) had pointed out, is one of the intensive aspects of attention and inasmuch as these various aspects are interrelated, formulations dealing with atypical arousal levels of autistic children and those that focus on a developmental lag in other aspects of attention are not incompatible.

Basic Defect or Developmental Disability?

Predictions about the development of autistic children depend on whether one views their condition as a basic defect or a developmental disability. If these children are defective in some fashion, one would expect their capacities to be severely limited, no matter what form of treatment was applied. If they have a developmental disability, on the other hand, one might expect that with appropriate teaching or training methods, instituted as early in the child's life as possible, they could be helped to function fairly adequately.

Unfortunately, research that might throw light on the nature of early infantile autism is made difficult by the fact that there is no general agreement on what children to include under this category and by the low incidence of this problem which limits the number of children any one investigator might study, even in a lifetime devoted to research. As a result, studies purporting to deal with early infantile autism often include children who do not display the four defining characteristics mentioned at the beginning of this chapter: early onset of autistic aloneness, absence or distortion of language, stereotyped insistence on sameness, and lack of demonstrable physical defect. Many studies, for example, label as autistic, children with obvious neurological disorders. Thus, Ritvo, Ornitz, and LaFranchi (1968), in a study of the repetitive behaviors in "early infantile autism and its variants," included among their fifteen subjects a child with chronic brain disease associated with phenylketonuria that had not been diagnosed until he was $4\frac{1}{2}$ years old. What all the children did have in common, in addition to the somewhat questionable diagnosis of early infantile autism, was a long history of repetitive behaviors.

The Ritvo et al. research showed that repetitive behaviors are not reactions to the environment but that they are initiated and maintained by involuntary processes in the central nervous system. This conclusion was based on analyses of motion pictures of the typically repetitive flapping, clapping, oscillating, and rocking movements of these children. The data showed a stable response rate from the beginning to the end of the episode. There was no speedup or slowdown in relation to changes in the child's presumed emotional state, as judged from his overt appearance. For all but body rocking, high consistency in rate was also noted when a given child's behavior was compared from one episode to the next and when comparisons between the rates of different children were made. One might assume that the variability in response rate within and between children would be far greater if, as some writers have held, the repetitive behavior were the symbolic representation of the child's hallucinatory fantasy. The authors of this study suggest that it is more likely that the behavior is involuntary and the result of a dysfunction (defect) of the central nervous system, possibly an imbalance between the excitatory and inhibitory control of motor responses. This view might lead one to fear that little can be done about these "involuntary" movements; yet, when Foxx and Azrin (1973b) and Rincover (1978) approached self-stimulatory, repetitive behaviors, such as head-weaving, hand-clapping, and object-mouthing, they were able to eliminate them by attending to their consequences.

Foxx and Azrin (1973b) and Foxx (1977) used a method they call *positive practice overcorrection*. This requires that the child engage in intensive practice of an overly correct form of appropriate behavior each time the self-stimulation is emitted. In the case of a 7-year-old autistic boy who clapped his hands almost continuously, the teacher instructed him to move his hands in one of five positions each time he engaged in this self-stimulation. Verbal instructions were accompanied by manual guidance and the child was required to hold his hands in the indicated position for 15 seconds after which another instruction would follow. This training had several objectives: it interrupted the self-stimulatory behavior; introduced an annoying (punishing) consequence; and taught the following of instructions. Once the self-stimulation had been successfully eliminated, the child encountered positive reinforcement for outward-directed activities which maintained the more appropriate behavior both over time and in a different setting.

Another study in which autistic children were mixed with other psychotic children was one reported by Hagen, Winsberg, and Wolff (1968). This work also illustrates the conceptual confusion that plagues this area of inquiry. It will be recalled that Rimland (1964) suggested that defective memory function precludes adequate language development. Hagen and his colleagues, on the other hand, reasoned that language is vital to such functions as memory for immediate past experience. They therefore compared the performance of ten psychotic children at various levels of language functioning with a group of normal controls. All but two of the psychotic children were described as autistic or with "autistic features," but several of them had demonstrable central nervous system damage. The children were tested on tasks requiring discrimination, transposition, generalization, reversal shift, and short-term memory with and without verbal cues. As expected, the psychotic children performed worse than the normals on all tasks, and language ability was directly related to the adequacy of performance of memory and discrimination learning tasks.

This study highlights the central role that deficient language plays in the behavioral difficulties of autistic children. A child who fails to develop language for whatever reason is obviously under a gross handicap. The study by Hagen et al. does not, of course, answer the question whether language deficit is the cause or the effect of the cognitive difficulties of autistic children. All it shows is that language impairment is correlated with other cognitive defects. To test the causal hypothesis, one would need to teach language to nonverbal children under carefully controlled conditions and then assess whether this learning produces improvement in their discriminative ability and memory. While not directly addressed to this issue, work by Stevens-Long (Stevens-Long & Rasmussen, 1974; Stevens-Long,

Schwarz, & Bliss, 1976), which follows the operant learning approach, has demonstrated that autistic children can be taught to produce both simple and compound sentences, which they are then able to use spontaneously in a classroom setting.

Viewing language disorder as the dominant problem of autistic children, Frith (1970) noted the paradox that these children fail to perceive structure, yet appear preoccupied with structure. They will, for example, fail to respond to the content of a verbal message, yet perseverate in repeating this message over and over again. Frith proposed that this paradox can be understood by postulating an imbalance between "feature extraction" and "pattern imposition." According to this hypothesis, the inability to perceive meaning would be explained by the failure of feature extraction, while the tendency to stereotyped behavior would be accounted for by a dominance of pattern imposition. To demonstrate the operation of this deficit in feature extraction, Frith conducted a study comparing immediate recall of binary verbal sequences of autistic, normal, and subnormal children. The children were asked to reproduce verbal sequences of two types. One type involved a cyclic pattern (*ababab*), as in "come here come here come here"; the other, a noncyclic pattern (*abbbaa*), as in "lets go go go lets lets." The results of the study were in line with the hypothesis in that the autistic children had little difficulty recalling quasi-random material but were impaired in processing meaningful material. While the normal, and to some extent the subnormal children were able to rely on the appropriate rule—depending on whether the sequence contained predominantly alternating or repeating elements—the autistic children would reconstruct the lists on the basis of a preservation rule, regardless of whether or not redundancy was the predominant feature of the list. In terms of the hypothesis, the control group showed feature extraction, while the autistic subjects showed evidence of pattern imposition, independent of input.

This work would seem to confirm the frequent observation that autistic children are unable to extract meaning from verbal messages; that is to say, to associate the sounds they hear with the objects, events, and relationships that these sounds symbolize. Whether this failure is due to the mechanisms postulated by Frith (1970) or to the difficulty in the realm of attention remains an unanswered question.

Several investigators (Cowan, Hoddinott, & Wright, 1965; Morrison, Miller, & Mejia, 1971; Wallace, 1975) have pointed to so-called negativism as a quality in the behavior of autistic children. This represents the observation that these children often fail to respond to simple commands and requests and at times do the opposite of what they have been asked to do. To call this negativism carries the implication that the child knows what the adult's verbal request means but purposely does the opposite or refuses to do anything. Wallace (1975) showed that a group of nine autistic children manifested that kind of behavior more frequently than children in a normal control group and that they had a greater tendency to negativism when the requested response was verbal than when it was nonverbal.

Negativism was investigated by Cowan et al. (1965), who studied the behavior of twelve children between the ages of 4 and 9 who had been carefully selected to meet the restricted definition of early infantile autism. The children were individually trained to pick up skeins of colored wool and deposit them in a box. The behavior was modeled by the examiner and reinforced with pieces of popcorn. After this response had been established, the child was given verbal instructions to place a specified object into the box. The objects were small colored tiles in the shapes of circles, squares, and triangles; and the requests were either for a square or for a red tile. The multiple-choice procedure used made it possible to compare the number of correct choices made by each child with the number of correct choices possible by chance. Only two of the twelve subjects obtained perfect scores; all others made *fewer* correct choices than chance would allow. That is, they were wrong more often than they would have been had they picked up the objects with their eyes closed. Since the correct choice was thus studiously avoided, it seemed clear that the children must have understood the request and known which object was the correct one. The authors conclude somewhat precipitately that "negativism, rather than indifference, lack of capacity, or lack of experience, is the only possible way of accounting for the failure of the ten *S*s to give correct responses" (p. 919).

In the first part of the experiment just described, every response, regardless of correctness, had been rewarded "in order to keep *S* interested in the task" (ibid., p. 916). Other than the experimenter's request, "Put a red one in the box," the condition thus did not contain any cues as to the correctness of the response. With red, blue, yellow, and green tiles of various shapes before them, the children were presented with the above request. Regardless of the tile picked up, they would receive a reward. This means that if they picked up a blue tile on the first trial, they were reinforced for *not* following the experimenter's instructions. Reinforcement theory would predict that on the next trial they should pick up the same blue tile, but the test conditions prevented this because the tile picked up on the immediately preceding trial was withheld during the next trial in order to prevent *S*s "from perservative responding" (ibid.). With the response that had just been reinforced thus prevented from being emitted, the children may well have learned a response class, that is, *not* following instructions. The fact that group data showed a decline in the number of correct choices in each succeeding block of five trials adds plausibility to this explanation. What is demonstrated, then, need not be called *motivational negativism*; it may simply be learning of a reinforced response class.

The second part of the Cowan et al. experiment seems to lend further support to the interpretation just advanced. The purpose was to test whether "the negativism could be overcome when the incentive conditions were changed" (p. 920). Instructions and task remained the same, but reinforcement was given *only* when the child emitted a correct response. Working only with the children who had given significantly few correct responses in the earlier sessions, five were now trained to present red tiles and five to present square tiles. Two days later, all children were retested on both the "red" and the "square" trials from the first part of the study. With this procedure, four of the ten subjects learned to make nothing but correct responses on both kinds of posttests. That is, those who had been trained on squares presented not only squares but also red appropriately. They had learned to follow the experimenter's instructions because following instructions had been reinforced during training trials. To say that the procedure had "overcome the negativistic behavior" (p. 921) seems to invoke an unnecessary construct. As for the six children who failed to learn to follow instructions, it is quite possible that, as Cowan et al. themselves suggest, different or larger rewards might have been more effective in establishing compliant responses.

Cowan et al. pointed out that the two children who had given correct responses throughout the first part of the experiment were the only ones in the sample who were able to use some language. These, plus five of the six who learned the compliance response in the second part of the study, also had the highest intelligence test scores. All six compliers are also reported to have succeeded on a concept learning task—which the six noncompliers had failed—and, in yet another study, compliers seemed to learn cooperative behavior more readily than noncompliers. All of this seems to suggest consistent differences in learning ability rather than resistance or negativism. Individual differences in learning ability would, of course, be expected from a formulation of early infantile autism as a developmental disability, since children, whether normal or autistic, develop the capacities one needs for learning at different rates and in varying qualities.

RECAPITULATION

Early infantile autism is manifested by profoundly disturbed, psychotic behavior which interferes with almost every area of a child's functioning. A variety of theories about the etiology of this disorder have been offered. These theories range from the purely biological to the strictly environmental, with some falling between these extremes in that they propose an interaction between genetic-constitutional and environmental factors. Inductive theories are difficult to test. A deductive approach, which takes as its point of departure empirically established psychological knowledge and applies it to autistic children, may prove more fruitful. The development of selective attention in normal children can be related to the problems of autistic children who might be operating on the immature level of overexclusive attention. Many laboratory studies seem to support this formulation and there is some evidence that it leads not only to a better understanding of the behavior of autistic children but also to viable approaches to their training and treatment.

Research on early infantile autism is complicated by the fact that the incidence of this disorder is low and agreement on whom to include in this category is not uniform. Studies often include not only autistic children but also those who are more appropriately classified as cases of childhood schizophrenia. We must therefore discuss that other form of psychotic behavior before we can return to a more detailed consideration of the treatment of both kinds of psychotic children.

Chapter 11

Psychotic Behavior: Childhood Schizophrenia

DEFINING CHARACTERISTICS

As was pointed out at the beginning of the previous chapter, early infantile autism and childhood schizophrenia are two distinctly different disorders of psychotic proportions. This view is not shared by everyone however (Trefert, 1970), and both the capacity for accurate diagnosis and the terminology used in this field are, unfortunately, far from refined; therefore, one often finds the labels autism, schizophrenia, and psychosis used interchangeably when severely disturbed children are discussed.

Rimland (1964) has done more than anyone else to try and obtain a conceptual differentiation between early infantile autism and childhood schizophrenia. He lists some fifteen aspects on which the two conditions differ, the most concrete of these are the following. *Onset* of the disorder is late and gradual for childhood schizophrenia, early (as the name implies) in early infantile autism. The autistic child displays *autistic aloneness* and a desire for *preservation of sameness*, the schizophrenic child does not. Finally, the schizophrenic child displays normal speech (though it is often used to produce noncommunicative content), while the autistic child's *language ability* is either grossly *impaired* and characterized by pronominal reversal or totally absent. A great deal of confusion could be avoided and the study of psychotic children greatly facilitated if clinicians and writers would be more precise in their terminology. Since they do not, some of the children whose treatment has been described in the previous chapter might have been more correctly identified as childhood schizophrenics.

Despite differences in terminology, careful observers of children with psychotic disorders agree on a series of characteristics which many of these children have in common. Goldfarb (1970), citing the work of a British committee of psychiatrists, lists nine such "schizophrenic" characteristics. These are as follows:

1 Distorted interpersonal relationships, including aloofness and withdrawal.
2 Disorientation with respect to the child's own person and body in relation to the environment, including self-injurious and bizarre explorations of his body.
3 Bizarre preoccupation with specific objects without regard to their accepted function.
4 Demand for sameness in the environment and a concomitant resistance to change.
5 Atypical responses to sensory stimuli, such as apparent insensitivity to pain or excessive responses to stimulation.
6 Distorted and excessive fears in the absence of objective danger with a concomitant absence of fear in the face of real danger.
7 Use of speech to communicate bizarre and meaningless content; absence of or greatly immature language.
8 Poor coordination, locomotion, and balance; body whirling and toe-walking; and excessive motility, immobility, bizarre posturing, or rocking.
9 Extensive retardation with occasional "islands" of normal or near-normal intellectual function.

This list is presented in order to give an impression of the pervasive nature of psychotic disorders. Clearly, not all children with psychotic disorders will manifest all these problems, and at least two of them—preservation of sameness and language disturbance—will be recognized as among the defining characteristics of early infantile autism. The list should therefore not be used to attempt a differentiation among children with profound psychological disorders.

The variability among children with psychotic disorders is reflected in a paper by Brown (1960), who reports that among 40 children with "atypical development," 21 had some language, 36 showed low frustration tolerance, 26 had strong or unusual fears, while 20 displayed primitive object manipulation or diffuse aggression.

The following description of a "schizophrenic child" seen by this writer (Ross, 1955) places many of these behavioral aberrations in context:

The boy was brought to the clinic at age 5 years, 11 months, when his mother sought help because the child "embarrased her by his peculiar behavior," and because of certain purposeless movements of the upper extremities. She stated that there was something definitely wrong with him because he did not act like other children his age. She mentioned his fondness for examining women's purses, his running into rest rooms looking under commodes to explore the pipes, his getting on his knees to examine women's legs, and his desire to rub his hands over the hair of other children and then smelling his hands. Because of these actions, as well as a tendency to strike other children on the head, the mother stated that he "needs watching all the time." She added that the boy prefers to remain at home and to play by himself. When he occasionally joins other children, the shooting of a cap pistol creates intense fear in him. In playing hide-and-go-seek, he screams when the other child comes out of hiding and when it is his turn to hide, he insists that his mother accompany him.

During subsequent interviews with the mother further "strange behavior" was reported. The boy likes to listen to the radio and seems to prefer popular music with a pronounced rhythm. He is extremely preoccupied with the daily mail delivery and will ask constantly whether the mail has come and accosts the mailman when he arrives at the house. Fender aprons of trucks are of particular fascination to him and he will crawl under trucks to examine them. He calls these aprons "rainwater" and when he sees a vehicle without them, he'll get upset and cry, "Put the rainwater on, Mommy, put the rainwater on."

The mother dated the onset of the child's difficulties as occurring when he was two years old, although at another time she claimed that she first noticed something strange about the time a younger brother was born when the boy was one year old. As an infant, he was said to have shown anticipatory posture at feeding, reaching out for bottle and mother. He was friendly, would coo and look at everybody and notice everything so that the parents thought that he was a bright baby. His first smile is dated as occurring at three months; he took his first unassisted step around one year of age but had some difficulty in this area, and when seen at the clinic was wearing corrective shoes because of his "habit of walking on his toes." The child began to utter single words before he was 13 months old, and spoke in short sentences by two years although his speech remains difficult to understand even at this time, in part, because he has a high-pitched, squealy voice.

During a 20 minute interview with the boy he showed no evidence of any interpersonal contact. He ignored the psychiatrist and played oblivious to all distractions and external stimuli. He put strange objects into his mouth and evidently explored them in this way rather than by looking or with his hands. He was rather clumsy but there was no gross disturbance of motor behavior. Whenever he became excited, which was rather frequently, he would jump up and down and move his arms in a rapid, apparently purposeless, repetitive movement. He whirled about several times whenever his body was turned by the doctor. On two or three occasions, he became interested in the doctor's foot or hand if one of these was placed directly in front of him, but there was no evidence that he recognized it as a part of someone else's body.

This boy thus displayed each of the behavioral characteristics considered typical of the "schizophrenic syndrome" by the group cited in Goldfarb's (1970) review. The child's use of language is particularly noteworthy since, unlike most children with early infantile autism, he had developed speech but used it to communicate bizarre content, such as the references to "rainwater." Again, unlike the case of early infantile autism, this boy was aware of his environment but was confused, disoriented, and anxious about it, as in his concern about the mail delivery. His strong fears and hypersensitivity to noise are further characteristics of a schizophrenic child, as are his toe walking, whirling, and repetitive behaviors.

ETIOLOGICAL FACTORS

Little is known about the factors causing schizophrenic disorders, but available information strongly suggests that one is dealing here with a behavior cluster to which a genetically based impairment of central nervous system functions makes a significant contribution (Garmezy, 1975). Thus, while the specific fears and preoccupations are undoubtedly learned response patterns, the overreaction and inability to cope with the fears may very well be a function of a genetic predisposition (Kallman & Roth, 1956). An ambitious longitudinal study by Mednick and Schulsinger (1968) promises to throw some light on this topic. Assuming that children born of schizophrenic mothers have a high risk of becoming psychiatric casualties, these investigators examined 207 such children in 1962–1963. At the time these children were functioning normally. Data on 104 children of normal mothers were gathered for purposes of control and with the intention of following these 311 children for the next 20 to 25 years. It was estimated that during that period approximately 100 of the high-risk children would develop a psychological disorder, about 30 of these being diagnosed as schizophrenic.

When the project reached its sixth year, Mednick (1970) reported that twenty of the children of schizophrenic mothers had suffered severe psychiatric breakdown. An analysis of the data from the earlier assessment made it possible to identify a number of premorbid characteristics which distinguished these subjects from the controls. Two of the most clearly discriminating characteristics were (1) the presence of a poorly controlled, hyperresponsive autonomic nervous system as measured by a physiological conditioning-generalization-extinction test and (2) history of pregnancy and delivery complications at the time of birth. Since the association between these complications and the autonomic hyperresponsiveness was absent in the control group, Mednick (1970; Mednick, Schulsinger, & Schulsinger, 1975) speculates that birth complications trigger some characteristic that may be genetically predisposed. He suggests that these complications damage the modulatory control of the body's stress-response mechanism such that in an autonomic conditioning experiment the subject will display rapid response onset, poor habituation of the response, poor extinction, and very rapid recovery from the response. A review of various animal studies led Mednick to the hypothesis that the pregnancy and delivery complications result in damage to the hippocampus, an important inhibitory center of the brain. Defective hippocampal functioning "in combination with genetic and environmental factors could conceivably play a vital predispositional role in at least some forms of schizophrenia" (Mednick, 1970, p. 59). This carefully worded hypothesis is in line with Mednick's theoretical orientation, for he views schizophrenia as a pattern of well-learned avoidance responses. A defective stress-response mechanism might well increase avoidance responses, and the rapid recovery from stress that is typical of hippocampal lesions would occasion immediate reinforcement of this response.

While Mednick's formulation must await further data from his impressive study, other research points in the same direction. Thus, Goldfarb (1970) concluded from an extensive review of available studies on various psychotic disorders of children that "the accumulated data . . . provide rather indisputable evidence of impairment of the central nervous system" (p. 804), though he hastens to add that this evidence is not found in all the children diagnosed as psychotic.

It is a common clinical observation that mothers of children called *schizophrenic* are tense, anxious, and preoccupied with their child's problem. This has led some to the totally unwarranted conclusion that the mother's behavior is the sole cause of the child's disturbance. The term *schizophrenogenic mother* was coined to lend credence to this logical fallacy that leaps from an observed correlation of two variables to the conclusion that one of these variables is the cause of the other. It should be apparent from the description of a psychotic disorder given above that the task of coping with such a severely disturbed child is likely to be a strain that will be reflected in the behavior of most mothers. The explanation that the child's condition causes the mother's psychological state is thus as logical, though no more warranted, as the obverse conclusion.

A good deal of research has been directed at the question whether parents and particularly, mothers of schizophrenic children share some characteristic that might explain why their children became schizophrenic (Bindman, 1966; Connerly, 1967; McDermott, Harrison, Schrager, Lindy, & Killins, 1967; Shodell, 1967; Sloat, 1966). Nothing in these studies lends support to the notion that psychotic or schizophrenic children are basically normal children who "were made psychotic" by some peculiarity in the behavior of their "schizophrenogenic" mother. The most conservative conclusion one can draw is that this diverse group of children—variously called *atypical, schizophrenic,* or *psychotic*—includes a large number whose profoundly disturbed behavior so upsets the equilibrium of their family interaction that their parents, and particularly their mothers, display disturbances in their own behavior. This clearly leaves the etiology of the child's problem an open question.

Research on Child Characteristics

Studies devoted to parental behavior were usually guided by the investigators' desire to test the hypothesis of maternal contribution to the development of psychotic children. Studies devoted to the characteristics of the psychotic child are frequently more exploratory in nature, seeking to establish how children in this group respond to various sensory, cognitive, or motor tasks.

A number of investigators who evaluated psychotic children have reported finding perceptual deficits and distortions. Thus, Hermelin and O'Connor (1967), having matched normal and psychotic children for mental age and having compared their performance on position and length discrimination problems, report that the psychotic children have difficulties with such discriminations. Their results were similar to those of Berkowitz (1961) and Goldfarb (1961), who reported difficulties in directionality, 2-point threshold, figure-ground discrimination, and finger localization.

The impaired performance on tasks requiring responses to sensory stimuli can be interpreted as due to deficient sensory functions, limited integrative capacity, or impaired response facility. At the present time, it is impossible to conclude anything other than that the performance of children classified as psychotic differs from the performance of children considered normal. Whether one basic defect, such as impaired attention, underlies all of the performance deficits or whether the variety of children classified as psychotic or schizophrenic have a variety of deficits is a question only further research can resolve.

Clinical observers often report that children with psychotic disorders frequently explore objects by touch, smell, or taste, in seeming preference to visual examination. This apparent preference for the use of tactual and chemoreceptors was the basis of a study conducted by Schopler (1966) in which he compared visual and tactual receptor preferences of schizophrenic, normal, and retarded children. The thirty schizophrenic children ranged in age from 5 years, 6 months to 9 years, 5 months. A group of fifteen mentally subnormal children of similar mental age and a group of ninety normal children of similar chronological age were used to obtain comparison data. In four standardized situations, each child was given the choice of playing with a primarily visual or a primarily tactual toy. In one situation, for example, the choice was between pushing a button that would activate a slide projector showing colored pictures or pressing a lever that produced moderate hand vibration. In another situation, the child had the choice between watching toy animals which were individually exposed by means of a rotating disk or tactually exploring similar animals enclosed in separate, screened compartments. Schopler reports that the normal children spent more time with the visual than with the tactual tasks and that the length of time spent on the visual tasks increased with age. The retarded children also showed a preference for the visual over the tactual; but for the schizophrenic children, this relationship did not appear, for they spent slightly more time at the tactual than at the visual tasks. Comparisons between the normal and the schizophrenic children showed the latter to have displayed less visual preference than same-aged normal children, although the schizophrenic did not spend more absolute time on tactual exploration than did the normal controls. The difference between the two groups is largely the result of the greater absolute amount of time the normal children were willing to spend on the various tasks, and of this time, they devoted more to the visual activities. Thus, the mean time spent on tactual stimuli was about 6½ minutes (6.6) for the schizophrenic and a little over 6 minutes (6.2) for same-aged normal children. The mean time spent on visual stimuli, on the other hand, showed 6.2 minutes for the schizophrenic but 10.3 minutes for the normal comparison group of the same age.

Schopler (1966) concluded from his findings that "schizophrenic children will express less visual preference than normal children of the same age" (p. 113). A conclusion with somewhat better foundation in the data would seem to be that the normal children spent more time with the experimental tasks, and of that time, they spent more with the primarily visual than with the primarily tactual stimuli. The schizophrenic children spent less total time on the tasks than did the normal children, and the difference in total time represents the time the normal children spent with the visual stimuli. It seems tenuous to conclude that this is due to "less visual preference" on the part of the schizophrenic children. In the absence of significant differences between schizophrenics and normals on the tactual measures, the results may be as easily due to the characteristics of the stimulus material used in this study as to differences in receptor preference.

The comparatively limited amount of time a child with a psychotic disorder is willing to spend on tasks of interest to an experimenter—as opposed to the inordinate length of time they often spend on self-selected, repetitive, stereotyped activity—is frequently attributed to short attention span. Rutter and Lockyer (1967), for example, in comparing sixty-three children with infantile psychosis (probably including cases of early infantile autism) with a group of nonpsychotic, matched controls, list short attention span as one of the characteristics of their patients, but their list also includes stereotyped, repetitive mannerisms and non-distractibility. It would seem important to explore the dimension of stimulus characteristics before using the responses of psychotic children as a basis of drawing inferences about their preferences or ability to attend. Few investigators have addressed themselves to the question of the kinds of stimuli to which psychotic children do and do not respond. Work by Hermelin and O'Connor (1965, 1967) has some bearing on this, although their interest was primarily in discrimination learning. In one study (Hermelin & O'Connor, 1965), they compared speaking and nonspeaking psychotic children with normal controls of matched mental age on a series of visual discrimination tasks. They found that tasks that could be solved on the basis of kinesthetic, brightness, or size cues did not differentiate between the groups, while those tasks that required the discrimination of shape or direction presented difficulties for the psychotic subjects. In a later study (Hermelin & O'Connor, 1967), these investigators explored the dimensions of position and length in relation to the discrimination learning of thirty-two psychotic children and an equal number of normal controls of matched mental age. All subjects learned to discrminate position more readily than length, with the normal children superior to the psychotic children in the tasks requiring the discrimination of position.

When one wishes to investigate children's performance on tasks where verbal mediation may facilitate solution, as is the case in discrimination learning, matching groups on language development may be more relevant than matching them on the more general criterion of mental age. This inference emerged from a study conducted by Heller (1966), who investigated conceptual sorting of schizophrenic children. He initially matched 27 schizophrenic and 27 elementary school children by age, sex, intelligence, and socioeconomic status. The minimal measured IQ score was 78. These subjects were given an object-sorting test that requires the classification of objects and the verbalization of the principle used in the sorting. The test was scored in terms of the adequacy of the sorting and of the verbalizations. The schizophrenic subjects were found to give a significantly greater number of idiosyncratic verbalizations, but only the older schizophrenic children displayed less adequate sorting than their normal controls. These differences, however, became negligible when the two groups were equated for language development. This seems to suggest that such differences as had been found between the two groups were largely a function of the language impairment of the schizophrenic children. Heller concluded that the inadequate language development of schizophrenic children results in an inability to focus on relevant aspects of the environment, leading to irrelevant, idiosyncratic, maladaptive, and bizarre associations and responses. Unable to reduce stimulus complexity through verbal labeling, the schizophrenic child would have difficulty in dealing with the events around him and to orient himself in relation to his environment.

The importance of language in the development and course of children's psychotic disorders is also reflected in the finding of Rutter, Greenfeld, and Lockyer (1967) that psychotic children who fail to develop useful language by age 5 are far less likely to show later improvement than those whose language development is less impaired. This is, of course, another way of saying that the more severe the disorder, the greater the language impairment and the less favorable the prognosis. From this one might also conclude that the earlier one intervenes and gives the child systematic language training and other treatment aimed at enhancing the socialization process, the more likely one will be to promote adaptive development.

Critique   Studies such as those just reviewed throw some light on the differences in performance between normal children and a heterogenous group of profoundly disturbed children. Differences do seem to exist, but beyond that self-evident statement, there is little one can offer by way of an integrating conclusion. Aside from the problem of definition which, until solved, continues to lead different investigators to study different children while calling them by the same catchall labels, there is the handicap of doing research without a guiding theory that might permit one to generate testable hypotheses. With few exceptions (Schopler, 1965), studies of the sensory and response capacities of psychotic children seem to be approached in the exploratory spirit of "I-wonder-what-would-happen-if." This is a reflection of the rudimentary state of knowledge in which we find ourselves in this field, for such an approach is typical of a very early period in scientific endeavor. In addition to this lack of a theory, there are methodological issues that must be solved before much progress can be expected.

One methodological problem that faces investigators interested in the learning capacity of psychotic children is the kind of control group that should be used in order to isolate the "psychotic" variable. Children with psychotic disorders are observed to have difficulty learning to discriminate objects by their shape, for example. It is also known, however, that these children obtain very low mental-age scores on tests of intelligence. If one now desired to demonstrate that shape discrimination is more difficult for psychotic than for normal children, what kind of "normal" children should one use for comparison? This question arises because investigators wish to study whether the difficulty with shape discrimination is "due to" the psychotic condition or "caused by" the psychotic child's low mental age. Hermelin and O'Connor (1967) attempted to solve this issue by matching for mental age. Since the measurable mental age of the psychotic subjects was less than half their chronological age, this meant that they had to select very young, normal children for their control group. As a result, the mean chronological age of the normal children was 4 years, 4 months, while the mean chronological age of their patient group was 11 years. This discrepancy in chronological age introduces factors into the study that may grossly distort the results. For example, the nature of the game, toy, or reward or the size of a manipulandum appropriate for an 11-year-old will be inappropriate for a 4-year-old and vice versa, regardless of psychotic condition or intelligence level. Such differences as may be found between these groups may thus be due to a variety of factors other than or in addition to the psychotic condition of the patient group.

The study by Schopler (1966), discussed above, used two control groups—one matched for mental age, the other matched for chronological age. Since the difference in time spent on the visual, as opposed to the tactual, tasks was found to hold regardless of the mental age of the control group, Schopler concluded that the difference was not a function of the low intelligence level of his psychotic children, implying that it was therefore a function of the fact that they were psychotic or schizophrenic. While two control groups permit one to make statements about the effect of the intelligence variable, they still do not provide a basis for speculations about the effect of the psychotic condition on, say, shape discrimination. This is the case because mental age is not a measure that is independent of the psychotic condition. Mental age is no more than a score a child achieves on an intelligence test. When a child with a psychotic disorder is tested, his test performance is going to be influenced by his disorder and his score is going to reflect his condition. If this child is then also tested on a shape-discrimination task and he is found to have difficulty with this, it is meaningless to ask whether his difficulty is the result of his "low intelligence" or due to his psychotic condition. The most parsimonious statement one can make is that the poor performance on the test of intelligence (which calls for shape discriminations, among other things) and the poor performance on an experimental task requiring shape discrimination are some of the many forms of maladaptive behavior that, together, have come to be called *psychosis* or *schizophrenia*.

The various behaviors making up the vague cluster labeled *psychotic disorders* are described in the nine characteristics cited at the beginning of this chapter. Ultimately, studies, such as those by Schopler (1966) and Hermelin and O'Connor (1967), do no more than show that some of these characteristics are indeed intercorrelated and that children who are called *normal* do not show these characteristics. What makes some children manifest these characteristics so that they come to be called *psychotic* or *schizophrenic*—the "cause" of the condition—remains to be discovered.

FOLLOW-UP STUDIES ON PSYCHOTIC CHILDREN

The work of Rutter and Lockyer (1967) and Rutter et al. (1967) represents one of the more ambitious attempts to provide information on the development of children with psychotic disorders. These reports provide a 5- to 15-year follow-up of children who had been designated as cases of "infantile psychosis." These children had been hospitalized between 1950 and 1958, and the follow-up was conducted in 1963 and 1964. Because the issue of nomenclature was even more confused in the 1950s than it is now, the cases included children with a variety of psychotic disorders, including early infantile autism. "Most" had shown psychotic development in early infancy, and their principal characteristics were distorted relationships with people; marked retardation of language; echolalia and pronominal reversal; stereotyped, repetitive mannerisms; a lack of responsiveness to auditory stimuli; and a tendency to self-injurious behavior. Rutter and his colleagues (1967) compared the later status of sixty-three such children with that of a matched, nonpsychotic control group of children who, at one time, had been patients at the same psychiatric hospital during that 8-year period. The psychotic children had a mean age of 5 years, 11 months at the time of the original hospitalization. The average intelligence quotient of the fifty-three who could be tested had been 62.5. None had shown "unequivocal" signs of central nervous system abnormality during the physical examination at time of admission. The male/female ratio was 4.25 to 1, reflecting the repeatedly reported disproportionate representation of boys among severely disturbed children. When the mean age of the psychotic children was 15 years, 7 months, they were reexamined, with Rutter and his colleagues personally conducting the examination in all but two instances. The most noteworthy result of the study is that the follow-up revealed a high incidence of brain damage among the psychotic. Of the 63 children who, on original examination, had shown no clear-cut abnormality, only 29 showed no evidence of brain damage when they were reexamined. The presence of brain damage was considered a "strong likelihood" in 12 cases, 10 of whom had developed epileptic seizures. In six cases, brain damage was deemed "probable," and in another 16 cases the presence of such impairment was classified as "possible."

This change in diagnostic picture may, of course, be an artifact of more sophisticated examination, but the finding of high incidence of brain damage among psychotic children is in line with data presented by Eaton and Menolascino (1967) on the basis of their 5-year follow-up of 32 psychotic children. Eaton and Menolascino view brain-damaged children as unusually reactive to stress and suggest that some psychotic reactions of childhood are secondary to central nervous system impairment.

The primary interest of the research by Rutter and his associates (1967) was to ascertain the social adjustment of their two groups of children. For this purpose they assigned Social Adjustment Ratings on a 4-point scale. These ratings are shown in Table 1. As can be seen from this table, the psychotic group had attained a far worse level of adjustment than the comparison group of nonpsychotic psychiatric patients. Only 1 case in the psychotic group was reported to have fully normal peer relations, and only 7 were able to relate to adults in a fully normal manner. The social-adjustment ratings, which may be subjectively biased, receive more objective support from the data on the settings in which the subjects were located at the time of follow-up (Table 2). All but 5 (8 percent) of the psychotic group were in some specialized, sheltered, or institutional setting. In the comparison group 21 individuals (34 percent) were either employed or attending ordinary school. When those over age 16 are separately scrutinized, one finds

Table 1   Social Adjustment Ratings at Follow-up*

Rating	Percent psychotic	Percent nonpsychotic
Normal/Good	14	33
Fair	25	31
Poor	13	11
Very Poor	48	25

*After Rutter, Greenfeld, and Lockyer, 1967, p. 1184.

Table 2   Status at Follow-up*

Status	All subjects		Subjects over age 16	
	Psychotic	Control	Psychotic	Control
Employed	2	14	2	12
Regular school	3	7	1	...
Special school	11	6	1	3
Living in village trust	3	...	3	...
Training center	7	10	4	6
At home, not working	9	2	7	1
Institutionalized	28	22	20	14
Total	63	61	38	36

*After Rutter, Greenfeld, and Lockyer, 1967, p. 1184.

that only 2 (5 percent) of the psychotic but 12 (33 percent) of the nonpsychotic expatients are listed as employed. A large proportion of both groups (44 percent of the psychotic and 36 percent of the nonpsychotic) were found on follow-up to be institutionalized, primarily in institutions for the mentally retarded. This reflects both the shortage of appropriate facilities for severely disturbed children and youth, and the low reliability of nomenclature and resulting arbitrary dispositions in this field. The bimodal distribution for the comparison group (34 percent in regular school or employment and 36 percent in institutions) reflects the heterogenous nature of this group, some of whom had originally come into psychiatric care because of severe acting out and delinquency, while others had been hospitalized because of questionable retardation or brain damage.

Rutter et al. (1967) point out that their results are similar to those of other investigators, such as Eisenberg (1956), who conducted follow-up studies on severely disturbed, autistic children and found some 50 percent to have been institutionalized by adolescence, again usually in institutions for the mentally retarded. Only from between 5 and 17 percent of these children were rated as "well adjusted," and even those whose autistic withdrawal was attenuated continued to show a lack of perceptiveness for the nuances of social behavior, such as interpersonal tact.

The low rate of positive outcomes in cases of childhood psychosis is, of course, closely related to the inadequacy, inefficiency, and sheer lack of available treatment resources. The children in the study by Rutter et al. (1967) had been exposed to an extremely heterogenous range of "treatments," including prolonged, daily psychoanalytic therapy, routine institutional care, medications of various kinds, and—in one instance—a leucotomy (accounting for one case of brain damage!). Treatment form seemed unrelated to outcome, with one notable exception: the amount of schooling. This, together with initial intelligence level, the presence or absence of speech by age 5, and the overall severity of the disorder, was a main variable that was clearly related to outcome. All children in the "good" outcome category (Table 2) had attended school for at least 2 years. This was true of only 63 percent of the "fair," 38 percent of the "poor," and 20 percent of the "very poor" outcome groups. The ability to attend school was only partly related to original intelligence level, as indicated by the fact that intelligence level did not differentiate between the "good" and "fair" groups who differed significantly on the school attendance variable. It would thus seem incorrect to attribute the positive relationship between school attendance and outcome to the fact that the less severely disturbed who were able to attend school had a higher probability of receiving a good adjustment rating on follow-up. Schooling appeared to contribute to positive outcome in its own right, somewhat independent of the initial level of the disturbance. As Rutter and his colleagues point out, "schooling probably did have some effect on the child's social adjustment in adolescence and early life" (p. 1195). In the group these investigators had studied, fewer than 50 percent of the psychotic children had as much as 2 years of regular school attendance, while 33 percent had never been exposed to school, 10 percent had gone to school for less than 6 months, and 6 percent had received some schooling only during their original, short hospitalization. Greater efforts at providing these children appropriate, individualized, systematic educational opportunities might well increase their chances for greatly improved functioning, justifying the "limited optimism" of Rutter et al. that with better facilities, better results might be obtained.

THE TREATMENT OF AUTISTIC AND SCHIZOPHRENIC CHILDREN

Because clinical investigators rarely differentiate among severely disturbed children when they describe their treatment efforts and since, from the point of view of treatment, it matters little whether a child bears the label early infantile autism or childhood schizophrenia, we shall discuss the treatment approaches under one heading.

Early infantile autism is a very severe disorder and children whose problems place them into this category have a generally poor prognosis. A follow-up study conducted at the Indiana University School of Medicine (DeMyer, Barton, DeMyer, Norton, Allen, & Steele, 1973) revealed that of 126 children who had been diagnosed as autistic, 42 percent were residents of institutions some 6 years later. Only 1 percent of these children were classified as normal, while 50 percent had their condition identified as "very poor." Combining their results with those of the follow-up study conducted by Rutter and Lockyer (1967), the Indiana investigators concluded that the outcome predictions for autism were that 1 to 2 percent would recover to normal, while 5 to 15 percent would remain in borderline, 16 to 25 percent in fair, and 60 to 75 percent in poor condition. Not too surprisingly, the better a child is functioning at the time his or her condition is identified as autistic and intervention is begun, the better are the chances that the child will improve. The best predictor of outcome for the children included in the study by DeMyer et al. (1973) had been their level of functioning in the school setting.

With such a poor prognosis, what are the chances of providing autistic children with effective treatment? The answer to this seems to depend on what one chooses as the focus of treatment, what one sets as one's treatment goal, and, most importantly, how early in the child's life treatment can be initiated. Most of the therapeutic attempts on which the just cited outcome studies were based aimed at "treating autism" and had as their goal the "curing of the disease." These approaches were predicated on the dual assumptions that there is such an entity as early infantile autism and that this entity is a disease. Both of these assumptions can be questioned. Despite certain common features, there is a great variation among children labeled as autistic and if one conceives of their difficulties as a developmental disability, the analogy to a physical disease that can be cured becomes meaningless.

Behavior Therapy and Its Goals

Investigators who study psychological disorders from a behavioral point of view do not ask, "How do I treat infantile autism?" but "What skill does this particular child lack and how do I best teach that skill?" The goal of behavior therapists is therefore not to cure autism or schizophrenia but to teach a variety of skills and their criterion of success then becomes whether the child has learned these skills, not whether he or she is no longer psychotic.

Imitation   One of the deficits frequently found in autistic children is their failure to imitate other people. In operant terminology: people do not serve as discriminative stimuli that might control the behavior of the child. Since the discriminative characteristic of a stimulus has to be learned, this represents an instance where the autistic child has failed to learn a skill—the lack of which, in turn, prevents the child from acquiring other, more complex response patterns through observational learning. In a study reported in 1965, Metz used operant methods to teach two autistic children to imitate simple behaviors of an adult. The children, a boy and a girl, both 7 years old, had been hospitalized for 1 and 2½ years, respectively, and had shown little, if any, response to conventional therapeutic programs. Working with them at lunchtime on days when they had not been given breakfast, Metz used food, tokens that could be traded for food, and the word "good" to reinforce imitative behavior and to establish generalized imitation.

To qualify as generalized imitation, a response must meet the following conditions: it must be topographically similar to the response demonstrated by the model; it must be emitted on the occasion of the specific example shown by the model; the model's behavior must serve as discriminative stimulus for the subject who must respond differentially to different responses by the model; and the behavior being imitated must be relatively novel as an item under the control of the model's exemplar; that is, it must be an item that the child has not been specifically taught to perform in response to the model's presentation.

Metz used such items as kicking a beanbag, putting a blanket on a doll, riding a hobby horse, placing a block into a box, and blowing a whistle. Working with each child individually, Metz used one list of such items to pretest for imitative behavior. At this point, the boy emitted five imitative responses, the girl none. The children were then taught a repertoire of six tasks, using passive demonstration and shaping procedures, with correct responses followed by the delivery of reinforcement. A task was considered learned when it was correctly performed six times in a row when presented in a series with the five other tasks. To reach this criterion, the boy required ten sessions and the girl five; the sessions were one-half to three-quarters of an hour in length. The six learned tasks were next interspersed with fourteen new tasks. Ten of these were reinforced when correctly imitated; four were nonrewarded tasks which were included to test for extinction. A task was considered imitated when it had been correctly performed on two out of three trials. This phase of the study was followed by further, more intensive training on additional items, further testing for generalization, and finally a post-testing with an entirely new list. On that occasion, the boy made eleven, the girl thirteen correct, imitative responses out of a possible total of sixteen. Generalized imitation had thus increased for both children although, without a control, it is not entirely certain that this increase was the result of the training procedures employed. One must nonetheless concur with Metz that the results suggest that autistic children can learn to imitate, that such learning can generalize to similar but new behaviors without specific training, and that the generalized imitative response can persist—in the context of reinforcement of *other* imitative behavior—without specifically being reinforced (p. 397).

Therapists using operant procedures to teach autistic children are frequently accused of ignoring the affective element of the child's behavior, particularly by those who, like DesLauriers and Carlson (1969), place heavy emphasis on affective aspects in their own therapeutic efforts. In this light, the following subjective observations, reported by Metz, are of particular interest:

> . . . as appropriate learning occurred, "inappropriate" motor and emotional behavior spontaneously disappeared. Not only did the children learn to do what was required by the task, but appropriate emotional responses also seemed to appear. For example, the children expressed joy or delight upon "solving" a problem, an affect rarely seen in these children in other situations. The children eventually appeared to enjoy the whole procedure, sought *E* out whenever he appeared on the ward, ran eagerly to the experimental room, etc. [Metz, 1965, p. 398].

While operant methods do not specifically deal with joy and delight, it seems that when these methods succeed in teaching a child adaptive responses that lead to positive reinforcement, positive affect appears spontaneously, as if the child enjoyed the newfound competence.

For many autistic children the learning of social imitation is the first step in learning other socially desirable and useful skills. Lovaas, Freitas, Nelson, and Whalen (1967) describe an operant procedure for teaching imitation which was then used in building such social and self-help skills as showing affection, giving friendly greetings, dressing and feeding oneself, brushing one's teeth, and so forth. The procedure entails shaping whereby the child is rewarded for making closer and closer approximations of the behavior modeled by the teacher (Lovaas, Schreibman, & Koegel, 1974).

Establishing Social Reinforcers   A statement of praise, a smile, or a compliment are social reinforcers that acquired their reinforcing properties by having been regularly paired with stimuli that already had such properties. Initially, such stimuli were the primary reinforcers, like food, warmth, and body contact, and it may be that all secondary or higher order reinforcers derive their reinforcing properties from these by the process of conditioning. For this reason, secondary reinforcers are also known as conditioned reinforcers. A similar development can be postulated for such social punishers as reprimands, frowns, and criticism whose effectiveness may ultimately derive from primary aversive stimulation, such as pain.

For some reason, whether because of their overexclusive attention or not, it is extremely difficult to establish conditioned reinforcers and punishers with autistic children. As a result, the acquisition and maintenance of behavior, which depends on the availability of conditioned and, especially, social reinforcers, are greatly hindered. When behavior is taught to autistic children by using such primary reinforcers as food (Risley & Wolf, 1967) or pain reduction (Lovaas, Schaeffer, & Simmons, 1965), the behavior is maintained only as long as these reinforcers are continued; that is, in the artificial situation set up in the school or clinic. In the outside world where these reinforcers are not normally dispensed such behavior very quickly undergoes extinction. To maintain that behavior, it is necessary either to teach those who interact with the child, like parents or teachers, to use the primary reinforcers with which the responses were originally taught or to teach the child to respond under contingencies normally available in the social environment, like smiles and praise, frowns and scoldings.

Ferster (1967) has drawn a useful distinction between arbitrary and natural reinforcers. An arbitrary reinforcer is one that is not the logical consequence of the behavior. Thus, it is not logical to receive a spoonful of cereal upon saying one's name when asked, "What's your name?" When Lovaas (1966) dispensed cereal in a program designed to develop speech with autistic children, he was using an arbitrary reinforcer. A natural reinforcer for this response would be to have the person who asked the question smile and say something like, "That's a nice name," but the reinforcing value of such a compliment must be acquired; otherwise, it is a meaningless, nonfunctional consequence. In order for a response to generalize to and be maintained in the environment outside of therapy, it is necessary to develop the effectiveness of natural consequences the child is likely to encounter in that environment by explicit efforts at establishing them as conditioned reinforcers (Rincover & Koegel, 1975). What is more, beyond making a smile, for example, into a conditioned reinforcer by pairing it with the delivery of food, one must also see to it that a smile, not only from the original teacher but from any other person, becomes reinforcing. When this is the case, the smile has become a *generalized conditioned reinforcer*, making it an extremely valuable response consequence which, because it is an interpersonal event, is also called a *generalized social reinforcer*.

The technology for establishing generalized social reinforcers is known and has been demonstrated with retarded children (Stokes, Baer, & Jackson, 1974). It entails pairing a social event like a smile with a primary reinforcer, which is delivered contingent on the production of a desired response. This pairing must be done by different people and in different settings. The primary reinforcer is then gradually withdrawn (this is called *fading*) and the social reinforcer is continued but on a gradually less regular schedule, thereby taking into consideration the fact that people in the natural social environment do not smile every time one says, "Good morning."

Work in this direction has also begun with autistic children, but with them primary reliance for the generalization of clinic-established behavior to the family environment is still being placed on training the children's parents to use the reinforcers that were effective in the clinic (Lovaas, et al., 1974). The reason for this lies primarily in the fact that it is extremely difficult and cumbersome to establish social reinforcers for autistic children in the first place. This was shown in work with two identical twins "with marked autistic features" who were 4 years old at the time (Lovaas, Freitag, Kinder, Rubenstein, Schaeffer, & Simmons, 1966). These investigators attempted to establish social reinforcement functions for the word "good." At first they used the respondent conditioning paradigm. Yet, in spite of several hundred trials during which the word was paired with the delivery of food, there was no change in the child's behavior. "Good" failed to acquire secondary reinforcement properties. The child continued to seem oblivious to the social stimulus; he apparently failed to attend to it.

Having found the classical conditioning paradigm to be ineffective in establishing social reinforcers, Lovaas et al. (1966) turned to the operant model to establish a discriminative social stimulus for the primary reinforcer. That is, the child learned that the presence of the social stimulus (the word "good") signaled the availability of food. Discriminative stimulus training thus forced the child to attend to the social stimulus. Once Lovaas had established the discrimination (presence of social stimulus = availability of food), he was able to use the social stimulus as an acquired reinforcer to maintain a simple motor response. With intermittent delivery of food, these investigators were able to show that the social stimulus retained its acquired reinforcement property over extended sessions as long as it continued to be discriminative for food.

The success of the operant approach, where the respondent approach had failed, might be due to the autistic child's problem with overexclusive attention, discussed earlier. In respondent conditioning, the unconditioned and conditioned stimuli occur almost simultaneously and may appear as a stimulus complex to the child. Should the child attend only to one of the two components, no conditioning would result. In the operant situation, on the other hand, discriminative and reinforcing stimuli are separated in time by the emission of the response, conceivably making learning easier for an autistic child.

Establishing Language   The highly complex behavior we call language can be analyzed in operant terms (Skinner, 1957). Accordingly, a word or words emitted by the child are reinforced by the social environment. Whether or not this formulation applies to the language acquisition of normal children, it has served as the basis for therapeutic techniques with children who had failed to acquire language and were either totally nonverbal or engaged in echolalia, the noncommunicative parroting of words just uttered by another person. In this approach, reinforcement is made contingent on the production of sounds or words. Because a response must occur before it can be reinforced, the child must actively participate in the treatment. The therapist can do little to elicit a word, and when a child is completely nonverbal, speech must be shaped by using any available vocalization and reinforcing successive approximations of language. In some instances (Risley & Wolf, 1967), the child's echolalic behavior can be used as a starting point, while in others (Hewett, 1965; Schell, Stark, & Giddan, 1967), training in social imitation or the therapist's prompts or both must precede speech training (Lovaas, 1966, 1977).

Like many children with as gross a disorder as absence of speech, Peter, the 4½-year-old boy treated by Hewett (1965), manifested other deviant behaviors that interfered with attempts to develop language. His high distractibility and low attention span made it necessary to train him in a specially constructed booth that not only reduced extraneous stimuli but also permitted the introduction of isolation and darkness contingent upon inappropriate responses. Appropriate responses were reinforced with candy and light, but these arbitrary reinforcers were soon supplemented by the natural reinforcers dispensed by the social environment when a child engages in acceptable and nonaversive behavior. Peter had acquired a 32-word vocabulary after 6 months of speech training, and after a further 8 months, his speaking vocabulary had grown to 150 words, the beginnings of spoken language. During the latter part of training, generalization to the natural environment was stressed—the boy's parents participating in the program. It is significant that Peter's change in behavior altered the reactions of others toward him. The nursing staff came to seek him out for verbal interaction, giving him cues for imitation and insisting on speech before granting requests. Generalization of appropriate speech from the therapy setting to the child's own environment can be enhanced if the therapist sees to it that speech is reinforced under a variety of conditions.

Work with children who exhibit echolalia raises the question of the reason for this behavior. The children can obviously produce words. What makes these productions occur in this atypical, noncommunicative fashion? An answer to this question was furnished by a study conducted by Carr, Schreibman, and Lovaas (1975), who tested the assumption that echolalic speech represents a response strategy these children employ in communicative situations where they are unable to make a more appropriate response. These investigators presented five severely disturbed and five normal children with two sets of verbal stimuli. One set consisted of verbal stimuli composed of nonsense words to which no response was possible (e.g., "Bot ni ork"), the other set were simple questions or instructions, such as "What's your name" or "Touch your head." The results showed that the psychotic children tended to echo the nonsense sentences but responded appropriately to the meaningful questions and instructions. The normal children, on the other hand, typically echoed neither type of statement.

Following this demonstration, the investigators taught three psychotic children appropriate responses to some of the nonsense sentences but not to others. For example, "La kels bes chern" was taught to be the instruction to touch a toy horse, while the question "What is a tas poo grot?" was to be answered by "shoe." In general, the results demonstrated that when the children had been taught to make an appropriate response to such sentences, their tendency to echo them disappeared, while they continued to echo those sentences to which no meaning had been attached. What is more, the appropriate response was also produced when someone other than the person who had been involved in the training addressed the nonsense statements to the children.

From this work it can be concluded that psychotic children tend to echo statements to which they have no appropriate response. Treatment of this problem should therefore be aimed at teaching these children the appropriate response to statements they echo; to teach them what the sentences mean. At the same time, as Carr et al. (1975) suggest, it would be economical to teach echolalic children to say "I don't know" or to ask "What?" when presented with questions or instructions to which they have not yet learned an appropriate response. It seems that these children use the echoing as their way of indicating that they do not know the meaning of a statement that has been addressed to them.

There remains the question how the echoing was acquired in the first place. Here, of course, one can only speculate, although a suggestion made by Carr et al. (1975) seems very plausible. They point out that in the earliest verbal interaction between parent and child, the parent points to a cat and says, "Look at the kitty." When the child then responds with "kitty" the parent indicates pleasure and says, "Right, kitty" thus reinforcing the echo. Echolalia may thus represent an early developmental stage of verbal behavior beyond which the autistic child has, for some reason, never been able to develop. Yet, given special training, as in the study just discussed, they may be able to grow beyond it.

The verbal mode is, of course, not the only way through which communication is possible. If it were the case that some autistic children have a particular difficulty in comprehending and/or producing words, it might be possible to teach them receptive and expressive skills by using another mode, such as the sign language employed by Gardner and Gardner (1969) to teach a rudimentary language to a chimpanzee. This reasoning underlies an approach used by De Villiers and Naughton (1974), who taught autistic children a symbol language similar to the one Premack (1970) had used in his work with the chimpanzee, Sarah. This involves associating so-called particles varying in shape, size, and color with different concepts and reinforcing the student for the correct use of these particles. De Villiers and Naughton (1974) worked with two autistic children whose verbal language was limited to echolalia in one case and infantile babbling in the other. Over the 9-month period during which this experiment was conducted, the echolalic child progressed to the point where he was able to produce and comprehend 4-word-long verbal sentences and to use the basic communication functions of naming, commanding, describing, and questioning. This had been accomplished by pairing the particle symbols with spoken words that stood for the same object or concept. The other child, who was younger and more severely impaired, advanced more slowly and did not progress that far. Though able to arrange four particles correctly, he did not use more than occasional single-syllable words in his own speech. Since the entire work done by these investigators took place in two 15-minute sessions per week, their results suggest that with more intensive efforts considerably more could be accomplished. The method may derive its effectiveness from the fact that visually presented symbols remain the same each time they are used and can therefore be more easily discriminated. Spoken words, on the other hand, vary in loudness or inflection from time to time and thus lack consistency as stimuli to which specific responses are to be learned. Furthermore, the symbol method requires the child to focus attention on the behavior of the other person. This combination of qualities may help an autistic child who, as we have seen, has difficulty in attending to the central aspects of a stimulus situation.

Reducing Excess Behavior   While most of the problems of autistic children stem from deficient behaviors, such as the absence of language or the inability to learn by imitation, there are some characteristic problems involving excess behavior which must be reduced, often before deficient behavior can be established. Such excess behavior often takes the form of self-stimulatory or self-injurious activities. Self-stimulatory behavior includes such stereotyped, repetitive behavior as spinning objects, flapping of fingers or arms, and rhythmic rocking. Since this behavior is often very persistent, it greatly interferes with therapeutic attempts to teach adaptive responses. It must therefore be reduced before much else can be done for the child. Self-injurious behavior, on the other hand, must be eliminated because it represents a real danger to the child's health and may, in fact, be life-threatening. This behavior consists of head banging, hitting one's eyes, biting parts of one's body, or repeated scratching to the point of creating deep and open wounds.

Self-Stimulatory Behavior   The word *autistic*, in its essential meaning of preoccupation with oneself, is nowhere more appropriate than in describing self-stimulatory behavior which seems to have no relationship to anything going on around the child and preempts the child's attention from all other matters. Only highly intrusive stimuli, such as a loud shout or a slap, can disrupt such behavior and (temporarily) bring the child to attend to stimuli a parent, teacher, or therapist wishes to present.

The principles of reinforcement tell us that behavior that is so tenaciously maintained must be receiving some kind of reinforcement. What, then, is it that is reinforcing self-stimulatory behavior? If we knew this we might, by withdrawing this reinforcement, be able to reduce this activity through extinction. This would certainly be more desirable than using punishment to suppress it, even if the punishment is no more than shouts and slaps or time-out.

The time-out procedure, it will be recalled, is technically a withdrawal of the opportunity to obtain positive reinforcement. Because it reduces the response on which it is made contingent, time-out is a form of punishment. To use time-out properly, one must have ascertained what it is that is serving as the positive reinforcer, since it is the access to this that is supposed to be temporarily suspended. In common use, however, only cursory attempts are made to find out what the positive reinforcer is that maintains the behavior one seeks to reduce (MacDonough & Forehand, 1973). It is usually assumed that the presence of other individuals in the room or the therapist's interest and attention are reinforcing and these are therefore made the object of the time-out procedure. When the behavior in question then decreases in frequency, it is assumed that the positive reinforcers have been correctly identified. Risley and Wolf (1967) were able to eliminate disruptive, self-stimulatory behavior in this manner. In working on the development of speech in echolalic children, they found that self-stimulatory behavior interfered with the training process. They were able to bring mildly disruptive behavior under control by simply looking away until the child once again sat quietly in the chair. More severe forms of disruptive behavior were dealt with by having the therapist leave the room for a brief period of time, reentering only when the child had not engaged in the self-stimulatory behavior for a few moments. The therapist's coming back into the room thus served as a negative reinforcer for desired behavior. This assumes that being left alone was an aversive condition which was terminated contingent on the production of the desired behavior. Whether the therapist's presence is indeed a positive reinforcer must be ascertained for each individual child by a controlled functional analysis. The pragmatic fact that a procedure, such as the one used in the Risley and Wolf (1967) approach, leads to success (in the sense of teaching some communicative speech) is not in itself proof that the relevant reinforcers had been correctly identified.

If one does not know what it is that maintains self-stimulatory behavior, one really does not know what is to be temporarily withheld by a time-out procedure. The therapist's leaving the room is based on the assumption that something about the therapist's presence is reinforcing, but whether that is so remains in the realm of speculation. In fact, as Solnick, Rincover, and Peterson (1977) have pointed out, without a functional analysis of the stimulus events, what one expects to be a time-out (punishing) procedure may, in fact, turn out to be a reinforcing event. These authors describe their work with a 6-year-old autistic child whose tantrum behavior disrupted attempts to teach her the discrimination of colors. Whenever the child engaged in a tantrum, the teacher would pick up the reinforcers in use for the training (candy) and leave the room for 10 seconds. Contrary to expectations, this procedure served to increase rather than reduce the number of tantrums; it reinforced, rather than punished this disruptive behavior. Careful observations revealed that the child would engage in self-stimulatory behavior during the time-out periods, leading to the assumption that the opportunity to engage in that behavior made the putative time-out intervals a positive rather than a negative experience. Following this discovery, a new procedure was introduced and its effectiveness tested. Whenever the girl engaged in a tantrum, the teacher would physically restrain all self-stimulatory behavior for 10 seconds by holding the child's hands or arms so that she could not weave, flap, or wave them. With this, tantrums quickly declined in frequency and disappeared altogether during the last four treatment sessions. There is apparently something about self-stimulation that is reinforcing. The question remains what this is.

Rincover (1978) conducted a study based on the assumption that self-stimulatory behavior is reinforced by the sensory feedback that the behavior itself produces and that the reinforcement is thus under the child's control. This assumption was tested by masking or removing various types of sensory feedback in order to see whether this would have an effect on the behavior. One child, for example, would incessantly spin objects, such as a plate, on the table. There are, of course, several senses that are stimulated by this action. One sees the plate twirling, feels the sensation in one's fingers and hand as the plate is given its spin, hears the sound it makes, and experiences the slight current of air that is set in motion by the spinning. In order to eliminate the reinforcing sensation, it must be identified. Theoretically, this can be done by removing or masking one of these feedbacks at a time until the one is found which, when removed, results in a reduction of the behavior's frequency. Careful observation, however, can accelerate such a functional analysis. In the case described by Rincover (1978), it was observed that the boy would cock his head to the side and lean toward the spinning plate, as if he was listening to the sound it made. A procedure, called *sensory extinction*, was then experimentally introduced to test the hypothesis that the sound of the plate was indeed the reinforcing consequence. The table at which the child was sitting was therefore covered with a thick but hard and flat carpet which made the spinning of the plate inaudible. As soon as this was done the percentage of time this boy spent on this self-stimulatory behavior dropped from a high of 72 percent to near zero. As part of a reversal design, the carpeting was then removed whereupon the spinning increased, taking up some 83 percent of the time in the testing session. Experimentally eliminating only the visual feedback by placing a blindfold over the boy's eyes had little effect on the self-stimulatory behavior, the plate spinning remaining around the 58-percent level. Only when the carpet was replaced and the auditory feedback thereby eliminated did the behavior return to and remain at the zero level over a follow-up period of 2 months. Similar work with other children who engaged in different forms of self-stimulatory behavior confirmed the assumption that such behavior is maintained by the sensory consequences and that sensory extinction can be used to reduce or eliminate it.

An experiment such as the one just discussed is not a treatment; it merely provides clues for the direction treatment should take. One of these directions is to include sensory extinction in a comprehensive program where new and adaptive responses are taught while the child is not engaging in the self-stimulatory behavior. Any undesirable behavior one eliminates must always be replaced by explicitly planned desirable alternatives. Another direction indicated by this work lies in the identification of potent reinforcers for use in strengthening desired behaviors. If a child's plate-spinning is reinforced by the sound that this action produces, one must conclude that this sound is a powerful reinforcer. As Rincover (1978) suggests, such an auditory consequence might well be used for constructive purposes. Why not, for example, record the noise of a spinning plate and permit the child to listen to it contingent on the emission of a desired response? This would be a readily available alternative to the commonly used edible reinforcers for which children tend to become satiated and which, for their effectiveness, depend on prior deprivation.

Self-Injurious Behavior   Unlike self-stimulatory behavior which, though it may be irritating to the adult observer, does no more harm than that it precludes other, more constructive and desirable behavior, self-injurious, self-mutilating, or self-destructive behavior often represents an immediate or long-range, physical danger to the child. Some children use their teeth to rip large amounts of tissue from their shoulders and arms, others have chewed off parts of their fingers, some hit their heads so violently against walls or furniture that their retinas become detached. As Lovaas et al. (1974) pointed out, some would accidentally kill themselves if they were not physically restrained or kept sedated by strong medications. Many of these children, some only 8 or 9 years old, "have spent most of their lives in restraints, tied down both by their feet and arms" (ibid., p. 116). Therapists, regardless of theoretical persuasion, find self-injurious behavior to head the list of problems that require immediate intervention.

Before a behavior can be eliminated, it is necessary to discover what maintains it. To do so, the behavior must be observed in the context of its antecedents and consequences. When this is done, what will be observed is that whenever a child engages in self-injurious behavior, whatever adult is nearby will immediately seek to intervene by holding the child, talking to him or her, or introducing a physical restraint. Self-injurious behavior invariably elicits such a response; it has demand characteristics. Lovaas and Simmons (1969) demonstrated that such, usually sympathetic attention actually increases the frequency of self-injurious behavior but that if such attention is withdrawn, the behavior decreases. At least for some children, the social consequences of self-injurious behavior serve as reinforcers (Bachman, 1972). If this is the case, then withdrawing such reinforcement should lead to the gradual extinction of that behavior. This is true from a theoretical standpoint, but in practice it is not advisable to rely on extinction as a means of dealing with self-injurious behavior. Not only is there the phenomenon of an initial increase in the response frequency or intensity when reinforcement is first withdrawn but the decrease follows only when no further reinforcement is forthcoming over a period of time. With as dangerous a behavior as self-injury, one cannot countenance this spurt at the beginning of the extinction regimen. In addition, as Lovaas et al. (1974) pointed out, self-mutilation that had become extinguished in a specific setting where it was no longer reinforced, reemerged in other situations where the child had previously been comforted following such behavior. Clearly, some other form of intervention than extinction will have to be used in order to deal with self-injurious behavior.

While Lovaas, Freitag, Gold, and Kassorla (1965) furnished convincing demonstrations of the potency of social reinforcement in maintaining self-injurious behavior, it appears that other motivations may also play a role or that different children engage in self-injurious behavior for different reasons. A detailed review by Carr (1977) suggests that a negative reinforcement hypothesis may also have merit. In this formulation, the child would be under some aversive stimulation that is terminated contingent on the emission of a self-injurious response. Carr, Newsom, and Binkoff (1976) demonstrated this functional relationship with a mildly retarded but not autistic boy who would hit his head with his fist to the extent that his face was bruised and cut. This behavior was particularly intense in a teaching situation immediately after the teacher issued a request that he do something (e.g., "Point to the window"). Typically, a teacher will interrupt the session and not insist that the demand be carried out in order to get the child to stop hitting himself. In fact, the entire lesson may be terminated when the self-injurious behavior rises to an intolerable level. In that way, the child escapes from the demanding situation in consequence of the self-injurious behavior which, having thus been reinforced, is likely to recur the next time the teacher tries to undertake a lesson.

When self-injurious behavior is attributed to social reinforcement where, in fact, it is maintained by negative reinforcement, attempts to deal with it by withdrawing the social consequences (ignoring it) would clearly be counterproductive. The more correct procedure in these cases would be to ascertain what aversive stimulation the child succeeds in terminating by the self-mutilating behavior and to attempt a reduction of the aversive nature of these stimuli. When Carr et al. (1976) had the teacher present her requests in the positive context of an animated, entertaining story, the frequency of the boy's self-hitting decreased dramatically.

Self-injurious behavior is apparently maintained by such *extrinsic* consequences as positive social reinforcement and the negative reinforcement entailed in escape from aversive stimulation. Carr (1977) suggests that there may also be instances where self-injurious behavior is maintained by *intrinsic* consequences. It is possible that for some children self-injurious behavior is merely a more extreme form of self-stimulatory behavior and that the contingencies that were discussed under that heading are also operating here. Obviously, when a child engages in self-injurious behavior because it provides sensory stimulation and an adult then comes rushing over with solicitous ministrations and attention, the behavior receives both extrinsic and intrinsic reinforcement, making it doubly difficult to reduce. From a therapeutic standpoint, if self-injurious behavior were maintained by its intrinsic consequences, attempts should be made to substitute other, less injurious, more constructive forms of sensory stimulation. Unfortunately, there is no technology currently available that would permit the attenuation or masking of the sensory stimulation a child can derive from headbanging or finger biting short of constant physical restraint or deep sedation, neither of which can be deemed to be therapeutic.

Punishment Procedures By far the quickest and most effective method of suppressing self-injurious behavior is by introducing an immediate, powerful negative consequence each time this behavior is emitted. We come thus to a discussion of the use of aversive stimuli in the treatment of this potentially life-threatening behavior. It is drastic treatment for a drastic problem. Various investigators (Lovaas et al., 1965; Lovaas, Schaeffer, & Simmons, 1965, Lovaas & Simmons, 1969; Risley, 1968; Tate & Baroff, 1966) have reported rapid response suppression when a painful electric shock is made contingent on self-injurious responses, particularly when this approach is combined with the positive reinforcement of incompatible, adaptive behavior. This "electric shock" should not be confused with the electroconvulsive therapy used by many psychiatrists wherein electrodes are attached to a patient's temples and a powerful current is transmitted through the brain, resulting in a convulsion which is followed by loss of consciousness. The shock used in work with autistic children is usually administered by means of a hand-held, battery-operated rod that is applied to the legs or other exposed parts of the body, except for face and head. This delivers between 4 and 5 milliamperes of current which, though painful, is entirely safe and harmless. The pain is localized to the point of contact and ends immediately when the current is turned off a moment later.

The effectiveness of this procedure raises the interesting question why a relatively mild and exceedingly brief pain should terminate the far more severe physical abuse that results from a child's self-injurious behavior. Lovaas et al. (1974) have suggested that over the years these children have adapted to the pain from their self-inflicted injuries, which may have started in a mild form and gradually increased in severity. The electric shock, on the other hand, being new and coming on full-strength, as it were, offers no opportunity for adaptation. At any rate, what seems clear is that if these children were hurting themselves because they enjoy or needed pain, the shock should be a sought-after experience. This not being the case, formulations that invoke masochism or guilt-assuaging as explanations do not seem to have much merit.

Those who employ electric shock as a punisher for self-injurious behavior are well aware of the ethical and moral questions that are raised by this procedure (e.g., Lovaas & Newsom, 1976). Clearly, physical punishment should be used as a form of treatment only when the behavior in question must be quickly suppressed because delay would endanger the child or make the learning of adaptive responses impossible. In a case reported by Risley (1968), for example, a child engaged in climbing behavior that not only endangered her safety but also thwarted all attempts to teach constructive responses. Before introducing punishment with electric shock, Risley had tried time-out procedures, extinction, and reinforcement of incompatible behaviors without success. When punishment seemed the only means left, careful records were kept to assure that it had no undesirable side effects, such as suppressing other behaviors, and the use of shock was discontinued as soon as the target behavior had been brought under control. For less dangerous undesirable behaviors, such as that child's autistic rocking, less severe forms of negative consequences, such as time-out, continued to be the method of choice.

In the work of Risley (1968) just cited, concern was expressed about undesirable side effects of the punishment procedure, yet none were found. Negative emotional responses on the part of the child, such as fear of the teacher, might have been expected but, as Risley tells us, the child recovered from the shock episodes much faster than the adult who administered the shock! In general, a review of the side effects of using electric shock in work with autistic children (Lichstein & Schreibman, 1976) supports the contention that negative side effects are minimal and transitory, while positive side effects are far more frequent. These include increases in social behavior, affection, cooperation, smiling, and playfulness, which generalized to extratherapy situations.

It is extremely important to remember that shock *suppresses* self-injurious behavior, it does not eliminate it. Therefore, any therapeutic use of this method must be accompanied by explicitly planned and systematic efforts to teach the child new and adaptive responses which can take the place of the temporarily suppressed behavior. As Lovaas and Newsom (1976) stress, no one should undertake to use punishment in dealing with self-destructive behavior unless they are willing to invest considerable time and effort in developing adaptive behaviors which can take the place of self-destructive behavior as a means of obtaining social reinforcement from the environment and which thus have a chance to be maintained in the child's repertoire.

Comprehensive Treatment Programs

Thus far, we have discussed the treatment of psychotic children in terms of work with specific aspects of their problem, such as developing imitation or language, and reducing self-stimulatory or self-injurious behavior. Individual children will obviously be receiving help with these and other problems in various combinations, depending on the specific nature of their particular disorder. Browning (1971), Lovaas, Koegel, Simmons, and Long (1973), and Nordquist and Wahler (1973) are among many authors who have reported their work in the comprehensive treatment of psychotic children. This often includes training parents and teachers in the behavioral methods used by the clinician because only in that way can the newly learned skills become generalized to the child's natural settings (Miller & Sloane, 1976). Because of the inordinate expense which is entailed in treating these profoundly disturbed children over a period as long as 2 or 3 years, attempts have begun to be made to explore treating small groups of such children in class-roomlike settings (Koegel & Rincover, 1974; Rincover & Koegel, 1977).

At the beginning of this discussion of the treatment of autistic children we cited the discouraging statistics from the follow-up study conducted by DeMyer et al. (1973), which showed that the prognosis for such children is rather poor. What happens to such children when they receive behavior therapy aimed not at "curing autism" but at establishing adaptive responses in specific areas of difficulties?

What is probably the most massive study of the effectiveness of behavior therapy with these severely disturbed children was reported by Lovaas et al. (1973), who treated twenty autistic children and took careful, reliable, quantitative measures of behavior. These measures reflected self-stimulation, echolalic speech, appropriate speech, social nonverbal behavior, and appropriate play. In addition, data on intelligence test scores and the results from the Vineland Social Maturity Scale were assessed. The authors report that during treatment disordered behavior decreased, while prosocial behavior increased for all twenty children, although the changes were not equally great for all. Some of the children developed spontaneous social interaction and the spontaneous use of language. Intelligence and social quotients showed large gains during treatment. When the same measures were used in a follow-up 2 years after treatment, large differences emerged that depended on whether or not the children had been institutionalized at the conclusion of their exposure to behavior therapy. Those children whose parents had been taught to use contingency management in the home continued to improve, while those children who had been sent to institutions where the contingencies were totally different from those under which the constructive behavior had been learned and whose parents had not learned to be their behavior therapist, regressed and deteriorated.

This report by Lovaas et al. (1973) also mentions the generalization of improvement to areas that had not been specific treatment targets. Thus, children who had been chronic toe-walkers began to walk normally after 4 to 5 months of treatment; those who had never slept through the night began to clock 10 hours of uninterrupted sleep, etc. At the same time, the authors clearly state that their treatment was not a "cure for autism." They made remarkable progress with children for whom other forms of treatment had been ineffective, and they were able to demonstrate that for children whose home environment can take over the treatment program by applying systematic contingency management, dramatic improvement can be recorded.

Regardless of the conditions under which the grossly atypical behavior of psychotic children first arose, reinforcement serves to maintain and modify it over time. It stands to reason that the longer such reinforcement is in effect, the more difficult it will be to reduce the psychotic behavior and to replace it by adaptive responses. For this reason, it is very important to begin therapeutic intervention as early in the child's life as possible. Prognosis is best for those children whose early infantile autism is identified during the first 2 years of life so that treatment can be undertaken while they are still that young. This consideration led Lovaas to institute a young-autism treatment project for children whose treatment is begun while they are still under 40 months of age. Lovaas, Young, and Newsom (1978) report that improvements in these children's behavior usually occur within the first year of treatment. These therapeutic changes include the full range of social, emotional, and intellectual aspects of behavior and "appear to be quite permanent" (ibid., p. 413).

RECAPITULATION

Childhood schizophrenia, a behavior disorder of profound, psychotic proportions, differs in several distinct features from early infantile autism, but the two disorders continue to be viewed as closely related or the same by many investigators and clinicians. The best available data suggest that childhood schizophrenia has a genetic basis and that its development involves an interaction between neurophysiological and environmental factors. There is little to substantiate the hypothesis that either or both parents "cause" the child's problem. On the contrary, it may well be that the presence of a profoundly disturbed child in the home has a disrupting effect on family equilibrium and parental behavior.

From the point of view of eventual prevention it is important to distinguish between early infantile autism and childhood schizophrenia, but in terms of the treatment of the individual child it matters little which label happens to apply. The aim of a behavioral approach to treatment is not to "cure" childhood schizophrenia or early infantile autism but to modify the child's deviant response repertoire so as to facilitate more appropriate functioning. The treatment of both types of psychotic disorders was therefore discussed under the same heading. Treatment entails the development of such important aspects of behavior as imitation, conditioned social reinforcers, and language. Since such excess behaviors as self-stimulation and self-injury not only interfere with the acquisition of adaptive responses but often endanger the child's health, they must be reduced if anything else is to be accomplished. To do so, it is necessary to discover what stimuli control and maintain these behaviors by conducting a careful functional analysis. Where slower methods represent a risk to the child, rapid suppression of self-injurious behavior can be achieved by punishment procedures, but these must always be accompanied by active efforts to develop adaptive responses. When treatment is initiated early in the child's life or where a treatment program can be continued in the child's home environment, behavior therapy has led to some dramatic improvements for psychotic children.

Chapter 12

Learning Disabilities

Whether a behavior is to be defined as deviant is a function of the implicit norms and role expectations a society holds for its members. For children of school age the role expectation is that they be adequately performing students. The adequacy of their performance is, in turn, defined and evaluated by the school that the child attends in terms of the requirements of that school and the expectations of the community that it serves. In a highly technological, knowledge-oriented society, which views education as the key to social mobility and success, inadequate performance in the role of student comes to be viewed as a serious problem by school and family alike. This concern about educational failure has made school-related difficulties the one most frequently cited problem of children brought to the attention of professionals concerned with psychological disorders of children (Gilbert, 1957). For reasons to be discussed below, it is very difficult to obtain accurate data on the prevalence of school children whose academic performance is below expectations, but informed estimates have placed their numbers as high as 20 percent of the school-age population (McCarthy & McCarthy, 1969).

PROBLEMS OF DEFINITION

Learning is a hypothetical construct that refers to a function that can only be inferred from observed changes in performance when they follow certain antecedent events called *training, teaching,* or *experience.* In order to demonstrate this function, one must (among other controls) measure a child's performance before and after an event that one presumes capable of changing (enhancing) his performance. It stands to reason that change should be expected only if the intervening event has relevance for this particular child in his current condition in terms of his developmental level, capacity, and learning history. A gross example may serve to illustrate this point. If, unknown to her teacher, a girl were to be totally deaf and the teacher presented her with a verbal statement designed to teach her something, the child would fail to learn. It would make no sense to say that the child has a learning disability; it might be more appropriate to say that the problem is the teacher's. If, and only if, an appropriate teaching method was used and the child failed to learn, is it appropriate to say the child has trouble learning. Because of this need to assure that the material to be taught and the method by which it is taught are appropriate to the child's condition, the study of learning disabilities encounters problems of major proportions. One can never be certain that a particular teaching method is appropriate as long as a child fails to learn. The onus is on those who try to teach; for they must exhaust all possible methods before opting for the easy vindication of blaming their teaching failure on the child's learning difficulty (Ross, 1967).

But the problem of appropriate instruction is not the only complication in this field. Another is the issue of measurement. A learning disability represents a discrepancy between a child's estimated academic potential and his or her actual level of academic performance. This calls not only for a measure of actual performance but also for an index that will permit a valid estimate of potential performance. To determine learning potential one would need a measure of a child's inherent endowment: *there is no such measure.*

The usual mode of estimating children's learning potential is to analyze their performance on a standard intelligence test. If the score is near the average or above-average range, it is assumed that the child's potential is at that level; but, as Haring and Bateman (1969) have pointed out, children who fail to score near the average on intelligence tests have, upon further examination, been shown to be capable of performance at a higher level. What an intelligence test measures is essentially how much of what the child has learned is capable of being displayed at the time of testing. These tests are, in other words, no more than measures of attainment or achievement, and if a child has difficulties in learning, for whatever reasons, this deficit will be reflected in the intelligence test score. A somewhat more sophisticated approach to ascertaining potential than that involved in looking at the overall intelligence test score is the analysis of the relationship of different subtest scores, as on such instruments as the revised Wechsler Intelligence

Scale for Children (Wechsler, 1974); but even here psychologists are only guessing when they assume the highest subtest scores to reflect the child's "true" potential, particularly in view of the low validity of profile interpretation (Ross, 1959).

There is, as was pointed out, no measure of learning potential, and the intelligence test is a poor substitute. The actual level of performance, with which the presumed "potential" is to be compared in establishing a learning disability, is usually measured by achievement tests; thus, a statement about learning disabilities is ultimately based on a comparison of scores on two kinds of achievement tests. Since performance on both kinds of tests can be interfered with by the same factors, it is possible that there will be no discrepancy between achievement test scores and intelligence test scores simply because both scores are equally depressed. On the other hand, when a discrepancy does appear, it need not necessarily mean that the child has a learning disability; for the problem may lie in test performance or in error of measurement or in the previously suggested teaching failure. The dilemma is not solved when the measure of school achievement is based not on test scores but on actual classroom performance because this only substitutes the unreliability of teachers' grading and often arbitrary promotion policies for the unreliability of formal achievement tests.

Bateman and Schiefelbusch (1969) cogently observe that it is often important to ascertain the general achievement level of a particular classroom before one can understand why a child's performance is perceived as less than adequate by teacher or parent. If a girl of average intelligence is placed in a class where the mean ability level is extremely high, she may appear to be performing quite poorly. On the other hand, it is possible that a severe learning difficulty remains undetected when a child of very high ability is placed in a low or low-average classroom or school. These writers also point out that the significance of a discrepancy between ability and performance may depend on whether "there is, in fact, something that can be done about the child's achievement problem. If there is, then the discrepancy is significant and the child has a learning disability. If there is not, perhaps he should not be so labeled" (p. 8).

Despite the difficulties in identifying and defining a child with a learning disability, and such misgivings of concerned investigators as Bateman and Schiefelbusch (1969) notwithstanding, it became necessary to develop a definition of learning disabilities. This need arose from the fact that the U.S. Congress passed a law, the 1969 Children with Specific Learning Disabilities Act (PL 91-230), which provides for the funding of services for learning-disabled children. Clearly, with money appropriated one had to know whom that money was for; the definition worked out for this purpose reads as follows:

> Children with specific learning disabilities exhibit a disorder in one or more of the basic psychological processes involved in understanding or using spoken or written language. These may be manifested in disorders of listening, thinking, talking, reading, writing, spelling, or arithmetic. They include conditions which have been re-

ferred to as perceptual handicaps, brain injury, minimal brain dysfunction, dyslexia, developmental aphasia, etc. They do not include learning problems which are due primarily to visual, hearing, or motor handicaps, to mental retardation, emotional disturbance, or to environmental disadvantage.

A few years later, when the U.S. Congress passed a law (the Education for All Handicapped Children Act (PL 94-142)) in which educational opportunities in the least restrictive environment were mandated for every child, regardless of handicap, this definition of learning disabilities was incorporated with some minor changes in wording. The vague "et cetera" was deleted and environmental disadvantage was broadened by the addition of the words cultural and economic. In an apparent attempt to clarify how learning-disabled children were to be identified, the lawmakers added the following sentence:

> A child who exhibits a discrepancy of 50 percent or more between expected achievement based on his intellectual ability and actual achievement, determined on an individual basis, shall be deemed to have a specific learning disability.

Even with the addition of this sentence, this definition remains extremely broad. In fact, by not indicating how the 50-percent discrepancy between expected and actual achievement is to be calculated, that sentence only compounded the confusion. From the standpoint of making help available to as many children as possible, the breadth of this legislation is a good thing—provided enough funds are appropriated to implement the good intentions. From the standpoint of knowing what to do for learning-disabled children and of finding out more about them, however, the definition is an utter failure. It fails to tell us how a disorder in one or more of the "basic psychological processes" involved in understanding language is to be identified, nor does it indicate how the manifestations of such a disorder in such areas as listening and thinking are to be recognized. Even more unfortunate are the references to brain injury and minimal brain dysfunction. These phrases extend the definition to a wide range of children whose inclusion under the category of learning disability will greatly complicate any attempts to study this problem for the purposes of treatment and prevention. For political and administrative reasons, one may wish to seek a broad definition; for educational and research purposes, however, a narrow and highly specific definition is the only kind that will help to advance knowledge and improve teaching.

Eventually, as Senf (1972) has pointed out, it will be necessary to identify subcategories within the area of learning disability. At that point, we should be able to make specific statements about what educational approach is best for children in a given group. Until such time, "learning disability" as a label for an individual child can be deemed useful only if it serves as an administrative key that gives the child access to available resources. Otherwise, there is not much point in the label; for if a child has trouble learning and someone labels him or her learning-disabled, there is the risk that, having found an impressive-sounding label for the child, efforts at providing help will cease because the label is viewed as an explanation for the problem. The statement "She has a learning disability, so, of course, she can't be expected to learn" all too often serves as an excuse for giving up on efforts to teach such a child. When used in this manner, the term "learning disability" is clearly objectionable. As with all other labels of psychological disorders, the term learning disability is no more than a description of what has been observed; it is not an explanation.

Selective Attention

The definition that has been written into law is, as we have said, of little value to those who seek to bring order out of the chaos that the field of learning disabilities currently represents. One way of approaching such an ordering is to review available research on learning-disabled children and to ask whether there is anything that many of them might have in common. Were this to be the case, this common factor might provide a basis for specifying one of the subcategories called for by Senf (1972). Such a review of research does indeed point in a certain direction (Ross, 1976). Available studies suggest that many learning-disabled children share a developmental delay in the ability to sustain selective attention (Pelham & Ross, 1977; Tarver, Hallahan, Kauffman, & Ball, 1976). From this recognition, it is possible to derive a definition of learning disability that is more restrictive than the one that has become encased in statutory concrete. It is that a learning-disabled child is

> . . . a child of at least average intelligence whose academic performance is impaired by a developmental lag in the ability to sustain selective attention. Such a child requires specialized instruction in order to permit the use of his or her full intellectual potential (Ross, 1977, p. 11).

The development of the cognitive processes that culminate in selective attention was traced in the chapter dealing with early infantile autism (Chapter 10). There we suggested that children with that profound disorder might be those who have developmentally remained at the level of overexclusive attention. It was further pointed out that in the normal process of development the child goes through a phase characterized by overinclusive attention before mature selective attention is attained. Children who progress through this development more slowly than most others would be handicapped in coping with the academic demands of the school, which usually operates on the assumption that all children function more or less at the same level of perceptual development. Construing learning disability as due to a lag in the development of selective attention implies that learning disability lies on a continuum with early infantile autism where problems with attention also seem to play a central role. This obviously does not mean that learning-disabled children are autistic. It does mean that early infantile autism represents a most profound impairment of learning because of which the child acquires hardly any coping skills and continues to function at the level of a preverbal child. The learning-disabled child, on the other hand, functions very well in all areas except for those, such as reading, that place a premium on the ability to employ selective attention.

The Brain-Dysfunction Hypothesis

The statutory definition of learning disability cited earlier makes reference to brain injury and minimal brain dysfunction, reflecting the fact that children with learning disabilities are at times said to have something wrong with their brains. Upon close examination, children with learning disabilities manifest a variety of difficulties, not only with attention, but also with motor control and coordination. They have been described as hyperactive, distractible, perseverative, impulsive, and disoriented. This has led some writers (e.g., Wender, 1971) to declare that the basic problem of these children is that they have an abnormality in the brain, although attempts to substantiate this hypothesis have been unsuccessful (Crinella, 1973; Owen, Adams, Forrest, Stolz, & Fisher, 1971). While there are children who do have damaged brains and who thus have trouble learning, it only confuses matters to group them in an undifferentiated category with other learning-disabled children who have no demonstrable brain damage. For the vast majority of learning-disabled children such terms as minimal brain dysfunction add nothing to the understanding of the problem and largely serve to give the misleading impression that there is a medically identifiable syndrome—and a known (and irreversible) cause of the difficulty.

   The assumption of neurological impairment in children who manifest learning disabilities is, at least in part, based on the following unsound syllogism: children with learning disabilities often display hyperactivity and distractibility; children with demonstrable brain damage often display hyperactivity and distractibility; therefore, children with learning disabilities have brain damage, even if it is not otherwise demonstrable. That this reasoning is fallacious was underscored in a careful study by Kaspar, Millichap, Backus, Child, and Schulman (1971), who showed that while brain-damaged children are more active and distractible than normal controls in a structured test situation, brain damage does not lead to hyperactivity and distractibility under any and all stimulus conditions "but rather to certain forms of hyperactivity in certain children, certain forms of distractibility in others, and so on" (p. 337).

   It is, of course, a truism to say that learning involves the brain and it follows that if a child has trouble with learning, that trouble must somehow involve the brain. But this does not necessarily mean that the brain is damaged, either minimally or in a gross fashion. When learning disability is construed as a developmental problem, which is to say that the learning-disabled child is functioning at the level of a child who is chronologically younger, one can expect that such a child's brain also functions like the brain of a younger child. In fact, some evidence is emerging that this may be the case (John, Karmel, Prichep, Ahn, & John, 1977), but this does in no way mean that one is dealing with a damaged or even a dysfunctioning brain. A developmental immaturity certainly does not call for treatment by the administration of the potent drugs as those who speculate about brain dysfunctions would advise (Wender, 1971).

Hyperactivity and Distractibility Support for the brain-dysfunction hypothesis is often sought by pointing to the presumably high correlation between learning disability and hyperactivity because hyperactivity is said to be symptomatic of brain damage. Aside from the fact that there does not seem to be such a high correlation (Minde, Webb, & Sykes, 1968; Routh & Roberts, 1972) and that brain-damaged children are not necessarily hyperactive (Werry, 1972), the observations on which statements about hyperactivity and learning disability are based may well be due to a bias in the selection of the children who are being studied.

Among the children who are referred to clinics that specialize in work with the learning disabled, a high percentage are also hyperactive; but the stress in this sentence should be on the fact that these children have been referred to such clinics. In order for a child to become identified as learning disabled, someone must first suspect that this child is having trouble learning; that the child is not performing as well as he or she could. Someone must have established that there is a discrepancy between the child's learning potential and learning performance. Estimates of learning potential are not made routinely in the ordinary school situation. Only when a child does very poorly in a given subject matter will a psychologist be brought into the picture who, on the basis of individual tests of intelligence and other measures, may discover that this child should be doing much better work. The label learning disabled may thus enter the picture. Now let us assume that a child is performing at an average level and is keeping up with the class but unbeknown to anyone, this child is actually very bright and ought to be doing superior work in school. Though actually learning disabled in the sense of achievement that is considerably below potential, this child's problem would go undetected *unless* he or she did a lot of fidgeting, spoke out of turn, moved around a lot, occasionally hit other children, and otherwise invited the teacher's attention by disrupting classroom routine. As Algozzine (1977) has demonstrated, the child who disturbs others is often the one who comes to be labeled as disturbed. It is such a child who is likely to be singled out for referral to a specialist whose examination may then lead to the discovery that there is a discrepancy between potential and performance. The child is learning disabled. Thus, if there were two children in the same classroom both of whom are doing less well than they should, referral to a specialty clinic for learning-disabled children is far more likely for the one who is hyperactive than for the one who sits quietly and does not disturb the class. As a result of this bias in the labeling and referral process, those who work in the specialty clinics would see far more learning-disabled children who are also hyperactive than there actually are among learning-disabled children in general.

Why one of the two children in the above example exhibited hyperactive behavior while the other did not might be due to one of several factors or a combination of factors. Fidgeting might be a reaction to repeated failure experiences. It might be the random response pattern one can observe in an aroused person or animal who has not discovered the operant response that leads to termination of noxious stimulation. It might be that this child simply finds it constitutionally difficult to learn in the sedentary position which schools deem so essential for the acquisition of knowledge (Werry, Minde, Guzman, Weiss, Dogan, & Hoy, 1972). In this connection, it is of considerable interest to note the results of a survey conducted by Tuddenham, Brooks, and Milkovich (1974), who administered a 100-item behavior inventory to more than 3,000 mothers of 10-year-old children who represented a sample of the normal population. One of the items on this inventory read, "Hates to sit still, restless." Mothers of boys checked this as true for their child in 42 percent of the cases; mothers of girls, 30 percent of the time. There was a significant difference between white and black children for both sexes. For boys from black families, this item was checked as descriptive 52 percent of the time; for girls, 44 percent of the time. With such a high prevalence of this behavior among presumably normal children, one must be extremely circumspect in drawing conclusions about brain functions when the same behavior is observed in some learning-disabled children.

If one restricts the term learning disability to children who have difficulty sustaining selective attention, hyperactivity might simply be due to a chlid's attending to what, from the teacher's point of view, is the wrong stimulus. Body movements are quite appropriate responses to such stimuli as the pressure of the seat on one's buttocks, a growling stomach, an itchy foot, or a strain in the neck; they just happen to be inappropriate responses when the teacher has asked one to read, or write, or do arithmetic. Similarly, distractibility may be no more than such a child attending to stimuli in the room other than those the teacher has designated as the things to look at or listen to. Seen in this fashion, problems designated as hyperactivity or distractibility are expressions of problems in not selectively attending to the "right" stimuli.

Nonetheless, there *are* hyperactive children. The problem is real, but it should not be confused with learning disability to the extent that the two terms actually become used interchangeably as if they were synonymous (Senf, 1977). In order to make it quite clear that learning disability and hyperactivity are distinctly different problems, the latter will receive detailed discussion in Chapter 13.

BEHAVIORAL ASSESSMENT

In a behavioral approach to helping a learning-disabled child, the child's difficulty in learning is taken as the problem that must be solved. No attempt is made to find "underlying causes" or to speculate about the etiology of the difficulty. Lovitt (1967) outlined four steps essential for such an approach to the assessment of children with learning difficulties. First, the child must be observed over a period of time so that a stable baseline of his or her school performance can be obtained. If the problem is in reading, this behavior is measured, using such indexes as rate, accuracy, retention, and comprehension. The second step is an assessment of the components of the behavior that has been identified as presenting difficulty. This includes ascertaining relevant stimulus events, as, for example, the child's preference for letter size in the case of reading difficulty; determining the child's responses to the stimuli; finding the contingency system or reinforcement schedule under which the child is operating; and noting the events that follow the child's behavior. If the problem is described as a failure to follow verbal instructions, one should assess such components as auditory discrimination, immediate auditory memory, attention to auditory stimuli, integration of auditory symbols and visual stimuli, temporal sequencing, and comprehension of structure and function of various linguistic patterns (Bateman & Schiefelbusch, 1969). The third step, following this analysis of the problem behavior, is to involve the referring agent, usually the teacher, to ascertain his or her ability to modify the conditions under which the child is working and to engage this agent's cooperation in the helping procedures to be instituted. The fourth, and last, step in the assessment is to generalize the findings from the assessment situation to the day-to-day classroom conditions since, knowing how the child reads, the reading behavior can now be modified. With the kind of specific suggestions possible on the basis of such a behavioral analysis, the teacher is able to institute concrete changes that are designed to help the child overcome the problem.

The assessment of learning disability is often complicated by a child's secondary psychological reactions to the pressures represented by puzzled, frustrated, and anxious parents or teachers who cannot understand the discrepancy between the child's intelligence level and scholastic achievement. The child's reactions may take various forms, such as avoidance, escape, or attack responses and when these are viewed as the cause rather than the effect of the learning problem, treatment efforts may be misdirected and, hence, ineffective. A boy may not be able to learn and, consequently, become anxious. This anxiety may further reduce his capacity to learn or to perform what he has learned, thus setting up a viscious cycle and complicating the assessment process.

Help for children who manifest secondary psychological reactions to learning disabilities calls not only for the introduction of special educational techniques but also for attention to the confounding secondary reaction. Both efforts must be coordinated and carefully paced if they are to be effective. For example, a girl who has developed a fear of failure as a result of repeated failure experiences in her academic endeavors is unlikely to benefit from special education until she can face learning tasks without their eliciting avoidance responses. She will also need to acquire some degree of confidence in her own abilities, and she is unlikely to gain such confidence until she has had some success experiences. Learning tasks must therefore be so arranged that the child can be sure of experiencing re-peated success. Since this is the principle that underlies programmed learning using so-called teaching machines, such programs, used in conjunction with rein-forcement principles, have been successfully applied in complex cases of learning difficulties.

SENSORY-MOTOR INTEGRATION

Among the steps in assessment outlined by Lovitt (1967) is the need to ascertain relevant stimulus events and the child's responses to these stimuli. Almost all of the stimulus events presented to a child by the school situation are in the visual or auditory realm, and the responses to be emitted by the child are largely in the motor realm, as in the production of spoken or written verbal or quantitative language. Most learning dysfunctions, particularly those identified in the primary grades, thus emerge along the sensory-input–motor-output process, an observa-tion reflected in the terms *sensory-motor dysfunction* and *perceptual-motor dif-ficulties*, which have had wide currency in the literature on learning difficulties. The usual implication (Kephart, 1960) is that the source of the difficulty is in the child's inability to perform the function necessary to relate sensory stimuli to motor responses. As with other inferences about central processes, it has been difficult to study sensory-motor integration objectively. Their review of research in this area led Chalfant and Scheffelin (1969) to the conclusion that there is "lit-tle empirical evidence that would support the contention that basic perceptual-motor training leads to improvement in perceptual-motor abilities or to better academic performance" (p. 28).

The role of sensory-motor activity in the learning of reading was investi-gated by Koenigsberg (1973), who worked with 120 children between the ages of 4 and 6 who had not yet acquired the ability to discriminate "b" from "d," seeking to identify the conditions under which such children can be aided to learn the discrimination between mirror-image stimuli. Studies by other investigators had demonstrated that it is possible to teach the discrimination to such children by having them engage in a motor response relative to the stimuli, such as tracing them or aligning a stencil over the letters. Success with these training procedures was usually explained in terms of Piagetian sensorimotor development. As Koe-nigsberg points out, all these methods of training have in common that they help focus the child's attention on the visual stimulus; thus, the sensorimotor aspect of the experience might not be an essential part of the procedure.

The method Koenigsberg (1973) devised for her study involved matching stimuli that differed in orientation, the child being asked whether these were the same or different. Training involved the placement of a transparent copy of the stimulus over both the standard and the comparison. In one group this was done by the experimenter, in another group by the child. In every case, the experimenter verbalized the correct answer (same or different) and explained the relationship

in terms of the fit of the overlay. Control groups received various modifications of this procedure, such as the inclusion of hand contact with the stimuli or of a motor response toward the stimuli.

This design permitted Koenigsberg to assess the relative effectiveness of sensorimotor activity and mere observation on the part of the child. The results indicated "that the principal factor responsible for improvement in performance was the demonstrations. Training using some form of sensorimotor activity appeared to add little to the benefits of demonstrations" (p. 768). Koenigsberg (1973) concludes that it is possible to teach preschool children to discriminate orientation and that their "performance depends to a large degree on the manner in which the task is presented" (p. 768), particularly "when the child's interest is adequately aroused and his attention is properly focused" (p. 769).

Occasionally, a study demonstrates a relationship between reading difficulty and some other functions, such as finger localization (Croxen & Lytton, 1971), but the meaning of such findings, either in causal or remedial terms, remains unclear. Beery (1967), for example, explored the ability of average and retarded readers to match auditory and visual stimuli. In this study fifteen children, whose reading achievement was at least 2 years below the age-appropriate grade level, were matched for intelligence test scores, age, and sex with a control group of normal readers. All the children were within the normal range of tested intelligence. The experimental tasks required that they match visually presented patterns of dots with an analogous pattern of discrete, recorded tones coming from a speaker and vice versa. In one test, the auditory stimuli were presented first, followed by the visual patterns; in a second test the presentation was reversed. The test pattern was presented, and after it had been withdrawn, the child had to recognize the correct representation from among three choices in the case of the auditory-visual sequence, then two in the visual-auditory sequence. The task thus involved not only matching but also immediate recall and, of course, attention. The results showed that on both series the normal controls performed significantly better than the retarded readers.

LEARNING AND ATTENTION

The work by Koenigsberg (1973) and by Beery (1967), which we just cited, suggested that attention is a crucial element in learning to read. Conversely, problems in the area of attention have been repeatedly shown to play a role in the most frequent of all learning disabilities, difficulties in reading. Extensive work by Dykman, Ackerman, Clements, and Peters (1971) has indicated that problems in focusing attention represented the most pronounced difference between a large group of learning-disabled boys and their normal controls. If attention, and specifically, selective attention is a problem for learning-disabled children, remedial work with such children should aim at enhancing that aspect of information processing.

Remedial Work

One way of enhancing selective attention is by modifying stimulus aspects. This can take the form of exaggerating the differences between the stimuli. A method of doing this is by using a series of graded steps where the critical features are first presented in isolation and irrelevant features are added gradually (faded in), as was done by Schreibman (1975). In teaching a child to differentiate the letters "b" and "d," for example, the perpendicular line is irrelevant from the standpoint of telling the letters apart. The critical feature is the relation of the vertical line to the rounded portion. One would thus want to emphasize the direction of the rounded portion by exaggerating its size in the beginning of training and then reduce its size in stepwise fashion until the letters come to be presented in their normal form. Such a fading technique was used by Caron (1968), who thereby succeeded in teaching 3-year-old children to differentiate between roundness and angularity, concepts that children of this age group are usually unable to handle. During early trials, the corners of the angular figures and analogous portions of the rounded figures were emphasized; the rest of the outlines were barely visible. As trials progressed, the outlines were made more and more pronounced until the full figures appeared on the final trials. This and similar studies have demonstrated that even very young children can learn to make difficult discriminations if they are provided with opportunities to learn to attend to the relevant aspects of the stimuli.

Another way of enhancing attention is by using novelty in presenting the stimuli (Berlyne, 1960). If one wishes to teach a child to differentiate between "b" and "d," for example, it is preferable to present these letter pairs in a variety of sizes and degrees of brightness, as well as in different parts of the writing surface, than to repeat the presentation of the same pair over and over again. There is, of course, a limit to the amount of novelty that can be introduced into a learning task and there are many routine and repetitious situations in which learning is nonetheless required. When this is the case, children cannot only be kept at the task but their attention can also be maintained at a high level if correct responses are followed by a reinforcing consequence. For older children this need be no more than knowledge of results; but for younger and learning-disabled children a more concrete reward appears to be necessary. The function of a reward in such a situation may be both motivational (keeping the child at a dull task) and informational (providing feedback as to response accuracy).

For a child who has difficulty in reading, a situation involving reading is often one of repeated presentation of the same familiar stimuli. Unable to obtain information from the symbols in front of him, the child has little if any interest in the task; accumulated failures may, in fact, have made the situation aversive. Under these circumstances, the introduction of extrinsic and, from the point of view of reading, arbitrary reinforcers may serve to enhance selective attention to the relevant aspects of the reading material. This may account for the success of remedial programs that apply reinforcement principles to the teaching of reading (Heiman, Fischer, & Ross, 1973; Staats & Butterfield, 1965). With young children and with learning-disabled children who may be functioning at an immature level in terms of selective attention, it appears best if one seeks to enhance their attention by modifying the stimuli.

Reading can be conceptualized as operant behavior in that the printed letter, word, or sentence is the stimulus to which the child must learn to make the appropriate response, which is then followed by reinforcement. In the usual process of learning to read, the reinforcement is no more than the word "good" or "right" said by the teacher. Later on, the meaning, knowledge, or information one gathers by reading come to serve as so-called natural reinforcers which, because they are consequences directly related to the activity of reading, are also referred to as intrinsic reinforcers.

When reading is viewed as operant behavior and analyzed in terms of its component tasks, highly successful remedial approaches can be demonstrated (Goldiamond & Dyrud, 1966). Using minimally trained adult volunteers and high school seniors as therapy technicians, Staats, Minke, Goodwin, and Landeen (1967) accelerated the reading rate of eighteen junior high school students who had been retarded readers. The desired responses were reinforced with small amounts of money, the amount per reading response being reduced as the reading rate accelerated and the material became more difficult.

Staats and Butterfield (1965) applied operant principles to the treatment of a 14-year-old boy with a long history of school failures and delinquencies. He was reading at second-grade level when treatment began. Following 40 hours of training, he not only read at the 4.3-grade level but also passed all of his courses for the first time, and his misbehavior in school had completely stopped. This case not only demonstrated once again that improvement generalizes to areas not specifically designated as treatment targets but it also illustrates how arbitrary extrinsic reinforcers (in this case money) can be gradually withdrawn as reading itself becomes reinforcing and other sources of reinforcement come into play to maintain the newly established behavior.

When reading is defined as making the correct verbal response to a particular written stimulus, it can be readily monitored. This, however, is not the case in silent reading where only subsequent changes in performance permit one to infer that reading has taken place. The boy in the Staats and Butterfield (1965) study had been reinforced for silent reading, and, as these authors point out, there is the danger of reinforcing the behavior of just looking at a printed page when no actual reading is going on. A double contingency was introduced in an attempt to guard against this possibility. Several levels of reinforcers (tokens representing different amounts of money) were used, so that for looking at a page, a low-value token was presented, while higher-value reinforcers were made contingent on correctly answering questions about the content of the reading material. Unfortunately, the design used here still does not permit an unequivocal answer to the question whether the boy was attending to the printed words instead of merely staring at them because the questions he had to answer were based on the story used for silent reading that had previously been the material for oral reading. This makes it barely conceivable that he had learned the answers to the questions during the readily monitored oral phase, after which he did no more than sit and look at the story when he presumably engaged in silent reading.

There is, of course, an easy way to find out whether a child has attended to the reading material and that is by including instructions for easily accomplished motor tasks ("look at the ceiling," "point to the door") among the material being read. This method of testing comprehension was used by Rosenbaum and Breiling (1976) who taught reading to a severely retarded 12-year-old girl.

The reinforcers usually used in the early stages of a remedial reading program based on operant principles are tokens which, in themselves, have no value but derive their value from the fact that they can be traded in later on for backup reinforcers of the child's own choosing. Initially, the tokens (which may be poker chips, checkmarks, paper scrip, or similar symbols) are delivered on a continuous or near-continuous schedule. Later they are "thinned out" so that they may be given as infrequently as once for every 30 correct responses. Once the child has reached sufficient proficiency that reading becomes intrinsically reinforcing, these extrinsic reinforcers are, of course, withdrawn altogether. The reinforcement schedules and the nature of the backup reinforcer must be individualized, since it is well known that something that is reinforcing for one child is not necessarily reinforcing to another. Sibley (1967) found that the less successful, less persevering children perform best under lower reinforcement ratios (1 reinforcement for every 2 responses), while the more able readers perform better at higher ratios (1 reinforcement for every 30 responses).

A flexible use of reinforcement schedules in the course of training is also illustrated in a study by Hewett, Mayhew, and Rabb (1967), who taught basic reading skills to mentally retarded, neurologically impaired, emotionally disturbed, and autistic children. During the first three lessons, reinforcement was on a continuous basis, with one unit of reinforcement for each correct response. After this, each child had to make five correct responses before receiving one unit of reinforcement (a 1 to 5 fixed ratio schedule). Reinforcements were such tangibles as candy or money at this point, but in addition, the experimenters began to phase in a token reward in the form of marks on a card, given on a 1 to 1 ratio schedule. The tangible reinforcers were later placed on a 1 to 10 schedule, and ultimately, 200 check marks were needed before they could be exchanged for 1 tangible reinforcer; a 1 to 200 schedule with a delay until the end of the session was thus in operation.

Teaching Response Strategies   Among the skills children must acquire in order to be efficient learners is how to approach a given task. In reading, for example, it is necessary not only to decode written symbols into words and sentences, the children must also learn to hold back their response until they have arrived at the correct solution to the task. It is a characteristic of many learning-disabled children that they blurt out the first answer that comes to mind, an answer that is more often wrong than right. This has led many observers to speak of these children as impulsive, or as having difficulty with impulse control (Douglas, 1972). Controlling the tendency to give the first answer that comes to mind is thus a response strategy that these children must learn.

One way of teaching this strategy is to induce these children to instruct themselves to "stop, look, and think" before answering (Palkes, Stewart, & Kahana, 1968). Such self-directed verbal commands represent a form of training in self-control, and they have been found to be effective both in laboratory studies (Meichenbaum & Goodman, 1971; Ridberg, Parke, & Hetherington, 1971) and in classroomlike settings (Camp, Blom, Hebert, & van Doorninck, 1977; Egeland, 1974).

Whether a child uses an impulsive or a reflective response style is often assessed by the Matching Familiar Figures (MFF) test developed by Kagan (1966), which requires the child to identify which of a series of six representations of a familiar object matches a standard when standard and variants are displayed at the same time. Children who respond rapidly and make many mistakes are classified as "impulsive," while those who respond slowly and make few mistakes are called "reflective." It can be shown (Kagan, Pearson, & Welch, 1966) that it is not enough to teach impulsive children to delay their response ("take your time") because this does not automatically make their answers more correct. What must also be done, as Egeland (1974) demonstrated, is to teach the child what to do in the time thus "taken."

Egeland (1974) administered the MFF test to 260 second-grade children, which led to the identification of 72 "impulsive" children who ranged in age from 6 years 10 months to 8 years 11 months. These children were randomly assigned to one of two training groups or to a control group that received no training. The training groups received eight 30-minute training sessions over a 4-week period. These sessions entailed exercises on matching tasks involving geometric designs and nonsense words, drawing geometric designs from memory, and describing geometric designs.

One training group was instructed to wait 10 to 15 seconds before responding; to "think about your answer and take your time." The other training group was given a set of rules and basic strategies that the children were to follow in responding to the training tasks. These rules were designed to induce the children to attend to the relevant features of the stimuli, to examine alternatives, to break the alternatives down into component parts, to look for similarities and differences, and to eliminate alternatives until only the correct alternative remained. This scanning strategy was designed to overcome the impulsive child's tendency to attend to only one alternative without considering others before deciding on the response.

The important difference between the two training groups used by Egeland

(1974) is that one group was told to delay their responses while the other group was taught what to do during the delay. The former thus received a general admonishment, much like those often used by adults in hopes of improving a child's performance, "Take your time; pay attention; think," while the latter group was given explicit training in a specific skill that is applicable to the task at hand.

When an alternate form of the MFF test was administered upon completion of the 4-week training period, the results revealed that both groups had increased response times and a corresponding decrease in errors, while no such changes were found with the control group. Two months later, however, when the children were once again tested on the MFF, only the group that had received training in the use of scanning strategies had maintained the improved performance. What is more, this group also achieved significantly higher scores on a test of reading comprehension (Gates-MacGinitie Reading Test) that was administered to the classes 5 months after completion of training.

As the author points out, these results prove most encouraging, since they indicate that impulsive children can be trained to alter the way in which they process information and solve problems. It is of interest to note Egeland's comment that when the children encountered a more difficult problem, they would revert back to an impulsive way of responding, as if they had learned to respond in that fashion in situations where they anticipated failure. This seems to suggest that the newly learned "reflective" response style was still too tenuous and that further training under conditions of intermittent positive reinforcement might have made it more resistant to extinction. Egeland's (1974) work strongly suggests that the basis of the performance deficit of the so-called impulsive child lies not so much in the precipitous nature of the responses as it does in the failure to use adaptive strategies of attention.

We have suggested elsewhere (Ross, 1976) that impulsivity may well be a learned response style of learning-disabled children; that it may be the result and not the cause of their learning problem. A response style that is characterized by rapidly produced, unreflective answers which are usually wrong (the operational definition of impulsivity used on the MFF test) might be typical of a child who has had a long history of failure experiences when he or she is faced with a cognitive task.

These failure experiences could be a function of the child's not having developed sufficient capacity to use selective attention in dealing with such a task. Repeated failures might result in making cognitive tasks aversive; therefore, such children might experience anxiety whenever they are faced with problems that they know they cannot solve. The quickest way of reducing such anxiety, to get out of the unpleasant situation and thus to be reinforced, would be to come up with a quick answer. "Better to give a wrong answer quickly than to struggle for a long time only to find that the answer is wrong anyway," might be the logic by which such children would operate. Moreover, physically removing oneself from the situation or, at least, turning away from the task would further serve to reduce anxiety engendered by being faced with a problem one knows one is unable to solve. Such moving or turning away might well be the behavior that often earns such children the labels "hyperactive" and "distractible."

It is only when these children are taught the attentional strategies required to solve cognitive problems that they will encounter sufficient success experiences to make it attractive for them to spend enough time on such problems to arrive at the right answers. Such performance will then earn them the label "reflective" on the MFF test, and observers will assume that they have acquired impulse control.

THE IMPORTANCE OF EARLY INTERVENTION

A crucial aspect of learning disabilities is that they represent a cumulatively worsening process owing to the pyramidal nature of education. A child who has been unable to learn the basic tool subjects in the primary grades experiences an ever increasing disability, since later teaching is always based on competencies presumed to have been established earlier. Concomitantly, continued exposure to the situations in which the child is expected to learn but encounters failure will make these situations ever more aversive and, hence, ever more likely to elicit escape or avoidance behavior. In 1967 Coleman and Sandhu published a report describing 364 children with learning difficulties who had been referred to a clinic specializing in these problems. They pointed out that 41 percent of these children were 2 or more years behind in their school work by the time they were brought to the clinic. It is also of interest that in this group boys outnumbered girls 6 to 1. Similar ratios are reported from other sources, suggesting either that boys tend to encounter greater difficulty under the prevailing educational system or that parents and teachers are more readily concerned when a boy rather than a girl exhibits problems in learning. In view of the possible relationship between learning difficulties and other behavior problems of boys to which Miller, Hampe, Barrett, and Noble (1971) have called our attention, the importance of preschool screening, early detection, and immediate help for learning-disabled children cannot be given enough stress.

RECAPITULATION

Despite their prevalence and the degree of concern they occasion, learning disabilities are a form of psychological disorder that is poorly understood. Problems in measurement and confusion in definition have contributed to this state of affairs. The definition promulgated by the U.S. federal government, which has been widely adopted because the receipt of support funds is contingent on using that definition, has done little to clarify matters because it is too all-inclusive. For purposes of research, a more restrictive definition is needed and one was proposed

in this chapter. It takes account of the fact that learning-disabled children manifest a discrepancy between their intellectual potential and their academic achievement, recognizes that for many this involves a developmental lag in the ability
to sustain selective attention, and stresses the need for specialized teaching methods.
Children with learning disabilities are often described as having poor motor
control and as being hyperactive, distractible, and impulsive. These characteristics
have led some to speculate that these children might have a central nervous system
dysfunction, but such a neurological hypothesis has never been confirmed. On
the other hand, remedial efforts aimed at enhancing such children's ability to
focus their attention on the distinctive features of the stimuli that are crucial for
learning have, in many instances, shown considerable promise. We now turn to an
examination of hyperactivity which, as we have said, is not the same thing as learning disability, although many learning-disabled children are also described as
hyperactive.

Chapter 13

Hyperactivity

WHO IS HYPERACTIVE?

As the term reveals, hyperactivity refers to a condition where a child is excessively active. Having said this, however, we must immediately ask what is meant by an excess of activity. Presumably, such a child's activity level exceeds an established norm, but in any quantitative sense no such norm exists. We are thus brought back to the issue of what is normal, for, in order to say that a behavior is excessive or abnormal, one should be able to answer the question, "Compared to what?"

As with almost all other definitions of disorders, the definition of hyperactivity is arbitrary and relative, but this definition, probably more so than all others, depends almost exclusively on the tolerance level of the child's environment. As a study by Werry and Quay (1971) revealed, 49.7 percent of the boys in supposedly normal kindergarten, first-, and second-grade public school classes were described by their teachers as restless and unable to sit still. In the large-scale survey mentioned in the previous chapter (Tuddenham, Brooks, & Milkovich, 1974), the statement, "Hates to sit still, restless," was checked as descriptive of their child by 42 percent of the mothers of supposedly normal 10-year-old boys.

It is tempting to say that restlessness is the norm. What then is an activity level so excessive that it is called hyperactivity?

One answer to this must include a reference to the situation where the excess activity takes place. If a child runs about a lot while in the yard or on the playground, few would complain. But if that child moves about in the classroom or runs around inside the house, people become upset. The point, then, is that we are talking about activity that is excessive with respect to the circumstances under which it is observed. We are thus faced with yet another situation where the definition of a psychological disorder is a relative matter. Yet, since children who manifest an activity level that their environment deems excessive will almost invariably encounter negative consequences, such as criticism and punishment for their behavior, and since they nonetheless continue to exhibit hyperactivity, the question emerges whether they are unable to control and inhibit this behavior. Some have consequently spoken of these children as having problems with impulse control, or as being "driven." Such terms, of course, do not serve to explain anything; they simply raise further questions.

As usual, it is difficult to establish just when, during development, a hyperactive child became hyperactive. In order to do so, one has to have an objective longitudinal record which is rarely available. As a result, most of the information on the early development of children who are at some later stage labeled hyperactive is based on their parents' attempts to reconstruct events from the early years. It is impossible to know how much such recollections are distorted by the events of the more recent years, during which the child's hyperactivity was often the principal focus of parental concern. Reports of excessive crying and irregular sleep during infancy thus may or may not reflect early expressions of what later comes to be viewed as hyperactivity. In preschool years, when nursery school teachers begin to keep written records of children, the descriptions of the early behavior of hyperactive children may be more valid. Here, one finds reports of uncontrollable behavior, of being constantly "on the go" or "into things," of being aggressive and destructive.

A study conducted by Schleiffer, Weiss, Cohen, Elman, Cvejic, and Kruger (1975) presents an objective picture of the behavior of hyperactive children in the preschool years. These investigators observed and tested twenty-eight 3- and 4-year-old hyperactive nursery school children and compared them with a normal control group. Among the children who had been labeled as hyperactive because of their chronic, sustained activity, Schleiffer et al. (1975) distinguished two subgroups. One, called the true hyperactives, contained ten children. These were reported to be hyperactive at home and rated as hyperactive by both nursery school teachers and examining psychiatrists. The other group, containing eighteen children, was called situational hyperactives because they displayed excessive activity only at home but not while they were in the nursery school setting. All of the children in the study were placed in groups of six children (three hyperactives and three normals) who participated in weekly, 2-hour nursery school sessions over a period of 9 weeks. These sessions were observed by trained observers who recorded the children's behavior without knowing to which group the children belonged. The teacher and teacher's helper were similarly "blind" regarding the status of the children, and neither they nor the psychiatrists and psychologists who did the interviewing and testing knew the purpose of this well-designed study.

It is of considerable interest that neither of the two types of hyperactive children differed from the normal control children when their activities were observed in a *free-play situation*. It was only when observations were conducted during the *structured play period*, when the teacher introduced activities the children were expected to carry out while seated, that differences emerged. Now, the hyperactive children were out of their chairs significantly more often than the normal children and they also exhibited aggressive behavior with greater frequency than the controls. These characteristics were found in both types of hyperactive children, those categorized as situational and those considered true hyperactives. A significant difference between these two groups emerged in the frequency of leaving the table. The true hyperactives did this more often than the situational hyperactives who, it will be recalled, had been thus labeled because their mothers had reported them as hyperactive at home, while their teachers had not found them so in school. Since both of these types of children were out of their seats more often than the normal controls, the findings seem to reflect that nursery school teachers are able to tolerate activity that takes the child out of the seat as long as he or she remains at the table. This is another reflection of the relativity of our labeling processes. It is not so much excessive activity that differentiates the hyperactive child from the normal child as it is activity that adults consider inappropriate, irrelevant, or irritating. It is in particular the difference between the children's behavior in the free-play and the structured-play situations that make one wonder to what extent hyperactivity is a function of the environmental constraints we impose on these children. As Werry (Werry, Minde, Guzman, Weiss, Dogan, & Hoy, 1972) has speculated, it may be that the hyperactive child is a problem only because our society places a premium on controlled activity and lengthy periods of sitting still. Inasmuch as demands for remaining seated and working for sustained periods of time increase as the child enters the more formal setting of elementary school, it is not surprising that the number of children who are identified as hyperactive increases for those in the primary grades.

It has been reported (Stewart, Pitts, Craig, & Dieruf, 1966) that about one in every twenty-five children in first grade is a hyperactive child. Under the circumstances, it may be somewhat puzzling why interest in hyperactivity as a disorder in its own right began only in the late 1960s. Before that time, children whom we would now consider hyperactive were probably called unruly, incorrigible, restless, or discipline problems. Teachers used to try and deal with these problems by the negative sanctions usually employed in schools: reprimand, punishment, retention, and suspension. Like other problems dealt with in this manner, the irritating behavior did not diminish.

There was, however, another group of children whose excessive activity level had been noted by another profession. The profession is medicine. It had long been known (Goldstein, 1942) that a frequently found consequence of damage to the brain is the person's inability to sit still. Hyperactivity or, to use the term preferred in the medical literature, hyperkinesis (Laufer & Denhoff, 1957) is one of the symptoms of brain damage. Physicians had also discovered (Bradley, 1937) that certain amphetamine-related drugs when administered to severely disturbed and institutionalized children would reduce their agitated, disruptive behavior.

WHAT IS HYPERACTIVITY?

There came a point when the educator who was unable to control the disruptive behavior of unruly children discovered that the physician had a pill that would subdue such children. All that was needed to solve the educator's problem was to define the unruly child as a child who had a medical disease; for with a diagnosis of "hyperactive behavior syndrome," such a child was no longer the responsibility of the educator but the responsibility of the physician or psychiatrist.

The Syndrome and Its Cause

The change in labels led not only to a change in jurisdiction but also to two far-reaching and interrelated consequences. One was that the newly defined medical syndrome raised the question of its cause. The other consequence was that with the medical profession having assumed responsibility for the problem, a medical treatment in the form of drugs came to take precedence over attempts to educate these children.

Speculations about the cause of hyperactivity led to a series of logically unsound conclusions. Children with known brain damage as the result of illness or injury often, but by no means always, manifest hyperactive behavior. Strauss and Lehtinen (1947), for example, cited hyperactivity as a primary symptom of brain-injured, mentally retarded children. If brain-injured children are hyperactive, it was erroneously concluded, hyperactive children must be brain injured and the brain injury the cause of the hyperactivity. It is not surprising that this illogical formulation has never been verified through research. In the first place, as Werry (1972) concluded from his review of the literature, the link between hyperactivity and brain injury is quite weak. Studies of children with definitely known brain damage indicate that hyperactivity is neither an inevitable nor a very frequent consequence of brain injury. Beyond this, there is a growing body of evidence that speaks against the presence of brain damage in most hyperactive children (Ross & Ross, 1976).

Unfortunately, this evidence did not lead to an abandonment of the notion that hyperactivity is caused by some defect in the child's brain. Instead, it led to the semantic maneuver by which terms like "minimal cerebral dysfunction" or the initials MBD (for minimal brain damage) were substituted for brain injury. It was now no longer necessary to demonstrate the presence of brain damage; all that was needed was to demonstrate the presence of hyperactivity and that alone was taken for evidence of the presence of minimal cerebral dysfunction. The circularity of this illogical reasoning should be immediately apparent. A child is hyperactive; the question is asked why he or she is hyperactive; the answer is given in terms of brain dysfunctions. When one then asks about the evidence for brain dysfunction, one is referred back to the hyperactive behavior. Presumably, the adjective "minimal" relieves those who reason in this manner of the responsibility to provide external proof for the assertion that there is something the matter with the child's brain. Werry (1972) pointed out that a significant number of children who exhibit hyperactive behavior have no signs of cerebral dysfunction and that the behavior alone should in no sense be taken as indicating cerebral damage or dysfunction.

It is, of course, not surprising that speculations about the cause of hyperactivity have been so fruitless. In the first place, speculation can never uncover the cause of anything; only research can do that. But research into the cause of any behavioral manifestation must ultimately be longitudinal research. What is needed is a large-scale study that follows the development of a substantial number of children, beginning at the point of conception and recording in great detail all the many events and circumstances from prenatal nutrition to classroom environment that might affect the children's later behavior. When some of the children in such a study later manifest hyperactive behavior, one could go back into the record and ascertain whether there was an event in their development that differentiates them from children who did not become hyperactive. Such a study is very costly and extremely difficult to carry out. No wonder it has never been conducted. Retrospective studies which begin with children identified as hyperactive and seek to reconstruct their earlier developmental histories cannot possibly lead to definitive answers about the cause of the problem.

A second reason why the search for a cause of hyperactivity has led to little more than controversy is that hyperactivity or its various synonyms, such as hyperkinetic child syndrome, is nothing more than a statement describing behavior. It is not a disease entity, like pneumonia, and a search for the cause of hyperactivity, based on the model of medical research, is bound to lead to failure. It is as if one were to take all children who manifest a lot of coughing and classify them as coughers or, to make it sound more esoteric, as hypertussive children. Clearly, children cough for all sorts of reasons; thus, a search for *the* cause of the hypertussive child syndrome would be as vain as *the* search for the cause of the hyperkinetic child syndrome.

Before we can hope to arrive at an understanding of hyperactivity, we must learn to differentiate among the many different kinds of children who move around a lot in a restless fashion (Ney, 1974). Some of these children probably do have real brain damage, others may be neurologically immature, others are likely to suffer from the effects of environmental pollutants, such as lead or radiation. There are probably some among these children who have a genetic predisposition for hyperactivity (Morrison & Stewart, 1974) or whose congenital problems, being related to their prenatal or birth history, contribute to later hyperactivity (Waldrop, Bell, McLaughlin, & Halverson, 1978). Others may be allergic to certain food-additives and food-colorings, as Feingold (1975) has suggested. Environmental constraints, such as crowding at home (McNamara, 1972) or demands to sit still in the classroom for long periods of time (Werry et al., 1972), may be the basis of hyperactivity for still other children. Yet another group may have learned to be hyperactive because the contingencies operating in their environment reinforced increased levels of activity, possibly through differential teacher attention (O'Leary & O'Leary, 1977).

Is It a Syndrome?   Mention has been made of the term "hyperactive child syndrome," which is used by physicians interested in the problem of hyperactivity (Stewart et al., 1966). In medicine a syndrome is a cluster of symptoms, complaints, or difficulties that usually go together and, as such, identify a disease. Not all symptoms need necessarily be present in every instance, but they should coincide sufficiently often to present a consistent picture. In the hyperactive child syndrome certain behavioral characteristics are viewed as analogous to the symptoms of a disease. Among these are high activity level, inability to sit still, fidgeting, impulsivity, and distractibility. Also listed are short attention span, frequent fighting with peers, failure to respond to discipline, unpredictability, temper tantrums, and academic difficulty in school. It should be apparent that many of these descriptive terms are simply synonyms—different ways of expression the same thing—like fidgeting and inability to sit still. Others, such as temper tantrums and academic difficulty, may be secondary problems resulting from the conflict-frought interaction between the hyperactive child and the adults in his or her environment. At any rate, these observations are quite different in nature from such medical symptoms as a raised temperature, swollen glands, skin rash, and cough, which might form a syndrome identifying a disease. The confusion created by the disease analogy is further illustrated by the fact that the same behavioral cluster is used by some to identify the minimal-brain-dysfunction syndrome (Clements, 1966) and by others as characteristic of children with learning disabilities (Werry, Weiss, & Douglas, 1964).

The statistical technique of factor analysis is very suitable for testing assumptions about the clustering of such items as clinical symptoms or behavioral characteristics. Based on the principle of correlation, the technique helps an investigator identify items that correlate highly with some but not with other items. Such correlational clusters, or factors, describe relationships that may be difficult to notice by casual observation. Sroufe (1975) reviewed several factor-analytic studies that had been designed to substantiate the syndrome status of the behavioral characteristics of hyperactive children and he concluded that these studies provide little support for a syndrome. This view was also adopted by Ross and Ross (1976), who reject the notion of a syndrome and view hyperactivity as a class of heterogeneous, inappropriate responses that are caused or maintained by any variety of social and nonsocial factors. They define the hyperactive child as one who consistently displays a high level of activity in situations where it is clearly inappropriate, who is unable to inhibit this activity on command, and who often appears capable of only one speed of responding (Ross & Ross, 1976).

While factor-analytic studies fail to substantiate the existence of a hyperactive or minimal-brain-dysfunction syndrome, another interesting conclusion emerges from one such study (Langhorne, Loney, Paternite, and Bechtoldt, 1976). These investigators submitted the data on ninety-four hyperactive boys to a factor analysis. What emerged was not a clustering of behavioral characteristics ("symptoms") but of the sources of the information. That is, the items derived from observations by teachers correlated with each other; the items derived from parents' ratings correlated with each other; the items derived from people who had rated the boys' medical charts intercorrelated, and so forth. All in all, 64 percent of the variance for these data was contributed by the source of the information. When Langhorne et al. (1976) reanalyzed earlier studies they were able to confirm that source-related factors are more important than those related to specific child-characteristics. These findings should not be interpreted as reflecting biases that are unique to teachers or to parents. What should be concluded is that the children behave differently in the different situations in which these different people make their observations. While there are some children who are hyperactive no matter where they are, most children identified as hyperactive manifest this problem in some, but not in other situations. With such situational specificity, what one should study is not the inside of the child, for example, the brain, but the interaction between the child and the environment where the hyperactive behavior occurs. That, as we shall see later, is likely to lead to far better answers to the problem than the persistent search for pathology in the child.

Medication and Its Effects

As we have said, one of the consequences of defining hyperactive behavior as a medical problem was the fruitless search for a single cause of the supposed syndrome. The second consequence has been the use of drugs as the predominant form of treatment. The discovery by Bradley (1937) that drugs that act as stimulants on the central nervous system have the effect of reducing the activity level of agitated and disruptive children eventually led to making such drugs the treatment of choice for children labeled as hyperactive.

The drugs most widely used with hyperactive children are dextroamphetamine, methylphenidate, and magnesium pemoline, which are marketed under the trademarks Dexedrine, Ritalin, and Cylert, respectively. Of these, methylphenidate has been the most frequently prescribed, although it is less potent than dextroamphetamine and more toxic than pemoline. Its reduced potency means that higher doses of methylphenidate are needed in order to achieve the same effect. What dosage and what effect? The available literature on this question reveals remarkable confusion and lack of agreement (Barkley, 1976).

The Intricacies of Drug Research   It is very difficult to test the effectiveness of a drug, particularly when the problem that the drug is expected to affect is as poorly defined as hyperactivity. The first decision to be made by an investigator who wishes to study the effectiveness of a drug on hyperactive children is what children to include in the research. A measure is needed that can aid in the identification of hyperactive children. There are a variety of measures of activity level but since different investigators use different measures, their studies are difficult to compare because the measures do not correlate (Barkley & Ullman, 1976). The measures include radio transmitters (Ball & Irwin, 1976) and mechanical devices (Porges, Walter, Korb, & Sprague, 1975) that count the number of times a child moves in a chair; observational counts of the number of times a child crosses a grid system drawn on the floor of a laboratory room (Routh & Schroeder, 1976); and rating scales for use by teachers (Conners, 1969) or parents (Werry et al., 1964). Inasmuch as activity level lies on a continuum, it is necessary to decide on a point above which a child is to be considered *hyper*active and thus a candidate for inclusion in a study. Even when two investigators use the same measure, their decision as to where that point should be is often not the same.

Another decision investigators of drug effectiveness have to make is where to get the children to be studied. One obviously cannot go to a school and ask for all their hyperactive children (however defined) and then proceed to administer a medication to them. For ethical and legal reasons, investigators can study only those children whose parents are seeking professional help for the child's problem and who grant permission for the child's participation in the proposed study. Whatever conclusions might be drawn from such a study must therefore be limited to the group from which the sample was obtained.

Drug research is further complicated by the fact that the very act of giving someone a pill that he or she believes to be a medication can have psychological effects that often resemble the effect the drug is expected to have. This is known as the placebo effect of a drug, and a control for it must be included in the experimental design by giving some participants an inert substance with no known chemical potency, a so-called *placebo*. Whatever reaction these participants show can be attributed to the psychological effect, and the magnitude of it must be subtracted from the effect of the real drug.

Related to the placebo effect, which involves the person who is taking the drug, is the effect on the people who dispense the drug and those who are to provide the measures of the effect. Since there may be subtle differences in the behavior of the dispenser when giving the drug and when giving the placebo, he or she must also be kept ignorant of what the pill being handed out really is. Similarly, since the person, such as parent or teacher, who is rating the child's behavior might be influenced in the ratings by knowing when the drug had been given, this individual must also be kept in the dark about the particular phase of the experiment in which the child is participating at any given time. An experiment in which these safeguards are used is said to be following a *double-blind design*. But still another safeguard is needed if the results are to have meaning. This precaution is known as a *crossover design*. Each child in the study must be evaluated under both the placebo and the drug condition, some receiving first the placebo and later the drug, while others experience these conditions in reverse order. The order must be carefully randomized so that whatever effects are found can really be attributed to the effect of the drug and are not an artifact of the research design.

In evaluating the effect of the drug, one must of course use a reliable and valid measure of hyperactivity. We have touched on the measurement problem when we spoke of the selection of children to be included in the study, This is now complicated by the necessity of obtaining effectiveness measures before and after the administration of the drug or placebo; that is, under each of the experimental conditions. Many of the tests in use are affected by repeated administration. A person filling out the same rating scale time and again on the same child does not retain the same perspective. A child repeatedly taking the same test responds to the items in different ways, but the difference may be due not to changes in what the test is supposed to measure but to the child having learned how to take the test. Ideally, alternate forms of the tests ought to be available, but they rarely are.

The many steps necessary in conducting a good study require many clinic visits and contacts between child and physician. To be well controlled, a study should also assess the effect of these contacts by including a condition where the children receive neither medication nor placebo but merely the personal attention involved in the research procedure. In practice, many of these methodological refinements are sacrificed for various reality considerations and this, as Sroufe (1975) pointed out, has resulted in a host of inconclusive or contradictory drug studies. When Barkely (1976) reviewed thirty-six research reports of various investigators, he found ten studies where a placebo control had either not been used or where unambiguous information on this point had not been provided. Thirteen of the studies had failed to use a double-blind design and only nineteen entailed a full crossover design.

There is yet another requirement that a truly good study of the effectiveness of a medication should meet; it is the use of a normal control group. In ordinary drug research such a control group would be unnecessary. If one wants to test the effectiveness of a new medication for the treatment of skin cancer, there is little point in testing this medication on people with normal skin because they would never be given that medication. Not so in the case of hyperactivity. There is an unknown number of normal children who are being given drugs such as methylphenidate. One reason for this is that some physicians prescribe these medications for children solely on the basis of a complaint by parents or teachers who say that a child moves around "too much." Many of these children are probably normal in the sense that they do not have a medical condition that calls for a medical treatment in the form of drugs. This irresponsible use of medication has been rightfully decried (Schrag & Divoky, 1975).

Another group of normal children who are given central nervous system stimulants stems from the use of such medications as a diagnostic device. Because there is no laboratory test that can tell us without a doubt that a child "has" hyperactivity, the line between normal restlessness and presumably pathological hyper-activity is a line drawn by subjective judgment. As a result, some physicians (Wender, 1971) advocate that hyperactive children be placed on a trial regimen of a drug such as methylphenidate in order to observe its effect. If the child's activity level shows some reduction, the physician concludes that the hyperactive behavior is due to "minimal brain dysfunction," even though there is no other evidence supporting this diagnosis. It is this deplorable practice that calls for studies of the effect of such central nervous system stimulants as methylphenidate on normal children. Unless one knows how normal children react to the drug, one cannot possibly draw conclusions about the cause of hyperactivity from observing hyper-active children's responses to the medication. Studies of the effect of amphetamines and similar drugs on the behavior of normal children are extremely difficult to conduct because of the obvious ethical issues this entails.

Having scrupulously followed the ethical requirements for conducting re-search with human participants, Rapoport, Buchsbaum, Zahn, Weingartner, Ludlow, and Mikkelsen (1978) studied the responses of fourteen normal, pre-adolescent boys to a single dose of dextroamphetamine. They found that these children reacted in ways highly similar to those usually reported for hyperactive children. The effects included decreased motor activity, faster reaction time, im-proved memory, and greater vigilance on laboratory tasks. Approximately 5 hours after the medication had been given, most of the children displayed a "re-bound effect," consisting of excitability and talkativeness. In hyperactive children, such behavior is typically attributed to the therapeutic effect of the drug wearing off. The fact that normal children also display this rebound suggests that it is due to drug-induced changes in receptor sensitivity that outlast the immediate chemical action of the drug. The authors draw several important conclusions from their study. One of these is that is is impossible to draw diagnostic conclusions from the fact that a child's activity level or attention span changes after the ad-ministration of a central nervous system stimulant, since normal children, too, manifest such changes. The diagnostic use of such drugs, as recommended by Wender (1971), would thus seem unwarranted. Another conclusion Rapoport et al. (1978) draw is that the reaction to amphetamine shown by hyperactive children cannot be used as a basis for speculations about the functions or con-dition of their brains or central nervous systems.

The Effect of CNS Stimulants   Central nervous system (CNS) stimulants are used with hyperactive children in order to help them settle down. Do these drugs have this effect? Given the aforementioned difficulties involved in drug re-search with children, the answer to this question must be hedged in several quali-fiers. Depending on what measure one uses, and depending on the child to whom the drug is given, and depending on the situation in which the child's response is measured, and depending on the amount of the drug and the kind of the drug one uses, CNS stimulants help some children to be less hyperactive. Activity level may be reduced, motor performance may become better controlled, periods during which attention can be sustained may increase, but most of these improvements are found in only well-structured situations and on tasks that call for mechanical, repetitious performance (Sroufe, 1975). Since many hyperactive children also have trouble learning, it is important to note that there is no evidence that CNS stimulants improve a child's learning *capacity*. While the ability to concentrate better on routine tasks in highly structured situations can be helpful to a child in school, this ability alone does not do much to help a child master such complex material as, for example, the meaning of a written paragraph.

This point was underscored by Rie and Rie (1977), who make the important distinction between acquisition (learning) and performance (test-taking ability). These investigators taught a group of twenty hyperactive children a story before any drug had been prescribed for them. They recorded the number of questions about the story each child could answer correctly after the first presentation and the number of trials needed before all could be answered without error. Two hours later and again 2 days later, they tested for recall of the story, using the same questions. The children were then put on medication (Ritalin) and after some 15 weeks had elapsed the entire procedure was repeated, using a different story of equivalent difficulty. The results revealed that the children's ability to learn the story was no better under the drug than the no-drug condition but that their performance on the test given 2 hours after learning was significantly better when they were on medication. This facilitation of test performance had, however, disappeared by the time the test was administered 2 days later. At that point, the children's performance was indistinguishable from the one they had produced before they had been placed on medication. Rie and Rie (1977) conclude from this and their earlier study (Rie, Rie, Steward, & Ambuel, 1976) that Ritalin fails to facilitate scholastic achievement. They stress the importance of evaluating the effect of Ritalin by taking both baseline and outcome measures while a child is on medication.

A similar issue has been raised by Swanson and Kinsbourne (1976), whose research suggests that when material is learned under the influence of methylphenidate, recall of that material at a later time may depend on whether the child is once again under that influence. This effect, called *state-dependent learning*, had been shown with laboratory animals, but Swanson and Kinsbourne (1976) report having demonstrated it with hyperactive children. They studied thirty-two hyperactive and sixteen nonhyperactive children who had been referred to a clinic for learning problems. Both groups of children were presented with a paired-associate learning task involving pictures of animals and names of cities. This is the kind of rote learning task on which the correct dosage of methylphenidate facilitates learning for many hyperactive children by enhancing their ability to sustain attention (Campbell, Douglas, & Morgenstern, 1971). The task was presented to the two groups of children under two conditions; once after administration of methylphenidate and once after having taken a placebo. On the following day, the children were tested for retention of the previously learned material; again, under both the drug and the placebo conditions. A crossover design generated four combinations of learning and retention states. These were drug-drug and placebo-placebo, the "same" states; and drug-placebo, placebo-drug, the "different" states. Comparisons of these four conditions for the two groups of children revealed a number of interesting effects.

For the hyperactive children, initial learning was facilitated by the drug. That is, they learned the lists with fewer errors after having ingested methylphenidate than when having taken the placebo. The nonhyperactive (control) children, on the other hand, were not helped by the drug. In fact, their learning was slightly worse under the drug than under the placebo condition. Since the control children were learning disabled but not hyperactive, this result has bearing on the practice of prescribing stimulant drugs to learning-disabled children regardless of whether they are hyperactive.

The state-dependent effect was demonstrated when the children were given tests of retention on the following day. For the hyperactive group, items learned under the drug condition were more readily relearned under the drug condition than under the placebo condition, while items learned under the placebo condition were more readily relearned under the placebo condition than under the drug condition. The readiness with which a previously learned list is relearned is a measure of retention and provides a test of memory. It is important to note that the placebo control permits one to rule out the explanation that the drug simply enhances a hyperactive child's capacity to attend on both the original learning task and on the retention test. Because lists had been learned to the same criterion of two errorless trials, regardless of condition, an overall facilitating effect of the medication should have produced better performance on retesting in the drug state than in the placebo state, regardless of the state under which the list had been learned on the previous day.

The error scores of the children in the control group on the retention tests again showed trends towards impaired performance due to the medication, but neither this nor reflections of state dependency were statistically significant for this group. The learning-disabled hyperactive children and the children who were learning disabled but not hyperactive thus revealed different patterns of results, suggesting that these children should be viewed as different populations when treatment by stimulant drugs is under consideration. Even among the hyperactive children, Swanson and Kinsbourne (1976) found more than 25 percent for whom the drug impaired the initial learning, but facilitated the subsequent relearning. State-dependent learning is therefore not a universal phenomenon, even among hyperactive children.

Considering the fact that the majority of the hyperactive children in their study showed good retention only for material learned in the drug condition when they were tested for it under the same condition, the conclusion Swanson and Kinsbourne (1976) reached is somewhat puzzling. They suggest that their work shows "the benefit of consistent medication," saying that "long-term retention of learned material may occur only when medication is applied consistently over time" and "advise the constant normalization of hyperactive behavior by stimulants in order to provide full benefit from the therapy" (p. 1356). For someone less convinced of the benefits of medication, their results might suggest that once a school-age child is placed on stimulant medication he or she had better be kept on medication for as long as the things the child learns in school are to be retained. In that case, might it not be better to seek alternatives to medication, especially in view of the fact that the placebo-placebo condition also showed state-dependent learning?

The Swanson and Kinsbourne (1976) study entailed three different dosages of methylphenidate; 10, 15, or 20 mg. The amount of the drug a given child receives is usually based on his or her body weight because the effect of a drug is a function of the dosage in which the drug is administered. That is, how much of the medication is given how many times a day. As Ross and Ross (1976) have pointed out, there is a dearth of research on this issue. Physicians often use either a standard dosage based on the child's age or body weight or they approach the decision about dosage in a trial-and-error method where the dosage is determined by the observed effects on the child's behavior. Neither of these methods is entirely satisfactory. There are great individual variations in drug response, variations that are functions of far more than such gross indicators as age or body weight. In using the effect on behavior as an index of appropriate dosage, one encounters the criterion difficulties mentioned earlier. What aspect of behavior is to be the determining factor? How valid and reliable are the reports on activity level that are obtained from teachers or parents?

It appears that different aspects of a child's behavior respond differently at different dosage levels. Sprague and Sleator (1977) report that at low dosage levels of methylphenidate a child's performance on a laboratory test of short-term memory shows improvement. At this dosage level, however, there is no noticeable effect on that child's hyperactive behavior. Only when the dosage level is increased is there a noticeable reduction in hyperactivity but by the time the dosage is high enough to accomplish this, the child's performance begins to suffer. In using a trial-and-error method for adjusting dosage, the criterion is usually the parents' or teacher's report of the child's behavior which is readily observed and not the adequacy of the child's academic performance, which often can be evaluated only over a relatively long period of time, such as a marking period. As the result of this approach to determining dosage level, the dosage usually recommended by physicians is well above the optimal range for cognitive performance; it is, in fact, deleterious to it (Sprague & Sleator, 1975). There thus appears to be a trade-off effect, and those dispensing medications may have to choose whether they want children sitting quietly but performing poorly, or performing better but wiggling more. At the same time, and as we shall see later in this chapter, it appears possible to reduce hyperactive behavior *and* improve academic performance by the judicious application of reinforcement principles (Ayllon, Layman, & Kandel, 1975).

Drugs and Attitudes

Before concluding this discussion of the use of medication in treating hyperactive children, it seems important to consider some of the more subtle implications of this practice, even though the absence of relevant research forces one to rely on speculative generalizations from related work.

People who experience a change in how they feel will usually seek to attribute this change to some cause. To what they attribute the change is a function of a variety of factors, including their expectations, the behavior of other people around them, and the situation in which they find themselves. For example, when people experience the physiological arousal that results from the discharge of adrenaline into the blood, it is likely that they attribute this to anger in one social situation and to excitement in another. Similarly, when a person stops smoking after taking a pill that is advertised as a "cure" for smoking, he or she may attribute this change in behavior to the pill, even though it was a totally inert substance. That same person might attribute overcoming the smoking habit to "self-control" if the change followed participation in a training program that was touted as having that as its goal. It is important to note that a change in behavior is maintained for a longer time if the change is attributed by the person to his or her own efforts than if it is held to be due to an external agent, such as a drug. Davison and Valins (1969), who conducted a study in which they found such a difference, pointed out that this attribution of effect might be a major reason why positive changes in behavior brought on by a drug so often tend to disappear as soon as the medication is withdrawn. They urge that whenever a drug is used to change a person's behavior, careful attention be paid to how the individual explains that change. When the person who receives the drug is also given something to do— such as exercising, relaxing, or following a set routine—so that he or she can attribute the change to that activity rather than to the drug, the positive change can be maintained even after the drug has been withdrawn. This was demonstrated in a study by Davison, Tsujimoto, and Glaros (1973), who worked with adults who had trouble falling asleep.

If one extrapolates from these studies to the effect of drugs used to reduce the hyperactive behavior of children, one can speculate that such a child will attribute the newly acquired ability to sit still and attend to lessons to the effect of the drug and that such a child will have a different attitude toward this achievement than a child who attributed the change to something he or she has learned to accomplish. What is more, it is likely that the reduced activity level will be maintained only for as long as the child remains on the drug. Indeed, drug treatment of hyperactive children is often continued for as long as 3 to 5 years (O'Malley & Eisenberg, 1973), even though we know very little about the long-term consequences in psychological or physical development of such continued use of CNS stimulants.

When children's hyperactivity is treated by drugs and they attribute the improvement to the medication, it may not only make the maintenance of the improvement depend on continued and regular administration of the drug but it may also affect the children's perception of themselves and lead them to believe that drugs are the way to solve personal problems. Children who, for years, have been criticized and reprimanded because of their restlessness and who often have a long history of poor school work will frequently have a poor self-image and low self-esteem. When drug-induced reduction in activity level then leads to their being better accepted and even praised, such children are likely to say, "The only reason I am behaving so well is because of my medicine." They will thus attribute their success to an external, chemical agent instead of viewing their behavior as under their own control. People who see the locus of control as external to themselves tend to adopt an attitude of helplessness and passivity, and they tend to look to external agents for the solution of problems (Bugental, Whalen, & Henker, 1977).

We began this discussion by referring to the consequences of viewing hyperactive behavior as a problem that belongs in the realm of medicine. This view has led to a search for a cause of the presumed syndrome, a search that has thus far been fruitless. It has also given rise to the widespread use of medication as the treatment of choice for hyperactive children. It would not be particularly constructive to take issue with this view were it not for the fact that an alternative method of treatment is available, which derives from the view that hyperactive behavior is not a medical disease but a behavior that can be changed by the application of principles of learning.

HYPERACTIVITY AS BEHAVIOR

Whatever definition of hyperactivity is used, it ultimately refers to the fact that a child moves around more often than other children with whom he or she is compared. Whether the measure is a rating scale filled out by teachers, a count of the number of quadrants on the playroom floor that the child traverses, or parents' reports, it is always the child's behavior that is the ultimate criterion. Behavior, whether it is hyperactive, aggressive, withdrawn, or fearful should be amenable to modification through the application of the same psychological principles. The relevant questions to ask are therefore those that deal with the antecedents and consequences of the behavior. What are the circumstances that precede hyperactive behavior? What are the events that immediately follow it? We might be curious about why some children are hyperactive while others are not or about the cause of hyperactivity, but the answers to such questions are not needed if the aim is to help an individual child reduce or redirect his or her activity level.

Behavior Therapy

As pointed out in several other places in this book, whenever the goal of treatment is the elimination of an undesirable behavior, it is essential to ask what one would like to see taking the place of that behavior and to take positive steps to establish desirable replacement behavior. In the case of the child whose hyperactive behavior is the target of intervention, it is necessary to ask what that child should be doing once the hyperactive behavior is no longer taking place. Behavior at a normal level of activity is not necessarily the obverse of hyperactive behavior. It is conceivable that a child who is no longer hyperactive will become hypoactive, simply sitting still and staring into space. For this reason, any intervention aimed at reducing hyperactivity must include a systematic plan to replace the hyperactive behavior with goal-directed, attentive, and constructive behavior.

Visualize a pie diagram that represents the total time in a child's school day. A "slice" representing one-quarter of this time might be taken up with disruptive behavior. Under specialized treatment conditions, such as a token program, this quarter slice of disruptive time might be reduced, but something—some other behavior—will have to fill that space; there cannot be a behavioral vacuum. If the person in charge of the treatment program does not make explicit and systematic plans to develop behavior to fill this "space," the behavior most likely to move into the vacant time is whatever behavior happens to be reinforced, often accidentally when it is emitted. Without a systematic plan, this behavior is very likely to be something the teacher or others find objectionable; it is unlikely to be constructive studying behavior. In working with a hyperactive child on reducing the hyperactivity by means of a reinforcement program, it is possible to reward and thus increase, periods of sitting still. But simply sitting still should not be the goal of the program, for sitting still is only a necessary step toward attending to a task to be learned. For this reason, reinforcement should quickly be made contingent not merely on sitting still, but on sitting still *and* working; otherwise, the outcome might be a child who has simply learned to "sit and do nothing."

An early demonstration of the use of behavioral principles in working with a hyperactive child was presented by Patterson, Jones, Whittier, and Wright (1965). They treated a 10-year-old brain-injured, retarded boy who was enrolled in a special school for physically handicapped children. This boy's teacher described him as being hyperactive with a short attention span and a tendency to be aggressive toward younger children. Raymond, as this boy is called in the paper by Patterson et al. (1965), was clearly more severely impaired than most children usually classified as hyperactive, but if one can demonstrate the effectiveness of a method for reducing such behavior in an extreme case, it stands to reason that the principles involved should also be applicable with less severe problems.

In order to ensure that changes in Raymond's behavior were indeed the result of the experimental manipulation, Patterson and his coworkers (1965) also gathered data on a control subject, a child in the same class who had problems and behaviors similar to those of Raymond. At the beginning of the project, Raymond was spending most of his classroom time staring into space, walking about the room, almost continuously moving his arms or legs, and displaying other behavior typical of hyperactive children. Such behavior is obviously in-compatible with attending to academic tasks. Since attending is the desirable behavior to be established in such cases, it was selected as the target of interven-tion. Observers behind a one-way screen used a checklist to record such "nonat-tending" behaviors as swinging of arms, twisting in chair, looking out of window, wiggling feet, fingering objects, talking to self, and walking around. Baseline data, collected before any intervention was started, showed that both boys en-gaged in a mean of approximately five such nonattending responses per minute.

Following the baseline period, Raymond was introduced to the conditioning procedure, which was described to him as a way of teaching him to sit still so that he could study better. He would wear an earphone (connected to a small radio receiver strapped to his back) through which he would receive a signal that in-dicated when he had earned a piece of candy. He was given a series of training trials outside the classroom during which the experimenter would activate the ear-phone and deliver a piece of candy for each 10-second period during which the boy did not display any of the hyperactive, nonattending behavior. Reinforcement was thus contingent on brief periods of attending to the work that had been as-signed. The reason for phrasing the contingency as a double negative (not dis-playing nonattending behavior) is that wiggling and other nonattending responses are readily observable, while "attending" is difficult to define in such a way that one is not merely reinforcing a child for directing glances toward the workbook.

After the initial adaptation to and training with the conditioning apparatus, Raymond wore the equipment in his classroom, the rest of the children having been told that it was to help him learn things by telling him when he was sitting still. They were also informed that Raymond would be earning candy, which he could share with the class at the end of the period. This involvement of the other children had led to much peer support and social reinforcement in earlier work conducted by Patterson, who reasons that many of a child's behaviors, both posi-tive and negative, are maintained by the reactions they elicit from the social en-vironment. The conditioning phase of his study lasted for 3 weeks, during which data were collected on 8 days for both subjects, with actual conditioning carried out for periods ranging from 5 to 18 minutes.

The results of this study showed that during the conditioning phase Raymond made significantly fewer nonattending responses than the control child. The mean number of such responses per minute was approximately 3.3 for Raymond, while those for the other child remained at the baseline level, near 5.0. After the end of the conditioning phase, the observations were continued over a 4-week period and this revealed that the difference between Raymond and the control child was maintained, although the latter's behavior also showed a decrease in the occur-rence of nonattending behavior. This is an intriguing phenomenon, which might be attributed to the fact that the two children sat close to each other in the class; thus, Raymond's improved behavior may have reduced the number of distracting stimuli to which the other child had previously reacted with hyperactivity of his own. Such an influence on the part of a disruptive child on the rest of the class is not unknown to classroom teachers.

Working with Groups of Children   Patterson et al. (1965) have thus demonstrated that it is possible to strengthen the attending behavior of a brain-injured, hyperactive boy by a relatively simple conditioning procedure. However, the use of a radio receiver and the need for an observer who signals the delivery of reinforcements limit this approach to highly specialized situations. It is thus important to note that other investigators, working in the behavior modification framework, have demonstrated that behavioral principles can also be applied under more normal classroom conditions. These applications usually involve a token reinforcement program, where the immediate reinforcer is a readily dispensable symbol (token) that can be exchanged for backup reinforcers in the form of tangible prizes or special privileges. With children who can comprehend verbal instructions, the relationship between backup reinforcer, tokens, and the means for earning these are usually announced in a clearly stated set of rules. When tokens, such as plastic disks, checkmarks, or paper scrip are handed out, they are accompanied by statements of praise, approval, smiles, and other social gestures which, being paired with the more concrete reinforcer, come to acquire greater strength in their own right. This is an important aspect of such a program because the tangible reinforcers and their backups are scheduled for eventual withdrawal, at which point social reinforcement and more "natural" reinforcers, such as highly favored classroom or recess activities or privileges, must take the place of the token program (Kazdin, 1977).

In a study reported by O'Leary, Pelham, Rosenbaum, and Price (1976) nine hyperactive children were treated over a 10-week period by home-based reward programs operated by the teachers in regular classrooms. Eight other hyperactive children served as a control group. The children's behavior was evaluated, both before and after treatment, using an abbreviated version of a teacher rating scale developed by Conners (1969) and a rating scale of problem behaviors that was individually prepared for each child to provide a measure of the severity of four or five problems that the particular child manifested.

The average age of the children in this study was 10 years: the youngest was 8 years, 11 months; the oldest 10 years, 11 months. In order to be selected for participation in the study, a child had to receive a score of at least 15 on the Conners scale. The hyperactive children had an average score of 19.7, while randomly selected normal controls who came from the same classroom as the hyperactives, had an average score of 5.1. There are ten items on the abbreviated Conners scale, consisting of the following descriptive statements:

Restless or overactive
Excitable, impulsive
Disturbs other children
Fails to finish things he starts, short attention span

Constantly fidgeting
Inattentive, easily distracted
Demands must be met immediately—easily frustrated
Cries often and easily
Mood changes quickly and drastically
Temper outbursts, explosive and unpredictable behavior

Each of these items is rated for the degree of activity displayed by the child. Zero represents "not at all" one "just a little," two "pretty much," and three "very much." If a child earned a score of three on every item, the total score would be 30. To be classified as hyperactive, a child must have a score of 15 points or more.

The children in the O'Leary et al. (1976) study were of average intelligence, but seven of the nine in the treatment group scored below average on an achievement test. None showed definite symptoms of brain damage and none were receiving medication for hyperactivity at the time the study was being conducted. The treatment focused on strengthening desirable behavior, such as completing a math assignment, helping another child with a class project, not fighting, and bringing completed homework to school. It is noteworthy that direct opposites of hyperactivity, such as sitting still, not fidgeting, or attending to a task were not the direct targets of the intervention.

The program involved the participation of the child's teacher and parents. The teacher would daily specify each child's classroom goals and praise the child's efforts to reach these goals. At the end of the day, the teacher prepared a progress report on the child's behavior in terms of the specified goals. The daily progress reports were sent to the child's parents, who were responsible for delivering rewards for the child's progress toward the goals. The role of the parents in this program had been explained to them during a conference with the therapist at the start of the intervention. Appropriate rewards were selected during this interview and modified, when needed, in the course of weekly telephone contacts.

The choice of rewards and their consistent delivery by the parents is probably the most critical element in such a treatment program. Unless the child receives meaningful positive consequences for the behavior one seeks to establish and strengthen, progress is unlikely. Rewards must therefore be selected for each individual child and their potency must be continually monitored. Examples of rewards used in the study here under discussion were such privileges as a half hour's extra television viewing, getting a special dessert, playing a favorite game with one of the parents, or receiving money. These were daily rewards. At the end of each week in which the child had earned at least four daily rewards, an end-of-week reward was also forthcoming. This might consist of going on a fishing trip with the father, or eating a family meal at a drive-in restaurant.

O'Leary and his colleagues (1976) point out that no single reward program will work for every case. Programs must be modified when one approach fails to produce significant improvement in the child's behavior. The range of possible rewards, they say, is limited only by reality constraints and the ingenuity of the therapist. For the hyperactive children in this study, the reward program appears to have been highly effective. At the start of the program the treated children and their controls had not differed in mean hyperactivity rating on either the Conners scale or the scale of problem behaviors. When these instruments were administered again after 10 weeks of treatment, the two groups differed significantly on both scales. On the individualized problem-behavior rating scale, only the treated group showed a significant ($p < .005$) improvement from before to after treatment. On the Conners scale, both groups showed significant improvement ($p < .005$), but the treated children had significantly lower posttreatment scores than the controls ($p < .066$).

The improvement on the part of the untreated controls who had no contact with the therapy team at any time during the study, while less dramatic than that of the children who had been treated, represents somewhat of a puzzle. It may be, of course, that hyperactive children become less hyperactive after 10 weeks of the school term have passed. We have no data to support this speculation of spontaneous improvement. In fact, anecdotes from teachers suggest that this does not take place. Another possibility is that hyperactive children stimulate one another and that, as one of them settles down, the other one does too. It will be recalled that Patterson et al. (1965) had reported the same phenomenon in their work with Raymond.

The work we have just discussed entailed the participation of parents. In fact, the children had, in part, been selected for participation in the study on the basis of their parents' willingness to cooperate with the therapists. Since the participation of parents may not always be feasible, one must ask whether a similar treatment program could be conducted without them. O'Leary, Becker, Evans, and Saudargas (1969) had investigated the effect of a token program that operated only in the school. It dealt with the behavior of seven disruptive children in a second-grade class of twenty-one students. Following a 6-week period, during which baseline data were gathered, the teacher gradually introduced systematic changes in classroom management. These changes consisted of rules for behavior, structuring of the program, praising appropriate and ignoring disruptive behavior, and, finally, the contingent delivery of tokens that were exchangeable for backup reinforcers. The results showed that disruptive behavior did not manifest a decrease until the introduction of the delivery of tokens, thus demonstrating that changes in classroom management that usually accompany a token program (rules, structure, and social reinforcement) are not, by themselves, responsible for behavior change. After 5 weeks, the token program was experimentally withdrawn; reinstated, and again withdrawn, and the disruptive behavior showed changes commensurate with these manipulations. As a final step, the token program was replaced by a procedure in which children received stars for appropriate behavior, with extra stars awarded to the best behaved row of children. At the end of the week, one piece of candy was awarded to the child with the greatest number of stars and to each member of the group (boys versus girls) that had earned the most stars. This procedure added peer competition to the awarding of tokens and served to maintain the improvement for some of the children. While successful for the 8 months during which this program was in effect, it is not known whether it resulted in any long-range changes in child behavior. What is more, the effects of this program, which was conducted only in the afternoon sessions of the class, did not generalize to the morning session when the token program was not in operation.

The Generalization of Progress   The issue of the generalization (carryover) of behavior changes achieved in token programs was discussed by O'Leary and Drabman (1971), who reviewed the use of token reinforcement programs in schools. They pointed out that generalization should not be expected to take place automatically, but that it must be built into the treatment plan in the same careful and systematic manner in which one works toward treatment effect in the first place. These authors make a number of suggestions for achieving generalizations from a treatment setting, such as a special resource room where a token economy is operating, to the child's regular classroom.

Follow-through   The first of these suggestions stresses the importance of providing children with a good academic program that is designed to teach the skills and knowledge commensurate with their level of achievement. This is important for any child who returns to the regular classroom after having had remedial help with academic work or special training in acquiring more adaptive behavior. Unless the regular classroom provides such children with the wherewithal to engage in constructive activity—if needed, by special tutoring—the probability that they will once again engage in disruptive behavior is quite high, unless, as O'Leary and Drabman (1971) put it, they have "simply learned to sit 'doing nothing'."

Attribution of Progress   The second suggestion for achieving generalization offered by O'Leary and Drabman (1971) deals with the expectations a child has for his or her own behavior. If a boy attributes his improvement to the setting in which he is acquiring his desirable response repertoire—his "good behavior and ability to learn"—he will expect that once he is out of that setting all he has gained is likely to be lost. For this reason, it is important that children be given the expectation that they themselves are capable of doing well, that their success is their accomplishment, not something somebody else has done for them. In order to ensure that a child will attribute improvement to himself and not to others, one must explicitly structure the entire helping situation from the start as one designed to increase the child's sense of competence. Attributions of success cannot be taken for granted, particularly not with a child who has had a long history of failure experiences which, because adults will usually have blamed him, may have resulted in low self-expectations and a poor self-image. A child who has come to be convinced that he "can't do it" is very likely to attribute success experiences to external causes. For this reason, O'Leary and Drabman (1971) advocate that one use exaggerated excitement when the child succeeds, pointing out that if he works he *can* succeed. Similarly, such children must be given the expectation that they will be able to work without a token program. Since a good token program is gradually faded by thinning out the schedule of reinforcement and shifting the burden of maintaining the behavior to such reinforcers as praise, approval, and privileges, this expectation is given considerable support. A token program is a temporary crutch, not a permanent prosthesis.

Another way of making sure that the children attribute improvements to themselves and will thus be able to carry them to other settings is to involve them in planning the specifics of the program, making it "their" program rather than the teacher's. They can aid in the selection of the behaviors to be reinforced, in evolving the rules under which the class is to function and, as the program progresses, in the specification of contingencies.

Enhancing Generalization   Generalization is also enhanced if children receive reinforcement for desirable behavior not only in the specialized environment of the token classroom but also in a variety of other situations and settings. Furthermore, it is important that the treatment setting be as similar as possible to the regular classroom setting so that the difference between the two is reduced. The ideal setting where a child should learn adaptive classroom behavior is, of course, the classroom itself but where this is not feasible, the special resource room or treatment class should not be so distinctly different as to have desirable behavior become associated with these distinct features. For example, if children in the regular class are used to calling their teachers by their last names, the resource-room teacher should not be addressed by the first name. As children are phased back from the special resource room to their regular classes, their teachers should be prepared to make it a point to praise good behavior, thus providing a similarity of settings and maintaining the adaptive behavior. (It would, of course, be good if the regular classroom teacher were to make it a practice to praise desirable behavior of all children most of the time.)

The Participation of Parents   Yet another means of enhancing transfer of progress by building a "bridge" between the special and the regular classroom is to involve the child's parents in the treatment plan. The parents can provide a constant background factor and their potential contribution to a treatment plan cannot be sufficiently stressed. Provided they are included in the planning from the start and given a thorough understanding of the principles and rationale involved, parents can be a primary source for the delivery of backup reinforcers. When this is done, the child brings home the tokens earned during a given period and there exchanges them for whatever it is that has been agreed upon. This procedure has the advantage that backup reinforcers can be highly personalized and consistent with the family's values and standards. More importantly, however, the parents can add their own social reinforcement to the delivery of the tangible reinforcer, and this social reinforcement can and should continue to be available long after the child has left the special treatment class and returned to regular class.

Self-Evaluation Self-evaluation by children played an important role in a study conducted by Drabman, Spitalknik, and O'Leary (1973), who demonstrated reduction of disruptive behavior that generalized over brief periods of time. The children in this study were eight boys, ages 9 to 10, who attended "adjustment" classes for students with academic and emotional problems. All were at least 1 year below grade level in reading skills and their teachers viewed them all as very disruptive, even in their small, special classes. For the purpose of the study, these children were enrolled in an after-school remedial reading class which met for 1 hour, five times a week and where the principles of token reinforcement were applied. Programs of this nature had demonstrated improvements in behavior, but those improvements had failed to generalize to situations other than those in which the token program was conducted (e.g., O'Leary et al., 1969). For this reason, Drabman et al. (1973) wanted to determine whether self-evaluation by children would lead to transfer of improvements in social and academic behavior to periods of the day when the token program was not in effect. The study was therefore designed to teach honest and veridical self-evaluation skills so that the teachers could transfer the responsibility for behavior evaluation to the students in a manner that would produce long-range maintenance of appropriate behavior.

To accomplish the goal of this study, Drabman and his colleagues (1973) proceeded in several stages. After recording baseline measures on disruptive behavior; the scores from the California Achievement Test Reading-Vocabulary; and the Sullivan reading series, they had the teacher introduce a standard token program in which the children could earn points for "good behavior" and completion of assignments. Each hour-long class was broken into four 15-minute periods, during one of which the token program was not in effect. At the beginning of each period, the teacher would announce whether it was a token period or not; the no-token episodes served as a control.

With the implementation of the conventional, teacher-administered token program, disruptive behavior decreased and academic performance improved. After 5 days of this regime, the teacher announced that henceforth the children were to rate their own behavior and to attempt to match the ratings she was giving them. During this matching phase, the children could earn extra points if their ratings matched those of the teacher. After 10 days of this training in self-rating, the teacher's checking of the students' ratings was gradually faded out, thereby fading out the bonus points that accompanied successful matches. During the last 12 days of the study, all checking was completely discontinued and the earning of points depended solely on the ratings the children had awarded themselves. Throughout the study, trained observers continued to record disruptive behavior. During the self-evaluation phase, such behavior showed an 88-percent decrease from baseline while points were in effect; for the no-token control periods, the improvement was even greater, disruptive behavior showing a 90-percent decrease. The group gained an average of .72 years on the reading vocabulary test during the 2½ months of the study, and similar improvement was reflected on the Sullivan reading series.

This work highlights the fact that honest self-evaluation can be taught to very disruptive children, who thus acquire sufficient self-control to maintain improved behavior even when this behavior receives no extrinsic reinforcement. In discussing their work, Drabman et al. (1973) write as follows:

> Several factors may have contributed to this maintenance of appropriate behavior during the self-evaluation phase: (a) The teachers continually praised the students for appropriate behavior, and their praise may have become more reinforcing over the course of the study; (b) Similarly, peer reinforcement for appropriate behavior increased with time, and the children did not want to be bothered by other pupils; (c) Honest self-evaluation was socially reinforced by the teachers and later by peers. It is quite likely that these self-evaluations became cues which served as self-instructional or mediational statements which guided appropriate behavior; (d) The children's academic skills were improved; their involvement in academic activities was partly incompatible with inappropriate behavior. Particularly toward the beginning of the self-evaluation phase, when the rate of disruptive behavior was lowest, the children could easily see that they had made academic progress; (e) The self-evaluations may have become secondary reinforcers for appropriate classroom behavior [Drabman et al., 1973, pp. 15f].

Despite the impressive finding regarding self-evaluation, this study is not really very convincing on the issue of generalization. The test for generalization of improved behavior was based on the 15-minute control periods during which the token program was not in effect. For most of these time segments a token period preceded and followed; therefore, the finding that disruptive behavior also decreased during the control sessions is not very strong evidence for generalization. It is more convincing if one can demonstrate that the positive effects of a token program are retained after a token program is terminated altogether. Such a demonstration was reported by O'Leary, Drabman, and Kass (1973), who found improved behavior to be maintained over a 20-day follow-up period after termination of a token program.

From Tokens to Praise   Most of the early token programs used with children in classroom situations employed tangible rewards, such as money, candy, and toys, as backup reinforcers. This not only introduces a highly artificial element into the school setting but it has also been thought that the magnitude of these reinforcers might be one of the reasons why improvements in behavior are rarely maintained once the reinforcements are withdrawn. For these reasons, O'Leary et al. (1973) decided to test whether appropriate behavior, developed in a token program, could be maintained if the reinforcers used were those readily available to any classroom teacher, such as extra recess or free time in a special-activity area of the classroom.

Twenty-two third- and fourth-grade children were selected for this study on the basis of their being the most disruptive in the school. All of them were deficient in reading and/or arithmetic. After they had been observed in their own classroom for the purpose of establishing a baseline for disruptive behavior, these children were assigned to three separate resource-room classes where they received special instruction in reading or arithmetic for 1 hour per day in supplementation of their regular academic program, which they continued in the homeroom. Following observations during a baseline phase in the resource room, token programs were introduced, lasting for 4 months. As is the case in all studies by O'Leary and his colleagues, disruptive behaviors observed and recorded were: not sitting in the seat, inappropriate noise, playing, turning around, noncompliance, vocalization, aggression, and not attending to task.

When the token reinforcement program was initiated, the teacher announced the introduction of a point system. Points could be earned for completion of assignment, completion of homework, coming to class on time, and behaving well in class. The emphasis was on the academic tasks, which served as the largest single source of potential point-earning. Points were awarded at the end of the first 45 minutes of the 1-hour resource-room period and the points thus earned were exchangeable (one point for 1 minute) for free time during the last 15 minutes of the free-activity period. A variety of games, such as checkers, paints, and building blocks were available during this free time.

The token programs in the resource room were continued for 4 months. During the last 3 weeks, all children were again observed in their home class to determine if the improved behavior developed in the resource room had influenced home-class disruptive behavior. In addition, the homeroom teachers repeated a rating of each child that had been gathered at the beginning of the study. Finally, one of the resource room classes was monitored for 8 weeks following termination of the program in order to investigate maintenance of the appropriate behavior generated by the token system.

The results reported by O'Leary et al. (1973) clearly show a decrease in disruptive behavior with the initiation of the token program. In one class, for example, the average frequency for disruptive behavior decreased by 57 percent and this improvement was maintained throughout the follow-up period when the token program was no longer in effect. An interesting phenomenon was revealed in the investigation of generalization to the home-class situation. While the ratings by the teachers in the homerooms showed a reduction in disruptive behavior for a significant number of children, no significant generalization of appropriate behavior to the homeroom classes was reflected in the independent observer recordings. These recordings showed that 14 of the 22 children manifested less disruptive behavior than they had during baseline, but this change did not reach statistical significance. It is likely that the teacher ratings were influenced by their expectations based on the knowledge that these children were participating in a special program. This raises the question whether, for practical purposes, it is more important to demonstrate a statistically significant effect or to influence the perceptions of teachers regarding the behavior of the children in their class. A statistically significant difference can have little practical significance. On the other hand, an event of practical significance may have little statistical significance. The two are not the same. At any rate, if 14 out of 22 disruptive children improve their behavior following a 1-hour-per-day experience over a 4-month period, the method used would seem to merit further investigation.

It is likely that generalization to the homeroom could have been enhanced if certain steps that the investigators had planned could have been carried out. They had hoped that the homeroom teacher might also award points based on homeroom behavior that could be exchanged for time in the special-activity area of the resource room. These ratings were then to be gradually faded out so that appropriate behavior might be maintained in the homeroom without such special treatment. Administrative difficulties kept this plan from being implemented. Another "bridge" between a special-class situation and a child's regular schoolroom would be the use of praise and teacher attention for desirable behavior. The special-class teacher usually pairs the awarding of points or tokens with much social reinforcement and this is continued even when the tangible rewards are eliminated. If classroom teachers could be helped to see the merit of frequent and explicit praise and attention for constructive behavior, they would be using the reinforcers made effective in the special class, thus enhancing generalization of progress a child has made. Unfortunately, as O'Leary, Kaufman, Kass, and Drabman (1970) have documented, classroom teachers are much more likely to deliver reprimands and to attend to undesirable behavior than they are to bestow praise and to attend to desirable behavior. The effect of this paradoxical approach is that undesirable behavior is strengthened and maintained.

Another aspect of this paradox has been documented in a study by Worland (1976) who compared the effect of different kinds of feedback on hyperactive and normal boys. He recorded both the amount of time a child spent on a task and the accuracy with which this task was accomplished. The results showed that negative feedback in the form of a loud, unpleasant noise whenever the child was not working on the task served to increase the time spent on the task. However, while increasing the on-task behavior, the negative feedback also decreased the accuracy of the work accomplished. Criticizing or punishing hyperactive children for not attending to a task may increase the amount of time they spend on the task, but this apparently happens at the expense of how well they do their work.

This study again illustrates that it is important to decide on the goal of an intervention and to focus this intervention on that goal. If it is desired that a child "pay attention," reprimands for not attending may result in the child's focusing on the task, but this does not mean that the task will be accurately accomplished. Since the quality of the work done is, after all, the real goal, the quality should be the target of intervention and here positive feedback seems more effective than reprimands or criticism. A moment's reflection leads to the recognition that in order to do accurate work a child must attend to the task, but attending to the task will not in and of itself result in accurate task completion.

On the other hand, if the focus of intervention is on work accuracy, attention to the task will take care of itself. This is another way of saying that attention is only the means to an end, not the end in itself. It is not enough to teach a child to pay attention; one must also teach what he or she is to do while engaging in the behavior we call paying attention.

Because attending to the task (that is, looking as if one were paying attention) is more quickly and easily monitored than the accuracy with which the work is being done (because accuracy can only be checked at completion), attention is often the primary focus of people who are concerned about hyperactive children. When such a child is attending to something other than that which the teacher considers to be the task at hand, it has often been inferred that the task-irrelevant object has distracted the child. This assumption has led to the use of various ways of reducing the number of possible "distractors" in the hyperactive child's classroom environment. Some have advocated placing such a child in a three-sided cubicle, a procedure originally introduced by Strauss and Lehtinen (1947) for work with brain-injured children. There is very little evidence that this approach has merit with hyperactive children. Not only will the cubicle reduce only the extraneous visual stimuli in front and on the sides of the child but it also tends to magnify the auditory stimuli coming from the rest of the classroom. In fact, a study by Zentall and Zentall (1976) has shown that it may be understimulation rather than overstimulation that precipitates hyperactive behavior; therefore, the elimination of so-called distractors may be an error. The notion of a distractor implies that a stimulus pulls the child away from the task as if by some magnetic force. What is more likely is that the child shifts his or her attention to another point, which can be a pattern in the grain of the cubicle wall as easily as a picture on the wall of the classroom.

MEDICATION OR BEHAVIOR THERAPY?

We have discussed the different implications for treatment of the hyperactive child that arise from the view of hyperactivity as the symptom of a physical disorder and the view of hyperactivity as a form of behavior. The first view leads to treating the problem with medications; the second calls for intervention based on principles of learning. These two approaches have been debated, both in the professional literature (Sroufe & Stewart, 1973; Wender, 1971) and in writings aimed at the general audience (Schrag & Divoky, 1975). Debating cannot settle this issue; only research can. In the final analysis, it may not be a question of whether one form of treatment is better than the other but whether certain children are helped best by one form, others by the other, while for yet a third group the optimal treatment entails a combination of approaches.

There has, unfortunately, been remarkably little research aimed at comparing the relative effectiveness of chemical and behavioral methods for treating hyperactive children. Pelham (1976) reported on the case of one child whom he treated under two conditions, first with behavior therapy and methylphenidate and then with behavior therapy alone. This 9-year-old boy had been receiving the medication since he was 6 years old, but his problems at home and in school (which had been attributed to his hyperactivity) had continued. Behavior therapy consisted of a home-based reward program, which was placed in the parents' hands after they had been trained in its appropriate use. The teacher's ratings of the boy's school behavior reflected gradual improvement during the first 7 weeks of treatment when medication was given concurrently with the behavioral treatment. After these 7 weeks, the medication was withdrawn and the behavioral program continued. It was found that the boy's behavior continued to improve, and it did so even after contact between the therapist and the parents had been terminated.

A similar comparison between treatment with methylphenidate and treatment with a behavioral alternative was reported by Ayllon et al. (1975), who worked with three hyperactive children whose academic performance was very inadequate. A multiple-baseline design permitted these investigators to demonstrate the effectiveness of the introduction of a reinforcement contingency. During the first 17 days and while the children were on their medication, observations of their activity level during math and reading periods revealed that they spent an average of 24 percent of class time engaged in hyperactive behavior. During the same periods, their performance on math and reading problems was only 12 percent correct. When medication was withdrawn after 17 days, the time spent in hyperactive behavior increased drastically, going as high as 87 percent for one of the children. After 3 days, the teacher introduced a token reinforcement system for correct math performance, which immediately showed dramatic improvement. Hyperactive behavior, which was not under any reinforcement contingency, returned to the level where it had been while the children were on medication, but it did so only during the math period where the reinforcement for good performance was in effect. In the reading period, where reinforcement had not yet been introduced, hyperactivity remained high and academic performance low. After a 6-day period, following the multiple-baseline design, the teacher introduced reinforcement for both math and reading performance. At this point and for the following 6-day period, academic performance in both subject matters was high and hyperactivity low during both class periods. The combined hyperactivity measures for the three children showed them hyperactive only 20 percent of the time (compared to 24 percent under the earlier medication), while their academic performance was 85 percent correct (compared to the 12 percent obtained under medication). Though this study lacks follow-up data so that one does not know whether the results held up over time, it strongly suggests that the use of medication controls hyperactivity at the cost of poor academic performance and that it is possible to obtain the same level of control without drugs by focusing reinforcement contingencies on the child's academic performance.

The studies just cited, though highly suggestive, can serve as no more than demonstrations of the effectiveness of behavioral methods. They leave unanswered such questions as whether the effect is limited to the few children involved or to the sequence (medication before reinforcement procedures) in which the two treatments were applied. What is needed in order to answer these and other questions is a large-scale investigation, comparing representative groups of hyperactive children under various combinations of treatment conditions. A study designed to answer some of these questions was in progress when Gittelman-Klein, Klein, Abikoff, Katz, Gloisten, and Kates (1976) presented a preliminary report on 34 out of a projected total of 75 hyperactive children. The children were between the ages of 6 and 12 and had been randomly assigned to one of three treatment conditions in which they remained for an 8-week period. One condition was a combination of methylphenidate and behavior therapy that followed the typical model of a home-based classroom token program. A control condition consisted of the same kind of behavior therapy combined with a placebo, which everyone except the experimenters believed to be "the real thing." The third condition involved the administration of methylphenidate in the manner of individualized drug treatment for hyperactivity.

When the entire study is completed, the authors intend to analyze a variety of measures on which the children's behavior before and after treatment can be compared. For the preliminary report only classroom observations and the post-treatment evaluations based on teacher, parent, and psychiatric ratings of activity level were available. The ratings were based on an 8-point scale, ranging from "completely well" to "much worse," which was further reduced to a dichotomy of "improved-unimproved." These ratings reflect only the child's behavior and give no information about academic performance. This crude analysis, on which the preliminary report was based, compounds other shortcomings of this study. These include the fact that the design did not provide for an untreated control group of hyperactive children nor for a crossover so that each child could have been studied under each of the treatment conditions. In addition, the evaluators were aware whether or not a child was receiving behavior therapy and the design failed to include a condition where a placebo is administered without behavior therapy.

Despite these shortcomings, some of which are unavoidable, the results of the Gittelman-Klein et al. study (1976) warrant reporting. All treatments produced significant clinical improvement in children's activity level, but the combination of behavior therapy plus methylphenidate was regularly better than the others, followed by methylphenidate alone and behavior therapy plus placebo. The lack of an untreated control group or a placebo-only group makes it impossible to know whether any of these treatments are superior to doing nothing at all or to providing a child with an inert pill. Work by other investigators (O'Leary, Pelham, Rosenbaum, & Price, 1976), who did include an untreated control group in their studies, had found that time alone does not improve the behavior of hyperactive children; therefore, one can assume that the treatments used by the Gittelman-Klein group did make a difference.

As far as the comparison of the three methods of treatment is concerned, Gittelman-Klein et al. (1976) report that there was no evidence of behavioral treatment plus medication being significantly better than medication alone, while behavioral treatment plus placebo was significantly less effective than medication alone. The investigators conclude from their results that inasmuch as they found no statistically significant difference in effectiveness between behavior therapy plus methylphenidate and methylphenidate alone, the treatment of choice for severely hyperactive children, such as those in their study, should be medication in individualized dosages. This recommendation is based on the fact that medication is easier and less costly to administer than a program of individual behavioral intervention. They advocate behavior therapy only in cases where parents refuse to permit medication or a child cannot tolerate the drug, as was the case with one child in their study who developed hypertension and a marked increase in heart rate (tachycardia) on a very small dosage of methylphenidate. Adverse reactions to stimulant drugs have also been found by others (Rapoport, Quinn, Bradbard, Riddle, & Brooks, 1974).

Advocating the use of drugs as the treatment of choice for hyperactive children ignores not only that drugs do not seem to improve academic performance but also the psychological implications we have mentioned earlier. In fact, Gittelman-Klein et al. (1976) noted a positive shift in parental attitudes toward the children who were receiving the behavioral treatment in which parents played an active part. The report, based on an 8-week study, also leaves open the questions of a long-term maintenance of the behavior change or of the long-range effect of maintaining a child on a central nervous system stimulant. There have been reports of a decrease in growth rate of hyperactive children who had been taking stimulant drugs for several years (Safer, Allen, & Barr, 1972; Safer & Allen, 1973). Such an impairment of growth rate was also found by Weiss, Kruger, Danielson, and Elman (1975), who conducted a follow-up study of hyperactive children who had been on methylphenidate for 3 to 5 years. These investigators had compared the children on methylphenidate with a control group who had received no medication, and they reported the impression that this drug was "helpful in making hyperactive children more manageable at home and at school" (p. 159) but that neither their behavior nor their school performance differed significantly from that of the controls after 5 years of treatment. Similarly, when Riddle and Rapoport (1976) conducted a 2-year follow-up study of seventy-two hyperactive boys who had been on stimulant drug medication, they found that 70 of the 72 parents were still seriously concerned about their children and that the boys' academic achievement and peer acceptance were still low. In addition, the boys who had been on the drug showed more depressive symptoms than a control group. Given these unresolved issues, it seems premature to draw the conclusion

Gittelman-Klein and her colleagues (1976) offered on the basis of their interim report.

RECAPITULATION

Hyperactivity is a label applied to children who move about more than someone considers normal and its use is thus largely a function of the tolerance level of those who make judgments about the behavior of children. A child who fails to sit still for any length of time not only disturbs other children in a classroom but is also often unable to do adequate academic work. Hyperactivity is thus a matter of concern for the school.

When the problem is viewed as related to dysfunctions in the child's brain, treatment by medication becomes an obvious route, even though there is no evidence that the problem has, indeed, an organic basis. The administration of central nervous system (CNS) stimulants often seems to result in a reduction of hyperactive behavior. It is very difficult to conduct definitive research on this problem. Available studies seem to show that a dosage high enough to reduce activity to a tolerable level interferes with the child's cognitive functions, beyond rote, repetitious learning. Not only that, but what learning does take place while a child is on a medication may be state-dependent, which means that once a child has been put on a drug he or she may have to be continued on it for a long period of time.

A formulation of hyperactivity as behavior leads to an intervention that applies the principles of reinforcement. This has been shown not only to reduce hyperactivity but also to enhance academic performance. Behavioral approaches can be used with an individual and with groups of children, and research has pointed to procedures that enhance the generalization and maintenance of treatment effects. The few studies that have compared the effectiveness of behavioral and medical approaches to working with hyperactive children tend to show that behavioral methods may be equally effective in reducing hyperactivity but more effective in improving academic performance. In view of the possible side effects and negative psychological implications of using drugs for the treatment of hyperactive children, the drug-free behavioral alternative would seem to deserve serious consideration.

Mental Subnormality

Mental subnormality includes the conditions known as *mental retardation* and *mental deficiency* which, while often used as synonyms, have somewhat different connotations. To these we shall return later. All three of the labels—mental subnormality, mental retardation, and mental deficiency—make reference to inadequate mental processes; processes whose existence can only be inferred by observing a child's performance. We examined the logical and methodological problems that are encountered in drawing such inferences when we discussed the topic of learning disabilities in Chapter 12. Largely because of these problems, the realm of mental subnormality is fraught with disagreements and uncertainties about terminology and definition. When a child's observed performance falls short of some arbitrary standard, this inadequacy may have a host of reasons—only one of which might be a permanent defect in the child's mental processes.

The arbitrary standard with which a child's performance is compared is inevitably a reflection of the expectations society holds about what is appropriate performance for a child at that chronological age. If, in comparison with other children of the same age, a given girl's performance is deemed inadequate and if she approaches the tasks in a manner considered appropriate for children at a younger developmental level, she would be called *retarded* or *deficient*, implying that her development was somehow held back or impaired. On tests that have been developed in order to make the comparison between such a child's performance and that of her peers more uniform—that is, on tests of intelligence—she would achieve a significantly lower score than is the norm for her age, hence the term *mental subnormality*.

SOME MISCONCEPTIONS ABOUT TESTS OF INTELLIGENCE

Performance on an intelligence test is usually expressed in a numerical code, the intelligence quotient (IQ). Because this is a number it is easy to view it as a measure of an entity, forgetting that the number reflects no more than performance on a test and that intelligence is not an entity but a hypothetical construct. By observing a child's performance on an intelligence test a psychologist draws inferences about that child's intelligence, which is a convenient designation that subsumes such cognitive processes as learning, memory, problem solving, and abstract reasoning. It is a misconception to view intelligence as anything more than an inference about various covert (mental) processes on which certain observable behavior is presumed to be based.

Another misconception is that a low score on an intelligence test can explain a child's poor academic performance in school. When a child does not do well in school, people will wonder why this is the case. When on a test of intelligence that child then obtains a score that can be classified as in the subnormal range, it is a fallacy to say that the mental subnormality is the reason for the poor school performance. The test of intelligence is simply another measure of performance, one that depends heavily on prior academic achievement. A low test score, therefore, does no more than document the fact that the child's performance is subnormal not only in school but also on the test. Such a correlated documentation does not explain anything. The reason for the poor performance remains to be discovered.

Yet another misconception is that mental subnormality is some invariable entity, like a disease, instead of a performance that has been judged to be deficient. The label of subnormality, even when based on a test, reflects a social judgment that is made in the context of the child's social environment and the demands that environment places upon children of that age. Tests of intelligence are designed to measure the kind of skills our society deems important for survival in our time in history. We happen to consider it very important that a child do well in the academic subject matter that is taught in the schools. Hence, our tests of intelligence are designed to predict how well a child will do in school. That was the purpose for the development of the very first tests of intelligence and it has not changed. We are not interested in how well a child might be able to bait a fishhook, track an animal, milk a cow, negotiate a city's subway system, or get along with other children. Those skills somehow do not enter our conception of intelligence, but children who do very poorly on tests of intelligence often do very well in these other areas. Not only are our tests constructed to assess a rather narrow set of skills, they are also changed from time to time, their standardization changes, and, as we shall see, the very definition of retardation undergoes changes.

THE DEFINITION

The arbitrary and relative norms that define psychological disorders (see Chapter 1) are nowhere as apparent as in the definition of mental subnormality. The point in the range of IQ scores below which an individual is labeled as defective or retarded depends on the standard deviation of the test used to measure his or her performance. On such tests, such as the Stanford-Binet (Terman & Merrill, 1973) that point is 68; on others, such as the Revised Wechsler Intelligence Scale for Children, the WISC-R (Wechsler, 1974), it is 70. Whether a child with a given intelligence test score is eligible for special educational considerations or admission to a specialized institution depends on the school system, state, or country in which he or she happens to live. In fact, the definition may even depend on the year in which the decisive testing took place. When a test is revised, as was the case with the widely used Wechsler instrument, questions are eliminated and others added, tasks are modified, and standardization is based on a new normative sample. Thus, a child tested with the old WISC (Wechsler, 1949) in 1973 might have a different IQ score if the test had been given with the revised version in 1975. Lastly, as we indicated above, the very definition of mental retardation that is widely used in the United States changed in the short span of 14 years.

The American Association on Mental Deficiency (AAMD) is a prestigious and important organization that has long been in the forefront of seeking improved conditions and more enlightened legislation for retarded persons. In 1959 this group adopted a manual on terminology and classification (Heber, 1959; revised 1961) which defined a mentally retarded person as one who manifests "subaverage intellectual functioning . . . associated with impairment in adaptive behavior" (Heber, 1961, p. 3). In elaboration, the manual stated that "subaverage" meant an intelligence test score that is one standard deviation below the mean; that would be a WISC IQ-score below 85. In the 1973 revision of the AAMD manual (Grossman, 1973) this standard was changed so that the new definition reads: "Mental retardation refers to significantly subaverage general intellectual functioning existing concurrently with deficits in adaptive behavior, and manifested during the developmental period" (p. 11). The addition of the word "significantly" makes a crucial difference; for now the elaboration states that what is meant by "significantly subaverage" is a test performance that is more than two standard deviations below the mean. On the WISC-R, this would be represented by an IQ score below 70. As Hobbs (1975) has pointed out, for 14 years children with an IQ below 85 were regarded by AAMD standards as officially retarded. Now they no longer bear that label. Why the shift?

To find the answer to this question we must look at the political climate in the United States, for it was that which proved to be a major influence in the arbitrary change of definition.

When Heber's manual on terminology and classification appeared in 1959 and particularly when it was revised in 1961, there was much hope that the federal government would begin massive and well-financed social and educational programs in the area of mental retardation. Those interested in the problems of the mentally retarded therefore saw merit in having as many persons as possible become eligible for these programs. They therefore promulgated a definition which included among those expected to benefit anyone with an IQ below 85 and associated impairment in adaptive behavior. By the time Grossman's revised manual appeared in 1973, it had become apparent that the hopes of the early 1960s had not materialized. Instead of making more people eligible for government-supported help, the wider definition of mental retardation had done little more than attach a stigmatizing label to a larger number of individuals. The shift in definition, as Hobbs (1975) points out, removed the label from a number of children but, at the same time, created disruptions in public school programs. These programs were now expected to shift gears because a child who, in 1972 was to be treated as "mentally retarded" became, in 1973 a child in the borderline range of intelligence.

The current definition of mental retardation (Grossman, 1973), as did the earlier one, makes reference to the quality of a person's adaptive behavior. In 1959, "impairment in adaptive behavior" had to be associated with "subaverage intellectual functioning." In 1973, "significantly subaverage intellectual functioning" must exist "concurrently with deficits in adaptive behavior." The difference between "impairment" and "deficit" is, of course, another reflection of the attempt to limit the definition to the more serious cases of retardation.

It is an important aspect of the definition that a low IQ score by itself is never sufficient for making the decision that a person is mentally retarded. If the person functions adequately in whatever personal and social role is expected of people of that age and in that cultural group, the term mental retardation would be misapplied. The elaboration on the definition that is included in the Grossman (1973) manual makes this quite clear. This elaboration also stresses that, inasmuch as role expectations change as an individual's age increases, the individual's adaptive behavior may be deficient at one stage of development (in school, for example) but adequate at another (as in a job situation).

Another look at the definition reveals that the subaverage intelligence and deficient adaptive behavior must be "manifested during the developmental period" (Grossman, 1973, p. 11). The elaboration places the upper age limit of this definition at 18 years. This means that if someone did not manifest low intelligence and deficient adaptation sometime during these 18 years, a loss of intellectual functions at a later stage in life should not be viewed as mental retardation.

Lastly, the AAMD definition says nothing about the cause of the problem nor about the prognosis for a mentally retarded person. In that respect it is a very behavioral definition. It simply describes current behavior and recognizes that the future level of a person's functioning depends a great deal on the treatment and training opportunities that will be available to the person, on such personal factors as motivation, and on general environmental conditions.

The insistence of those who wrote the AAMD definition that inadequate adaptive behavior must go along with a low intelligence test score before a label of mental retardation is justified, takes cognizance of the fact that many things besides low cognitive ability can enter into producing a low score on an intelligence test. When a child fails to give correct answers to questions on an intelligence test and thus earns a low score, it may be for one of several reasons or because of a combination of reasons. The most obvious of these reasons is that the child has never been taught the expected responses. On the Revised Wechsler Intelligence Scale for Children (WISC-R) (Wechsler, 1974), for example, there appear such questions as "From what animal do we get bacon?" and "In what way are telephone and radio alike?" By about age 11, the average child is supposed to have no difficulty in answering these questions correctly. But what of the child in whose home bacon is never served or where there is no telephone? Furthermore, children who attended school only at irregular intervals or whose school is so inadequate that they have never had an opportunity to learn the answers to "Who discovered America?" or "How many things make a dozen?" will in all likelihood be unable to give the correct response. As a result, their test scores, when converted into IQ points, may well fall into the subnormal range. Provided they function adaptively in the nonacademic areas of their lives, if they are able to cope with the environment, the AAMD definition would not include them among the mentally retarded.

To have learned the skill or information one needs in order to be able to give the correct answer to intelligence test questions is not, however, the only condition necessary for doing well on such a test. The child must also attend to the questions being asked, hear them correctly, and understand what they mean. He or she must recall the information requested and be able to make the appropriate response. On top of it all, the child must be motivated and interested in giving the right responses. A hostile or negativistic attitude toward the test or the examiner, fear of possible failure, or anxiety about the consequences of giving the right response would all lead to the same outcome as would not knowing the correct answer. Unless the person who is administering the test and interpreting its result has been trained to be alert to these factors, the test score may be of questionable validity in the sense of not reflecting what it is supposed to reflect; namely, intelligence.

Retarded or Defective?

While the definition we have just examined speaks of *mental retardation*, the term *mental deficiency* is also widely used in referring to mental subnormality. Is there a difference? Although the two terms are often used interchangeably, it may be well to examine the different implications of the two expressions.

Some children, as we have just said, score in the subnormal range because they have never had the opportunity to learn the kind of things they are asked to do or say on an intelligence test. Others may fall in the subnormal range because, although they were exposed to opportunities for acquiring the expected skills around the same time as other children their age, they failed to learn them. Some children may learn these skills from months to years later than their age group; others may never master them. Those who acquire appropriate skills more slowly than their peers, whose development is retarded, might appropriately be called *mentally retarded*, while those who are incapable of acquiring these skills altogether might be categorized as *mentally defective*. This distinction was advanced by Masland, Sarason, and Gladwin (1958), but as with all labels, these terms are inadequate and beg a great many questions. What, for example, happens to the label when a child whose mental development had been retarded slows down more and then fails to make further progress? Does such a child cease being mentally retarded and become mentally defective?

The term "defective" implies that there is some defect in the children, that they are of limited potential or capacity, and that—no matter what one might try—they would be unable to acquire additional skills. The term "retardation" merely states an observation: The child is less advanced than his peers. The term "defective," on the other hand, carries implications of a limited potential. Potential, representing a projection into the future, can never be known; it can only be guessed and, given currently available tools, this guess is most hazardous. At best, one can make the statement that at the time and in the manner a given skill was taught, such a child did not learn it. The stress must be on present behavior and not on uncertain estimates of potential and future functioning. With that, the focus is placed not on the child's learning capacity but on the manner in which teaching is attempted.

Whether it be tying a shoelace, acquiring language, learning to read, write, or do arithmetic, the culture and its educational system generally make the assumption that all children can and should master these skills under the same conditions and in the same manner. Elementary school, in particular, operates on the unwarranted assumption that one mode of teaching is optimal for all of the children in a given class. The boy who fails to learn reading, writing, spelling, or arithmetic is assumed to have "something wrong with him." The problem is seen as *his* learning problem, not as his school's teaching problem. He is then usually given an intelligence test (which relies heavily on questions involving things one learns in school), and when he attains a low score, this "explains" why he has failed to learn: he is mentally retarded. The fact that this description is not an explanation is ignored, and the possibility that this particular child might have been able to learn if a different mode of teaching had been used is rarely, if ever, considered.

CLASSIFICATION

Since mental subnormality is a matter of degree, intelligence test scores and their standard deviation have been used to establish subclassifications. According to the American Association on Mental Deficiency (Grossman, 1973), scores from tests like the Wechsler Intelligence Scale for Children that have a standard deviation of 15 points divide the range of mental subnormality as follows:

Level of retardation	IQ score range
Mild	55–69
Moderate	40–54
Severe	25–39
Profound	under 25

Such a classification is, of course, no more than an assignment of verbal labels to ranges of test scores, ranges based on the statistical concept of one standard deviation. That is, scores between two and three standard deviations below the mean are called *mild*, between three and four *moderate*, and so forth. It is important to stress the arbitrary nature of these classifications. It is meaningless to call a child with an IQ score of 54 "moderately retarded," while with a score of 55 the same child would be called "mildly retarded." This is particularly apparent when one recalls that the standard error of measurement of most intelligence tests is around five points.

The issue is further complicated by the fact that the test scores and labels traditionally used in the area of mental subnormality are not merely statements describing observed facts but statements from which people draw inferences about the child's future behavior, about "potential." The inferential implications of IQ scores have found expression in the terms *trainable*, applied to children with scores between roughly 25 and 49, and *educable*, describing those with scores above 50 but below 76. The educable are expected to be able to do academic work at least to the third-grade level, occasionally to the sixth-grade level, by the time they are 16 years old. The trainable, on the other hand, are not expected to master academic skills. The goal of training for the latter is to teach them self-care and to cope with simple routines under supervision. Used in this manner, the test scores carry clear (and unfortunate) implications of potential.

When a young girl's measured intelligence quotient is 45, this not only means that she now functions at the level of moderate retardation, it also suggests to many psychologists and educators that she will be unable to benefit from academic instruction since her "potential" is viewed as below the expectations of elementary school (as currently constituted). *A test score reflects present performance; it is not a measure of future potential.* Yet once a child's present performance is measured and recorded, the inference about potential often becomes a self-fulfilling prophecy. Because of the low score the child will be excluded from elementary school. What training he or she receives will be gauged to the presumed capacity, and the end result will be that such children do not learn such academic subject matter as reading and arithmetic—just as their test scores had "predicted."

Estimates of potential for children in the subnormal range of intelligence are extremely hazardous; unless they are continuously questioned, they are likely to lead to standardized training procedures that are deemed successful when they permit a child to function at the level of the predicted potential. If one takes a low IQ score for what it is—a measure of present performance—and makes no assumptions about limited future potential, one is led to a continuous search for different training and teaching methods for all children, expecting that one can help them raise their present level of performance. In settings where preconceptions about limited potential are discarded, as in the program described by Birnbrauer, Wolf, Kidder, and Tague (1965), retarded children can achieve at levels previously thought "impossible." It is a salutary development that terms like trainable and educable as well as some of the more rigid uses of other classifications in the field of mental subnormality are beginning to be discarded.

ETIOLOGY

A great deal has been written about the cause or etiology of *mental subnormality* because it is hoped that knowing how this condition develops will permit its prevention. The trouble with that hope is that mental subnormality is not a *condition*, analogous to a disease; it is a term that describes observable behavior (i.e., behavior measured by an intelligence test). A low score on an intelligence test, in and of itself, says nothing about etiology. An intelligence test score is no more than a statement of how a child's test performance compares to the performance of other children of that age. Relative to those other children, a child's score may be higher or lower; why it is higher or lower is not revealed by the quantitative statement. If it is significantly lower, the child may be said to be mentally subnormal because the score is below the *normal*, but to say that the score is low *because* the child is mentally subnormal would be a fallacious circularity.

In order to discuss the possible meaning that might be attributed to a low intelligence test score, it is well to turn to a brief examination of how these scores are distributed. Measured intelligence is a complex function of the interaction of many genetic and environmental factors. *If* these factors were subject only to random variation, their interaction would generate the well-known bell-shaped curve of normal distribution. But such random variation does not take place. The variation of heredity is constrained by social obstacles to random breeding, and the variation of environment is constrained by the fact that social obstacles prevent random assignment of any individual to any environment. What is more, these social constraints are particularly potent in matters directly related to intelligence. The girl of high intelligence is likely to attend college where the choice of potential mates is biased in favor of intelligent boys, and the child of such a union is likely to be raised in an intellectually stimulating environment. Since the converse is likely to be true in the case of the girl of low intelligence, the actual picture is more that of selective breeding with selective assignment of environment than of random variation of factors.

The *normal* distribution of intelligence along a single, continuous, bisymmetrical curve is a theoretical ideal that probably bears little relationship to reality. It should be noted that it is impossible to ascertain the actual shape of this distribution given only existing tests of intelligence with which to conduct such an investigation. All standardized tests of intelligence are constructed on the assumption of normal distribution of "intelligence." Questions are carefully selected so that only a predetermined percentage of children at each age level will pass the items, and this percentage reflects the test constructors' theoretical assumption about the normal distribution of the construct they are trying to measure. Once test standardization is completed, the scores will generally distribute along the bell-shaped curve simply because that was the goal of the standardization. A test that failed to give a normal distribution of scores would be rejected as invalid; the validity of the underlying assumption is rarely questioned.

Leaving aside the question of the validity of the assumption of a normal distribution of intelligence, whatever the actual shape of the distribution that may be generated by the polygenic model and the nonrandom influences mentioned earlier, there are children whose intellectual development is disrupted by inborn or acquired physical damage or defect. The low intelligence of these children contributes disproportionately to the low end of the distribution of intelligence scores, further distorting its bisymmetry. A number of writers (Dingman & Tarjan, 1960; Penrose, 1963; Zigler, 1967) have pointed out that the low end of the distribution has many more cases than the theoretical normal curve would predict, and some have spoken of a "pathological bulge" in the curve representing the scores of retardates with physical defects whose extremely low scores, largely in the IQ range below 50, occur with disproportionate frequency.

Familial Retardation

Zigler (1967) advocates a two-group approach to mental retardation, stating that the polygenic model of intelligence generates a distribution from IQ 50 to 150. In such a distribution some individuals will be expected to have scores considerably above the mean, while the scores of others should be considerably below the mean. Those at this lower end of the range are viewed as individuals whose

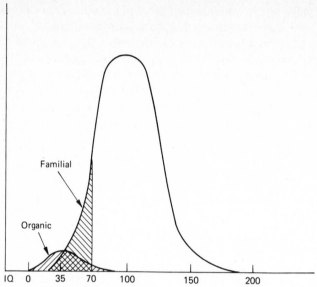

Figure 7 Distribution of intelligence test scores according to Zigler's two-group approach. (*After Zigler, 1967.*)

low intelligence is an expression of the same factors that contribute to *normal* intelligence. In Zigler's approach these form one group, the *familial retardates*, who represent about 75 percent of all retardates. Their intelligence scores fall roughly between 50 and 70, and they do not have demonstrable physical defects. The other group, whose scores range from 0 to 70–with a mean of approximately 35—do have physical, "organic" defects that severely impair their intellectual functioning. They are "abnormal" in the usual sense of that word in that their scores are not part of the hypothetical "normal distribution." Zigler's view is illustrated in Figure 7.

According to that view, the familial retardates are *normal* in the statistical sense; their scores are an integral part of the dispersion of intelligence test scores that one would predict from the manifestations of the gene pool in a population.

> Within such a framework it is possible to refer to the familial retardate as less intelligent than other normal manifestations of the genetic pool, but he is just as integral a part of the normal distribution as are the 3 percent of the population whom we view as superior, or the more numerous group of individuals whom we consider to be average [Zigler, 1967, p. 293].

The children whom Zigler called familial retardates come from families where many relatives also score in the subnormal range of intelligence. Such children's backgrounds are usually impoverished, they have had poor housing, inadequate medical care, poor nutrition, and little intellectual stimulation. The current AAMD definition (Grossman, 1973) speaks of the retardation manifested by these children as due to *psychosocial disadvantage*. While the environmental factors associated with poverty may alone be responsible for the development of mental retardation, the contribution of hereditary factors cannot be ruled out on the basis of existing knowledge. The failure of the AAMD definition of retardation due to psychosocial disadvantage to take this possibility into account would seem to be based more on political than on scientific considerations. What we call intelligence is undoubtedly the result of an interaction between genetic and environmental factors. What we do not know (and what is the basis of much heated argument) is how much each of these variables contributes to the end result.

Organic Retardation

While the familial retardates come largely from the retarded segment of the population, and usually tend to score in the mild to borderline range of subnormality, children with physical defects come from families at all levels of socioeconomic status and measured intelligence. Their defects are presumably caused by an accidental factor and not, as in the case of the familial retardates, by a combination of several adverse conditions. Organic retardation may be due to a single recessive gene, as in the case of *phenylketonuria*. This disorder, usually referred to as PKU, has received rather wide publicity although it occurs only about once in 13,000 to 20,000 live births (Robinson & Robinson, 1976). The interest in this condition stems from the fact that it represents one of the few types of severe mental retardation whose genetic-metabolic cause is well enough understood that preventive measures have become possible. Since these children have metabolisms that are incapable of transforming the protein substance phenylalanine, resulting in the release of phenylpyruvic acid into the body, ultimate injury to the brain and the resulting mental retardation can be prevented by placing the children on a diet that is low in phenylalanine.

Even in cases where the etiology is clearly identified and reducible to a single recessive gene, as in PKU, it would be a mistake to assume that the children who are afflicted with that condition form a homogenous group of retardates. The degree of retardation varies with PKU children; and, as Steisel, Friedman, and Wood (1967) have shown, PKU children are a heterogeneous group in terms of their social interaction; thus, behaviorally, phenylketonuria is not a unitary disorder.

Another type of mental retardation, *Down's Syndrome*, has been found to be related to a chromosomal aberration. This takes the form of a third chromosome 21, hence it is also known as *Trisomy 21*. In almost all cases, this third chromosome is due to an error in cell division that took place when the egg or sperm was being formed. For reasons not fully understood, this condition occurs more frequently in older than in younger parents. Because pregnancies among parents over 35 are beginning to decline and since prenatal detection by amniocentesis has become available, the incidence of this form of mental deficiency is decreasing (Richards, 1967).

In addition to the forms of mental retardation caused by genetic factors, only two of which we have mentioned above, other forms are the result of damage to the central nervous system caused by environmental factors. Here are included children whose mothers were exposed to radiation or who had rubella while pregnant, and cases of Rh incompatibility, congenital syphilis, encephalitis, lead poisoning, and accidental injury to the brain. We shall not attempt to present a complete list nor an exhaustive discussion of the various types of mental retardation. Instead, the reader is referred to such excellent books on the subject as that by Robinson and Robinson (1976).

Differentiating between familial and organic retardation and establishing other subcategories is important from the standpoint of our ultimate understanding of mental subnormality and the possibility of preventing these problems, which can only come through such understanding. For the individual child whose adaptive behavior and intelligence test scores are subnormal, it matters little whether we know that this is due to psychosocial disadvantage or brain injury. Since the familial and the organic groups overlap in the IQ range from 50 to 70 (see Figure 7), an individual in that range may come from either group, and attempts to differentiate among them on the basis of tests are probably futile. Large-scale studies (Birch, Belmont, Belmont, & Taft, 1976; Clausen, 1966) have been devoted to such attempts to little avail. As Clausen (1966) concluded after a 7-year-long project: "The differentiation of the mentally retarded into subgroups . . . has not been particularly successful" (p. 172). Extensive batteries of available tests thus do not permit a differentiation between retarded children in terms of presence or absence of organic impairment. But even if such differentiation were readily accomplished, the knowledge thus gained would hardly aid in making plans for helping an individual child. It may thus be well to turn our attention to other, more pragmatic questions.

THE REINFORCEMENT HISTORY OF THE MENTALLY SUBNORMAL

Mentally subnormal children, by definition, function at a less than adequate level of adaptation. This fact will color all of their interactions with the environment, and it will therefore influence their general pattern of behavior. This impact of impairment in adaptive behavior on the psychological development of the child would be the same regardless of whether the impairment is due to "organic" or "familial" reasons. If the experiences of these children are similar, no matter what the etiology of their retardation, they would acquire a response repertoire that would make them, as a group, more similar than different by the time they are tested at age 8 as was the case in Clausen's (1966) study.

The intelligence test performance of a mentally retarded child is usually similar to the performance of a child at a lower chronological age. For example, a retarded child who is 10 years old may be performing like a normal child who is 6 years old. This has led to the concept of *mental age*, and the retarded child in this example would be said to have a mental age of 6. When one seeks to study how retarded children differ from normal children in matters other than intelligence test scores, it is customary to compare retarded and normal children who have the same mental age. This is known as matching for mental age.

It is a well-established finding (Zigler, 1966*a*) that when retarded and normal children are matched for mental age, the retarded perform less well or differently than the normal on many learning and problem-solving tests. Since matching for mental age presumably equates intellectual functioning, the remaining differences in performance are thought to be due to other than intellectual factors. Those who hold what Zigler (1960) has called the "difference orientation" maintain that the familial retardate represents an inherently different type of organism who suffers from a basic defect in either physiological or cognitive structure. This defect is thought to be responsible for the child's impaired performance. The support for this position has been evaluated by Zigler (1966*a*), who is led to reject this view in favor of a motivational or developmental orientation. When, for purposes of research, one matches a 10-year-old child who functions at the mental age of 7 (IQ 70) with a 7-year-old child who also functions at the mental age of 7 (IQ 100), one may have matched test performance expressed in a mental-age score; but one has not matched reinforcement history, for, if nothing else, the retardate has lived 3 years longer. Moreover, these 3 years have been filled with failure experiences, as have all the other years of his or her life.

With this reasoning in mind, it is perhaps significant that the key variables in Clausen's (1966) test battery that differentiated between the retarded and the normal (though not between brain-injured and familial) were pure tone threshold and such simple motor tasks as lower-arm movement and reaction time. Approaching these findings from the standpoint of a difference theorist, Clausen sees these tests as reflecting the retardates' impairment of such general factors as arousal, vigilance, effort, and response initiation and—without any physiological evidence whatever—attributes this impairment to the ascending reticular activating system in the brainstem. A more parsimonious explanation would seem to be that the retarded children have learned not to trust their judgment or to initiate responses on their own initiative: attributes that are essential for adequate performance on pure tone discrimination, reaction time, and simple motor-task experiments. Zigler (1966*a*) views such performance deficit to reflect the retardate's learned "outer-directed response style."

According to Zigler (1966*a*), this outer-directed style of problem solving is acquired in the often repeated situation where retarded children are selectively reinforced for careful attentiveness to external cues. When, on the other hand, they base a response on their own meager cognitive resources, they almost invariably encounter negative consequences. They thus come to acquire an over-reliance on external cues—an outer-directedness, as Zigler would have it. As this outer-directedness generalizes, the children would come to attend in rapid succession to a wide variety of stimuli. Their behavior would then be characterized as "distractible," a characteristic that has often been attributed to the retarded child and has, in fact, been viewed by some as an inherent characteristic—basic deficit—of the retarded and as an indication of brain injury.

While this learned behavioral characteristic tends to interfere with the problem-solving ability of retarded children because they attend to misleading and distracting cues (Achenbach & Zigler, 1968), Turnure and Zigler (1964) have shown that retarded children's problem solving can be enhanced when extraneous stimuli are task-relevant or if, as Zeaman and House (1963) have pointed out, these stimuli increase attention by introducing novelty.

Investigators like Zeaman and House (1963), who have carried on extensive studies of various aspects of discrimination learning using retarded subjects, frequently point to deficits in attention-directing ability as a crucial factor in the poor performance of retarded children. When children of different mental ages are compared, those with lower mental age take considerably longer to attend to the relevant task dimensions. Once they attend to these dimensions, however, the children do not differ in their *rate* of learning the discrimination. Attending to the cues an experimenter considers relevant to his task would seem to be another learned form of behavior. An environment that does not provide sufficient opportunities for such learning for a child who learns more slowly than the normal may well provide the basis for developing an attention deficit. Again, it would seem to be unnecessary to postulate inherent, hence irreversible, defects in some inferred "attending mechanism." The presence of such an inherent defect in all retardates is particularly unlikely in view of the fact that investigators who study discrimination learning in institutions for the retarded rarely differentiate among their subjects in terms of familial and organic factors. When these different etiologic groups show a common deficit, it is far more parsimonious to look for the source of this deficit in common conditions of learning than in common structural impairment.

TEACHING THE MENTALLY SUBNORMAL

The research evidence mentioned so far supports the contention that the classification of the retarded in terms of presumed etiologies is neither feasible, using present-day psychological tools, nor necessary in terms of educational planning. As Birch et al. (1967) pointed out, the etiologic designation of brain damage does not lead to a clearly defined educational strategy, and so an assessment of the educational capacities and incapacities of a particular child is a more useful basis for a program of training than knowing whether he or she should be called *brain-damaged* or *familial*.

Not only does it seem irrelevant for the psychologist or educator to know the etiology of a child's maladaptive behavior but it also appears unnecessary to be too concerned with classification into intellectual categories, that is, by IQ test scores. Support for this statement can be found in the extensive literature that shows that the basic principles of learning operate at all levels of intelligence.

From the point of view of the applicability of learning principles, there are no inherent differences between the normal and the retarded, regardless of degree of retardation. Certainly, genetic and physiological conditions set limits on the speed of acquisition and on a child's ultimate response repertoire, but learning can take place and does take place according to the same principles whether the learner be profoundly or mildly retarded. Kingsley (1968), for example, demonstrated that on an associative-learning task a group of educable mentally retarded children performed in a qualitatively similar manner as other ability groups, while Morgan (1969) showed that there is no difference in responsiveness to stimulus complexity at different levels of intelligence. As Ullmann and Krasner (1969) have stated, not even the most severe defect rules out responses to the environment and alteration of behavior through training. From this point of view, it makes no sense to differentiate between the trainable and the educable—a pseudo-classification which, we must remind ourselves, is simply another arbitrary cutoff on the continuum of intelligence test scores that is no more valid than the discarded idiot, imbecile, moron trichotomy.

A demonstration of the applicability of principles of learning at even the most profound level of retardation can be found in the work of Bailey and Meyerson (1969), who worked with a 7-year-old boy. This child was blind, at least partially deaf, had no speech, was not toilet trained, and could neither feed himself nor walk. Virtually his entire waking hours were taken up with such stereotyped behaviors as slapping his face; hitting himself on the chin, ears, and side of the head; and banging his head, teeth, or a foot against the bars of his crib. Using vibration of the crib as a reinforcer, Bailey and Meyerson trained this boy to make a lever-pressing response. When he was working the lever, he would press it lightly with his hand or kick it with his foot and then lie motionless with an occasional giggle during the 6 seconds the vibrator was in operation. As soon as the vibration stopped, he would press the lever again. In this manner, he produced an average of 1,000 lever presses per day for a period of 3 weeks. When the vibration contingency was discontinued, the lever pressing showed a striking decrease. Clearly, this boy had learned something which, had the work with him continued beyond this demonstration, might well have been a first step toward enlarging his repertoire to include more complex and useful forms of behavior.

In working with the mentally retarded, as with any group who are identified by such a label, the aim is not to "treat retardation" but to teach individual children the behaviors they need in order to function more adaptively in their environment. For retarded children who are residents of special schools or institutions, the goal of intervention is often to teach them to follow simple commands, dress themselves, use eating utensils appropriately, use the toilet, and communicate with others. Some programs seek to work on several of these behaviors (Colwell, Richards, McCarver, & Ellis, 1973; Gray & Kasteler, 1969), while other reports focus on only one of them (Baer & Guess, 1971; Repp & Deitz, 1974; Stokes, Baer, & Jackson, 1974).

Toilet training was one of the first problems for which training methods based on reinforcement principles were applied. Giles and Wolf (1966), for example, used these principles to teach appropriate use of the toilet to five institutionalized, severely retarded boys. This study points to the importance of finding suitable reinforcers for each child. While candy is an effective reinforcer for many children, Giles and Wolf found one boy who refused candy but accepted baby food; for others, a ride in a wheelchair, taking a shower, or being permitted to return to bed were rewarding consequences. Giles and Wolf also point out that training can be improved if, in addition to the positive reinforcement of desired responses, inappropriate behavior is followed by aversive stimuli. Where positive reinforcement alone produced no results, they introduced physical restraint, the removal of which—contingent on appropriate toileting behavior—came to serve as a negative reinforcer. With this combination of techniques, all subjects learned consistently to eliminate in the toilet.

Another early example of such an approach was reported by Hundziak, Maurer, and Watson (1965), who made candy, paired with light and tone stimuli, contingent on elimination in the toilet. Eight mentally retarded boys between the ages of 7 and 14 with IQs ranging from 8 to 33, underwent such training. They showed a significantly greater increase in appropriate toilet use than a comparison group of boys who were trained by conventional techniques. The training had been conducted in a special cottage, but once the appropriate responses had been established they generalized to the boys' original living unit.

In these early studies training was usually based on having the child sit on the toilet for extended periods of time so that eventual urination or defacation could be followed by positive reinforcement. More recently, electronic devices, such as moisture sensitive pants and toilet chairs that emit a signal when they are activated, have been used to obviate this cumbersome procedure (Azrin & Foxx, 1971). With such devices, a child's failure to use the toilet can be followed by consequences such as overcorrection, while appropriate toileting or periods of remaining dry can be rewarded.

In addition to the application of reinforcement principles, procedures such as modeling, prompting, and demonstrations have been shown to be effective means of teaching retarded children self-help skills and other adaptive behavior. One aspect of a program described by O'Brien, Bugle, and Azrin (1972), for example, involved manually guiding the child's hand for self-feeding. Ross and Ross (1973), who worked with mildly retarded, noninstitutionalized children, describe the use of modeling procedures in establishing adaptive studying and working responses.

With retarded children who attend special education classes, methods of intervention often take the form of programs administered in classroom settings. Here, token systems (Birnbrauer, Bijou, Wolf, & Kidder, 1965), time-out procedures (Lahey, McNees, & McNees, 1973), and social reinforcement (Ross & Ross, 1973) have found successful application in decreasing disruptive behavior (Baer, Ascione, & Casto, 1977), improving academic performance (Dalton, Rubino, & Hislop, 1973), and enhancing listening skills (Ross & Ross, 1972).

The reason for referring to these studies is not merely to illustrate the constructive results that follow when psychological principles are applied to the training and education of the mentally retarded but also in order to stress that these principles apply regardless of the degree of a child's retardation. Establishing this degree in terms of test scores would thus seem a very secondary consideration, more useful for administrative-forensic than for therapeutic-educational purposes.

Reinforcer Effectiveness

Most of the studies and demonstrations mentioned above are based on the principle of reinforcement, which states that the consequences of a response are powerful factors in determining whether this response will be weakened or strengthened. If one seeks to modify the behavior of retarded children—or of any children, for that matter—one must first assess what consequences can serve as reinforcers.

We are indebted to Zigler (1966a) for pointing to the differential effectiveness of reinforcers when retarded children, and particularly institutionalized retarded children, are compared with normal children; for this difference can account for many of the performance deficits of retarded children. In fact, the differences appear to be a function of institutionalization itself. In a series of studies Zigler (1966b) and his coworkers have shown that the effectiveness of social reinforcement is a function of the retardate's preinstitutional background. While the social deprivation that characterizes the institutional setting tends to make social reinforcement more potent for all institutional children, this effect is enhanced for those who come from relatively nondeprived homes as compared to those from more socially deprived backgrounds (Zigler & Balla, 1972). In the long run, institutionalization is more socially depriving for children from good than for children from poor backgrounds, and follow-up studies (Zigler & Williams, 1963; Zigler, Butterfield, & Capobianco, 1970) demonstrate a decrease in social-reinforcer effectiveness that is greater for those with deprived preinstitutional histories. It thus appears that children from better backgrounds continue to be motivated by attention, praise, affection, and other social reinforcers, while for those from poorer backgrounds, these consequences gradually cease to be effective in maintaining behavior. When social reinforcers are ineffective, more tangible reinforcers, such as trinkets or food, can be used to reward behavior. Thus, Zigler and deLabry (1962), who found performance differences between normal and retarded children on a concept-switching task, demonstrated that when the consequences of success were changed to tangible reinforcers, these differences disappeared. When an effective reinforcer is used, deficient performance can often be overcome—bearing out the contention that it is at least as important to assess what constitutes a reinforcing consequence for a given child as to count how many correct responses he can give on an intelligence test or to see what kind of a pattern his EEG tracings make on a piece of paper.

RECAPITULATION

Mental subnormality is a performance deficit that is associated with impairment in adaptive behavior. It is neither a disease entity nor necessarily a permanent, immutable state. There are a great many reasons why a given individual may be functioning at a subnormal level on tasks such as intelligence tests. Some children may be culturally disadvantaged, some developmentally retarded, and some limited in their potential. From the point of view of grouping mentally subnormal children it is helpful to speak of *familial retardation* and *organic retardation*, but in any specific case it is often difficult to determine the origin of the problem. Regardless of origin, all mentally subnormal children share a type of experience that has to do with their inability to meet the expectations of their social environment. These common experiences may be more important determinants of the behavior of these children than is the original cause of their subnormality. Approaches to the training of subnormal children that ignore the question of etiology and focus instead on the behavioral assets and deficits of the child and address these in a systematic fashion have been shown to be very effective.

Psychophysiological Disorders

Every behavior involves the body in some fashion, whether it be the brain when a girl solves a puzzle or the legs when a boy runs across a room. From that standpoint it is possible to view all of psychology as an aspect of physiology and to speak of all behavior disorders as psychophysiological disorders. Traditionally, however, only a limited set of problems have been classified as psychophysiological disorders. They are primarily those instances where the problem entails a disordered bodily function such as breathing, eating, or eliminating. For some time these problems were called *psychosomatic disorders* and viewed as phenomena where psychological (emotional) factors had caused a bodily (somatic) difficulty. This formulation implies that mind and body are distinctly separate entities that influence one another in a cause and effect relationship. The body, however, with all of its functions is one unit, although we refer to some of its functions as psychological and to others as physiological. It is in keeping with the contemporary view of life to discard the anachronistic mind-body dualism which dates from the seventeenth century when René Descartes postulated it in order to prove the existence of the human soul. The term *psychophysiological*, as used here, is meant to convey no more than that we are dealing with interacting psychological and physiological aspects of life. No causal implication should be read into the term.

AN INTERACTIONAL FORMULATION

In a scholarly review of psychophysiological disorders of children, Lipton, Stein-schneider, and Richmond (1966) point to the complex interaction of individually differentiated constitutional predispositions and environmental situations. It has also been demonstrated (Richmond & Lustman, 1955) that there are marked individual differences in autonomic functions within the first days of life. Neonates differ in changes of skin temperature and heart rate in response to a variety of stimuli, and these differences follow a normal distribution with hyperreactors at one extreme and hyporeactors at the other. When such constitutional deviations from the norm interact with a given combination of environmental events, among which maternal behavior no doubt plays a major role, it is likely that a psychophysiological disorder can develop. On the other hand, a child with atypical autonomic reactions who encounters a different set of environmental events might well go through life without developing such a disorder.

This interactional formulation attributes the cause of psychophysiological disorders neither to purely biological nor to purely environmental factors. The complex development of such a disorder is next to impossible to analyze into its component interacting factors when an individual child with a psychophysiological problem is studied after having lived with this disorder for a number of years. Like any child with a persistent health problem that began in early childhood, the problem will have complicated the child's relationship to his or her parents and particularly to the mother whose caretaking efforts will have been affected. Like children with chronic diseases, the child may well have developed atypical dependency on the mother, but theories that view this dependency as the cause rather than the effect of the disorder are not well founded.

Psychological aspects of primarily physical disorders and the response of such disorders to psychologically based methods of intervention have been demonstrated in such diverse problems as organically based epilepsy (Balaschak, 1976; Zlutnick, Mayville, & Moffat, 1975), the spasmotic behaviors of Giles de la Tourette's syndrome (Hutzell, Platzek, & Logue, 1974), chronic hair pulling (Evans, 1976), asthma, obesity, and enuresis. Because of their greater frequency, the last three of these disorders have received a more thorough exploration than the former by psychologists, and we shall focus on them for detailed discussion.

ASTHMA

The physical symptoms of asthma are difficulty in inspiring and, particularly, expiring air. This is accompanied by sensations of chest tightening and a characteristic wheezing during the expiratory phase of breathing. These symptoms are observed in a variety of conditions, including so-called asthmatic bronchitis and some allergies, not all of which are appropriately classified as asthma (Lipton et al., 1966). It has been proposed (Turnbull, 1962) that asthma is a learned response, but while the onset of many asthmatic attacks appear related to social situations, it remains to be demonstrated that differential reinforcement can establish asthma in a child who does not have a constitutional predisposition.

Because many clinical observations have pointed to the parent-child relationship as an important factor in precipitating asthmatic attacks, Purcell, Brady, Chai, Muser, Molk, Gordon, and Means (1969) conducted a crucial study designed to assess the effect of experimentally separating the child from his family. In the past, such separations usually involved moving the child from his home. However this separation confounds the experiment because the child is also removed from potential allergic agents in the home, such as dust, pollens, or animal fur, which leaves unanswered the question whether asthmatic attacks are due to psychosocial or allergic factors, or both. In addition to separating these two factors, the Purcell study also throws light on the question whether asthmatic attacks are associated with impending or threatened separation from the mother (since some have speculated that the "wheeze" is a distorted cry for the mother). The study also supports the contention that asthmatic children do not form one homogenous group but that there are subgroups among these children for whom a variety of stimuli serve as a trigger for asthmatic attacks.

The subjects in the Purcell study were twenty-five asthmatic children with a mean age of 8 years, 4 months. On the basis of detailed interviews, the group was divided into two parts. The first included thirteen children whose asthmatic attacks were usually preceded by emotional arousal, such as anger, anxiety, excitement, or sadness. The other twelve had a history of asthmatic attacks that did not appear to be precipitated by emotional arousal. On the basis of earlier work (Purcell, 1963), the investigators predicted that separation from the family would result in improvement for the asthmatic children with emotional precipitants, while the others would show no change.

Two of the measures used to assess change—expiratory peak flow rate (gauging the speed with which the child is able to expel air) and scaled degree of wheezing—were taken during daily laboratory visits; the other two—daily medications and daily history of asthma—were based on reports from the adult caretaker. The investigators took the base-rate measures while the child was at home with his family and during a period when impending separation was explicitly discussed. The family then moved out of the home, and the child stayed there with a carefully selected substitute mother. The separation lasted 2 weeks, after which the family returned. The measures were collected during the entire time the family was absent, upon reunion, and into the postreunion period. Figure 8 shows the data for the expiratory peak flow rate for the thirteen children with emotional precipitants.

Contrary to the speculation that asthma is related to fear of separation from the mother, there was no increase on any of the measures during the preseparation period. Furthermore, and in confirmation of the investigators' predictions, the experimental separation resulted in improvement on all four measures for the thirteen children whose asthma appeared emotion related. Only one measure (daily asthma) reflected improvement for the other twelve children, suggesting

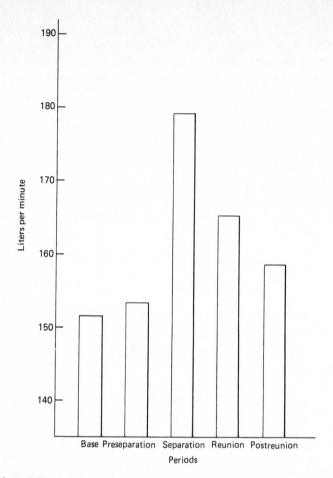

Figure 8 Mean daily expiratory peak flow rate for thirteen asthmatic children with emotional precipitants. (*After Purcell et al., 1969*, copyright 1969 by the American Psychosomatic Society and reproduced by permission.)

that even for these, psychosocial factors played some role in precipitating attacks. Using a rather stringent criterion of improvement for each individual child (as opposed to improvement on group-based measures), Purcell reports that during the period of separation seven of the thirteen emotion-related cases improved, while only three of the twelve for whom no improvement had been predicted showed a positive change. One of the most interesting aspects of this carefully conducted study is that following reunion with their families, all measures for all children returned to the base-rate, preseparation level. This strongly suggests that asthmatic attacks are under the control of stimuli associated with family members, but these results cannot be used to support an argument that psychosocial factors alone were originally responsible for the child's asthma.

A speculation based on the interaction hypothesis would lead one to assume that some children have a constitutional tendency for an atypical respiratory pattern and that this comes to interact with environmental conditions following the operant paradigm. The principles of operant learning require that a response must be emitted before it can come under the control of environmental stimuli. The higher the operant rate of a response (that is, its "natural" rate before conditioning has taken place), the higher the probability that the response will be emitted in the presence of a given set of circumstances that can come to serve as discriminative and reinforcing stimuli. Since breathing is one of the most frequently occurring responses and inasmuch as changes in rate of breathing are reflexive reactions to sudden changes in stimulation, it would not be unexpected that for children with an atypical breathing pattern, maternal behavior can come to be associated with respiratory distress, since such behavior would have countless opportunities to become contingent on the respiratory responses of the child.

Behavioral Treatment of Asthma

A demonstration that an environmental manipulation, such as separating an asthmatic child from his or her family, produces changes in such a problem as asthma cannot be used as proof that environmental factors were the original cause of that problem. Conversely, it is not necessary for a problem to have an environmental cause in order for it to be susceptible to an environmental manipulation. Specifically, as Shapiro and Surwit (1976) have pointed out, it is not necessary to establish a behavioral etiology of a disorder in order to devise a behavioral form of treatment for that problem.

With children whose asthmatic attacks are preceded by such emotional arousal as anger, anxiety, or excitement, training in systematic, progressive relaxation appears to be an effective way of reducing the severity of the attacks (Alexander, 1972). Such training, which is an integral part of the systematic desensitization treatment developed by Wolpe (1969), consists of teaching a person voluntarily to relax various muscle groups. Alexander, Miklich, and Hershkoff (1972) showed that children who had been given three sessions of such training had a higher expiratory flow rate than a control group of children who had merely been instructed to sit still for the length of time relaxation occupied for the others.

Respiratory problems similar to asthma have also been treated by behavioral methods. A 15-year-old boy who had suffered from a chronic cough for 14 months was treated by an avoidance conditioning procedure which eliminated the problem within 1 week (Alexander, Chai, Creer, Miklich, Renne, & Cardoso, 1973). A demonstration by Creer (1970) underscored the importance of the consequences of asthmalike wheezing in maintaining this behavior. In fact, as Creer, Weinberg, and Molk (1974) suggest, some children may have learned to use such wheezing as a means of avoiding stressful situations. By identifying and removing these maintaining consequences, as Creer (1970) did with a time-out procedure, one can effectively reduce the frequency of the wheezing, provided the child can now obtain such desired consequences as adult attention through more constructive behavior.

OBESITY

Eating is another response that, while not as frequent as breathing, takes place so many times in a child's early life that it would be surprising if the mother's behavior did not become an important discriminative and reinforcing stimulus. During the first few years of life, the presence of the mothering person is, in fact, an inevitable discriminative stimulus for food intake. In addition, food intake, after a period of relative food deprivation, represents a positive consequence for eating behavior, and so the behavior carries its own, natural reinforcer. This combination of circumstances, the reinforcing nature of eating and—at least in the early years—the inevitable presence of the mother while eating takes place, makes this situation a potent setting for learning.

Obesity, the physical state of overweight, is usually the result of overeating, although in some instances it may involve a metabolic disorder. It is not clear to what extent a constitutional predisposition plays a role in obesity; the fact that many obese children have obese parents can be explained, as we shall see, without recourse to genetic speculations. As with so many other psychological disorders, obesity is a relative concept. Except in extreme instances, the point at which a chubby, sturdy child should be considered "overweight" depends on the deviation from the age-height-weight norm for that sex in that society. Some investigators (e.g., Bruch, 1961) use an arbitrary cutoff point whereby a child's weight must be 25 percent above the norm before being classified as obese.

Food intake is positively reinforcing only to the point of satiation; beyond this, further eating becomes aversive and will be avoided unless powerful reinforcers are operating which, on balance, are stronger than the avoidance tendencies. In the case of the obese child, one must look for these postulated reinforcers in order to ascertain what maintains the overeating. In the absence of systematic research on this topic, clinical observations suggest that among the reinforcing conditions for excessive eating are the behavior of an oversolicitous mother who rewards the child's eating by offering extrinsic reinforcers, possibly because watching her child eat has reinforcing implications for her. It is also possible that feelings of comfort, associated with the feeding period in the child's early years have acquired secondary reinforcement value and serve to maintain eating behavior beyond the point of satiation, particularly when the child has limited alternate sources of comfort. One also observes that obese children often have one or two obese parents, leading to the speculation that these parents model or reward excessive eating or both. In some cases, overeating may be maintained by negative reinforcement, since obesity permits a child to avoid peer competition in physical activity and sports or in social interaction such as attending dances, skating parties, hikes and the like, any or all of which may be aversive to a given child. It is unlikely that the overeating was originally learned through avoidance conditioning (a child does not begin to overeat "in order to" have a reason for not joining the track team), but once learned, the behavior may well be maintained in this manner.

Being overweight is not only a health hazard but also a considerable social handicap; therefore, these reasons alone call for intervention in obesity aimed at reducing the child's weight. Another reason for such intervention, however, is that it has been established (Abraham & Nordsieck, 1960) that obese children become obese adults and that such "juvenile-onset obesity" in adults tends to be more severe, more resistant to treatment, and more likely to be accompanied by psychological problems than the obesity adults acquire in later life (Stunkard & Mahoney, 1976).

Treatment Approaches

The recognition of the importance of the family environment in the eating behavior of chidren is reflected in the fact that treatment programs for obese children usually involve the child's parents or, at least, the mother. Aragona, Cassady, and Drabman (1975), for example, showed parents of overweight children how to teach their children to eat more slowly, delay meals, and leave food on the plate. Through *contingency contracting*, the children and their parents negotiated each week which special non-food rewards the child might earn for losing specified amounts of weight. This demonstration project, which lasted for 12 weeks, resulted in impressive weight losses. When a follow-up was conducted 8 weeks after the program had ended, the experimental groups continued to be significantly below the weight of the control group, but 31 weeks later the differences were no longer statistically significant. As with weight-reduction programs for adults, programs aimed at children must be specially designed in order to ensure that the weight reduction is maintained over time. One important ingredient in such a design is the individualization of the approach, something that is not possible when the experimental design of a study demands that individuals be randomly assigned to the various treatment conditions. When Wheeler and Hess (1976) individualized treatment for a group of mother-child pairs in an obesity program, they were able to report positive and apparently sustained results.

Whether it is always necessary to work with child and parent has been investigated by Kingsley and Shapiro (1977), who compared three behavioral programs for control of obesity in children. In one of these programs, the treatment group was composed of mothers and their children; another group consisted of children only; and in a third group the mothers were being seen in a group without their children. All three of these groups lost considerably more weight than a no-treatment control group, but the experimental groups did not differ from one another in terms of the *children's* weight. On the other hand, the *mothers* in the group that had been seen without the children had lost significantly more weight than the mothers in the other treatment groups. It thus appears possible not only to help a mother lose weight but also to teach her to work on the weight reduction of her child without having the child directly participate in the program.

By the time an individual reaches adolescence, the mother's participation in a treatment program may no longer be desirable because the control of eating behavior should now be placed in the young person's own hands. A behavioral approach to the treatment of adolescent obesity was reported by Weiss (1977), whose program extended over 12 weeks and proved successful over a 1-year follow-up. An important aspect of this program was a *stimulus control procedure*. This procedure entails instructing the overweight person in practices that bring eating under the control of a limited number of stimuli. Among these practices are eating in only one room of the house and in a specific spot, setting a table before eating, and doing nothing else while eating. In the program described by Weiss (1977), the individual would provide self-reinforcement, earning points for each of these desirable eating behaviors. As in other token programs, these points could later be exchanged for individualized treats or privileges, such as going to a movie. Of various treatment combinations compared in this study, the one involving the stimulus control procedure plus a conventional diet proved the most effective.

FOOD REFUSAL

The logical opposite of overeating, *food refusal*, is traditionally known as anorexia nervosa, "nervous loss of appetite." The objective result of food refusal is loss of weight, and the definition of this problem usually includes a reference to excessive weight loss. Some (e.g., Bliss & Branch, 1960) define excessive weight loss in terms of absolute pounds, although setting the cutoff point in terms of a percentage would be a more useful criterion, particularly in the case of children. With the definitional emphasis placed on weight loss, this category also includes persistent vomiting following feeding, which can be viewed as a variant of food refusal. This discussion of excessive weight loss through food refusal or persistent vomiting is, of course, limited to instances where it is clearly a psychological problem and not the result of physical illness.

Clinical histories of children who display food refusal often include parents for whom food has some special significance, either in terms of their overeating or in their need to maintain a diet for medical reasons. As might be expected, eating or not eating has long played a role in such children's interaction with their parents, and many of these children have had periods of excessive food intake before they finally came to clinical attention because of the weight loss. Of interest is the fact that food refusal is one of the few disorders that have a higher frequency among girls than boys, some investigators (Bliss & Branch, 1960), reporting a ratio as high as 9 to 1. Another characteristic feature is that these underweight, often emaciated, children and adolescents maintain that they are not too thin, some, in fact, insisting that they are too fat (Blitzer, Rollins, & Blackwell, 1961).

There are probably a variety of developmental events and environmental conditions that will lead to the end state recognized as food refusal. One formulation, proposed by Bruch (1961, 1962), suggests that individuals have to learn appropriate labels for various bodily sensations and that these labels then come to guide behavior that is relevant to these sensations. According to this, children would have to learn the label *hunger* for the sensations related to food deprivation, and having learned this label, they could learn to engage in food-seeking behavior when they recognize the sensation. While this formulation has a distinctly counterintuitive quality (food seeking when hungry seems such a "natural" response), research supporting attribution theory (Schachter & Singer, 1962; Valins, 1967) lends some credence to this view. Attribution theory holds that people attribute their internal sensations to external stimuli; that is, they "explain" how they feel by circumstances under which the feeling is experienced. The theory further states that social influences and the learning of labels importantly affect a person's attributions (Nisbett & Valins, 1971). If some children fail to learn to label correctly the sensations accompanying nutritional need, they might literally not know when they are hungry and when they are sated. Reports that many anorexic children have gone through earlier periods of excessive eating would be consonant with this speculation.

Further support for the formulation that cognitive labeling factors may play an important role in anorexia nervosa comes from a study by Agras, Barlow, Chapin, Abel, and Leitenberg (1974), who found that information feedback about the effects of eating and not eating is the most potent variable in the treatment of this disorder. Yet another source of indirect support is the fact that food refusal is largely an adolescent phenomenon. Until adolescence, food intake tends to be controlled by the mother; the chlid does not have to know when to eat and when not to eat. With the increasing independence from maternal control that comes with adolescence, however, the girl who does not seek food when she is objectively hungry because she mislabels the subjective sensation would lose weight rather precipitously. When the mother then steps back into the picture, urging the adolescent to eat, conflict over control and independence may well complicate the problem. It must, of course, also be remembered that adolescence is a period of drastic changes in the biochemistry of the body and of great changes in body build, factors that have led some to attribute adolescent eating problems either to biochemical dysfunction (Anand, 1961) or to conflicts about becoming a woman (Bliss & Branch, 1960).

Treatment Approaches

While the efficacy of a given method of treatment does not throw light on the etiology of the disorder so treated, a careful analysis of the variables operating in the treatment approach does reveal some of the factors currently maintaining the disorder. One such analysis was reported by Leitenberg, Agras, and Thomson (1968), who treated two adolescent girls who manifested food refusal. Both complained of "lack of appetite," frequently vomited after eating, expressed fear of obesity, and had menstrual disturbances (amenorrhea), a frequent concomitant of anorexia. The first case, a 14-year-old girl weighed 76 pounds at the start of treatment, down 25 pounds from her usual weight. The other, a 17-year-old, weighed 69 pounds, which was 22 pounds below what she usually weighed. The therapeutic strategy called for ignoring all comments the girls would make related to such physical complaints as headaches, nausea, or cramps. This extinction procedure resulted in a drastic reduction of these complaints, but it did not increase food intake or body weight, suggesting that food refusal was not maintained by contingent attention from the environment. Only when verbal praise for food intake and such pleasurable activities as watching TV or taking walks were made contingent on food intake and weight gain, did the girls' body weights increase to near their normal levels.

Leitenberg et al. (1968) concluded from their work with these two girls that the positive reinforcement contingent on eating and weight gain had been responsible for the treatment success. Their procedure, however, had included more than the positive reinforcement entailed in verbal praise. Gaining the privileges of watching TV and going on walks only when a meal had been eaten, or being discharged from the hospital only if weight had been gained are not positive, but negative reinforcements; being in the hospital and not being allowed to have these privileges represents an aversive state of affairs which is terminated contingent on the required response. Further, since the girls were told how many calories they had eaten and how much weight they had gained, information feedback was another variable in that treatment program. In order to ascertain which of these several variables had been primarily responsible for the outcome of the earlier work, Agras et al. (1974) conducted a carefully controlled study with another group of young girls in which positive reinforcement, negative reinforcement, information feedback, and the size of available meals were isolated. As already mentioned, informational feedback turned out to be the most potent variable, although the other three also played a role in increasing food intake and consequent weight gain. Of note, too, and relevant to the possibility that one is here dealing with cognitive factors, was the finding that patients ate more when larger meals were served—even when the servings were so large that they could not eat all of the food.

With adolescents of normal intelligence, the spelling out of the contingencies ("If you gain weight, you can watch TV") and the information provided by calorie counters and weight charts play important roles in treatment programs based on the principles of operant learning (Garfinkel, Kline, & Stancer, 1973). When weight loss is a result not of refusing to eat but of vomiting what has been eaten, so-called *ruminative vomiting*, and when the individual is not a bright adolescent but a retarded child or an infant, treatment must take a different form. Kohlenberg (1970) and Luckey, Watson, and Musick (1968), who worked with severely retarded children, and Lang and Melamed (1969), who treated an infant, approached chronic ruminative vomiting through an avoidance conditioning paradigm. The somewhat drastic technique of introducing punishment contingent on vomiting is called for when, as in these cases, the continuing loss of bodily weight represents a threat to the child's life. Kohlenberg (1970) succeeded in reducing vomiting in a nonverbal mongoloid by delivering a shock to the thigh contingent on stomach tension that had been observed to precede the actual vomiting. This approach was later supplemented by confining the subject to a chair contingent on having vomited and resulted in a weight gain of 10½ pounds in 25 days. As is frequently the case when punishment of an undesired response is used in the absence of positive reinforcement of its functionally reciprocal desired response, vomiting again became a problem about a year later, highlighting the fact that while punishment is an effective emergency measure, it does not constitute treatment in the absence of a more positive approach.

In the case of a normally developing young child, as opposed to a retardate, the positive consequences normally contingent on nonvomiting behavior appear to support such behavior once the vomiting has been suppressed by avoidance conditioning. Lang and Melamed (1969) report on a 9-month-old male infant whose ruminative vomiting had reduced his weight to 12 pounds (from 17 pounds at 6 months of age). This infant had developed normally until his fifth month, when he first began vomiting. The problem increased in severity to the point where the child vomited within 10 to 15 minutes after every meal. This activity resulted in three brief hospitalizations for the purpose of various tests, including exploratory surgery. None of these procedures revealed a medical reason for the problem, nor did any of several treatment approaches reduce the frequency of vomiting. Conditioning procedures were introduced as a last resort and because the infant's life was endangered.

Treatment consisted of delivery of an electric shock through an electrode attached to the child's calf as soon as electromyographic recording indicated that vomiting was about to occur. The shock was paired with a loud tone, and the effect of the treatment was dramatic. After two sessions shock was rarely required, and by the sixth session the infant was no longer vomiting. He began to gain weight during the treatment and continued to improve thereafter. One month after discharge from the hospital he weighed 21 pounds, and 5 months later his weight was 26 pounds, 1 ounce. He was eating well and not vomiting, and a physician described him as alert, active, and attentive. He continued to thrive when followed up 1 year after treatment. Coincident with the successful conditioning therapy, the child's positive social behavior had increased; he had become more responsive to adults, smiled more frequently, and seemed to be more interested in toys and games than he had been previously. There seemed to have been no adverse consequences to the avoidance conditioning, and the positive reinforcers normally available in the social environment appear to have been sufficient to maintain the normal, nonruminative behavior.

ENURESIS AND ENCOPRESIS

Lack of appropriate control over the elimination of urine (*enuresis*) and feces (*encopresis*) has received considerable attention in the psychological literature, at least in part because Freudian tradition held that the conditions under which this control is learned ("toilet training") play a critical role in personality development. When a mother is faced with the task of teaching her child to eliminate in a place and under conditions the society happens to consider "appropriate," she uses the same skills (or lack of skill) at teaching that she brings to other aspects of child rearing. As such, she has an impact not only on the child's specific behaviors with regard to toilet functions but also on all the other behaviors, the constellation of which we come to call "personality." An impatient mother who insists on early and quick bowel control and punishes noncompliance by her baby is also likely to insist on and model such behavioral qualities as neatness, cleanliness, frugality, and orderliness. When her boy later exhibits these qualities, he does so not necessarily because of the way he was toilet trained but because of the similar manner in which the mother who toilet trained him also taught him other behaviors.

As is true of so many other psychological disorders, there is a problem in defining difficulties with elimination. It is, again, a rather arbitrary decision whether or not to call occasional bed-wetting by a 5-year-old a psychological problem. What is "occasional"? And at what age does it cease to be normal and become a problem? Among the school-age children studied by Lapouse and Monk (1959), 8 percent wet their beds at least once a month; yet these were normal children, if not being a patient at a psychiatric clinic can be taken as a definition of normality. There are families in parts of the United States where bed-wetting at any age is accepted as an expected, unremarkable event, and there are others who become concerned when a child of 3 is unable to sleep without wetting. In the final analysis, it is again the child's environment that defines the problem; and once any behavior is classified under the rubric of "problem," the responses of the environment make it a problem behavior, no matter what cutoff point or definition textbook writers might offer.

Enuresis and the related but rarer disorder, encopresis, are encountered in two forms, chronic and regressive. In both forms, wetting usually occurs at night (nocturnal enuresis or bed-wetting), but in more serious cases the child may also wet during the day. Encopresis, or soiling, on the other hand, usually occurs during the day and is often associated with periods of excessive bowel retention.

In *chronic enuresis* the child has never learned to hold the urine and to micturate only in appropriate places. In *regressive enuresis* the child will have learned urinary control at one time but has resumed wetting some time later. Such regression can be conceptualized in terms of a response hierarchy in which response patterns of increasing maturity have been acquired sequentially. At the top of the hierarchy the prepotent and most likely, but most recently learned, response to a distended bladder is to inhibit the innate elimination response until the appropriate stimulus conditions at the toilet are present. Like other instrumental responses, the sequence hold-wait-seek toilet-urinate was probably learned and maintained by positive consequences. During acquisition in childhood, these consequences may have included maternal attention and praise for being mature and self-sufficient. If these consequences should then be withdrawn before the mature response is fully established and maintained by the negative reinforcement of tension release and by positive consequences, such as pride in achievement that the child can deliver to himself, one would predict the mature response pattern to undergo extinction, with a less mature pattern—lower on the hierarchy—(i.e., wetting) becoming prepotent.

When a child resumes wetting after an earlier period of having been toilet trained, the consequences of the regressive response tend to be maternal consternation which, despite its negative content, is a form of attention and hence a potential reinforcer for the wetting behavior. Some mothers may attempt to punish the child for wetting, but since such punishment is administered a considerable time after the wetting response was made (i.e., when the wet bed is discovered in the morning), it is bound to be ineffective. Negative attention or punishment or both are unlikely to reestablish the desired "dry night" behavior at the prepotent position in the hierarchy. On the contrary, the attention may, in fact, strengthen the wetting behavior.

In order to teach the two responses that together represent adaptive toileting behavior—"hold" and "release in right place"—these responses must be strengthened by positive reinforcement, while their inappropriate reciprocals are weakened through nonreinforcement (extinction) or negative consequences (punishment). It is only in this combination and when administered as soon after the response as possible that punishment can have the desired effect. Even when properly timed, punishment alone is effective only in the inhibiting ("hold") aspect of the response sequence; it cannot develop the desired behavior of going to the toilet and eliminating. Since inhibition alone will ultimately be overwhelmed by the increasing physiological bladder tension with resulting elimination, punishment, when used, must be paired with teaching the positive response.

In encopresis, as was pointed out, one frequently finds periods of excessive fecal retention alternating with periods of soiling. It may be that these are children who have learned only the "hold" part of the response sequence, possibly because their toilet training emphasized aversive control (punishment). Extended periods of bowel retention can result in a hardening of fecal matter because of moisture absorption. The stools thus become so impacted that defecation becomes painful. To avoid this pain, the child may continue retention until, in some instances, defecation becomes physically impossible and medical intervention is required in order to induce evacuation.

Aversive control can, under certain circumstances, bring about the suppression of a response, but the more likely responses learned under these conditions are avoidance and escape. Some encopretic children learn to hide the evidence of their soiling, secreting dirty underwear in the most ingenious places—much to the understandable distress of their families. When a positive response is to be established—in this case, associating the internal cues of bladder or bowel tension with going to the toilet to eliminate—this positive response must be explicitly taught. When the contingencies are wrong, the wrong behavior will be strengthened. This was demonstrated in a case reported by Lal and Lindsley (1968). A 3-year-old boy had developed chronic constipation. Observation revealed that whenever the boy failed to eliminate, his parents would shower him with affection on the mistaken assumption that his constipation was the result of his feeling insecure and needing more love. With receiving affection thus contingent on *not* eliminating, the boy's condition became worse. Improvement came quickly once the parents were instructed to place the boy on the toilet and to leave him alone until he called to indicate that he had defecated and *then* to praise and caress him and to permit him to engage in the highly desired privilege of playing with his water toys in the bathtub.

The discussion thus far may have led to the impression that the only trouble with enuretic or encopretic chldren is that they eliminate too often in inappropriate places and that they merely have to learn the hold-wait-eliminate-in-toilet sequence of responses in order to be rid of their problem. By the time children who do not display age-appropriate toilet behavior come to clinical attention, they are likely to have acquired at least some conditioned anxiety to stimuli associated with wetting or soiling. Some of these stimuli, such as the sensation associated with sphincter release and urine passing through the urethra, are the same whether the elimination takes place in an appropriate or inappropriate place. Anxiety that has become associated with these stimuli thus represents an incompatible response when it is elicited while the child is on the toilet. One aspect of treating enuresis is thus the discrimination learning whereby toilet cues will no longer elicit the anxiety response and its toilet-avoiding consequences.

Another concomitant of wetting and soiling is found in the perceptions these children form of themselves and their capacity to cope with problems (Compton, 1968). Having failed to learn what "any baby can learn" (control over bladder and bowel functions), they are apt to see themselves as inadequate, incompetent, or worthless. Since their condition is also likely to limit their interactions with peers (no sleeping at a friend's house, no overnight camp), this area of their lives is also often disrupted. Inasmuch as these conditions are reversed once enuresis is successfully treated, there tends to be a marked improvement in areas such as peer relations, school behavior, academic performance, and general adjustment, even when none of these were subject to direct treatment (Baker, 1969).

Treatment Approaches

The treatment of *enuresis* by the application of the principles of learning has been available for many years, having been described by Mowrer and Mowrer in

1938. In their basic bell-and-pad approach, the child sleeps on a pad that is wired in such a fashion that a single drop of urine will close a circuit and activate a bell or buzzer which continues to sound until it is manually turned off, either by the child, a parent, or an attendant.

Treatment by the bell-and-pad method was originally conceptualized as an application of respondent conditioning principles, but it is very likely that operant learning is also involved, particularly since rewards for improvement and for dry nights are often a part of the procedure. It is, in fact, possible to treat bedwetting by methods based on operant learning alone, without resorting to the bell and pad. One such method was outlined by Kimmel and Kimmel (1970), who focus on teaching voluntary sphincter control during the day while the child is awake; for once this skill is acquired, it seems to generalize to when the child is asleep at night. Children who wet the bed appear to have a higher rate of urination during the day than children who can sleep through the night without wetting. Following this observation, Paschalis, Kimmel, and Kimmel (1972) instructed a group of parents to teach bladder control to their children. The parents held daily sessions in which the children were rewarded for holding their urine for 2 to 3 minutes longer than the day before, up to a total of 45 minutes. Treatment lasted from 15 to 20 days. When the children had succeeded in staying dry at night for 1 week, previously selected gifts were presented as a reward. Follow-up 3 months later showed that of the thirty-one children, of whom none had ever had a dry night before, fifteen were completely dry and eight had improved significantly. Reinforcement for dry nights may be an important part of the treatment for young children (Samaan, 1972), but with adolescents it may be sufficient to provide them with knowledge of the results of their efforts (Stedman, 1972).

Another method of dealing with enuresis that also teaches appropriate responses to the child in the waking state is the rapid toilet-training procedure introduced by Foxx and Azrin (1973a). As used by Azrin, Sneed, and Foxx (1974) with enuretic children, this method entails having the child drink a lot of fluids so that the frequency of needing to urinate is increased, thus massing the trials during which voiding in the toilet can be reinforced. One aspect of this approach is *positive practice overcorrection*, which consists of a period of practicing the correct response whenever the changeworthy response (in this case, wetting) has been emitted. As soon as the child has failed to use the toilet, the parent indicates disapproval and requires the child to practice walking to the toilet from various locations in the house for a total of ten rapidly conducted trials, during which all responses involved in the use of a toilet (except actual urination) are to be demonstrated. While this experience has educative aspects, it would seem that overcorrection is a form of punishment because it reduces the frequency of the behavior (wetting) on which it is contingent. When Bollard and Woodroffe (1977) applied this procedure with fourteen enuretic children, all achieved dry nights within a median of 12 days, although two of these children had resumed wetting when a follow-up was conducted 6 months later.

It is not uncommon for children whose enuresis had been successfully treated to suffer a relapse some months later (Doleys, 1977; Lovibond, 1963). This phenomenon may be viewed as the extinction of a learned response and, as such, can be counteracted by the use of intermittent reinforcement in the course of the training procedure (Finley, Besserman, Bennett, Clapp, & Finley, 1973). Overtraining is another method that has been used with the bell-and-pad system in order to prevent relapse (Young & Morgan, 1972). Here, once dryness has been initially achieved, the child is given large quantities of fluid to drink before retiring, thereby massing the number of learning trials with the wake-up alarm. Relapse is, of course, also a reflection of the fact that in this, as in similar cases of the treatment of behavior deficits, one is not merely establishing a response that was previously missing from the child's repertoire but one is introducing into the repertoire a response that is antagonistic to one already established. An enuretic boy is not simply one who lacks appropriate sphincter control; he is one who makes a micturition response to the stimulus of bladder distension. The therapeutic task must thus be viewed as establishing a complex series of behaviors that includes sustained sphincter contraction and micturition under appropriate stimulus conditions (toilet). One must thus strengthen an adaptive response pattern while simultaneously weakening its maladaptive reciprocal, and this would seem to involve a combination of respondent, avoidance, and operant factors— the latter coming into play in relation to the secondary reinforcements the child should receive for not wetting the bed. If these secondary reinforcements are not, at least intermittently, forthcoming, the staying-dry behavior may well undergo extinction, allowing the innate competing response to once again become prepotent, thus resulting in a relapse. For this reason it is important to reinforce dry nights either by such social reinforcement as praise or such self-reinforcement as pride of accomplishment. This can be furthered if, as Lovibond (1964) suggests, the child is an active partner in the treatment plan, helping with the essential record keeping and receiving praise for his progress.

Since relapse is not found in all children whose enuresis is treated by conditioning methods (Doleys, 1977), it is possible that those for whom relapse is recorded represent a different population of enuretics. As pointed out earlier, children who are enuretic can be divided into two groups: one, the chronic, is composed of those who had never been dry at night and the other, the regressed, contains those who had once learned to sleep through the night without wetting but resumed the innate response in later years. In the first group, treatment would consist of teaching a new response not previously available. In the second group, where one is dealing with children for whom an adaptive response had undergone extinction, a previously learned response must be relearned. It would stand to reason that the two groups should differ not only in acquisition rate but also in the resistance to extinction of the response pattern being established in the course of treatment.

Some support for the above speculation comes from a study by Novick

(1966), who treated twenty-two chronic and twenty-three regressed enuretics by a form of supportive therapy. For the 80 percent of the children who had failed to get help from this approach, he subsequently provided treatment with a bell-and-pad apparatus. In this manner, all but four of the children reached the cure criterion of 14 consecutive dry nights. Novick reports that the regressed enuretics, that is, those who had acquired enuresis after an initial period of dryness, had reached the cure criterion sooner and with more rapid decrease in wetting. This would suggest that those who merely had to reestablish a previously learned response learned more quickly than those who had to acquire an entirely new response. On the other hand, the regressed cases were also more likely than the chronic cases to display relapse or new problems, as revealed by follow-up interviews extending over a period of 1 year. It may well be that the relapsing cases reported in other studies are also primarily those for whom enuresis represents a regression. There may be at least two explanations for this phenomenon. The first is that the regressed children reach an acceptable level of dryness sooner than the chronic, thus receiving fewer reinforced training trials and evincing concomitant instability of the adaptive response. Further—and often quickly successful—courses of treatment would thus increase the number of training trials and more firmly establish the desired response. Indeed, DeLeon and Mandell (1966) reported this to be the case. The second (and related) explanation of the relapse phenomenon would seem to lie in the reinforcement contingencies that operate in the regressed child's environment. These may be such that the response of wetting or other maladaptive behavior is more strongly reinforced than the adaptive responses involved in staying dry. This might explain why these children not only regressed originally but relapsed after apparently successful treatment.

The treatment of *encopresis* by methods based on learning principles has usually taken the form of operant contingency management. Thus, Gelber and Meyer (1965) treated a 14-year-old by placing him in a hospital in order to be able to control the response consequences. Once in the hospital, the privilege of leaving the ward was used as the positive consequence for appropriate toilet behavior, while restriction to the ward became the punisher for soiling. Similar approaches to encopresis and stool retention were reported by Edelman (1971), Tomlinson (1970), Ayllon, Simon, and Wildman (1975), Plachetta (1976), and by Bach and Moylan (1975), all of whom trained the parents of encopretic children in the use of contingent reinforcement methods; all reported favorable results. Unfortunately, the absence of necessary experimental controls makes it impossible to conclude from such case studies that the reinforcement contingencies were indeed responsible for the observed improvement.

As is the case with other psychophysiological disorders, encopresis has both psychological and physiological components. Young (1973) discussed the neurophysiology of bowel control and pointed out that the encopretic children he treated "had no perception of the gastro-ileal or gastro-colic reflexes and could exercise no control over their bowel actions" (p. 501). He treated these children with a mild laxative, combined with having them sit on the toilet for 10 minutes after they had eaten 20 to 30 minutes earlier. When a bowel movement occurred, the parents rewarded the child with praise. This treatment was successful within a mean of 7 months for twenty-two of the twenty-four children in the study.

One of the difficulties in teaching children to control such physiological processes as sphincter contraction is that these functions can only be monitored indirectly. In the case of encopresis, one can only conclude that sphincter contraction was maintained when no soiling takes place for a period of time. Since training by operant methods is most effective when the response is reinforced as soon as it occurs, it would be best if one could reinforce sphincter contraction rather than periods of staying clean. This problem was solved by Kohlenberg (1973) who treated a 13-year-old encopretic boy. In order to be able to measure the pressure exerted by the anal sphincter, this investigator inserted a fluid-filled balloon attached to a pressure gauge into the boy's rectum. This not only permitted the immediate reinforcement of increases in sphincter pressure but it also enabled the boy to obtain external feedback of his internal responses. Kohlenberg was able to demonstrate that sphincter pressure was a function of the reinforcement schedule and he succeeded in gradually increasing this pressure in the course of his experiment. If, as Young (1973) has suggested, encopretic children have trouble knowing through internal feedback whether their sphincter muscles are contracted, such external feedback may help them learn to bring the necessary responses under voluntary control. Such *biofeedback* has a great variety of applications in helping people establish learned control over their physiological functions (Shapiro & Surwit, 1976), but thus far this approach has not been widely used in the treatment of children.

RECAPITULATION

The biological functions of the body, the physiological conditions, play a role in every form of human behavior, in every behavior disorder. In some behavior disorders the role of physiological functions is more prominent than in others, and such disorders can be singled out and called *psychophysiological disorders*. Asthma is a classic example of such a disorder, and there have been many speculations about the interaction and direction of causality between environmental and biological factors. Research suggests that in some children asthmatic attacks are under the control of environmental stimuli, but little is known about what it is that makes these children susceptible to these effects. Overeating and food refusal are often related to external stimuli, particularly parental behavior, and this seems also the case where a child lacks appropriate control over eliminatory processes, as in enuresis and encopresis. In these disorders it is useful to differentiate between chronic and regressive cases; for in the former, the child has never learned appropriate control, while in the latter, these controls, although once learned, have become lost. All of the disorders mentioned in this chapter have been successfully treated by the manipulation of environmental conditions but this success does not permit one to draw conclusions about the relative importance of biological and environmental factors in the original development of these disorders.

Summing Up

I have tried to present the topic of psychological disorders of children from a behavioral point of view and I hope that in so doing I have shown the strengths and the weaknesses, the problems and the promises of the behavioral approach to clinical child psychology. It seems to me that the strength of this approach lies in the insistence on defining problems in such a way that they can be investigated by the methods of science. Like science itself, this makes the approach a constantly changing, self-correcting process where old ideas that fail the test of empirical investigations are discarded to make room for new ideas that must, in turn, submit to that test. Yet this very insistence on empiricism is also the source of one of the problems with which those who subscribe to the behavioral approach must contend. It is that their system is incomplete so that many important questions remain unanswered. This makes some impatient and they would rather rely on their intuition or resurrect discarded formulations than wait for the painstaking process of science to provide the answers. If the past provides a guide to the future, there is no reason to suppose that questions that cannot be answered today because we lack the needed instruments or methods will not be answered in the future. It is here that I find much of the promise of the behavioral approach to clinical child psychology.

What are some of the unanswered questions? I believe that most of them are to be found in the area of what I called private events in one of the first pages of this book. I said there that behaviorally oriented psychologists do not deny the existence of thoughts and feelings but that they prefer, *as a matter of strategy*, to focus their attention on the observable. The most readily observable phenomenon, thus far, has been people's overt behavior. As a result, we have amassed information about the circumstances that surround observable behavior so that, where these circumstances can be modified, we are able to change behavior that is troubling those who seek our help. Yet we also know that thoughts and feelings are important. In fact, they probably are integral parts of what some have called the A-B-C unit (affect, behavior, cognition) that is the person. Most unanswered questions have to do with affective and cognitive aspects of life and our problem has been mainly our inability to develop trustworthy methods for making these aspects observable. Progress is being made, but we have a long way to go. As laboratory investigators make advances in the study of affect and cognition, those in the applied areas will be in the position to bring this accumulating knowledge to bear on the problems they face in the clinic. This, after all, has been the course of development with respect to behavior where laboratory research on conditioning and learning found successful clinical application.

Other questions awaiting answers are not so much internal to psychology as they are related to the interface between psychology and its neighboring sciences and between psychology and society-at-large. In the first chapter I spoke of the determinants of behavior and listed genetic-constitutional factors, past learning, current physiological state, and current environmental conditions as crucial to arriving at a full understanding of how people come to be what they are. Strictly speaking, only past learning is the province of psychology. For authoritative contributions regarding the other factors psychologists must turn to the various specialties within biology and the social-behavioral sciences. How do we best work with them? How can we learn what they have to contribute? Where is the boundary between their field and ours? And who is best equipped to take an integrative view of all these determinants so as to arrive at a full picture of the functioning person? All of these are questions with which we must grapple if duplication of effort, neglect of critical areas, and jurisdictional disputes are to be avoided. But these questions relate not only to the sources of our knowledge; analogous questions exist with respect to the application of knowledge. There we must find constructive ways of interacting with educators, physicians, penologists, others in the field of mental health, and—in no way least—parents, if the children about whom we all care are to derive maximum benefit from our knowledge.

The interface between clinical child psychology and society-at-large raises yet other questions and issues. First of all, one must recognize that there are limits to what psychology can accomplish with respect to the problems of children. The current environmental conditions that are one of the determinants of behavior are often beyond the reach of the psychologist who desires to change them in order to help a child. It would be folly to assume that the treatment a psychologist is able to provide can solve every conceivable human problem. The psychologist as a psychologist can do little or nothing about inadequate housing, unhealthy nutrition, poor schools, antiquated prison systems, disrupted social services, or poverty. The psychologist as a citizen can and should do something about these.

Another aspect of the interface between psychology and society has to do with the fact that in many ways society defines the disorders we seek to study and treat. I have touched on this in earlier chapters but it bears restating. We have seen how the definition of juvenile delinquency depends on court decisions and that whether a child is called mentally retarded is a function of shifting pronouncements by influential organizations. Similarly, the label *learning disabled* can serve to help or to hinder a child, depending on the changing regulations that govern the policies of school systems. These and similar influences affect the welfare of children, and those who are concerned about children, like clinical child psychologists, often find that they must enter the public arena in order to help shape reasonable laws and sensible regulations and to try to change those that influence children adversely. This is another aspect of child advocacy of which I spoke in the discussion of the rights of children.

THE EFFECTIVENESS OF BEHAVIOR THERAPY

Throughout this book I have attempted to show how the behavioral approach of psychology can be brought to bear on the psychological disorders of children. In the final analysis, the relevance of this approach hinges on whether it facilitates constructive intervention in the lives of troubled children; for they will benefit little from esoteric theorizing or fascinating research unless these lead to effective treatment. How good is the behavioral approach in that respect?

No treatment procedure can be said to have demonstrated its effectiveness until the stability of improvements has been analyzed over time. This calls for systematic follow-up studies, but these are exceedingly rare, not only for behavior therapy but for any kind of psychological treatment of disordered behavior. The few exceptions (Baker, 1969; Kennedy, 1965; Nolan, Mattis & Holliday, 1970) suggest that over such relatively short periods as 12 months, improvements attributed to behavior therapy have been maintained. At times, however, one finds reports of studies (Miller, Barrett, Hampe, & Noble, 1972a; Kent & O'Leary, 1976) that show that untreated children will also improve after a relatively brief period of time. On the other hand, children treated for one problem also show improvements in areas that had not been the focus of treatment (Baker, 1969; Nolan et al., 1970). This may be a reflection of the fact that problem behaviors prevent the children from engaging in behavior that might be a source of positive reinforcement, reinforcement that becomes available for building an adaptive repertoire once the problem behavior is removed. It is, of course, not possible to say for how long a treated case should be followed before one can speak with confidence about the stability of improvement. Nor would it necessarily be proof of the ineffectiveness of treatment if a former client developed new problems many years after apparently successful treatment. Therapy is not a form of immunization, and an individual may always encounter circumstances under which maladaptive behavior can once again be acquired.

The reasons for the dearth of well-controlled outcome and follow-up studies are well known. As Bergin (1966) and Paul (1967) have pointed out, it is difficult to meet the requirements of meaningful outcome research. Relevant control groups are hard to find, therapies and therapists are difficult to equate, a sufficient number of cases with the same problem behavior are rarely available, and tracing terminated clients for careful follow-up assessment is time-consuming and expensive.

Enuresis is a problem that lends itself more readily to experimental study than most psychological disorders. Bed-wetting is readily operationalized and objectively measured; it has a high enough frequency in the child population to permit a researcher to gather a reasonably large number of subjects in a relatively short time. Withholding treatment from an enuretic child for a period of months in order to have him or her in a control group does not raise major ethical qualms because his or her problem does not represent a danger to him or her or others and is unlikely to worsen without immediate treatment. Lastly, the behavioral treatment of enuresis entails a well-developed conditioning technique that requires minimal activity on the part of the therapist who can thus treat a relatively large number of children during a reasonably limited period of time. For all these reasons, the best outcome research available deals with the conditioning treatment of bed-wetting. Such studies (Baker, 1969; DeLeon & Mandell, 1966; Lovibond, 1964) have compared conditioning treatment with other modes of therapy and with no-treatment controls. In all instances, the children treated by the bell-and-buzzer conditioning methods reached cure criterion earlier than those treated by other methods or held in the control group.

One might, of course, question the necessity of proving the superiority of one form of treatment over another. There are now many studies that attest to the effectiveness of behavior therapy with the wide variety of problems where it has been applied. There is also no question that behavior therapists usually reach their defined treatment goal more quickly than psychotherapists reach their criterion for terminating a case. Even if behavior therapy were ultimately to prove to be no more effective than psychotherapy, it is certainly more efficient, in terms of both time and professional effort. Rather than studying the question whether one form of treatment is superior to another, it would seem wiser to investigate what, if anything, are the effective ingredients in various forms of treatment and what kinds of problems are best treated by which method. It is unlikely that behavior therapy as it is practiced today is the panacea for every conceivable psychological disorder. So far, only the conditioning and modeling paradigms have been widely applied to clinical problems in any systematic fashion. In all probability, other knowledge from the behavioral sciences has relevance to the treatment of psychological disorders, and it is to the gathering and application of such knowledge that efforts should continue to be directed.

REFERENCES

Abraham, S., Nordsieck, M. Relationship of excess weight in children and adults. *Public Health Reports*, 1960, *75*, 263–273.

Achenbach, T. M. The classification of children's psychiatric symptoms: A factor-analytic study. *Psychological Monographs*, 1966, *80* (6, Whole No. 615).

Achenbach, T. M., & Zigler, E. Cue-learning and problem-learning strategies in normal and retarded children. *Child Development*, 1968, *39*, 827–848.

Ackerson, L. *Children's Behavior Problems*. Chicago, Ill.: University of Chicago Press, 1931.

Ackerson, L. Children's behavior problems: II. Relative importance and interrelations among traits. *Behavior Research Fund Monograph*. Chicago, Ill.: University of Chicago Press, 1942.

Agras, W. S., Barlow, T. H., Chapin, H. N., Abel, G. G., & Leitenberg, H. Behavior modification of anorexia nervosa. *Archives of General Psychiatry*, 1974, *30*, 343–352.

Alexander, A. B. Systematic relaxation and flow rates in asthmatic children: Relationship to emotional precipitants and anxiety. *Journal of Psychosomatic Research*, 1972, *16*, 405–410.

Alexander, A. B., Chai, H., Creer, T. L., Miklich, D. R., Renne, C. M., & Cardoso, R. R. deA. The elimination of chronic cough by response suppression shaping. *Journal of Behaviour Therapy and Experimental Psychiatry*, 1973, *4*, 75–80.

Alexander, A. B., Miklich, D. R., & Hershkoff, H. The immediate effects of systematic relaxation training on peak expiratory flow rates in asthmatic children. *Psychosomatic Medicine*, 1972, *34*, 388–394.

Alexander, J. F., Barton, C., Schiavo, R. S., & Parsons, B. V. Systems-behavioral intervention with families of delinquents: Therapist characteristics, family behavior, and outcome. *Journal of Consulting and Clinical Psychology*, 1976, *44*, 656–664.

Alexander, J. F., & Parsons, B. V. Short-term behavioral intervention with delinquent families: Impact on family process and recidivism. *Journal of Abnormal Psychology*, 1973, *81*, 219–225.

Algozzine, B. The emotionally disturbed child: Disturbed or disturbing? *Journal of Abnormal Child Psychology*. 1977, *5*, 205–211.

Allen, K. E., Hart, B. M., Buell, J. S., Harris, F. R., & Wolf, M. M. Effects of social reinforcement on isolate behavior of a nursery school child. *Child Development*, 1964, *35*, 511–518.

Allen, M. K., & Liebert, R. M. Children's adoption of self-reward patterns: Model's prior experience and incentive for nonimitation. *Child Development*, 1969a, *40*, 921–926.

Allen, M. K., & Liebert, R. M. Effects of live and symbolic deviant-modeling cues on adoption of a previously learned standard. *Journal of Personality and Social Psychology*, 1969b, *11*, 253–260.

Anand, B. K. Nervous regulation of food intake. *Physiological Review*, 1961, *41*, 677–708.

Aragona, J., Cassady, J., & Drabman, R. S. Treating overweight children through parental training and contingency contracting. *Journal of Applied Behavior Analysis*, 1975, *8*, 269–278.

Aronfreed, J., & Reber, A. Internalized behavior suppression and the timing of social punishment. *Journal of Personality and Social Psychology*, 1965, *1*, 3–16.

Ayllon, T., Layman, D., & Kandel, H. J. A behavioral-educational alternative to drug control of hyperactive children. *Journal of Applied Behaviour Analysis*, 1975, *8*, 137–146.

Ayllon, T., Simon, S. J., & Wildman, R. W., II. Instructions and reinforcement in the elimination of encopresis: A case study. *Journal of Behaviour Therapy and Experimental Psychiatry*, 1975, *6*, 235–238.

Ayllon, T., Smith, D., & Rogers, M. Behavioral management of school phobia. *Journal of Behaviour Therapy and Experimental Psychiatry*, 1970, *1*, 125–138.

Azrin, N. H., & Foxx, R. M. A rapid method of toilet training the institutionalized retarded. *Journal of Applied Behavior Analysis*, 1971, *4*, 89–99.

Azrin, N. H., Sneed, T. J., & Foxx, R. M. Dry-bed training: Rapid elimination of childhood enuresis. *Behaviour Research and Therapy*, 1974, *12*, 147–156.

Bach, R., & Moylan, J. J. Parents administered behavior therapy for inappropriate urination and encopresis: A case study. *Journal of Behaviour Therapy and Experimental Psychiatry*, 1975, *6*, 239–241.

Bachman, J. A. Self-injurious behavior: A behavioral analysis. *Journal of Abnormal Psychology*, 1972, *80*, 211–224.

Baer, D. M., & Guess, D. Receptive training of adjectival inflections in mental retardates. *Journal of Applied Behavior Analysis*, 1971, *4*, 129–139.

Baer, R., Ascione, F., & Casto, G. Relative efficacy of two token economy procedures for decreasing the disruptive classroom behavior of retarded children. *Journal of Abnormal Child Psychology*, 1977, *5*, 135–145.

Bailey, J., & Meyerson, L. Vibration as a reinforcer with a profoundly retarded child. *Journal of Applied Behavior Analysis*, 1969, *2*, 135–137.

Baker, B. L. Symptom treatment and symptom substitution in enuresis. *Journal of Abnormal Psychology*, 1969, *74*, 42–49.

Balaschak, B. A. Teacher-implemented behavior modification in a case of organically based epilepsy. *Journal of Consulting and Clinical Psychology*, 1976, *44*, 218–223.

Ball, T. S., & Irwin, A. E. A portable, automated device applied to training a hyperactive child. *Journal of Behaviour Therapy and Experimental Psychiatry*, 1976, *7*, 185–187.

Bandura, A. Psychotherapy as a learning process. *Psychological Bulletin*, 1961, *58*, 143–159.

Bandura, A. *Principles of behavior modification*. New York: Holt, Rinehart & Winston, 1969.

Bandura, A. Vicarious and self-reinforcement processes. In R. Glaser (Ed.), *The nature of reinforcement*. New York: Academic Press, 1971, 228–278.

Bandura, A. *Aggression: A social learning analysis*. Englewood Cliffs, N.J.: Prentice-Hall, 1973.

Bandura, A. *Social learning theory*. Englewood Cliffs, N.J.: Prentice-Hall, 1977.

Bandura, A., Grusec, J. E., & Menlove, F. L. Vicarious extinction of avoidance behavior. *Journal of Personality and Social Psychology*, 1967, *5*, 16–23.

Bandura, A., & Menlove, F. L. Factors determining vicarious extinction of avoidance behavior through symbolic modeling. *Journal of Personality and Social Psychology*, 1968, *8*, 99–108.

Bandura, A., & Mischel, W. Modification and self-imposed delay of reward through exposure to live and symbolic models. *Journal of Personality and Social Psychology*, 1965, *2*, 698–705.

Bandura, A., & Rosenthal, T. L. Vicarious classical conditioning as a function of arousal level. *Journal of Personality and Social Psychology*, 1966, *3*, 54–62.

Bandura, A., Ross, D., & Ross, S. A. Imitation of film-mediated aggressive models. *Journal of Abnormal and Social Psychology*, 1963, *66*, 3–11.

Bandura, A., & Walters, R. H. *Adolescent aggression*. New York: Ronald, 1959.

Bandura, A., & Walters, R. H. Aggression. In H. W. Stevenson, J. Kagan, & C. Spiker (Eds.), *Child psychology, The 62nd yearbook of the National Society for the Study of Education*. Chicago, Ill.: National Society for the Study of Education, 1963, 364–415.

Barkley, R. A. Predicting the response of hyperkinetic children to stimulant drugs: A review. *Journal of Abnormal Child Psychology*, 1976, *4*, 327–348.

Barkley, R. A., Hastings, J. E., Tousel, R. E., & Tousel, S. E. Evaluation of a token system for juvenile delinquents in a residential setting. *Journal of Behaviour Therapy and Experimental Psychiatry*, 1976, *7*, 227–230.

Barkley, R. A., & Ullman, D. G. A comparison of objective measures of activity and distractibility in hyperactive and nonhyperactive children. *Journal of Abnormal Child Psychology*, 1976, *3*, 231–244.

Bateman, B. D., & Schiefelbusch, R. L. Educational identification, assessment, and evaluative procedures. In *Minimal brain dysfunction in children*, U.S. Public Health Service Publication No. 2015. Washington, D.C.: U.S. Department of Health, Education, and Welfare, 1969, 5–20.

Baum, M. Rapid extinction of an avoidance response following a period of response prevention in the avoidance apparatus. *Psychological Reports*, 1966, *18*, 59–64.

Becker, W. C. The relationship of parental ratings of self and each other to the behavior of kindergarten children as rated by mothers, fathers, and teachers. *Journal of Consulting Psychology*, 1960, *24*, 507–527.

Becker, W. C., & Krug, R. S. A circumplex model for social behavior of children. *Child Development*, 1964, *35*, 371–396.

Becker, W. C., Peterson, D. R., Luria, Z., Shoemaker, D. J., & Hellmer, L. A. Relations of factors derived from parent-interview ratings to behavior problems in five-year-olds. *Child Development*, 1962, *33*, 509–535.

Beery, J. W. Matching of auditory and visual stimuli by average and retarded readers. *Child Development*, 1967, *38*, 827–833.

Bergin, A. E. Some implications of psychotherapy research for therapeutic practice. *Journal of Abnormal Psychology*, 1966, *71*, 235–246.

Berkowitz, B. P., & Graziano, A. M. Training parents as behavior therapists: A review. *Behaviour Research and Therapy*, 1972, *10*, 297–317.

Berkowitz, P. H. Some psychological aspects of mental illness in children. *Genetic Psychology Monographs*, 1961, *63*, 103–148.

Berlyne, D. E. *Conflict, arousal and curiosity*. New York: McGraw-Hill, 1960.

Berlyne, D. E. Attention as a problem in behavior theory. In D. I. Mostofsky (Ed.), *Attention: Contemporary theory and analysis*. New York: Appleton-Century-Crofts, 1970, 25–49.

Bernal, M. Behavioral treatment of a child's eating problem. *Journal of Behaviour Therapy and Experimental Psychiatry*, 1972, *3*, 43–50.

Bettelheim, B. *The empty fortress*. New York: Free Press, 1967.

Bindman, S. S. Personality characteristics of the parents of children diagnosed as schizophrenic. *Dissertation Abstracts*, 1966, *27*, 298–299.

Birch, H. G., Belmont, L., Belmont, I., & Taft, L. T. Brain damage and intelligence in educable mentally subnormal children. *Journal of Nervous and Mental Disease*, 1967, *144*, 247–257.

Birch, H. G., & Gussow, G. D. *Disadvantaged children*. New York: Grune & Stratton, 1970.

Birnbrauer, J. S., Bijou, S. W., Wolf, M. M., & Kidder, J. D. Programed instruction in the classroom. In L. P. Ullmann & L. Krasner (Eds.), *Case studies in behavior modification*. New York: Holt, Rinehart & Winston, 1965, 358–363.

Birnbrauer, J. S., Wolf, M. M., Kidder, J. D., & Tague, C. E. Classroom behavior of retarded pupils with token reinforcement. *Journal of Experimental Child Psychology*, 1965, *2*, 219–235.

Bliss, E. L., & Branch, C. H. H. *Anorexia nervosa: Its history, psychology, and biology*. New York: Hoeber, 1960.

Blitzer, J. R., Rollins, N., & Blackwell, A. Children who starve themselves: Anorexia nervosa. *Psychosomatic Medicine*, 1961, *23*, 369–383.

Block, J., & Martin, B. Predicting the behavior of children under frustration. *Journal of Abnormal and Social Psychology*, 1955, *51*, 281–185.

Bollard, R. J., & Woodroffe, P. The effect of parent-administered dry-bed training on nocturnal enuresis in children. *Behaviour Research and Therapy*, 1977, *15*, 159–165.

Bornstein, M. R., Bellack, A. S., & Hersen, M. Social-skills training for unassertive children: A multiple-baseline analysis. *Journal of Applied Behavior Analysis*, 1977, *10*, 183–195.

Bradley, C. The behavior of children receiving benzedrine. *American Journal of Psychiatry*, 1937, *94*, 577–585.

Broden, M., Hall, R. V., & Mitts, B. The effect of self-recording on the classroom behavior of two eighth-grade students. *Journal of Applied Behavior Analysis*, 1971, *4*, 191–199.

Brown, J. L. Prognosis from symptoms of preschool children with atypical development. *American Journal of Orthopsychiatry*, 1960, *30*, 382–391.

Brown, P., & Elliott, R. Control of aggression in a nursery school class. *Journal of Experimental Child Psychology*, 1965, *2*, 103–107.

Browning, R. M. Treatment effects of a total behavior modification program with five autistic children. *Behaviour Research and Therapy*, 1971, *9*, 319–327.

Bruch, H. Conceptual confusion in eating disorders. *Journal of Nervous and Mental Disease*, 1961, *133*, 46–54.

Bruch, H. Perceptual and conceptual disturbances in anorexia nervosa. *Psychosomatic Medicine*, 1962, *24*, 187–194.

Buell, J., Stoddard, P., Harris, F. R., & Baer, D. M. Collateral social development accompanying reinforcement of outdoor play in a preschool child. *Journal of Applied Behavior Analysis*, 1968, *1*, 167–173.

Bugental, D. B., Whalen, C. K., & Henker, B. Causal attribution of hyperactive children and motivational assumptions of two behavior-change approaches: Evidence for an interactionist position. *Child Development*, 1977, *48*, 874–884.

Burchard, J., & Barrera, F. An analysis of time-out and response cost in a programmed environment. *Journal of Applied Behavior Analysis*, 1972, *5*, 271–282.

Burchard, J., & Tyler, V., Jr. The modification of delinquent behaviour through operant conditioning. *Behaviour Research and Therapy*, 1965, *2*, 245–250.

Camp, B. W., Blom, G. E., Hebert, F., & van Doorninck, W. J. "Think Aloud": A program for developing self-control in young aggressive boys. *Journal of Abnormal Child Psychology*, 1977, *5*, 157–169.

Campbell, S. B., Douglas, V. I., & Morgenstern, G. Cognitive styles in hyperactive children and the effect of methylphenidate. *Journal of Child Psychology and Psychiatry*, 1971, *12*, 55–67.

Caron, A. J. Conceptual transfer in preverbal children as a consequence of dimensional training. *Journal of Experimental Child Psychology*, 1968, *6*, 522–542.

Carr, E. G. The motivation of self-injurious behavior: A review of some hypotheses. *Psychological Bulletin*, 1977, *84*, 800–816.

Carr, E. G., Newsom, C. D., & Binkoff, J. A. Stimulus control of self-destructive behavior in a psychotic child. *Journal of Abnormal Child Psychology*, 1976, *4*, 139–153.

Carr, E. G., Schreibman, L., & Lovaas, O. I. Control of echolalic speech in psychotic children. *Journal of Abnormal Child Psychology*, 1975, *3*, 331–351.

Cattell, R. B. *Personality: A systematic theoretical and factual study.* New York: McGraw-Hill, 1950.

Chalfant, J. C., & Scheffelin, M. A. *Central processing dysfunctions in children: A review of research.* Bethesda, Md.: U.S. Department of Health, Education, and Welfare, 1969 (NINDS Monograph No. 9).

Clark, J. P., & Wenninger, E. P. Socio-economic class and area as correlates of illegal behavior among juveniles. *American Sociological Review*, 1962, *27*, 826–834.

Clausen, J. *Ability structure and subgroups in mental retardation.* New York: Spartan Books, 1966.

Clement, P. W., & Richard, R. C. Identifying reinforcers for children: A children's reinforcement survey. In E. J. Mash & L. G. Terdal (Eds.). *Behavior therapy assessment: Diagnosis, design, and evaluation.* New York: Springer, 1976. 207–216.

Clements, S. D. *Minimal brain dysfunction in children.* Washington, D.C.: U.S. Department of Health, Education, and Welfare 1966 (NINDM Monograph No. 3; USPHS Publication No. 1415).

Cloward, R., & Ohlin, L. *Delinquency and opportunity: A theory of delinquent gangs.* Glencoe, Ill.: Free Press, 1960.

Cohen, H. L., & Filipczak, J. *A new learning environment.* San Francisco, Calif.: Jossey-Bass, 1971.

Coleman, J. C., & Sandhu, M. A descriptive-relational study of 364 children referred to a university clinic for learning disorders. *Psychological Reports*, 1967, *20*, 1091–1105.

Colletti, G., & Harris, S. L. Behavior modification in the home: Siblings as behavior modifiers, parents as observers. *Journal of Abnormal Child Psychology*, 1977, *5*, 21–30.

Colwell, C. N., Richards, E., McCarver, R. B., & Ellis, N. R. Evaluation of self-help habit training. *Mental Retardation*, 1973, *11*, 14–18.

Compton, R. D. Changes in enuretics accompanying treatment by the conditioned response technique. *Dissertation Abstracts*, 1968, *28* (7-A), 2549.

Connerly, R. J. A comparison of personality characteristics for parents of brain-injured and normal children. *Dissertation Abstracts*, 1967, *28*, 1291–1292.

Conners, C. K. A teacher rating scale for use in drug studies with children. *American Journal of Psychiatry*, 1969, *126*, 884–888.

Conners, C. K. Symptom patterns in hyperkinetic, neurotic, and normal children. *Child Development*, 1970, *41*, 667–682.

Conroy, R. L., & Weener, P. The development of visual and auditory selective attention using the central-incidental paradigm. *Journal of Experimental Child Psychology*, 1976, *22*, 400–407.

Cowan, P. A., Hoddinott, B. A., & Wright, B. A. Compliance and resistance in the conditioning of autistic children: An exploratory study. *Child Development*, 1965, *36*, 913–923.

Cowan, P. A., & Walters, R. H. Studies of reinforcement of aggression: I. Effects of scheduling. *Child Development*, 1963, *34*, 543–551.

Crandall, V. C. Reinforcement effects of adult reactions and nonreactions on children's achievement expectations. *Child Development*, 1963, *34*, 335–354.

Creer, T. L. The use of time-out from positive reinforcement procedure with asthmatic children. *Journal of Psychosomatic Research*, 1970, *14*, 117–120.

Creer, T. L., Weinberg, E., & Molk, L. Managing a hospital behavior problem: Malingering. *Journal of Behaviour Therapy and Experimental Psychiatry*, 1974, *5*, 259–262.

Crinella, F. M. Identification of brain dysfunction syndromes in children through profile analysis: Patterns associated with so-called "minimal brain dysfunction." *Journal of Abnormal Psychology*, 1973, *82*, 33–45.

Croghan, L., & Musante, G. J. The elimination of a boy's high-building phobia by *in vivo* desensitization and game playing. *Journal of Behaviour Therapy and Experimental Psychiatry*, 1975, *6*, 87–88.

Croxen, M. E., & Lytton, H. Reading disability and difficulties in finger localization and right-left discrimination. *Developmental Psychology*, 1971, *5*, 256–262.

Dalton, A. J., Rubino, C. A., & Hislop, M. W. Some effects of token rewards on school achievement of children with Down's syndrome. *Journal of Applied Behavior Analysis*, 1973, *6*, 251–259.

Davison, G. C., Tsujimoto, R. N., & Glaros, A. G. Attribution and the maintenance of behavior change in falling asleep. *Journal of Abnormal Psychology*, 1973, *82*, 124–133.

Davison, G. C., & Valins, S. Maintenance of self-attributed and drug-attributed behavior change. *Journal of Personality and Social Psychology*, 1969, *11*, 25–33.

Davison, G. C., & Wilson, G. T. Processes of fear-reduction in systematic desensitization: Cognitive and social reinforcement factors in humans. *Behavior Therapy*, 1973, *4*, 1–21.

Davitz, J. L. The effects of previous training on post-frustration behavior. *Journal of Abnormal and Social Psychology*, 1952, *47*, 309–315.

DeLeon, G., & Mandell, W. A comparison of conditioning and psychotherapy in the treatment of functional enuresis. *Journal of Clinical Psychology*, 1966, *22*, 326–330.

DeMyer, M. K., Barton, S., DeMyer, W. E., Norton, J., Allen, J., & Steele, R. Prognosis in autism: A follow-up study. *Journal of Autism and Childhood Schizophrenia*, 1973, *3*, 199–246.

DesLauriers, A. M., & Carlson, C. F. *Your child is asleep: Early infantile autism, etiology, treatment, parental influences.* Homewood, Ill.: Dorsey, 1969.

De Villiers, J. G., & Naughton, J. M. Teaching a symbol language to autistic children. *Journal of Consulting and Clinical Psychology*, 1974, *42*, 111–117.

Dingman, H. F., & Tarjan, G. Mental retardation and the normal distribution curve. *American Journal of Mental Deficiency*, 1960, *64*, 991–994.

Doleys, D. M. Behavioral treatments for nocturnal enuresis in children: A review of the recent literature. *Psychological Bulletin*, 1977, *84*, 30–54.

Dollard, J., Doob, L. W., Miller, N. E., Mowrer, O. H., & Sears, R. R. *Frustration and aggression*. New Haven, Conn.: Yale University Press, 1939.

Douglas, V. I. Stop, look and listen: The problem of sustained attention and impulse control in hyperactive and normal children. *Canadian Journal of Behavioral Science*, 1972, *4*, 259–281.

Drabman, R., & Spitalnik, R. Training a retarded child as a behavioral teaching assistant. *Journal of Behaviour Therapy and Experimental Psychiatry*, 1973, *4*, 269–272.

Drabman, R. S., Spitalnik, R., & O'Leary, K. D. Teaching self-control to disruptive children. *Journal of Abnormal Psychology*, 1973, *82*, 10–16.

Dreger, R. M., Lewis, P. M., Rich, T. A., Miller, K. S., Reid, M. P., Overlade, D. C., Taffel, C., & Flemming, E. L. Behavioral classification project. *Journal of Consulting Psychology*, 1964, *28*, 1–13.

Dubey, D. R., Kent, R. N., O'Leary, S. G., Broderick, J. E., & O'Leary, K. D. Reaction of children and teachers to classroom observers: A series of controlled investigations. *Behavior Therapy*, 1977, *8*, 887–897.

Dykman, R. A., Ackerman, P. T., Clements, S. D., & Peters, J. E. Specific learning disabilities: An attentional deficit syndrome. In H. R. Myklebust (Ed.), *Progress in learning disabilities* (vol. 2). New York: Grune & Stratton, 1971, 56–93.

Eaton, L., & Menolascino, F. J. Psychotic reactions of childhood: A follow-up study. *American Journal of Orthopsychiatry*, 1967, *37*, 521–529.

Edelman, R. I. Operant conditioning treatment of encopresis. *Journal of Behaviour Therapy and Experimental Psychiatry*, 1971, *2*, 71–73.

Egeland, B. Training impulsive children in the use of more efficient scanning techniques. *Child Development*, 1974, *45*, 165–171.

Eisenberg, L. The autistic child in adolescence. *American Journal of Psychiatry*, 1956, *11*, 607–612.

Erickson, M. L., & Empey, L. T. Class position, peers and delinquency. *Sociology and Social Research*, 1965, *49*, 268–282.

Estes, W. K. *Learning theory and mental development*. New York: Academic Press, 1970.

Evans, B. A. A case of trichotillomania in a child treated in a home token program. *Journal of Behaviour Therapy and Experimental Psychiatry*, 1976, *7*, 197–198.

Eyberg, S. M., & Johnson, S. M. Multiple assessment of behavior modification with families: Effects of contingency contracting and order of treated problems. *Journal of Consulting and Clinical Psychology*, 1974, *42*, 594–606.

Eysenck, H. J. *The dynamics of anxiety and hysteria*. New York: Praeger, 1957.

Eysenck, H. J. (Ed.). *Behaviour therapy and the neuroses*. New York: Pergamon, 1960.

Fagot, B. I. Consequences of moderate cross-gender behavior in preschool chldren. *Child Development*, 1977, *48*, 902–907.

Feingold, B. F. *Why your child is hyperactive*. New York: Random House, 1975.

Ferster, C. B. Positive reinforcement and behavioral deficits of autistic children. *Child Development*, 1961, *32*, 437–456.

Ferster, C. B. Arbitrary and natural reinforcement. *Psychological Record*, 1967, *17*, 341–347.

Ferster, C. B., & DeMyer, M. K. A method for the experimental analysis of the behavior of autistic children. *American Journal of Orthopsychiatry*, 1962, *32*, 89–98.

Finley, W. W., Besserman, R. L., Bennett, L. F., Clapp, R. K., & Finley, P. M. The effect of continuous, intermittent, and "placebo" reinforcement on the effectiveness of the conditioning treatment for enuresis nocturna. *Behaviour Research and Therapy*, 1973, *11*, 289–297.

Firestone, P. The effects and side effects of timeout on an aggressive nursery school child. *Journal of Behaviour Therapy and Experimental Psychiatry*, 1976, *7*, 79–81.

Fixsen, D. L., Phillips, E. L., Phillips, E. A., & Wolf, M. M. The teaching-family model of group home treatment. Paper presented at the meeting of the American Psychological Association, Honolulu, Hawaii, September 1972.

Fixsen, D. L., Phillips, E. L., & Wolf, M. M. Achievement Place: The reliability of self-reporting and peer-reporting and their effects on behavior. *Journal of Applied Behavior Analysis*, 1972, *5*, 19–30.

Fixsen, D. L., Phillips, E. L., & Wolf, M. M. Achievement Place: Experiments in self-government with pre-delinquents. *Journal of Applied Behavior Analysis*, 1973, *6*, 31–47.

Flowers, J. V. Behavior modification of cheating in an elementary school student: A brief note. *Behavior Therapy*, 1972, *3*, 311–312.

Foxx, R. M. Attention training: The use of overcorrection avoidance to increase the eye contact of autistic and retarded children. *Journal of Applied Behavior Analysis*, 1977, *10*, 489–499.

Foxx, R. M., & Azrin, N. H. Dry pants: A rapid method of toilet training children. *Behaviour Research and Therapy*, 1973a, *11*, 435–442.

Foxx, R. M., & Azrin, N. H. The elimination of autistic self-stimulatory behavior by overcorrection. *Journal of Applied Behavior Analysis*, 1973b, *6*, 1–14.

Frith, U. Studies in pattern detection in normal and autistic children: I. Immediate recall of auditory sequences. *Journal of Abnormal Psychology*, 1970, *76*, 413–420.

Funkenstein, D. H., King, S. H., & Drolette, M. E. *Mastery of stress*. Cambridge, Mass.: Harvard University Press, 1957.

Gardner, R. A., & Gardner, B. T. Teaching sign language to a champanzee. *Science*, 1969, *165*, 664–672.

Garfinkel, P. E., Kline, S. A., & Stancer, H. C. Treatment of anorexia nervosa using operant conditioning techniques. *Journal of Nervous and Mental Disease*, 1973, *157*, 428–433.

Garmezy, N. The experimental study of children vulnerable to psychopathology. In A. Davids (Ed.), *Child personality and psychopathology: Current topics* (vol. 2). New York: Wiley, 1975, 171–216.

Garvey, W. P., & Hegrenes, J. R. Desensitization techniques in the treatment of school phobia. *American Journal of Orthopsychiatry*, 1966, *36*, 147–152.

Gelber, H., & Meyer, V. Behaviour therapy and encopresis: The complexities involved in treatment. *Behaviour Research and Therapy*, 1965, *2*, 227–231.

Gelfand, D. M., & Hartmann, D. P. Behavior therapy with children: A review and evaluation of research methodology. *Psychological Bulletin*, 1968, *69*, 204–215.

Gelfand, D. M., & Hartmann, D. P. *Child behavior analysis and therapy*. New York: Pergamon, 1975.

Gersten, J. C., Langner, T. S., Eisenberg, J. G., Simcha-Fagan, O., & McCarthy, E. D.

Stability and change in types of behavioral disturbance in children and adolescents. *Journal of Abnormal Child Psychology*, 1976, *4*, 111–127.

Gesell, A. The conditioned reflex and the psychiatry of infancy. *American Journal of Orthopsychiatry*, 1938, *8*, 19–29.

Gilbert, G. M. A survey of "referral problems" in metropolitan child guidance centers. *Journal of Clinical Psychology*, 1957, *13*, 37–42.

Giles, D. K., & Wolf, M. M. Toilet training institutionalized severe retardates: An application of operant behavior modification techniques. *American Journal of Mental Deficiency*, 1966, *70*, 766–780.

Gittelman-Klein, R., Klein, D. F., Abikoff, H., Katz, S., Gloisten, A. C., & Kates, W. Relative efficacy of methylphenidate and behavior modification in hyperkinetic children: An interim report. *Journal of Abnormal Child Psychology*, 1976, *4*, 361–379.

Glogower, F., & Sloop, E. W. Two strategies of group training of parents as effective behavior modifiers. *Behavior Therapy*, 1976, *7*, 177–184.

Glueck, S., & Glueck, E. *Unraveling juvenile delinquency*. Cambridge, Mass.: Harvard University Press, 1950.

Glueck, S., & Glueck, E. *Predicting delinquency and crime*. Cambridge, Mass.: Harvard University Press, 1959.

Glueck, S., & Glueck, E. *Family environment and delinquency*. Boston: Houghton Mifflin, 1962.

Goldfarb, W. *Childhood schizophrenia*. Cambridge, Mass.: Harvard University Press, 1961.

Goldfarb, W. Childhood psychosis. In P. H. Mussen (Ed.), *Carmichael's manual of child psychology* (3d ed.), vol. 2. New York: Wiley, 1970, 765–830.

Goldiamond, I., & Dyrud, J. E. Reading as operant behavior. In J. Money (Ed.), *The disabled reader: Education of the dyslexic child*. Baltimore, Md.: Johns Hopkins, 1966, 93–115.

Goldstein, K. *Aftereffects of brain-injury in war*. New York: Grune & Stratton, 1942.

Gottman, J. M. Toward a definition of social isolation in children. *Child Development*, 1977, *48*, 513–517.

Gottman, J., Gonso, J., & Schuler, P. Teaching social skills to isolated children. *Journal of Abnormal Child Psychology*, 1976, *4*, 179–197.

Gray, R. M., & Kasteler, J. M. The effects of social reinforcement and training on institutionalized mentally retarded children. *American Journal of Mental Deficiency*, 1969, *74*, 50–56.

Graziano, A. M. Introduction: Behavior therapy with children. In A. M. Graziano (Ed.). *Behavior therapy with children, II*. Chicago, Ill.: Aldine, 1975, 1–38.

Grossman, H. (Ed.). *Manual on terminology and classification in mental retardation, 1973 revision*. Washington, D.C.: American Association on Mental Deficiency, 1973.

Group for the Advancement of Psychiatry. Psychopathological disorders in childhood: Theoretical considerations and a proposed classification. *GAP Report* No. 62, 1966.

Hagen, J. W., & Hale, G. A. The development of attention in children. In A. D. Pick (Ed.), *Minnesota symposia on child psychology* (vol. 7), Minneapolis, Minn.: University of Minnesota Press, 1973, 117–140.

Hagen, J. W., Winsberg, B., & Wolff, P. Cognitive and linguistic deficits in psychotic children. *Child Development*, 1968, *39*, 1103–1117.

Hallsten, E. A., Jr. Adolescent anorexia nervosa treated by desensitization. *Behaviour Research and Therapy*, 1965, *3*, 87–91.

Hampe, E., Noble, H., Miller, L. C., & Barrett, C. L. Phobic children one and two years posttreatment. *Journal of Abnormal Psychology*, 1973, *82*, 446–453.

Haring, N. G., & Bateman, B. D. Introduction. In *Minimal brain dysfunction in children*. U.S. Public Health Service Publication No. 2015. Washington, D.C.: U.S. Department of Health, Education and Welfare, 1969, 1–4.

Hawkins, R. P., Peterson, R. F., Schweid, E., & Bijou, S. W. Behavior therapy in the home: Amelioration of problem parent-child relations with the parent in a therapeutic role. *Journal of Experimental Child Psychology*, 1966, *4*, 99–107.

Heber, R. F. A manual on terminology and classification in mental retardation. *American Journal of Mental Deficiency*, 1959, *64*. Monograph Supplement (rev. ed., 1961).

Heiman, J. R., Fischer, M. J., & Ross, A. O. A supplementary behavioral program to improve deficient reading performance. *Journal of Abnormal Child Psychology*, 1973, *1*, 390–399.

Heller, K. M. Conceptual sorting and childhood schizophrenia. *Dissertation Abstracts*, 1966, *26*, 6168.

Herbert, E. W., Pinkston, E. M., Hayden, M. L., Sajwaj, T. E., Pinkston, S., Cordua, G., & Jackson, C. Adverse effects of differential parental attention. *Journal of Applied Behavior Analysis*, 1973, *6*, 15–30.

Hermelin, B., & O'Connor, N. Visual imperception in psychotic children. *British Journal of Psychology*, 1965, *56*, 455–460.

Hermelin, B., & O'Connor, N. Perceptual and motor discrimination in psychotic and normal children. *Journal of Genetic Psychology*, 1967, *110*, 117–125.

Hersen, M. Behavior modification approach to a school-phobia case. *Journal of Clinical Psychology*, 1970, *20*, 395–402.

Hersen, M., & Bellack, A. (Eds.). *Behavioral assessment: A practical handbook*. Elmsford, N.Y.: Pergamon, 1976.

Hetherington, E. M. A developmental study of the effects of sex of the dominant parent on sex-role preference, identification, and imitation in children. *Journal of Personality and Social Psychology*, 1965, *2*, 188–194.

Hewett, F. M. Teaching speech to an autistic child through operant conditioning. *American Journal of Orthopsychiatry*, 1965, *35*, 927–936.

Hewett, F. M., Mayhew, D., & Rabb, E. An experimental reading program for neurologically impaired, mentally retarded, and severely emotionally disturbed children. *American Journal of Orthopsychiatry*, 1967, *37*, 35–48.

Hewitt, L. E., & Jenkins, R. L. *Fundamental patterns of maladjustment: The dynamics of their origin*. Springfield, Ill.: State of Illinois, 1946.

Hill, J. H., Liebert, R. M., & Mott, D. E. Vicarious extinction of avoidance behavior through films: An initial test. *Psychological Reports*, 1968, *22*, 192.

Hobbs, N. *The futures of children: Categories, labels, and their consequences*. San Francisco, Calif.: Jossey-Bass, 1975.

Hobbs, T. R., & Holt, M. M. The effect of token reinforcement on the behavior of delinquents in cottage settings. *Journal of Applied Behavior Analysis*, 1976, *9*, 189–198.

Hoffman, M. L. Moral development. In P. H. Mussen (Ed.), *Carmichael's manual of child psychology* (3d ed.), vol. 2. New York: Wiley, 1970, 261–359.

Holland, C. J. An interview guide for behavioral counseling with parents. *Behavior Therapy*, 1970, *1*, 70–79.

Hollenberg, E., & Sperry, M. Some antecedents of aggression and effects of frustration in doll play. *Journal of Personality*, 1951, *1*, 32–43.

Hops, H., & Walters, R. H. Studies of reinforcement of aggression: II. Effects of emotionally-arousing antecedent conditions. *Child Development*, 1963, *34*, 553–562.

Horton, L. E. Generalization of aggressive behavior in adolescent delinquent boys. *Journal of Applied Behavior Analysis*, 1970, *3*, 205–211.

Hundziak, M., Maurer, R. A., & Watson, L. S., Jr. Operant conditioning in toilet training of several mentally retarded boys. *American Journal of Mental Deficiency*, 1965, *70*, 120–124.

Hutt, S. J., Hutt, C., Lee, D., & Ornsted, C. A behavioural and electroencephalographic study of autistic children. *Journal of Psychiatric Research*, 1965, *3*, 181–197.

Hutzell, R. R., Platzek, D., & Logue, P. E. Control of symptoms of Giles de la Tourette's syndrome by self-monitoring. *Journal of Behaviour Therapy and Experimental Psychiatry*, 1974, *5*, 71–76.

Irwin, O. C. The amount and nature of activities of newborn infants under constant external stimulating conditions during the first ten days of life. *Genetic Psychology Monographs*, 1930, *8*, 1–92.

Ivanov-Smolenski, A. G. Neurotic behavior and teaching of conditioned reflexes. *American Journal of Psychiatry*, 1927, *7*, 483–488.

James, L. E., & Foreman, M. E. A-B status of behavior therapy technicians as related to success of Mowrer's conditioning treatment for enuresis. *Journal of Consulting and Clinical Psychology*, 1973, *41*, 224–229.

Jenkins, R. L., & Hewitt, L. Types of personality structure encountered in child guidance clinics. *American Journal of Orthopsychiatry*, 1944, *14*, 84–94.

John, E. R., Karmel, B. Z., Prichep, L. S., Ahn, H., & John, M. Neurometrics applied to the quantitative electrophysiological measurement of organic brain dysfunction in children. In C. Shagass, S. Gershon, & A. Friedhoff (Eds.), *Psychopathology and brain dysfunction*. New York: Raven, 1977, 299–337.

Johnson, C. A., & Katz, C. Using parents as change agents for their children. A review. *Journal of Child Psychology and Psychiatry*, 1973, *14*, 181–200.

Johnston, J. M. Punishment of human behavior. *American Psychologist*, 1972, *27*, 1033–1054.

Joint Commission on Mental Health of Children. *Crisis in child mental health: Challenge for the 1970s*. New York: Harper & Row, 1970.

Jones, H. G. The behavioral treatment of enuresis nocturna. In H. J. Eysenck (Ed.), *Behaviour therapy and the neuroses*. London: Pergamon, 1960, 377–403.

Jones, M. C. A laboratory study of fear: The case of Peter. *Pedagocial Seminary*, 1924*a*, *31*, 308–315.

Jones, M. C. The elimination of children's fears. *Journal of Experimental Psychology*, 1924*b*, *7*, 383–390.

Jurkovik, G. J., & Prentice, N. M. Relation of moral and cognitive development to dimensions of juvenile delinquency. *Journal of Abnormal Psychology*, 1977, *86*, 414–420.

Kagan, J. Reflection-impulsivity: The generality of conceptual tempo. *Journal of Abnormal Psychology*, 1966, *71*, 17–24.

Kagan, J., Pearson, L., & Welch, L. The modification of an impulsive tempo. *Journal of Educational Psychology*, 1966, *57*, 359–365.

Kallman, F. J., & Roth, B. Genetic aspects of preadolescent schizophrenia. *American Journal of Psychiatry*, 1956, *112*, 599–606.

Kanfer, F. H. Issues and ethics in behavior manipulation. *Psychological Reports*, 1965, *16*, 187–196.

Kanfer, F. H., Karoly, P., & Newman, A. Reduction of children's fear of the dark by competence-related and situational threat-related verbal cues. *Journal of Consulting and Clinical Psychology*, 1975, *43*, 251–258.

Kanfer, F. H., & Phillips, J. S. Behavior therapy: A panacea for all ills or a passing fancy? *Archives of General Psychiatry*, 1966, *15*, 114–128.

Kanner, L. Autistic disturbances of affective contact. *Nervous Child*, 1943, *2*, 217–240.

Kanner, L. The specificity of early infantile autism. *Zeitschrift für Kinderpsychiatrie*, 1958, *25*, 108–113.

Kaspar, J. C., Millichap, J. G., Backus, R., Child, D., & Schulman, J. L. A study of the relationship between neurological evidence of brain damage in children and activity and distractibility. *Journal of Consulting and Clinical Psychology*, 1971, *36*, 329–337.

Kazdin, A. E. *The token economy: A review and evaluation.* New York: Plenum, 1977.

Keeley, S. M., Shemberg, K. M., & Carbonell, J. Operant clinical intervention: Behavior management or beyond? Where are the data? *Behavior Therapy*, 1976, *7*, 292–305.

Keller, M. F., & Carlson, P. M. The use of symbolic modeling to promote social skills in preschool children with low levels of social responsiveness. *Child Development*, 1974, *45*, 912–919.

Kelly, G. *The psychology of personal constructs.* New York: Norton, 1955.

Kennedy, W. A. School phobia: Rapid treatment of fifty cases. *Journal of Abnormal Psychology*, 1965, *70*, 285–289.

Kent, R. N., & Foster, S. L. Direct observational procedures: Methodological issues in naturalistic settings. In A. R. Ciminero, K. S. Calhoun, & H. E. Adams (Eds.), *Handbook of behavioral assessment.* New York: Wiley, 1977, 279–328.

Kent, R. N., Kanowitz, J., O'Leary, K. D., & Cheiken, M. Observer reliability as a function of circumstances of assessment. *Journal of Applied Behavior Analysis*, 1977, *10*, 317–324.

Kent, R. N., & O'Leary, K. D. A controlled evaluation of behavior modification with conduct problem children. *Journal of Consulting and Clinical Psychology*, 1976, *44*, 586–596.

Kent, R. N., & O'Leary, K. D. Treatment of conduct problem children: BA and/or PhD therapists. *Behavior Therapy*, 1977, *8*, 653–658.

Kent, R. N., O'Leary, K. D., Diament, C., & Dietz, A. Expectation biases in observational evaluation of therapeutic change. *Journal of Consulting and Clinical Psychology*, 1974, *42*, 774–780.

Kephart, N. C. *The slow learner in the classroom.* Columbus, Ohio: Merrill, 1960.

Kessler, J. W., *Psychopathology of childhood.* Englewood Cliffs, N.J.: Prentice-Hall, 1966.

Kimmel, H. D. Instrumental conditioning of autonomically mediated responses in human beings. *American Psychologist*, 1974, *29*, 325–335.

Kimmel, H. D., & Kimmel, E. An instrumental conditioning method for the treatment of enuresis. *Journal of Behaviour Therapy and Experimental Psychiatry*, 1970, *1*, 121–122.

Kingsley, R. F. Associative learning ability in educable mentally retarded children. *American Journal of Mental Deficiency*, 1968, *73*, 5–8.

Kingsley, R. G., & Shapiro, J. A comparison of three behavioral programs for the control of obesity in children. *Behavior Therapy*, 1977, *8*, 30–36.

Klebanoff, L. B. Parents of schizophrenic children: I. Parental attitudes of mothers of schizophrenic, brain-injured and retarded, and normal children. *American Journal of Orthopsychiatry*, 1959, *29*, 445–454.

Koegel, R. L., & Rincover, A. Treatment of psychotic children in a classroom environment: I. Learning in a large group. *Journal of Applied Behavior Analysis*, 1974, *7*, 45–59.

Koegel, R. L., & Rincover, A. Some detrimental effects of using extra stimuli to guide learning in normal and autistic children. *Journal of Abnormal Child Psychology*, 1976, *4*, 59–71.

Koegel, R. L., & Schreibman, L. Teaching autistic children to respond to simultaneous multiple cues. *Journal of Experimental Child Psychology*, 1977, *24*, 299–311.

Koegel, R. L., & Wilhelm, H. Selective responding to the components of multiple visual cues by autistic children. *Journal of Experimental Child Psychology*, 1973, *15*, 442–453.

Koenigsberg, R. S. An evaluation of visual versus sensorimotor methods for improving orientation discrimination for letter reversal by preschool children. *Child Development*, 1973, *44*, 764–769.

Kohlberg, L. Development of moral character and moral ideology. In M. Hoffman & L. W. Hoffman (Eds.), *Review of child development research* (vol. 1). New York: Russell Sage, 1964, 383–431.

Kohlenberg, R. J. The punishment of persistent vomiting. *Journal of Applied Behavior Analysis*, 1970, *3*, 241–245.

Kohlenberg, R. J. Operant conditioning of human anal sphincter pressure. *Journal of Applied Behavior Analysis*, 1973, *6*, 201–208.

Kohn, M. Congruent competence and symptom factors in the preschool child. Paper presented at the meeting of the American Psychological Association, Washington, D.C., September 1969.

Kohn, M. *Social competence, symptoms and underachievement in childhood: A longitudinal perspective*. Washington, D.C.: Winston, 1977.

Kohn, M., & Rosman, B. L. A social competence scale and symptom checklist for the preschool child: Factor dimensions, their cross-instrument generality, and longitudinal persistence. *Developmental Psychology*, 1972a, *6*, 430–444.

Kohn, M., & Rosman, B. L. Relationship of pre-school social-emotional functioning to later intellectual achievement. *Developmental Psychology*, 1972b, *6*, 445–452.

Kohn, M., & Rosman, B. L. Cross-situational and longitudinal stability of social-emotional functioning in young children. *Child Development*, 1973, *44*, 721–727.

Koocher, G. P. (Ed.). *Children's rights and the mental health professions*. New York: Wiley, 1976.

Kornhaber, R. C., & Schroeder, H. E. Importance of model similarity on extinction of avoidance behavior in children. *Journal of Consulting and Clinical Psychology*, 1975, *43*, 601–607.

Krasner, L. The therapist as a social reinforcement machine. In H. H. Strupp & L. Luborsky (Eds.), *Research in psychotherapy* (vol. 2). Washington, D.C.: American Psychological Association, 1962.

Krasner, L. Behavior control and social responsibility. *American Psychologist*, 1964, *17*, 199–204.

Krasner, L. Behavior modification: Ethical issues and future trends. In H. Leitenberg (Ed.), *Handbook of behavior modification and behavior therapy*. Englewood Cliffs, N.J.: Prentice-Hall, 1976, 627–649.

Krasnogorski, N. I. The conditioned reflex and children's neuroses. *American Journal of Diseases of Children*, 1925, *30*, 753–768.

Krumboltz, J. D., & Krumboltz, H. B. *Changing children's behavior*. Englewood Cliffs, N.J.: Prentice-Hall, 1972.

Lahey, B. B., McNees, M. P., & McNees, M. C. Control of an obscene "verbal tic" through timeout in an elementary school classroom. *Journal of Applied Behavior Analysis*, 1973, *6*, 101–104.

Lal, H., & Lindsley, O. R. Therapy of chronic constipation in a young child by rearranging social contingencies. *Behaviour Research and Therapy*, 1968, *6*, 484–485.

Lang, P. J., & Melamed, B. G. Avoidance conditioning therapy of an infant with chronic ruminative vomiting: Case report. *Journal of Abnormal Psychology*, 1969, *74*, 1–8.

Langhorne, J. E., Jr., Loney, J., Paternite, C. E., & Bechtoldt, H. P. Childhood hyperkinesis: A return to the source. *Journal of Abnormal Psychology*, 1976, *85*, 201–209.

Lapouse, R., & Monk, M. A. Fears and worries in a representative sample of children. *American Journal of Orthopsychiatry*, 1959, *29*, 803–818.

Lapouse, R., & Monk, M. A. Behavior deviations in a representative sample of children: Variation by sex, age, race, social class and family size. *American Journal of Orthopsychiatry*, 1964, *34*, 436–446.

Laufer, M. W., & Denhoff, E. Hyperkinetic behavior syndrome in children. *Journal of Pediatrics*, 1957, *50*, 463–474.

Lavigueur, H. The use of siblings as an adjunct to the behavioral treatment of children in the home with parents as therapists. *Behavior Therapy*, 1976, *7*, 602–613.

Lazarus, A. A. The elimination of children's phobias by deconditioning. *Medical Proceedings of South Africa*, 1959, *5*, 261–265.

Lazarus, A. A., & Abramovitz, A. The use of "emotive imagery" in the treatment of children's phobias. In L. P. Ullman & L. Krasner (Eds.), *Case studies in behavior modification*. New York: Holt, Reinhart & Winston, 1965, 300–304.

Lazarus, A. A., Davison, G. C., & Polefka, D. A. Classical and operant factors in the treatment of a school phobia. *Journal of Abnormal Psychology*, 1965, *70*, 225–229.

Lefkowitz, M. M., & Burton, N. Childhood depression: A critique of the concept. *Psychological Bulletin*, 1978, *85*, 716–726.

Leitenberg, H., Agras, S., Butz, R., & Wincze, J. Relationship between heart rate and behavioral change during the treatment of phobias. *Journal of Abnormal Psychology*, 1971, *78*, 59–68.

Leitenberg, H., Agras, W. S., & Thomson, L. E. A sequential analysis of the effect of selective positive reinforcement in modifying anorexia nervosa. *Behaviour Research and Therapy*, 1968, *6*, 211–218.

Leitenberg, H., & Callahan, E. J. Reinforced practice and reduction of different kinds of fears in adults and children. *Behaviour Research and Therapy*, 1973, *11*, 19–30.

Levitt, E. E. The results of psychotherapy with children: An evaluation. *Journal of Consulting Psychology*, 1957, *21*, 189–196.

Levitt, E. E. Psychotherapy with children: A further evaluation. *Behaviour Research and Therapy*, 1963, *1*, 45–51.

Lewis, W. W. Continuity and intervention in emotional disturbance: A review. *Exceptional Children*, 1965, *31*, 465–475.

Lichstein, K. L., & Schreibman, L. Employing electric shock with autistic children. *Journal of Autism and Childhood Schizophrenia*, 1976, *6*, 163–174.

Liebert, R. M., Hanratty, M., & Hill, J. H. Effects of rule structure and training method on the adoption of a self-imposed standard. *Child Development*, 1969, *40*, 93–101.

Liebert, R. M., & Ora, J. P., Jr. Children's adoption of self-reward patterns: Incentive level and method of transmission. *Child Development*, 1968, *39*, 537–544.

Liebert, R. M., & Schwartzberg, N. S. Effects of mass media. *Annual Review of Psychology*, 1977, *28*, 141–173.

Lipinski, D., & Nelson, R. Problems in the use of naturalistic observations as a means of behavioral assessment. *Behavior Therapy*, 1974a, *5*, 341–351.

Lipinski, D., & Nelson, R. The reactivity and unreliability of self-recording. *Journal of Consulting and Clinical Psychology*, 1974b, *42*, 118–123.

Lipton, E. L., Steinschneider, A., & Richmond, J. B. Psychophysiologic disorders in children. In L. W. Hoffman & M. L. Hoffman (Eds.), *Review of child development research* (vol. 2). New York: Russell Sage, 1966, 169–220.

Lobitz, G. K., & Johnson, S. M. Normal versus deviant children: A multimethod comparison. *Journal of Abnormal Child Psychology*, 1975, *3*, 353–374.

Lorr, M., & Jenkins, R. L. Patterns of maladjustment in children. *Journal of Clinical Psychology*, 1953, *9*, 16–23.

Lovaas, O. I. Effect of exposure to symbolic aggression on aggressive behavior. *Child Development*, 1961a, *32*, 37–44.

Lovaas, O. I. Interaction between verbal and nonverbal behavior. *Child Development*, 1961b, *32*, 329–336.

Lovaas, O. I. A program for the establishment of speech in psychotic children. In J. K. Wing (Ed.), *Early childhood autism*. Oxford: Pergamon, 1966, 115–144.

Lovaas, O. I. *The autistic child: Language development through behavior modification.* New York: Irvington, 1977.

Lovaas, O. I., Freitag, G., Gold, V. J., and Kassorla, I. C. Experimental studies in childhood schizophrenia: Analysis of self-destructive behavior. *Journal of Experimental Child Psychology*, 1965, *2*, 67–84.

Lovaas, O. I., Freitag, G., Kinder, M. I., Rubenstein, B. D., Schaeffer, B., & Simmons, J. Q. Establishment of social reinforcers in two schizophrenic children on the basis of food. *Journal of Experimental Child Psychology*, 1966, *4*, 109–125.

Lovaas, O. I., Freitas, L., Nelson, K., & Whalen, C. The establishment of imitation and its use for the development of complex behavior in schizophrenic children. *Behaviour Research and Therapy*, 1967, *5*, 171–181.

Lovaas, O. I., Koegel, R., Simmons, J. Q., & Long, J. S. Some generalization and follow-up measures on autistic children in behavior therapy. *Journal of Applied Behavior Analysis*, 1973, *6*, 131–166.

Lovaas, O. I., & Newsom, C. D. Behavior modification with psychotic children. In H. Leitenberg (Ed.), *Handbook of behavior modification and behavior therapy*. Englewood Cliffs, N.J.: Prentice-Hall, 1976, 303–360.

Lovaas, O. I., Schaeffer, B., & Simmons, J. Q. Building social behavior in autistic children by use of electric shock. *Journal of Experimental Research in Personality*, 1965, *1*, 99–109.

Lovaas, O. I., & Schreibman, L. Stimulus overselectivity of autistic children in a two stimulus situation. *Behaviour Research and Therapy*, 1971, *9*, 305–310.

Lovaas, O. I., Schreibman, L., & Koegel, R. L. A behavior modification approach to the treatment of autistic children. *Journal of Autism and Childhood Schizophrenia*, 1974, *4*, 111–129.

Lovaas, O. I., Schreibman, L., Koegel, R., & Rehm, R. Selective responding by autistic children to multiple sensory input. *Journal of Abnormal Psychology*, 1971, *77*, 211–222.

Lovaas, O. I., & Simmons, J. Q. Manipulation of self-destruction in three retarded children. *Journal of Applied Behavior Analysis*, 1969, *2*, 143–157.

Lovaas, O. I., Young, D. B., & Newsom, C. D. Childhood psychosis: Behavioral treatment. In B. B. Wolman, J. Egan, & A. O. Ross (Eds.), *Handbook of treatment of mental disorders in childhood and adolescence*. Englewood Cliffs, N.J.: Prentice-Hall, 1978, 385–420.

Lovibond, S. H. The mechanism of conditioning treatment of enuresis. *Behaviour Research and Therapy*, 1963, *1*, 17–21.

Lovibond, S. H. *Conditioning and enuresis*. Oxford: Pergamon, 1964.

Lovitt, T. C. Assessment of children with learning disabilities. *Exceptional Children*, 1967, *34*, 233–239.

Luckey, R. E., Watson, C. M., & Musick, J. K. Aversive conditioning as a means of inhibiting vomiting and rumination. *American Journal of Mental Deficiency*, 1968, *7*, 139–142.

McCarthy, J. J., & McCarthy, J. F. *Learning disabilities*. Boston, Mass.: Allyn & Bacon, 1969.

McCord, W., & McCord, J. *Origins of crime: A new evaluation of the Cambridge-Somerville youth study*. New York: Columbia University Press, 1959.

McDermott, J. F., Jr., Harrison, S. I., Schrager, J., Lindy, J., & Killins, E. Social class and mental illness in children: The question of childhood psychosis. *American Journal of Orthopsychiatry*, 1967, *37*, 548–557.

MacDonald, M. L. Multiple impact behavior therapy in a child's dog phobia. *Journal of Behaviour Therapy and Experimental Psychiatry*, 1975, *6*, 317–322.

MacDonough, T. S., & Forehand, R. Response-contingent time out: Important parameters in behavior modification with children. *Journal of Behaviour Therapy and Experimental Psychiatry*, 1973, *4*, 231–236.

MacFarlane, J. W., Allen, L., & Honzik, M. P. *A developmental study of behavior problems of normal children between 21 months and 14 years*. Berkeley, Calif.: University of California Press, 1954.

McNamara, J. J. Hyperactivity in the apartment bound child. *Clinical Pediatrics*, 1972, *11*, 371–372.

Mallick, S. K., & McCandless, B. R. A study of catharsis of aggression. *Journal of Personality and Social Psychology*, 1966, *4*, 591–596.

Marchant, R., Howling, P., Yule, W., & Rutter, M. Graded change in the treatment of the behaviour of autistic children. *Journal of Child Psychology and Psychiatry*, 1974, *15*, 221–227.

Martin, B. The assessment of anxiety by physiological behavioral measures. *Psychological Bulletin*, 1961, *58*, 234–255.

Mash, E. J., & Terdal, L. G. (Eds.). *Behavior-therapy assessment: Diagnosis, design, and evaluation*. New York: Springer, 1976.

Masland, R. L., Sarason, S. B., & Gladwin, T. *Mental subnormality*. New York: Basic Books, 1958.

Masters, J. C., & Miller, D. E. Early infantile autism: A methodological critique. *Journal of Abnormal Psychology*, 1970, *75*, 342–343.

Mednick, S. A. Breakdown in individuals at high risk for schizophrenia: Possible predispositional perinatal factors. *Mental Hygiene*, 1970, *54*, 50–63.

Mednick, S. A., & Schulsinger, F. Some premorbid characteristics related to breakdown in children with schizophrenic mothers. *Journal of Psychiatric Research*, 1968, *6*, 267–291.

Mednick, S. A., Schulsinger, H., & Schulsinger, F. Schizophrenia in children of schizophrenic mothers. In A. Davids (Ed.), *Child personality and psychopathology: Current topics* (vol. 2). New York: Wiley, 1975, 217–252.

Meichenbaum, D. H., *Cognitive-behavior modification: An integrative approach*. New York: Plenum, 1977.

Meichenbaum, D. H., & Goodman, J. Training impulsive chlidren to talk to themselves: A means of developing self-control. *Journal of Abnormal Psychology*, 1971, *77*, 115–126.

Metz, J. R. Conditioning generalized imitation in autistic children. *Journal of Experimental Child Psychology*, 1965, *2*, 389–399.

Metz, J. R. Stimulation level preferences of autistic children. *Journal of Abnormal Psychology*, 1967, *72*, 529–535.

Miller, L. C. Dimensions of psychopathology in middle childhood. *Psychological Reports*, 1967a, *21*, 897–903.

Miller, L. C. Louisville Behavior Check List for males, 6–12 years of age. *Psychological Reports*, 1967b, *21*, 885–896.

Miller, L. C. Pittsburgh Adjustment Survey Scales: A Cross Validation and Normative Study. Unpublished manuscript, University of Louisville, 1968.

Miller, L. C. *School behavior checklist—Manual*. Los Angeles, Calif.: Western Psychological Services, 1977.

Miller, L. C., Barrett, C. L., Hampe, E., & Noble, H. Comparison of reciprocal inhibition, psychotherapy, and waiting list control for phobic children. *Journal of Abnormal Psychology*, 1972a, *79*, 269–279.

Miller, L. C., Barrett, C. L., Hampe, E., & Noble, H. Factor structure of childhood fears. *Journal of Consulting and Clinical Psychology*, 1972b, *39*, 264–268.

Miller, L. C., Hampe, E., Barrett, C. L., & Noble, H. Children's deviant behavior within the general population. *Journal of Consulting and Clinical Psychology*, 1971, *37*, 16–22.

Miller, S. J., & Sloane, H. N., Jr. The generalization effects of parent training across stimulus settings. *Journal of Applied Behavior Analysis*, 1976, *9*, 355–370.

Miller, W. B. Lower class culture as a generating milieu of gang delinquency. *Journal of Social Issues*, 1958, *14*, 5–19.

Minde, K., Webb, G., & Sykes, D. Studies on the hyperactive child VI—Prenatal and paranatal factors associated with hyperactivity. *Developmental Medicine and Child Neurology*, 1968, *10*, 355–363.

Mischel, W. Preference for delayed reinforcement and social responsibility. *Journal of Abnormal and Social Psychology*, 1961, *62*, 1–7.

Mischel, W. Theory and research on the antecedents of self-imposed delay or reward. In B. A. Maher (Ed.), *Progress in experimental personality research* (vol. 3). New York: Academic Press, 1966, 85–132.

Mischel, W. *Personality and assessment*. New York: Wiley, 1968.

Mischel, W. Toward a cognitive social learning reconceptualization of personality. *Psychological Review*, 1973, *80*, 252–283.

Mischel, W., & Gilligan, C. Delay of gratification, motivation for the prohibited gratification, and responses to temptation. *Journal of Abnormal and Social Psychology*, 1964, *69*, 411–417.

Mischel, W., & Liebert, R. M. The role of power in the adoption of self-reward patterns. *Child Development*, 1967, *38*, 673–683.

Mischel, W., & Metzner, R. Preference for delayed reward as a function of age, intelligence, and length of delay interval. *Journal of Abnormal and Social Psychology*, 1962, *64*, 425–431.

Moore, D. J., & Shiek, D. A. Toward a theory of early infantile autism. *Psychological Review*, 1971, *78*, 451–456.

Morgan, S. B. Responsiveness to stimulus novelty and complexity in mild, moderate and severe retardates. *American Journal of Mental Deficiency*, 1969, *74*, 32–38.

Morris, R. J. *Behavior modification with children: A systematic guide*. Cambridge, Mass.: Winthrop, 1976.

Morrison, D., Miller, D., & Mejia, B. Effects of adult verbal requests on the behavior of autistic children. *American Journal of Mental Deficiency*, 1971, *75*, 510–518.

Morrison, J. R., & Stewart, M. A. Bilateral inheritance as evidence for polygenicity in the hyperactive child syndrome. *Journal of Nervous and Mental Disease*, 1974, *158*, 226–228.

Mowrer, O. H. Two-factor learning theory: Summary and comment. *Psychological Review*, 1951, *58*, 350–354.

Mowrer, O. H., & Mowrer, W. M. Enuresis—A method for its study and treatment. *American Journal of Orthopsychiatry*, 1938, *8*, 436–459.

Nedelman, D., & Sulzbacher, S. I. Dicky at 13 years of age: A long-term success following early application of operant conditioning procedures. In G. Semb (Ed.), *Behavior analysis and education*. Lawrence, Kans.: University of Kansas Press, 1972, 3–10.

Nelson, R. O. The use of intelligence tests within behavioral assessment. Paper presented at the meeting of the American Psychological Association, Chicago, Ill., September 1975.

Newsom, C. D., & Lovaas, O. I. Studies of overselective attention in autistic children. Paper presented at the meeting of the American Psychological Association, Montreal, Canada, August 1973.

Ney, P. G. Four types of hyperkinesis. *Canadian Psychiatric Association Journal*, 1974, *19*, 543–550.

Nisbett, R. E., & Valins, S. *Perceiving the causes of one's own behavior*. New York: General Learning Press, 1971.

Nolan, J. D., Mattis, P. R., & Holliday, W. C. Long-term effects of behavior therapy: A 12-month follow-up. *Journal of Abnormal Psychology*, 1970, *76*, 88–92.

Nordquist, V. M., & Wahler, R. G. Naturalistic treatment of an autistic child. *Journal of Applied Behavior Analysis*, 1973, *6*, 79–87.

Novick, J. Symptomatic treatment of acquired and persistent enuresis. *Journal of Abnormal Psychology*, 1966, *71*, 363–368.

Novick, J., Rosenfeld, E., Bloch, D. A., & Dawson, D. Ascertaining deviant behavior in children. *Journal of Consulting Psychology*, 1966, *30*, 230–238.

Nye, F. I. *Family relationships and juvenile delinquency*. New York: Wiley, 1958.

Nye, F. I., Short, J. F., & Olson, V. J. Socioeconomic status and delinquent behavior. *American Journal of Sociology*, 1958, *63*, 381–389.

O'Brien, F., Bugle, C., & Azrin, N. H. Training and maintaining a retarded child's proper eating. *Journal of Applied Behavior Analysis*, 1972, *5*, 67–72.

O'Connor, R. D. Relative efficacy of modeling, shaping, and the combined procedures for modification of social withdrawal. *Journal of Abnormal Psychology*, 1972, *79*, 327–334.

O'Connor, R. D. Modification of social withdrawal through symbolic modeling. *Journal of Applied Behavior Analysis*, 1969, *2*, 15–22.

O'Dell, S. Training parents in behavior modification: A review. *Psychological Bulletin*, 1974, *81*, 418–433.

O'Leary, K. D. Behavior modification in the classroom: A rejoinder to Winett and Winkler. *Journal of Applied Behavior Analysis, 1972, 5*, 505–511.

O'Leary, K. D. & Becker, W. C. Behavior modification of an adjustment class: A token reinforcement program. *Exceptional Children*, 1967, *33*, 637–642.

O'Leary, K. D., Becker, W. C., Evans, M. B., & Saudargas, R. A. A token reinforcement program in a public school: A replication and systematic analysis. *Journal of Applied Behavior Analysis*, 1969, *2*, 3–13.

O'Leary, K. D., & Drabman, R. Token reinforcement programs in the classroom. *Psychological Bulletin*, 1971, *75*, 379–398.

O'Leary, K. D., Drabman, R., & Kass, R. E. Maintenance of appropriate behavior in a token program. *Journal of Abnormal Child Psychology*, 1973, *1*, 127–138.

O'Leary, K. D., Kaufman, K. F., Kass, R. E., & Drabman, R. The effects of loud and soft reprimands on the behavior of disruptive children. *Exceptional Children*, 1970, *37*, 145–155.

O'Leary, K. D., & O'Leary, S. G. *Classroom management: The successful use of behavior modification* (2 ed.). Elmsford, N. Y.: Pergamon, 1977.

O'Leary, K. D., Pelham, W. E., Rosenbaum, A., & Price, G. H. Behavioral treatment of hyperkinetic children: An experimental evaluation of its usefulness. *Clinical Pediatrics*, 1976, *15*, 510–515.

O'Leary, K. D., Turkewitz, H., & Taffel, S. J. Parent and therapist evaluation of behavior therapy in a child psychological clinic. *Journal of Consulting and Clinical Psychology*, 1973, *41*, 279–283.

Oltmanns, T. F., Broderick, J. E., & O'Leary, K. D. Marital adjustment and the efficacy of behavior therapy with children. *Journal of Consulting and Clinical Psychology*, 1977, *45*, 724–729.

O'Malley, J. E., & Eisenberg, L. The hyperkinetic syndrome. In S. Walzer & P. H. Wolff (Eds.), *Minimal cerebral dysfunction in children*. New York: Grune & Stratton, 1973, 95–103.

Owen, F. W., Adams, P. A., Forrest, T., Stolz, L. M., & Fisher, S. Learning disorders in children: Sibling studies. *Monographs of the Society for Research in Child Development*, 1971, *36*, (Serial No. 144).

Palkes, H., Stewart, M., & Kahana, B. Porteus maze performance of hyperactive boys after training in self-directed verbal commands. *Child Development*, 1968, *39*, 817–829.

Parke, R. D. Rules, roles, and resistance to deviation: Recent advances in punishment, discipline, and self-control. In A. D. Pick (Ed.), *Minnesota symposia on child psychology* (vol. 8). Minneapolis, Minn.: University of Minnesota Press, 1975, 111–143.

Pasamanick, B., & Knobloch, H. Retrospective studies on the epidemiology of reproductive casualty: Old and new. *Merrill-Palmer Quarterly*, 1966, *12*, 7–26.

Paschalis, A. Ph., Kimmel, H. D., & Kimmel, E. Further study of diurnal instrumental conditioning in the treatment of enuresis nocturna. *Journal of Behaviour Therapy and Experimental Psychiatry*, 1972, *3*, 253–256.

Patterson, G. R. An empirical approach to the classification of disturbed children. *Journal of Clinical Psychology*, 1964, *20*, 326–337.

Patterson, G. R. Retraining of aggressive boys by their parents: Review of recent literature and follow-up evaluation. *Canadian Psychiatric Association Journal*, 1974, *19*, 142–158.

Patterson, G. R. Naturalistic observation in clinical assessment. *Journal of Abnormal Child Psychology*, 1977, *5*, 309–322.

Patterson, G. R., Helper, M. E., & Wilcott, R. C. Anxiety and verbal conditioning in children. *Child Development*, 1960, *31*, 101–108.

Patterson, G. R., Jones, R., Whittier, J., & Wright, M. A. A behavior modification technique for the hyperactive child. *Behaviour Research and Therapy*, 1965, *2*, 217–226.

Patterson, G. R., Littman, R. A., & Bricker, W. Assertive behavior in children: A step toward a theory of aggression. *Monographs of the Society for Research in Child Development*, 1967, *32* (Whole No. 113).

Patterson, G. R., & Reid, J. B. Intervention for families of aggressive boys: A replication study. *Behaviour Research and Therapy*, 1973, *11*, 383–394.

Paul, G. L. Strategy of outcome research in psychotherapy. *Journal of Consulting Psychology*, 1967, *31*, 109–118.

Peed, S., Roberts, M., & Forehand, R. Evaluation of the effectiveness of a standardized parent training program in altering the interaction of mothers and their noncompliant children. *Behavior Modification*, 1977, *1*, 323–350.

Pelham, W. E. Behavioral treatment of hyperkinesis. *American Journal of Diseases of Children*, 1976, *130*, 565.

Pelham, W. E., & Ross, A. O. Selective attention in children with reading problems: A developmental study of incidental learning. *Journal of Abnormal Child Psychology*, 1977, *5*, 1–8.

Penrose, L. S. *The biology of mental defect*. London: Sidgwick & Jackson, 1963.

Perry, D. G., & Bussey, K. Self-reinforcement in high- and low-aggressive boys following acts of aggression. *Child Development*, 1977, *48*, 653–657.

Perry, D. G., & Perry, L. C. Denial of suffering in the victim as a stimulus to violence in aggressive boys. *Child Development*, 1974, *45*, 55–62.

Peterson, D. R. Behavior problems of middle childhood. *Journal of Consulting Psychology*, 1961, *25*, 205–209.

Phillips, D., Fischer, S. C., & Singh, R. A children's reinforcement schedule. *Journal of Behaviour Therapy and Experimental Psychiatry*, 1977, *8*, 131–134.

Phillips, E. L. Achievement Place: Token reinforcement procedures in a home-style rehabilitation setting for "pre-delinquent" boys. *Journal of Applied Behavior Analysis*, 1968, *1*, 213–223.

Phillips, E. L., Phillips, E. A., Fixsen, D. L., & Wolf, M. M. Achievement Place: Modification of the behaviors of pre-delinquent boys within a token economy. *Journal of Applied Behavior Analysis*, 1971, *4*, 45–59.

Pinkston, E. M., Reese, N. M., LeBlanc, J. M., & Baer, D. M. Independent control of a preschool child's aggression and peer interaction by contingent teacher attention. *Journal of Applied Behavior Analysis*, 1973, *6*, 115–124.

Plachetta, K. E. Encopresis: A case study utilizing contracting, scheduling, and self-charting. *Journal of Behaviour Therapy and Experimental Psychiatry*, 1976, *7*, 195–196.

Porges, S. W., Walter, G. F., Korb, R. J., & Sprague, R. L. The influences of methylphenidate on heart rate and behavioral measures of attention in hyperactive children. *Child Development*, 1975, *46*, 727–733.

Powell, J., Martindale, B., Kulp, S., Martindale, A., & Bauman, R. Taking a closer look: Time sampling and measurement error. *Journal of Applied Behavior Analysis*, 1977, *10*, 325–332.

Powers, E., & Witmer, H. *An experiment in the prevention of delinquency: The Cambridge-Somerville youth study*. New York: Columbia University Press, 1951.

Premack, D. A. Toward empirical behavior laws: I. Positive reinforcement. *Psychological Review*, 1959, *66*, 219–233.

Premack, D. A. A functional analysis of language. *Journal of Experimental Analysis of Behavior*, 1970, *14*, 107–125.

Purcell, K. Distinctions between subgroups of asthmatic children: Children's perceptions of events associated with asthma. *Pediatrics*, 1963, *31*, 486–494.

Purcell, K., Brady, K., Chai, H., Muser, J., Molk, L., Gordon, N., & Means, J. The effect on asthma in children of experimental separation from the family. *Psychosomatic Medicine*, 1969, *31*, 144–164.

Rachman, S. Clinical applications of observational learning, imitation, and modeling. *Behavior Therapy*, 1972, *3*, 379–397.

Rapoport, J. L., Buchsbaum, M. S., Zahn, T. P., Weingartner, H., Ludlow, C., & Mikkelsen, E. J. Dextroamphetamine: Cognitive and behavioral effects in normal prepubertal boys. *Science*, 1978, *199*, 560–563.

Rapoport, J. L., Quinn, P. O., Bradbard, G., Riddle, D., & Brooks, E. Imipramine and methylphenidate treatments of hyperactive boys. *Archives of General Psychiatry*, 1974, *30*, 789–793.

Reid, J. B., & Hendricks, A. F. Preliminary analysis of the effectiveness of direct home intervention for the treatment of predelinquent boys who steal. In L. A. Hamerlynck, L. C. Handy, & E. J. Mash (Eds.), *Behavior change: Methodology, concepts, and practice*. Champaign, Ill.: Research Press, 1973, 209–220.

Reisinger, J. J., Ora, J. P., & Frangia, G. W. Parents as change agents for their children: A review. *Journal of Community Psychology*, 1976, *4*, 103–123.

Rekers, G. A. Stimulus control over sex-typed play in cross-gender identified boys. *Journal of Experimental Child Psychology*, 1975, *20*, 136–148.

Rekers, G. A. Sexual problems: Behavior modification. In B. B. Wolman, A. O. Ross, & J. Egan (Eds.), *Handbook of treatment of mental disorders in childhood and adolescence*. Englewood Cliffs, N. J.: Prentice-Hall, 1978, 268–296.

Rekers, G. A., & Lovaas, O. I. Behavioral treatment of deviant sex-role behaviors in a male child. *Journal of Applied Behavior Analysis*, 1974, *7*, 173–190.

Rekers, G. A., Lovaas, O. I., & Low, B. The behavioral treatment of a "transsexual" pre-adolescent boy. *Journal of Abnormal Child Psychology*, 1975, *2*, 99–116.

Rekers, G. A., Yates, C. E., Willis, T. J., Rosen, A. C., & Taubman, M. Childhood gender identity change: Operant control over sex-typed play and mannerisms. *Journal of Behaviour Therapy and Experimental Psychiatry*, 1976, *7*, 51–57.

Repp, A. C., & Deitz, S. M. Reducing aggressive and self-injurious behavior of institutionalized retarded children through reinforcement of other behaviors. *Journal of Applied Behavior Analysis*, 1974, *7*, 313–325.

Rescorla, R. A., & Solomon, R. L. Two-process learning theory: Relationships between Pavlovian conditioning and instrumental learning. *Psychological Review*, 1967, *74*, 151–182.

Reynolds, B. S., Newsom, C. D., & Lovaas, O. I. Auditory overselectivity in autistic children. *Journal of Abnormal Child Psychology*, 1974, *2*, 253–263.

Richards, B. W. Mongolism: The effect of trends in age at childbirth on incidence and chromosomal type. *Journal of Mental Subnormality*, 1967, *13*, 3–13.

Richmond, J., & Lustman, S. Autonomic function in the neonate: I. Implications for psychosomatic theory. *Psychosomatic Medicine*, 1955, *17*, 269–275.

Ridberg, E. H., Parke, R. D., & Hetherington, E. M. Modification of impulsive and reflective cognitive styles through observation of film-mediated models. *Developmental Psychology*, 1971, *5*, 369–377.

Riddle, K. D., & Rapoport, J. L. A 2-year follow-up of 72 hyperactive boys. *Journal of Nervous and Mental Disease*, 1976, *162*, 126–234.

Rie, E. D., & Rie, H. E. Recall, retention, and Ritalin. *Journal of Consulting and Clinical Psychology*, 1977, *45*, 967–972.

Rie, H. E., Rie, E. D. Stewart, S., & Ambuel, J. P. Effects of methylphenidate on under-achieving children. *Journal of Consulting and Clinical Psychology*, 1976, *44*, 250–260.

Rimland, B. *Infantile autism: The syndrome and its implications for a neural theory of behavior.* New York: Appleton-Century-Crofts, 1964.

Rincover, A. Sensory extinction: A procedure for eliminating self-stimulatory behavior in autistic children. *Journal of Abnormal Child Psychology*, 1978, *6*, 299–310.

Rincover, A., & Koegel, R. L. Setting generality and stimulus control in autistic children. *Journal of Applied Behavior Analysis*, 1975, *8*, 235–246.

Rincover, A., & Koegel, R. L. Classroom treatment of autistic children: II. Individualized instruction in a group. *Journal of Abnormal Child Psychology*, 1977, *5*, 113–126.

Rinn, R. C., Vernon, J. C., & Wise, M. J. Training parents of behaviorally-disturbed children in a group: A three years' program evaluation. *Behavior Therapy*, 1975, *6*, 378–387.

Risley, T. R. The effects and side effects of punishing the autistic behaviors of a deviant child. *Journal of Applied Behavior Analysis*, 1968, *1*, 21–34.

Risley, T. R., & Wolf, M. M. Establishing functional speech in echolalic children. *Behaviour Research and Therapy*, 1967, *5*, 73–88.

Ritter, B. The group desensitization of children's snake phobias using vicarious and contact desensitization procedures. *Behaviour Research and Therapy*, 1968, *6*, 1–6.

Ritvo, E. R., Ornitz, E. M., & LaFranchi, S. Frequency of repetitive behaviors in early infantile autism and its variants. *Archives of General Psychiatry*, 1968, *19*, 341–347.

Robbins, L. C. The accuracy of parental recall of child development and child rearing practices. *Journal of Abnormal and Social Psychology*, 1963, *66*, 261–270.

Roberts, A. H., & Erikson, R. V. Delay of gratification. Porteus Maze Test performance, and behavioral adjustment in a delinquent group. *Journal of Abnormal Psychology*, 1968, *73*, 449–453.

Robins, L. N. *Deviant children grown up*. Baltimore, Md.: Williams & Wilkins, 1966.

Robinson, H. B., & Robinson, N. M. *The mentally retarded child: A psychological approach* (2d ed.). New York: McGraw-Hill, 1976.

Romanczyk, R. G., Diament, C., Goren, E. R., Trunell, G., & Harris, S. L. Increasing isolate and social play in severely disturbed children: Intervention and postintervention effectiveness. *Journal of Autism and Childhood Schizophrenia*, 1975, *5*, 57–70.

Romanczyk, R. G., Kent, R. N., Diament, C., & O'Leary, K. D. Measuring the reliability of observational data: A reactive process. *Journal of Applied Behavior Analysis*, 1973, *6*, 175–184.

Rosenbaum, M. S., & Breiling, J. The development and functional control of reading-comprehension behavior. *Journal of Applied Behavior Analysis*, 1976, *9*, 323–333.

Ross, A. O. A schizophrenic child and his mother. *Journal of Abnormal and Social Psychology*, 1955, *51*, 133–139.

Ross, A. O. Confidentiality in child guidance treatment. *Mental Hygiene*, 1958, *42*, 60–66.

Ross, A. O. *The practice of clinical child psychology*. New York: Grune & Stratton, 1959.

Ross, A. O. The issue of normality in clinical child psychology. *Mental Hygiene*, 1963, *47*, 267–272.

Ross, A. O. Learning theory and therapy with children. *Psychotherapy: Theory, Research and Practice*, 1964a, *1*, 102–108.

Ross, A. O. *The exceptional child in the family*. New York: Grune & Stratton, 1964b.

Ross, A. O. The application of behavior principles in therapeutic education. *The Journal of Special Education*, 1967, *1*, 275–286.

Ross, A. O. The rights of children as psychotherapy patients. In G. P. Koocher (Chair), *Children's rights and the psychologist's role*. Symposium presented at the meeting of the American Psychological Association, New Orleans, La., 1974.

Ross, A. O. *Psychological aspects of learning disabilities and reading disorders*. New York: McGraw-Hill, 1976.

Ross, A. O. *Learning disability: The unrealized potential*. New York: McGraw-Hill, 1977.

Ross, A. O., Lacey, H. M., & Parton, D. A. The development of a behavior checklist for boys. *Child Development*, 1965, *36*, 1013–1027.

Ross, D. M., & Ross, S. A. The efficacy of listening training for educable mentally retarded children. *American Journal of Mental Deficiency*, 1972, *77*, 137–142.

Ross, D. M., & Ross, S. A. Cognitive training for the EMR child: Situational problem solving and planning. *American Journal of Mental Deficiency*, 1973, *78*, 20–26.

Ross, D. M., & Ross, S. A. *Hyperactivity: Research, theory, and action*. New York: Wiley, 1976.

Routh, D. K., & Roberts, R. D. Minimal brain dysfunction in children: Failure to find evidence for a behavioral syndrome. *Psychological Reports*, 1972, *31*, 307–314.

Routh, D. K., & Schroeder, C. S. Standardized playroom measures as indices of hyperactivity. *Journal of Abnormal Child Psychology*, 1976, *4*, 199–207.

Ruebush, B. K. Anxiety. In H. W. Stevenson, J. Kagan, & C. Spiker (Eds.), *Child psychology: The 62nd yearbook of the National Society for the Study of Education*. Chicago, Ill.: National Society for the Study of Education, 1963, 460–516.

Rutter, M., Greenfeld, D., & Lockyer, L. A five to fifteen year follow-up study of infantile psychosis: II. Social and behavioural outcome. *British Journal of Psychiatry*, 1967, *113*, 1183–1199.

Rutter, M., & Lockyer, L. A five to fifteen year follow-up study of infantile psychosis: I. Description of sample. *British Journal of Psychiatry*. 1967, *113*, 1169–1182.

Safer, D. J., & Allen, R. P. Factors influencing the suppressant effects of two stimulant drugs on the growth of hyperactive children. *Pediatrics*, 1973, *51*, 660–667.

Safer, D. J., Allen, R. P., & Barr, E. Depression of growth in hyperactive children on stimulant drugs. *New England Journal of Medicine*, 1972, *287*, 217–219.

Salapatek, P., & Kessen, W. Prolonged investigation of a plane geometric triangle by the human infant. *Journal of Experimental Child Psychology*, 1973, *15*, 22–29.

Salter, A. *Conditioned reflex therapy.* New York: Farrar, Straus & Giroux, 1949.

Samaan, M. The control of nocturnal enuresis by operant conditioning. *Journal of Behaviour Therapy and Experimental Psychiatry*, 1972, *3*, 103–105.

Sameroff, A., & Chandler, M. Reproductive risk and the continuum of caretaking casualty. In F. D. Horowitz, M. Hetherington, S. Scarr-Salapatek, & G. Siegel (Eds.), *Review of child development research* (vol. 4). Chicago, Ill.: University of Chicago Press, 1974, 187–244.

Saposnek, D. T. An experimental study of rage-reduction treatment of autistic children. *Child Psychiatry and Human Development*, 1972, *3*, 50–62.

Sattler, J. M. *Assessment of children's intelligence.* Philadelphia, Pa.: Saunders, 1974.

Schachter, S., & Singer, J. E. Cognitive, social and physiological determinants of emotional state. *Psychological Review*, 1962, *49*, 379–399.

Schaefer, E. S. Converging conceptual models for maternal behavior and for child behavior. In J. C. Glidewell (Ed.), *Parental attitudes and child behavior.* Springfield, Ill.: Thomas, 1961, 124–146.

Schaefer, E. S., & Bayley, N. Maternal behavior, child behavior, and their intercorrelations from infancy through adolescence. *Monographs of the Society for Research in Child Development*, 1963, *28* (Whole No. 87).

Schaefer, H. H. Self-injurious behavior: Shaping "headbanging" in monkeys. *Journal of Applied Behavior Analysis*, 1970, *3*, 111–116.

Schell, R. E., Stark, J., & Giddan, J. J. Development of language behavior in an autistic child. *Journal of Speech and Hearing Disorders*, 1967, *32*, 51–64.

Schleiffer, M., Weiss, G., Cohen, N., Elman, M., Cvejic, H., & Kruger, E. Hyperactivity in preschoolers and the effect of methylphenidate. *American Journal of Orthopsychiatry*, 1975, *45*, 38–50.

Schlichter, K. J., & Ratliff, R. G. Discrimination learning in juvenile delinquents. *Journal of Abnormal Psychology*, 1971, *77*, 46–48.

Schopler, E. Early infantile autism and receptor processes. *Archives of General Psychiatry*, 1965, *13*, 327–335.

Schopler, E. Visual versus tactual receptor preferences in normal and schizophrenic children. *Journal of Abnormal Psychology*, 1966, *71*, 108–114.

Schover, L. R., & Newsom, C. D. Overselectivity, developmental level, and overtraining in autistic and normal children. *Journal of Abnormal Child Psychology*, 1976, *4*, 289–298.

Schrag, P., & Divoky, D. *The myth of the hyperactive child.* New York: Pantheon, 1975.

Schreibman, L. Effects of within-stimulus and extra-stimulus prompting on discrimination learning in autistic children. *Journal of Applied Behavior Analysis*, 1975, *8*, 91–112.

Schreibman, L., Koegel, R. L., & Craig, M. S. Reducing stimulus overselectivity in autistic children. *Journal of Abnormal Child Psychology*, 1977, *5*, 425–436.

Schreibman, L., & Lovaas, O. I. Overselective response to social stimuli by autistic children. *Journal of Abnormal Child Psychology*, 1973, *1*, 152–168.

Schwitzgebel, R. *Street-corner research: An experimental approach to the juvenile delinquent.* Cambridge, Mass.: Harvard University Press, 1964.

Schwitzgebel, R. Short-term operant conditioning of adolescent offenders on socially relevant variables. *Journal of Abnormal Psychology*, 1967, *72*, 134–142.

Senf, G. M. An information-integration theory and its application to normal reading acquisition and reading disability. In N. D. Bryant & C. E. Kass (Eds.), *Leadership training institute in learning disabilities: Final report* (vol. 2). Tucson, Ariz.: University of Arizona, 1972, 305–391.

Senf, G. M. Review of *Psychological aspects of learning disabilities and reading disorders* by A. O. Ross. *Contemporary Psychology*, 1977, *22*, 374–375.

Serbin, L. A., O'Leary, K. D., Kent, R., & Tonick, I. J. A comparison of teacher response to the preacademic and problem behavior of boys and girls. *Child Development*, 1973, *44*, 796–804.

Shapiro, D., & Surwit, R. S. Learned control of physiological function and disease. In H. Leitenberg (Ed.), *Handbook of behavior modification and behavior therapy.* Englewood Cliffs, N.J.: Prentice-Hall, 1976, 74–123.

Shirley, M. M. *The first two years; a study of twenty-five babies.* vol. 3: *Personality manifestations. Institute of Child Welfare Monograph Series*, No. 8. Minneapolis, Minn.: University of Minnesota Press, 1933.

Shodell, M. J. Personalities of mothers of nonverbal and verbal schizophrenic children. *Dissertation Abstracts*, 1967, *28*, 1175.

Short, J. F., & Strodtbeck, F. L. *Group process and gang delinquency.* Chicago, Ill.: University of Chicago Press, 1965.

Sibley, S. A. Reading rate and accuracy of retarded readers as a function of fixed-ratio schedules of conditioned reinforcement. *Dissertation Abstracts*, 1967, *27*, 4134–4135.

Sines, J. O., Pauker, J. D., Sines, L. K., & Owen, D. R. Identification of clinically relevant dimensions of children's behavior. *Journal of Consulting and Clinical Psychology*, 1969, *33*, 728–734.

Skinner, B. F. *The behavior of organisms: An experimental analysis.* New York: Appleton-Century-Crofts, 1938.

Skinner, B. F. *Science and human behavior.* New York: Macmillan, 1953.

Skinner, B. F. *Verbal behavior.* New York: Appleton-Century-Crofts, 1957.

Sloat, S. C. Child rearing practices in childhood schizophrenia: A comparison of ten schizophrenic children and their non-psychotic siblings. *Dissertation Abstracts*, 1966, *27*, 1296–1297.

Smith, R. E., & Sharpe, T. M. Treatment of a school phobia with implosive therapy. *Journal of Consulting and Clinical Psychology*, 1970, *35*, 239–243.

Snyder, J. J. Reinforcement analysis of interaction in problem and nonproblem families. *Journal of Abnormal Psychology*, 1977, *86*, 528–535.

Solnick, J. V., Rincover, A., & Peterson, C. R. Some determinants of the reinforcing and punishing effects of time-out. *Journal of Applied Behavior Analysis*, 1977, *10*, 415–424.

Solomon, R. L., & Brush, E. S. Experimentally derived conceptions of anxiety and aversion. In M. R. Jones (Ed.), *Nebraska symposium on motivation*. Lincoln, Nebr.: University of Nebraska Press, 1956, 212–305.

Spates, C. R., & Kanfer, F. H. Self-monitoring, self-evaluation and self-reinforcement in children's learning: A test of a multi-stage self-regulation model. *Behavior Therapy*, 1977, *8*, 9–16.

Sprague, R. L., & Sleator, E. K. What is the proper dose of stimulant drugs in children? *International Journal of Mental Health*, 1975, *4*, 75–104.

Sprague, R. L., & Sleator, E. K. Methylphenidate in hyperkinetic children: Differences in dose effects on learning and social behavior. *Science*, 1977, *198*, 1274–1276.

Sroufe, L. A. Drug treatment of children with behavior problems. In F. D. Horowitz, E. M. Hetherington, S. Scarr-Salapatek, & G. M. Siegel (Eds.), *Review of child development research* (vol. 4). Chicago, Ill.: University of Chicago Press, 1975, 347–407.

Sroufe, L. A., & Stewart, M. A. Treating problem children with stimulant drugs. *New England Journal of Medicine*, 1973, *289*, 407–413.

Staats, A. W., & Butterfield, W. H. Treatment of nonreading in a culturally deprived juvenile delinquent: An application of reinforcement principles. *Child Development*, 1965, *36*, 925–942.

Staats, A. W., Minke, K. A., Goodwin, W., & Landeen, J. Cognitive behavior modification: "Motivated learning" reading treatment with sub-professional therapy-technicians. *Behaviour Research and Therapy*, 1967, *5*, 283–299.

Stampfl, T. G., & Levis, D. J. Essentials of implosive therapy: A learning-theory-based psychodynamic behavioral therapy. *Journal of Abnormal Psychology*, 1967, *72*, 496–503.

Stedman, J. M. An extension of the Kimmel treatment method for enuresis to an adolescent: A case report. *Journal of Behaviour Therapy and Experimental Psychiatry*, 1972, *3*, 307–309.

Steisel, I. M., Friedman, C. J., & Wood, A. C., Jr. Interaction patterns in children with phenylketonuria. *Journal of Consulting Psychology*, 1967, *31*, 162–168.

Stevens-Long, J., & Rasmussen, M. The acquisition of simple and compound sentence structure in an autistic child. *Journal of Applied Behavior Analysis*, 1974, *7*, 473–479.

Stevens-Long, J., Schwarz, J. L., & Bliss, D. The acquisition and generalization of compound sentence structure in an autistic child. *Behavior Therapy*, 1976, *7*, 397–404.

Stevenson, H. W. *Children's learning*. New York: Appleton-Century-Crofts, 1972.

Stewart, M. A., Pitts, F. N., Craig, A. G., & Dieruf, W. The hyperactive child syndrome. *American Journal of Orthopsychiatry*, 1966, *36*, 861–867.

Stokes, T. F., & Baer, D. M. An implicit technology of generalization. *Journal of Applied Behavior Analysis*, 1977, *10*, 349–367.

Stokes, T. F., Baer, D. M., & Jackson, R. L. Programming the generalization of a greeting response in four retarded children. *Journal of Applied Behavior Analysis*, 1974, *7*, 599–610.

Stover, D. O., & Giebink, J. W. Inter-judge reliability of the Pittsburgh Adjustment Survey Scales. *Psychological Reports*, 1967, *21*, 845–848.

Strain, P. S., Shores, R. E., & Timm, M. A. Effects of peer social initiation on the behavior of withdrawn preschool children. *Journal of Applied Behavior Analysis*, 1977, *10*, 289–298.

Straughan, J. H. Treatment with child and mother in the playroom. *Behaviour Research and Therapy*, 1964, *2*, 37–41.

Strauss, A. A., & Lehtinen, L. E. *Psychopathology and education of the brain-injured child*. New York: Grune & Stratton, 1947.

Stuart, R. B. Behavioral contracting with the families of delinquents. *Journal of Behaviour Therapy and Experimental Psychiatry*, 1971, *2*, 1–11.

Stuart, R. B., Tripodi, T., Jayaratne, S., & Camburn, D. An experiment in social engineering in serving families of predelinquents. *Journal of Abnormal Child Psychology*, 1976, *4*, 243–261.

Stumphauzer, J. S. Elimination of stealing by self-reinforcement of alternative behavior and family contracting. *Journal of Behaviour Therapy and Experimental Psychiatry*, 1976, *7*, 265–268.

Stunkard, A. J., & Mahoney, M. J. Behavioral treatment of eating disorders. In H. Leitenberg (Ed.), *Handbook of behavior modification and behavior therapy*. Englewood Cliffs, N.J.: Prentice-Hall, 1976, 45–73.

Swanson, J. M., & Kinsbourne, M. Stimulant-related state-dependent learning in hyperactive children. *Science*, 1976, *192*, 1354–1356.

Tahmasian, J., & McReynolds, W. Use of parents as behavioral engineers in the treatment of a school-phobic girl. *Journal of Counseling Psychology*, 1971, *18*, 225–228.

Talbot, M. Panic in school phobia. *American Journal of Orthopsychiatry*, 1957, *27*, 286–296.

Tarver, S. G., Hallahan, D. P., Kauffman, J. M., & Ball, D. W. Verbal rehearsal and selective attention in children with learning disabilities: A developmental lag. *Journal of Experimental Child Psychology*, 1976, *22*, 375–385.

Tasto, D. L. Systematic desensitization, muscle relaxation and visual imagery in the counterconditioning of a four-year-old phobic child. *Behaviour Research and Therapy*, 1969, *7*, 409–411.

Tate, B. G., & Baroff, G. S. Aversive control of self-injurious behavior in a psychotic boy. *Behaviour Research and Therapy*, 1966, *4*, 281–287.

Terman, L. M., & Merrill, M. A. *The Stanford-Binet Intelligence Scale Third Revision*. Boston, Mass.: Houghton Mifflin, 1973.

Tharp, R. G., & Wetzel, R. J. *Behavior modification in the natural environment*. New York: Academic Press, 1969.

Thomas, A., & Chess, S. *Temperament and development*. New York: Brunner/Mazel, 1977.

Thomas, A., Chess, S., & Birch, H. G. *Temperament and behavior disorders in children*. New York: New York University Press, 1968.

Thomas, A., Chess, S., Birch, H. G., Hertzig, M. E., & Korn, S. *Behavioral individuality in early childhood*. New York: New York University Press, 1963.

Thoresen, C. E., & Mahoney, M. J. *Behavioral self-control*. New York: Holt, Rinehart & Winston, 1974.

Tomlinson, A. The treatment of bowel retention by operant procedures: A case study. *Journal of Behaviour Therapy and Experimental Psychiatry*, 1970, *1*, 83–85.

Trefert, D. A. Epidemiology of infantile autism. *Archives of General Psychiatry*, 1970, *22*, 431–438.

Tuddenham, R. D., Brooks, J., & Milkovich, L. Mothers' reports of behavior of ten-year-olds: Relationship with sex, ethnicity, and mother's education. *Developmental Psychology*, 1974, *10*, 959–995.

Turnbull, J. W. Asthma conceived as a learned response. *Journal of Psychosomatic Research*, 1962, *6*, 59–70.

Turnure, J., & Zigler, E. Outer-directedness in the problem solving of normal and retarded children. *Journal of Abnormal and Social Psychology*, 1964, *69*, 427–436.

Tyler, V. O., Jr., & Brown, G. D. The use of swift, brief isolation as a group control device for institutionalized delinquents. *Behaviour Research and Therapy*, 1967, *5*, 1–9.

Tyler, V. O., Jr., & Brown, G. D. Token reinforcement of academic performance with institutionalized delinquent boys. *Journal of Educational Psychology*, 1968, *59*, 164–168.

Ullman, L. P., & Krasner, L. *A psychological approach to abnormal behavior*. Englewood Cliffs, N.J.: Prentice-Hall, 1969.

Valins, S. Emotionality and information concerning internal reactions. *Journal of Personality and Social Psychology*, 1967, *6*, 458–463.

Van Hoose, W. H., & Kottler, J. A. *Ethical and legal issues in counseling and psychotherapy*. San Francisco, Calif.: Jossey-Bass, 1977.

Vurpillot, E. The development of scanning strategies and their relation to visual differentiation. *Journal of Experimental Child Psychology*, 1968, *6*, 632–650.

Wahler, R. G. Some structural aspects of deviant child behavior. *Journal of Applied Behavior Analysis*, 1973, *8*, 27–42.

Wahler, R. G., & Cormier, W. H. The ecological interview: A first step in out-patient child behavior therapy. *Journal of Behavior Therapy and Experimental Psychiatry*, 1970, *1*, 279–289.

Waldrop, M. F., Bell, R. Q., McLaughlin, B., & Halverson, C. F., Jr. Newborn minor physical anomalies predict short attention span, peer aggression, and impulsivity at age 3. *Science*, 1978, *199*, 563–565.

Wallace, B. R. Negativism in verbal and nonverbal responses of autistic children. *Journal of Abnormal Psychology*, 1975, *84*, 138–143.

Walters, R. H., & Brown, M. Studies of reinforcement of aggression: III. Transfer of responses to an interpersonal situation. *Child Development*, 1963, *34*, 563–571.

Walters, R. H., & Brown, M. A test of the high-magnitude theory of aggression. *Journal of Experimental Child Psychology*, 1964, *1*, 376–387.

Ward, A. J. Early infantile autism: Diagnosis, etiology, and treatment. *Psychological Bulletin*, 1970, *73*, 350–362.

Watson, J. B., & Rayner, R. Conditioned emotional reactions. *Journal of Experimental Psychology*, 1920, *3*, 1–14.

Wechsler, D. *Wechsler Intelligence Scale for Children*. New York: The Psychological Corp., 1949.

Wechsler, D. *Wechsler Intelligence Scale for Children—Revised*. New York: The Psychological Corp., 1974.

Weiss, A. R. A behavioral approach to the treatment of adolescent obesity. *Behavior Therapy*, 1977, *8*, 720–726.

Weiss, G., Kruger, E., Danielson, R., & Elman, M. Effect of long-term treatment of hyperactive children with methylphenidate. *Canadian Medical Association Journal*, 1975, *112*, 159–165.

Wenar, C. The reliability of mothers' histories. *Child Development*, 1961, *32*, 491–500.

Wender, P. H. *Minimal brain dysfunction in children*. New York: Wiley, 1971.

Werry, J. S. Organic factors in childhood psychopathology. In H. C. Quay & J. S. Werry (Eds.), *Psychopathological disorders of childhood*. New York: Wiley, 1972, 83–121.

Werry, J. S., Minde, K., Guzman, A., Weiss, G., Dogan, K., & Hoy, E. Studies on the hyperactive child—VII: Neurological status compared with neurotic and normal children. *American Journal of Orthopsychiatry*, 1972, *42*, 441–451.

Werry, J. S., & Quay, H. C. The prevalence of behavior symptoms in younger elementary school children. *American Journal of Orthopsychiatry*, 1971, *41*, 136–143.

Werry, J. S., Weiss, G., & Douglas, V. Studies on the hyperactive child: I. Some preliminary findings. *Canadian Psychiatric Association Journal*, 1964, *9*, 120–130.

Wheeler, M. E., & Hess, K. W. Treatment of juvenile obesity by successive approximation control of eating. *Journal of Behaviour Therapy and Experimental Psychiatry*, 1976, *7*, 235–241.

Whitehill, M., DeMyer-Gapin, S., & Scott, T. J. Stimulation seeking in antisocial preadolescent children. *Journal of Abnormal Psychology*, 1976, *85*, 101–104.

Winett, R. A., & Winkler, R. C. Current behavior modification in the classroom: Be still, be quiet, be docile. *Journal of Applied Behavior Analysis*, 1972, *5* 499–504.

Wing, J. K. (Ed.), *Early childhood autism: Clinical, educational, and social aspects*. Oxford: Pergamon, 1966.

Wolf, M. M., Risley, T., Johnston, M., Harris, F., & Allen, E. Application of operant conditioning procedures to the behavior problems of an autistic child: A follow-up and extension. *Behaviour Research and Therapy*, 1967, *5*, 103–111.

Wolf, M. M., Risley, T., & Mees, H. L. Application of operant conditioning procedures to the behavior problems of an autistic child. *Behaviour Research and Therapy*, 1964, *1*, 305–312.

Wolff, W. M., & Morris, L. A. Intellectual and personality characteristics of parents of autistic children. *Journal of Abnormal Psychology*, 1971, *77*, 155–161.

Wolpe, J. *Psychotherapy by reciprocal inhibition*. Stanford, Calif.: Stanford University Press, 1958.

Wolpe, J. *The practice of behavior therapy*. New York: Pergamon, 1969.

Worland, J. Effects of positive and negative feedback on behavior control in hyperactive and normal boys. *Journal of Abnormal Child Psychology*, 1976, *4*, 315–326.

Yarrow, M. R., Waxler, C. Z., & Scott, P. M. Child effects on adult behavior. *Developmental Psychology*, 1971, *5*, 300–311.

Young, G. C. The treatment of childhood encopresis by conditioned gastro-ileal reflex training. *Behaviour Research and Therapy*, 1973, *11*, 499–503.

Young, G. C., & Morgan, R. T. T. Overlearning in the conditioning treatment of enuresis. *Behaviour Research and Therapy*, 1972, *10*, 147–151.

Zaslow, R. W., & Breger, L. A therapy and treatment of autism. In L. Breger (Ed.), *Clinical-cognitive psychology: Models and integrations*. Englewood Cliffs, N.J.: Prentice-Hall, 1969, 246–291.

Zeaman, D., & House, B. J. The role of attention in retardate discrimination learning. In N. R. Ellis (Ed.), *Handbook of mental deficiency*. New York: McGraw-Hall, 1963, 159–223.

Zentall, S. S., & Zentall, T. R. Activity and task performance of hyperactive children as a function of environmental stimulation. *Journal of Consulting and Clinical Psychology*, 1976, *44*, 693–697.

Zigler, E. Developmental versus difference theories of mental retardation and the problem of motivation. *American Journal of Mental Deficiency*, 1960, *73*, 536–556.

Zigler, E. Mental retardation: Current issues and approaches. In L. W. Hoffman & M. L.

Hoffman (Eds.), *Review of child development research* (vol. 2). New York: Russell Sage, 1966*a*, 107–168.

Zigler, E. Research on personality structure of the retardate. In N. R. Ellis (Ed.), *International review of research in mental retardation* (vol. 1). New York: Academic Press, 1966*b*.

Zigler, E. Familial mental retardation: A continuing dilemma. *Science*, 1967, *155*, 292–298.

Zigler, E., & Balla, D. Developmental course of responsiveness to social reinforcement in normal children and institutionalized retardates. *Developmental Psychology*, 1972, *6*, 66–73.

Zigler, E., Butterfield, E. C., & Capobianco, F. Institutionalization and the effectiveness of social reinforcement: A 5- and 8-year follow-up study. *Developmental Psychology*, 1970, *3*, 255–263.

Zigler, E., & deLabry, J. Concept-switching in middle-class, lower-class, and retarded children. *Journal of Abnormal and Social Psychology*, 1962, *65*, 267–273.

Zigler, E., & Phillips, L. Psychiatric diagnosis: A critique. *Journal of Abnormal and Social Psychology*, 1961, *63*, 607–618.

Zigler, E., & Williams, J. Institutionalization and the effectiveness of social reinforcement: A three-year follow-up study. *Journal of Abnormal and Social Psychology*, 1963, *66*, 197–205.

Zlutnick, S., Mayville, W. J., & Moffat, S. Modification of seizure disorders: The interruption of behavioral chains. *Journal of Applied Behavior Analysis*, 1975, *8*, 1–12.

Name Index

Name Index

Subject Index

Subject Index